RISKY
BUSINESS?

AMERICAN POLITICAL INSTITUTIONS AND PUBLIC POLICY

Stephen J. Wayne
Series Editor

VICTORY
How a Progressive Democratic Party Can Win and Govern
Arthur Sanders

THE POLITICS OF JUSTICE
The Attorney General and the Making of Legal Policy
Cornell W. Clayton

A KINDER, GENTLER RACISM?
The Reagan–Bush Civil Rights Legacy
Steven A. Shull

CONGRESS, THE PRESIDENT, AND POLICYMAKING
A Historical Analysis
Jean Reith Schroedel

RISKY BUSINESS?
PAC Decisionmaking in Congressional Elections
Robert Biersack, Paul S. Herrnson, and Clyde Wilcox, Editors

PUBLIC ATTITUDES TOWARD CHURCH–STATE RELATIONS
Clyde Wilcox and Ted G. Jelen

AMERICAN POLITICAL INSTITUTIONS AND PUBLIC POLICY

RISKY BUSINESS?

PAC Decisionmaking in Congressional Elections

ROBERT BIERSACK
PAUL S. HERRNSON
CLYDE WILCOX
editors

M.E. Sharpe
Armonk, New York
London, England

This book is dedicated to
Neil Cotter, Leon Epstein,
Herbert Asher, and Aage Clausen

Library of Congress Cataloging-in-Publication Data

Risky Business? : PAC decisionmaking in congressional elections /
p. cm. — (American political institutions and public policy)
Includes bibliographical references and index.
ISBN 1-56324-294-X. — ISBN 1-56324-295-8
1. Campaign funds—United States.
2. Political action committees—United States.
I. Biersack, Robert, 1954– . II. Herrnson, Paul S., 1958– .
III. Wilcox, Clyde, 1953– . IV. Series.
JK1991.R57 1994
324.7′8′0973—dc
94-18902
CIP

Printed in the United States of America
The paper used in this publication meets the minimum
requirements of American National Standard for
Information Sciences—Permanence of Paper for
Printed Library Materials, ANSI Z 39.48-1984.

∞

BM (c)   10   9   8   7   6   5   4   3   2   1
BM (p)   10   9   8   7   6   5   4   3   2   1

Contents

Foreword

Political action committees—PACs—are villains in contemporary electoral politics, at least from the public's perspective. They get blamed for much of what is wrong with the system: the incumbency advantage in elections, the weakening of political parties, and the pernicious effect of money on the cost and conduct of elections and on the public policy decisions of those who have been elected.

With regularity and often righteous indignation, public interest groups, journalists, and even politicians, who have been the recipients of their largess, have bemoaned PACs' evil influence and urged reforms that include limiting or eliminating their campaign contributions. There have even been proposals to ban them altogether, proposals of dubious constitutionality.

Are these accusations justified? Do PACs exercise an undue and unhealthy influence? Under the guise of a democratic electoral process, do they contribute to undemocratic election results and to unrepresentative government, government of, by, and for the few? Should PACs be constrained? Should they be prohibited altogether?

We need data to answer these questions. In *Risky Business? PAC Decisionmaking in Congressional Elections*, Robert Biersack, Paul S. Herrnson, Clyde Wilcox, and the other contributors provide that data in a set of fascinating case studies, based in part on personal interviews with PAC decisionmakers, that examine PAC decisionmaking and activities during the 1992 election cycle.

The authors are interested in understanding how PACs work, how they choose those whom they are going to support. Obviously the type of PAC, the structure of its organization, the involvement of its membership, the method by which it obtains information about the candidates, their positions, and their chances, and the extent to which it exploits particular electoral opportunities are all factors that potentially affect a PAC's decisions about whom to support and how much to give.

The PACs studied in this book are diverse. They include public and private groups, communities with broad and with narrow memberships, ones with economic interests, and others with social concerns. Large and small contributors, business, labor, and trade associations, ideological and issue-specific committees are all examined to provide a cross-section of the more than 4,000 PACs that participated in the 1992 elections.

Some of the findings of the case studies are surprising. As the title suggests, PAC activity can be risky business. PACs' objectives are to further their organizations' interests. They can be expected to act rationally when trying to do so. The issue is whether this self-interested behavior is antithetical to the democratic process and to democratic outcomes. Readers of this book will be able to decide better how risky PACs' business is for the political system.

Risky Business? is an important book that broadens our understanding of PAC activity and thereby enhances our capacity to evaluate it within the context of the principles and practices of American democracy.

Stephen J. Wayne
Georgetown University

Preface

In recent years congressional elections have become fairly predictable and stable events. Incumbents who run for reelection have generally won, often with ever-increasing margins. People and organizations who give financial support to congressional campaigns have observed this pattern and found it in their interest to back winners—almost irrespective of their own partisan or ideological beliefs. Political scientists have developed theories about how these groups might react in competitive elections—where the likely winner was truly unknown—but these races have become more unusual with each election year.

One of the frustrations of social science is that it usually is very difficult to change, and thereby test, the factors that are thought to affect political behavior: elections cannot be mixed and matched in test tubes. The 1992 election cycle presented a rare opportunity to test some of the theories that have been advanced to explain how campaign contributors might respond to an election season marked by the potential for tremendous congressional turnover.

In early 1991 we began to think of ways to study how political action committees (PACs)—the most talked-about source of congressional election funding—would participate in an election heavily influenced by redistricting, incumbent retirements, and voter hostility toward Congress. We wondered whether many PACs would jump at their first real chance in many years to influence the makeup of Congress. Would they be willing to risk angering entrenched representatives and senators by aggressively supporting challengers and open-seat candidates who shared their specific policy concerns or general political inclinations?

We chose to involve as many colleagues and students as possible in a series of case studies of PACs. Fortunately many of our colleagues and students were also interested in the financing of the 1992 election. Eighteen scholars participated in the study by conducting research on one or more PACs. The contributors followed these committees from the early stages of the election cycle through the frantic final days of the campaign.

The study proceeded through several stages, beginning with the selection of a diverse group of PACs—some large and some small—that represented different economic and political interests. The authors of the case studies first interviewed the directors of the PACs in late 1991, when most were concentrating on fundraising and planning their contribution strategies. The authors asked the directors the same basic questions: how the PAC was structured, how it made its contribution decisions, and how the director expected the 1992 election would unfold. The PAC directors were interviewed again in early summer, as the fall campaign was beginning to take shape. In this interview the authors concentrated on how the committees were reacting to the changing nature of the election. Another set of interviews was conducted just before the election, and postmortems were held after election day to assess whether the experience had changed the PAC directors' perspectives on their committees' role in funding congressional campaigns. These interviews were particularly instructive, as we learned that some PACs had disbanded, some had grown far beyond their own expectations, and some had already begun planning for 1994.

The twenty-one chapters in this book were written with a variety of audiences in mind, including undergraduate students, scholars who specialize in congressional elections or campaign finance, and political practitioners. As a group, the chapters reveal a PAC community with widely diverse goals and capabilities. Each PAC is influenced by its own structure as well as by the political framework in which it works. In general, we find that it is a mistake to think of the actions of PACs as strictly electoral: the motivations for their actions often reach far beyond the next election, and these other considerations lead them to make contributions sometimes at odds with the possibilities posed by a particular campaign.

Like any highly collaborative enterprise, this book would not have been possible without the cooperation of many individuals. We must first thank our friends, colleagues, and students who participated in the project. They put some of their own research aside in order to attend meetings, meet deadlines, and write the chapters that follow. We would also like to thank the PAC directors and other officials who willingly agreed to interrupt their busy schedules to meet with our authors and attend a conference held in the spring of 1993. Without their candor and assistance, this book would not have been possible. The Consortium of Universities of the Washington Metropolitan Area and the Department of Government and Politics at the University of Maryland deserve special thanks for cosponsoring the PAC conference. Paul Herrnson and Clyde Wilcox received support for this research from the National Science Foundation under grants SES-9210169 and SES-9209342, respectively. Our editor at M. E. Sharpe, Michael Weber, and the copyeditor, Susanna Sharpe, played an important role in moving the project along.

Finally, a note about the persons to whom this book is dedicated. Each of us was supported and encouraged as a graduate student by scholars who gave us the opportunity to benefit from their wisdom and experience and also develop our own skills by actively conducting research. Neil Cotter was Robert Biersack's mentor at the University of Wisconsin–Milwaukee; Leon Epstein mentored Paul Herrnson at the University of Wisconsin–Madison, and Herbert Asher and Aage Clausen played a similar role for Clyde Wilcox. The important role that our students played in the development of this book reflects our attempt to continue the tradition from which each of us has so richly benefited.

RISKY BUSINESS?

1

Introduction

Robert Biersack

Political action committees—commonly called PACs—are the major organized financiers in congressional elections. During the 1992 elections the 4,792 members of the PAC community gave more than $187 million to 1,890 congressional candidates. Although PACs play an important role in American politics, journalists and scholars who write about them often describe them in the most general terms—how much money they raise, to whom they contribute, and whether the recipients of PAC money win or lose their elections. Rarely do they inform readers about why particular PACs gave contributions to the candidates they supported, or how these committees reached their contribution decisions.

The purpose of this book is to take a close-up look at a number of PACs that are representative of the PAC community. Instead of using a broad brush to paint a general picture of PACs, each of the contributors to this book focuses on one or at most two committees. Each chapter addresses three general questions: How do PACs select the candidates to whom they contribute? Where do PACs turn for the information they use when selecting candidates for support? How do they respond to the opportunities that emerge in particular elections? From this series of close studies of PAC decisionmaking, it is possible to draw broader conclusions about the role of PACs in the campaign finance system.

The 1992 elections offered a unique setting for studying PACs. Redistricting, widespread congressional retirements, and scandal created a climate of uncertainty for candidates and those who might support them. These conditions offered those PACs whose managers were interested in changing the composition of Congress the opportunity to break from the comfortable pattern of giving most of their money to incumbents. The uncertainties that resulted from these conditions had the potential to make the 1992 congressional elections more competi-

tive than any others in the past decade. They also created the opportunity for
PACs to inject some new lines into the script that has guided most PAC activity
in the last four election cycles. In its simplest form, this script reads, "Incumbents always win, so contributions to challengers are wasted; PACs seek access
to congressional decisionmakers, so PACs give to incumbents." In 1992, it appeared to be reasonable for some PACs to add to the script the following phrase:
". . . except when prospects for drastically changing the composition of Congress
are good, and additional policy or ideological goals can be met by backing
open-seat or challenger candidates. Under these circumstances some PACs give
to competitive nonincumbents as well." The PAC community is not monolithic,
and discerning which PACs are willing to change the "script" and take risks is
one of the goals of this book.

PACs and Democracy

PACs are probably the most studied and certainly the most criticized actors in
the campaign finance system. They represent one mechanism through which
people who share some common interest can participate as a group in the political process. By pooling the financial resources of many individuals, PACs can
turn $10, $100, or larger donations from their contributors into $1,000 or $5,000
contributions to congressional candidates. In so doing, PACs give their supporters an opportunity to voice their concerns to candidates, to reward members of
Congress who have supported their positions, or to try to change the makeup of
the Congress to better reflect their views.

While this description of PAC activity sounds like the very core of what
Americans consider to be democratic politics, it is also true that people and
groups have unequal abilities to participate in the financing of elections. Financial resources are not evenly distributed, and the ability to organize as a group is
easier for some types of people and causes than others. As a result, the kinds of
groups that have formed the most influential PACs do not represent all points of
view on various issues. If PACs have greater influence on who serves in Congress and how members of Congress view issues because they help finance
campaigns, then individuals and groups with greater financial resources have the
potential to have a bigger impact on policymaking than others. The conclusion
one comes to about these two contradictory views of PACs—that they are useful
vehicles to pool small contributions and allow groups to express themselves, or
that they represent a way for financial elites who hold strong views to have
unfair influence in the political process—determines how one approaches the
controversial issues inherent in campaign finance reform.

The Rules of the Game

The basic rules that govern how interest groups, corporations, labor unions, and
other associations participate in federal election campaigns have been virtually
unchanged since the Federal Election Campaign Act (FECA) was amended in

1974 and the Federal Election Commission (FEC) handed down its landmark *SUNPAC* Advisory Opinion in 1975. As a result of these legislative and regulatory acts, all kinds of organizations are allowed to create voluntary political institutions (popularly called PACs) that can raise money from their members and make contributions to candidates for federal office. Further, corporations, unions, and membership groups that create PACs can use their corporate profits, union dues, or membership fees to pay their PACs' overhead expenses.

Any PAC that has existed for at least six months, has received contributions from at least fifty people, and has made contributions to at least five federal candidates is entitled to contribute up to $5,000 to any federal candidate for each election in which that candidate participates. In most cases this means a maximum contribution of $10,000 (because primary and general elections count as separate races) from a PAC to any candidate. Individuals are permitted to give up to $5,000 each year to a PAC, but PACs sponsored by corporations, unions, and groups with regular members can only accept contributions from certain "members" of the organization. Corporations can only receive contributions from management and executive employees or stockholders, and unions and other membership groups can only accept donations from members.

Within these basic rules are several variations and options that permit different kinds of PAC activities. The Supreme Court decision in *Buckley* v. *Valeo* established the right of any individual or PAC to make unlimited expenditures advocating the election or defeat of a federal candidate so long as those expenditures are made without the candidate's prior knowledge or consent. Any PAC can therefore contribute $5,000 per election to any candidate and also make unlimited "independent expenditures"—anything from mailings to television advertisements—so long as no coordination takes place between the PAC and the campaign.

Most PACs are sponsored by an organization, such as a corporation, a trade association, a labor union, a professional association, or a membership group. Some PACs, however, are formed independently to influence the electoral process. These are known as "nonconnected" PACs. They are formed by individuals who care about specific issues or government policies and seek to promote their views by organizing groups that directly lobby members of Congress. PACs formed by these nonconnected, ideological, or issue groups must pay for their overhead using voluntary contributions. Moreover, these and other groups that are organized primarily for political purposes do not receive the same tax advantages as other charitable organizations. As a result, many issue-oriented groups create several organizations, some of which can receive tax-exempt contributions for public education and other purposes, and others, including PACs, that are primarily political. Nonconnected PACs have the same limits on contributions to candidates, but they may seek contributions from any individual, not just group members. It is these committees that have popularized the direct-mail solicitation techniques that fill America's mailboxes.

In addition, the courts have ruled that these organizations can, in some instances, spend funds received by the organization itself, not just contributions to the PAC, for political purposes so long as the activity does not involve expressly advocating the election or defeat of a specific federal candidate. Pro-life organizations, for example, can spend their treasury money to send their members or others information about the positions that candidates take on abortion without counting that spending as a campaign contribution, so long as they do not specifically advocate the election of an identified candidate.

Campaign finance is a complex process, with the formal rules providing only a general framework within which PACs must operate. These rules are complex, and some of the managers of the PACs in the studies herein appear to have misunderstood some of the implications of these regulations. As we will see in the chapters that follow, the rules leave many choices available to committees about whom to support and how. Before looking at the individual committees we have selected to study in detail, we should consider the kinds of factors that might affect their decisions and the results that their collective choices have had on congressional elections.

The State of Nature

The world of campaign finance has been characterized by rapid change and development since the FECA was amended in 1974. For PACs, the period began with several years of rapid growth in both the number of committees and the amount of money they raised and spent. From 608 committees at the end of 1974, the number of PACs rose steadily, reaching 4,009 by the end of 1984 (see Figure 1.1).

There was substantial growth in the number of corporate-sponsored PACs after the FEC officially sanctioned their existence (from 89 in 1974 to 1,682 in 1984). Ideological (nonconnected) PACs also grew dramatically in number during this period, from 110 at the end of 1977 (when this type was first counted separately) to 1,053 at the end of 1984. Considerable if less dramatic growth also occurred among trade association PACs, such as the National Association of Realtors PAC. The numbers of union PACs grew the most slowly, from 201 in 1974 to 294 ten years later. This slower growth may be partially explained by the longer tradition of PAC activity among unions. Most of the larger unions had already established PACs before the passage of FECA, while most corporations had not.

Since the mid-1980s growth in the number of PACs has slowed considerably. There were 1,715 corporate PACs in mid-1993, only 33 more than in 1984 and down from a high of 1,816 at the end of 1988. Similarly, nonconnected committees totaled 1,011 in mid-1993—42 fewer than existed seven years earlier, and down from a high of 1,145 in 1992.

The financial activity of PACs shows a similar pattern of considerable growth in the early years followed by slower growth more recently (see Figure 1.2).

Figure 1.1. **Number of Registered PACs, 1974–92**

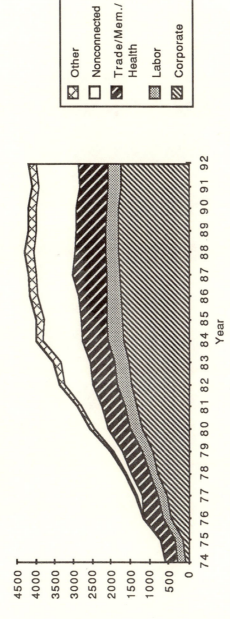

Source: Federal Election Commission.

8

Figure 1.2. **PAC Receipts and Contributions to Candidates, 1978–92**

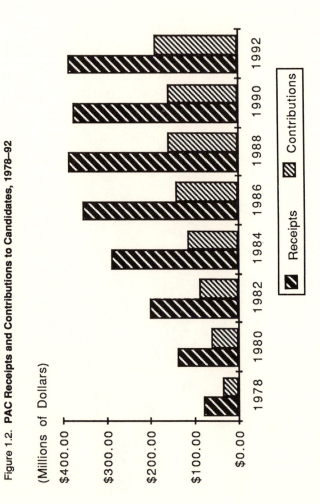

(Millions of Dollars)

Source: Federal Election Commission.

PACs raised a total of about $80 million during the 1977–78 election cycle, the first for which reliable information is available, and they contributed a total of $35.2 million to federal candidates. By the 1984 election cycle, these totals had increased to $289 million in receipts and $113 million contributed to candidates. By 1990, the rate of growth in financial activity had also slowed considerably, with PAC receipts totaling $372 million and contributions equaling $159.1 million. Thus, while receipts had increased by 260 percent in the six years from 1978 to 1984, they grew by only 29 percent during the next six years.

Such broad measures of activity can often hide as much as they reveal, however, and major changes in PAC activity were continuing during the last half of the 1980s. One of the important characteristics of PAC behavior in the early years was the surprisingly dynamic nature of their support for candidates. There was a willingness among many PACs to support a variety of types of candidates, including members of both parties, incumbents, challengers, and candidates involved in races for open seats.[1] Simplistic expectations that certain types of PACs would behave monolithically—for example, that corporate PACs would give only to Republicans—proved to be incorrect. This diversity in PAC decisions was attributed to differences in size of the organizations (with large numbers of small PACs making decisions independently) as well as the geography of the PAC community, for many committees outside Washington presumably focused on local concerns and candidates.[2]

PAC activity in recent years indicates a reduction in the diversity that existed earlier. First, there has been an increasing concentration of activity among a relatively small number of PACs. During 1984 there were 73 committees who made contributions to candidates totaling at least $250,000 each, and they represented just over 41 percent of all PAC contributions. By the 1990 election cycle, there were 124 committees making contributions of this size, and these represented over 51 percent of all contributions made by the 4,769 PACs in existence. The fact that there are many PACs with widely divergent interests tells only part of the story. A much smaller number of PACs make a disproportionate share of PAC contributions.

In addition, the types of candidates to whom contributions are made has evolved over the years. During the 1978 election cycle PACs gave 57 percent of their contributions to incumbents, 22 percent to challengers, and 21 percent to open-seat candidates. By 1990 these percentages had moved to 79 percent for incumbents, 10 percent for challengers, and 11 percent for open-seat candidates (see Figure 1.3). PACs now concentrate most of their financial assistance on candidates already in Congress to the exclusion of all others, including those for open seats.

How Decisions Are Made

Several factors are influential in PACs' decisionmaking processes.[3] The first factor is the amount of money in a PAC's treasury. Committees with limited

Figure 1.3. **PAC Support of Nonincumbent House Candidates, 1980–92**

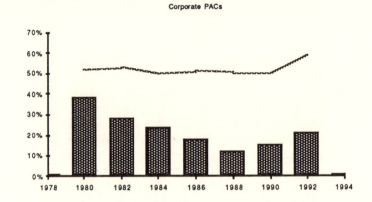

Corporate PACs

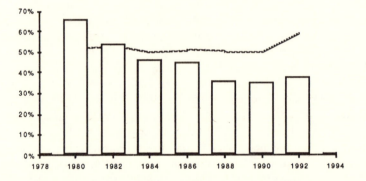

Non Connected PACs

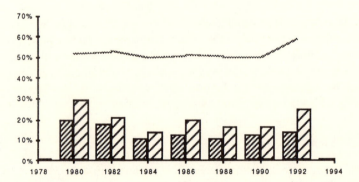

Cooperative and Corp w/out Stock PACs

Figure 1.3 *(continued)*

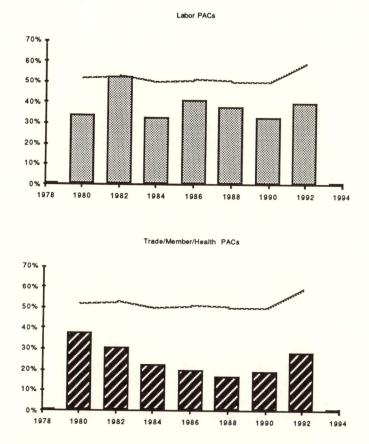

Source: Federal Election Commission, Reports on Financial Activity.
Notes: The line represents the proportion of all House candidates who were not incumbents. Bars indicate the proportion of PAC contribution to those candidates.

resources can prioritize candidates easily and are often unable to proceed very far down the list before they exhaust their available funds. In contrast, wealthier PACs, which make the majority of all PAC contributions, have more opportunities to give money, and this sometimes makes their decisions more complicated. Some PACs are so large that the limits on how much they can contribute to any single candidate play a role in their allocation decisions. They have the capability to give the maximum allowed to all of their most favored candidates and then contribute to others as well. For them, choosing between candidates who are lower on their priority lists is more than an academic question. It involves deciding whether to give small contributions to a great many candidates or to give big contributions to a few. It also involves deciding whether to spend money on activities beyond making contributions, such as independent expenditures or communicating to members.

Another factor that is important in PAC decisionmaking is the structure of the PAC and the organization sponsoring it. Whether an organization has a broad geographic base or focuses its business in a smaller area, as well as the level of involvement of its membership in its decisionmaking, both influence the distribution of PAC contributions.[4] Committees sponsored by groups where a broad geographic membership is involved in decisionmaking may be less likely than other PACs to focus only on "inside the Beltway" considerations, such as subcommittee assignments or other issues that may be important to the organization's lobbyist.

The politics of the sponsoring organization can also have other effects. The traditionally partisan political involvement of labor unions enables labor PACs to back nonincumbent candidates only so long as they are Democrats.[5] Corporations, on the other hand, represent a diverse public that might object to a corporate PAC's taking strong political stands. This has encouraged them to become risk-averse, contributing to few challengers in order to avoid offending stockholders, employees, clients, and other PAC supporters. This book includes studies of PACs that represent several different points on the spectrum of organizational complexity and participatory structure.

A third general factor important for decisionmaking is the information available to PAC managers. One plausible explanation for the greater concentration of PAC contributions among incumbents in recent years is that PAC decisionmakers may have developed better and more organized sources of information about likely election outcomes, and these all point to the fact that incumbents almost always win. This book explores the networks within which PAC managers work—with whom they communicate among their colleagues, party leaders, and other cue-givers, and what other sources of information they consult.

Finally, both electoral conditions and habit can influence PAC decisionmaking. The strategic actor theory suggests that all of the players in the electoral process anticipate the most likely general outcome when planning their election strategies.[6] Potential candidates check the environment for signs that a decision to run might lead to success. If an incumbent is vulnerable or the seat is open, the pool of "quality" candidates (those with experience and political skills) is generally larger than when the probability of success is slim. Similarly, potential contributors examine the environment, see who the likely candidates are, judge whether the economy or other political conditions are favorable to incumbents or challengers, and make decisions about whom to support based upon the candidates' probability of winning. This suggests that any significant change in the political environment might lead to changes in the pattern of PAC contributions.

Another theory suggests that PACs make decisions incrementally, drawing upon their most successful decisions and the successes and failures of other PACs. Since these decisions are based on that prior learning, sudden changes in the electoral environment do not necessarily lead to significant changes in PAC behavior. Rather, PACs are expected to follow the same old rules, in spite of the different opportunities and risks that emerge in the current election cycle.

Moreover, PACs view the electoral process differently than they do candidates, parties, voters, and even each other. PACs are interested in specific policy outcomes and have developed a working relationship with members. They typically see the electoral process as a threat to the sets of relationships they have built up over the years. Thus, big electoral changes can represent a threat to a PAC's influence, and PACs may react to uncertainty by trying to protect threatened incumbents rather than carefully examining the issue positions of unknown challenger and open-seat candidates to determine who might better represent them.

The 1992 Election

The 1992 election differed from the ones preceding it in several ways. First, it was the first congressional election after the reapportionment and redistricting that followed the 1990 census. As a result, virtually all House district lines were changed at least somewhat, raising the level of uncertainty surrounding reelection prospects of incumbents. This effect was magnified by the unusually heavy involvement of the judiciary in the redistricting process. Several states left the final decisions about district boundaries to the courts or to court-appointed representatives, in part because of the requirements for minority representation contained in the Civil Rights Act and in part because of divided government in many states. As a result, some of the partisan maneuvering was removed from the process in some states, and the boundaries drawn were very different from those used in earlier elections.

Magnifying the effect of redistricting was the rising level of dissatisfaction voters expressed toward Congress. This feeling first took form near the end of the 1990 campaign when attention was focused on the congressional pay raise. Scandals erupting in 1991 and 1992 involving the House Bank and Post Office also increased this dissatisfaction and the uncertainty that incumbents would be easily reelected early in the 1992 election season.

Finally, the combination of legislative stalemate, relatively few retirements, and high reelection rates during the 1980s led to a record number of retirements from the House prior to the 1992 election. All of these events reduced the feeling of certainty that had developed in recent years among those trying to predict the outcomes of congressional elections. The simple fact that incumbents usually win, which had come to dominate the way in which PACs and most others viewed congressional elections, was called into serious question for the first time since many of the PACs currently in existence were created. From 1974 through 1990, a trend toward more convincing reelection margins for House members developed, and this lesson was not lost on PAC managers. In 1992, it appeared that this pattern could be changing, creating a greater potential for PACs to follow different strategies. Nevertheless, PAC managers who were considering employing a new strategy could not do so without taking tremendous risks.

Studying PACs in 1992

In order to get a complete picture of the decisionmaking processes of the PACs they were studying, the contributors to this book interviewed the managers of their PACs at four specific points in the election cycle: September 1991, April 1992, September 1992, and after the election. The core of their discussions with PAC managers followed a common interview protocol, but participants were also instructed to inquire as to the unique aspects of the PAC or PACs they were studying. The contributors were also given FEC reports documenting the history of their PACs' activity prior to 1992 and over the course of the 1992 election cycle.

The Organization of This Book

The following chapters examine in detail the structure and behavior of nineteen different political action committees. The committees were selected with an eye toward the factors that are most important in shaping PAC decisions, including the political environment in which the 1992 elections were staged. The PACs examined are of different sizes and organizational types, have different decisionmaking rules and levels of "democratization," have varying degrees of involvement in the Washington political community, and are concerned about different interests or issues. The contributions and expenditures of these committees for the past seven election cycles are detailed in the Appendices.

The four chapters in Part One focus on committees generally identified as opinion leaders among PACs. The AFL-CIO Committee on Political Education (COPE), Business and Industry Political Action Committee (BIPAC), National Committee for an Effective Congress (NCEC), and Free Congress PAC (FCP) emphasize communications with other PACs but also get directly involved in campaigns. They are sought out by other PAC leaders when information about competitive races or individual candidates is needed. This extends their influence beyond the dollars they raise and spend in elections.

The second group of PACs, discussed in Part Two, represent the "big hitters" among the PAC community. These committees, including the National Education Association (NEA) PAC, AT&T PAC, Eaton's Corporation's EPPA, the National Association of Realtors PAC (RPAC), the National Abortion Rights Action League (NARAL) PAC, and the National Right to Life (NRL) PAC are among those 100 or so committees that make the majority of all PAC contributions to congressional candidates. They also possess highly developed organizational structures and use elaborate decision rules to guide their political involvement. They are representative of large PACs that are concerned with traditional economic interests, as well as groups organized around social-cultural issues.

Finally, in Part Three we include several chapters describing the "great un-washed" of the PAC community. These are committees with modest but not insignificant resources that reflect the diversity of most organizations. Within this group are traditional corporate PACs, such as FHP Corporation's PAC; labor organizations, such as the National Federation of Federal Employees' NFFE PAC, the National Air Traffic Controllers' Association's NATCA PAC; trade associations such as the Association of American Publishers; and issue-focused groups representing many different perspectives on abortion, the environment, and other important issues.

While these committees are of modest size, they have very different decisionmaking styles and approaches to the political process. Many are essentially one-person shops, where a single representative makes most decisions about whom to support without much input from others. They also have different political goals, ranging from maintaining access to powerful committee chairs to changing the composition of Congress. The diversity of these PACs, and that of the other PACs included in this volume, enables us to present a representative picture of how PACs make their contribution decisions and how they responded to the dynamics of a unique election cycle.

Notes

1. Larry J. Sabato, *PAC Power: Inside the World of Political Action Committees* (New York: W.W. Norton, 1984).

2. Theodore Eismeier and Phillip Pollock III, *Business, Money, and the Rise of Corporate PACs in American Elections* (New York: Quorum Books, 1988).

3. Theodore Eismeier and Phillip Pollock III, "Political Action Committees: Varieties of Organization and Strategy," in Michael J. Malbin, ed., *Money and Politics in the United States* (Chatham, NJ: Chatham House, 1984); Clyde Wilcox, "Organizational Variables and the Contribution Behavior of Large PACs: A Longitudinal Analysis," *Political Behavior* (1989): 157–73.

4. John Wright, "PACs, Contributions, and Roll Calls: An Organizational Perspective," *American Political Science Review* 79 (1985):400–414.

5. Frank J. Sorauf, *Inside Campaign Finance* (New Haven, CT: Yale University Press, 1992), p. 108.

6. Gary Jacobson and Samuel Kernell, *Strategy and Choice in Congressional Elections* (New Haven, CT: Yale University Press, 1983), pp. 19–48.

Part One
Lead PACs

Some PACs attempt to influence the contributions of others by providing information and other cues. These lead PACs are generally older, larger, and more institutionalized than other PACs. At least part of their behavior during an election cycle consists of gathering and disseminating information on the positions and prospects of candidates. Beyond these similarities, however, there is a fair amount of diversity among lead PACs. We have chosen four in this section to represent the most important broad types of committees. The Committee on Political Education (COPE) and the Business and Industry Political Action Committee (BIPAC) represent traditional economic interests and have parent organizations as sponsors. They provide cues to labor union and business committees. The National Committee for an Effective Congress (NCEC) and the Free Congress PAC represent a broad spectrum of ideological concerns and have no parent organizations. They provide cues to ideological PACs of the right and left. Other PACs in this volume may also serve as lead PACs within more narrowly defined communities.

Although lead PACs attempt to influence the contribution behavior of other PACs, they cannot safely assume that other PACs sharing their economic or ideological perspective will merely follow their example and direction. Rather, lead PACs must make substantial efforts to exert some influence on the flow of campaign money. Most lead PACs assign ratings to members of Congress based on their roll-call voting and other legislative behavior, and many assign ratings to nonincumbent candidates based on their responses to surveys. Most send newsletters and memos about the status of specific contests to other allied committees. They also issue press releases and grant interviews to journalists and reporters who work for specialized publications, such as the *Political Report* and the *Cook Political Report*, which serve the Washington, D.C., political community. As the election cycle gets under way, lead PACs hold briefings with increasing frequency in order to update other committees about the status of close congressional races or to introduce promising candidates to PAC managers.

A number of lead PACs get involved in activities that extend beyond the contribution or direction of campaign money. The NCEC provides detailed precinct-level demographic analyses and campaign advice to House and Senate candidates. COPE mobilizes large numbers of volunteers that provide the manpower for telephone banks, voter registration drives, and other grassroots activities. The Free Congress PAC, once the premier lead PAC of the right and now little more than a shadow of its former self, conducts campaign seminars to train nonincumbents on how to run a congressional campaign. These activities, which overlap with those presently conducted by the parties' congressional and senatorial campaign committees, are conducted to improve the quality of the candidates' campaigns and help them raise even more support from other PACs.

2

Coping with Increasing Business Influence: The AFL-CIO's Committee on Political Education

Clyde Wilcox

The 1980s was not a good decade for organized labor. Although Ronald Reagan was the first former labor union head to serve as president, he dismantled the Air Traffic Controllers Union in his first term. An overwhelming majority of unions endorsed Walter Mondale in the Democratic primaries in 1984, but nearly one-third of union members voted for Reagan in the general election. Union membership declined throughout the decade. Corporations increasingly fired striking workers and replaced them with nonunion labor. When collective bargaining did take place, it frequently resulted in a "give-back" of benefits or salary. Corporate PACs increased in number throughout the eighties. It was clearly a better decade for the business community than for organized labor.

Despite these setbacks, labor PACs continued to play an important role in the financing of American elections. During the 1980s, labor funds provided crucial seed money to Democratic nonincumbent candidates. The direct contributions by the AFL-CIO Committee on Political Education (COPE) in the 1990 election cycle totaled more than $830,000, and many PACs associated with member unions made even larger contributions. The true value of communications by the AFL-CIO to its members on behalf of candidates, and of the volunteer activities of union members, is difficult to estimate.

Although COPE is not the largest of the many labor PACs, it is the most influential. A COPE endorsement can help persuade other PACs to contribute, and when COPE puts its entire financial and nonfinancial resources into a race, it is formidable.

History

COPE can trace its roots to the early twentieth century. When John L. Lewis created Labor's Nonpartisan League (LNL) to help coordinate Congress of Industrial Organizations (CIO) support for Franklin Roosevelt in 1936, he began a long tradition of labor financial backing of Democratic presidential and congressional candidates.[1] After Lewis left the CIO (taking the LNL with him), the organization's leaders established the CIO Political Action Committee (CIO-PAC). Although the American Federation of Labor (AFL) was more reluctant to become directly involved in electoral politics, it eventually formed Labor's League for Political Education (LLPE). When the AFL and CIO were reunited in 1935 to form the AFL-CIO, the LLPE and the CIO-PAC were merged into COPE.

Long before the Federal Election Campaign Act (FECA) imposed the current regulatory regime on campaign finance activity, COPE endorsed candidates, made campaign contributions, politicized its members and their families through various means of communications, and mobilized its membership to vote.[2] When Congress considered campaign finance reform, the AFL-CIO pushed its Democratic allies to accommodate political action committees in the legislation, allowing COPE to continue.[3] COPE's $2.7 million dollars in contributions in 1972 had gone almost entirely to congressional Democrats, so their arguments found receptive ears among party leaders.

Throughout the 1970s and 1980s, COPE continued its strong support of Democratic candidates. In every election cycle since the passage of the FECA, more than 95 percent of COPE contributions have gone to Democratic candidates (see Table A.1). Moreover, while corporate and trade association PACs have abandoned Republican challengers in favor of incumbents of both parties, COPE has generally acted as a strategic political actor—supporting vulnerable Democratic incumbents when electoral conditions favor the Republicans, and backing promising Democratic nonincumbents when conditions favor the Democrats. Figure 2.1 shows the total COPE contributions going to different types of candidates in each election cycle.

In 1982 and 1986, COPE directed approximately two-thirds of its Democratic contributions to nonincumbent candidates, while in 1984 COPE directed half of its Democratic contributions to incumbents who appeared vulnerable to possible Reagan coattails. In elections in which neither party was advantaged (e.g., 1988 and 1990), COPE directed slightly under half of its Democratic contributions to nonincumbents.

This pattern of regular support for nonincumbents is typical of PACs that want to change the composition of Congress. COPE's leaders have no difficulty securing access to Democratic party leaders and committee chairs, so they see little to gain in supporting safe incumbents. Instead, they seek to maximize the number of Democratic seats in the House and Senate by contributing in those

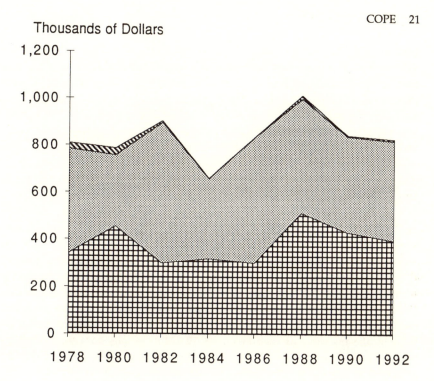

Thousands of Dollars

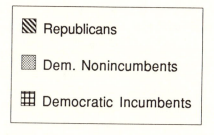

Figure 2.1. **Total Contributions by COPE** (by candidate type)

races where their funds are most needed. The few COPE contributions to Republican candidates are made to those incumbents who are the strongest friends of labor; COPE rarely supports Republican nonincumbents. Since 1982, only 5 percent of the small amount that went to Republican candidates went to non-incumbents.[4] Table A.1 shows the total contributions and the number of candidates to which COPE contributed between 1978 and 1992.

In all presidential elections except 1972, the AFL-CIO has endorsed and aided the Democratic candidate. In 1984, labor went even further, endorsing

Walter Mondale during the Democratic presidential nomination process. When Gary Hart surprised Mondale in New Hampshire, labor support was crucial to Mondale's ability to eventually win the nomination. Labor unions formed the core of many of the "delegate committees" that aided the Mondale campaign in certain key states such as Pennsylvania. In 1992, labor was initially divided in supporting various Democratic presidential candidates, but despite Clinton's mixed record on labor issues in Arkansas, COPE rallied to support his candidacy.

Organization and Decisionmaking

The AFL-CIO is a federation composed of other federated labor organizations. The members of AFL-CIO are ninety-eight major national and international unions with state affiliates, more than 55,000 total local affiliates, and more than 13 million members. A number of these member unions have their own PACs, which can contribute their own funds to candidates. COPE raises its money directly from its member unions: each union is assessed a certain amount based on its total membership. These contributions are treated as earmarked contributions by the members of each union's PAC. Most unions raise their funds by payroll deduction, and those who elect to contribute through this mechanism are informed that a small percentage of their contribution will go to COPE.[5]

The AFL-CIO is federated in another way: it has local and state organizations, which have as members the unions active in that state or area. The Joint Council of local unions in an area has the power of endorsement, and state AFL-CIO councils are often involved in ratifying these choices. In principle, all endorsements originate at the local level. Local unions can vote to recommend endorsement by the national union, and a few locals make endorsements distinct from that of the national organization. Local recommendations are then passed along to the central labor councils (CLCs). The CLCs are intermediate organizations that represent one area of the state, and they recommend endorsements to the state federation. If two-thirds of the unions on the state executive board vote to endorse a candidate, the state federation of the AFL-CIO then recommends that COPE support the candidate.[6] Voting in the CLCs and in the state federations is weighted by per capita payments by each union, so larger unions have more influence. Generally, endorsements by state organizations are honored by the national committee.

Occasionally, however, the national organization will prefer a different candidate. In 1992, the tension between local and national actors surfaced in the Senate race between incumbent Republican Robert Packwood and challenger (and House incumbent) Les AuCoin. Both Packwood and AuCoin had strong labor records, and many PAC directors preferred to support the incumbent Packwood. The state committee endorsed AuCoin in the primary and then in the general election, but the Senate marginal committee was deadlocked for some time before eventually endorsing AuCoin.[7] Packwood eventually received $94,000 in labor PAC contributions, and AuCoin received $288,000.

National officials consider the voting record of the incumbents (COPE has its own roll-call rating scale), as well as the willingness of the incumbent to work with COPE lobbyists in committee. Yet it is quite rare for COPE to override the endorsement of the state organizations. COPE has a national director of a staff that usually numbers between thirty and forty, and an operating committee of eighty members. The heads of the various member unions serve on the operating committee. More important are two subcommittees of the operating committee that determine the amount of financial and other assistance that COPE will provide. The House and Senate marginal committees are each composed of approximately thirty to thirty-five members. These committees determine which candidates will receive COPE funds and the level of support that will flow to endorsed candidates. The committees operate by consensus, but if one union strongly supports a candidate, its director may lobby other committee members.[8] If a union proposes a candidate for inclusion on the marginal list, a vote is taken at the next meeting. If there is insufficient support to place the candidate on the marginal list but several union representatives find the candidate promising, she or he is placed on the watch list, and the campaign is scrutinized for signs of momentum. During the heart of the political season, the marginal committees often meet every two to three weeks. If a candidate appears to be either falling behind or pulling away from her or his opponent, the race may be removed from the marginal list to the watch list.

The marginal committees gather information from a variety of sources. State and local union officials provide valuable insights into the candidates and the electoral climate in the state or district. Members of the marginal committees are assigned to consider candidates from particular states and to report back to their committees. Thus the primary source of information for COPE decisionmaking is union PAC directors, who get their information from local labor activists. At times this local information can be indispensable. George Gould of the Letter Carriers Union noted that local mail carriers were able to carefully monitor the reaction to the House Post Office scandal, and this information was shared with party leaders and directly with members.

COPE considers information from NCEC and Democratic (and sometimes Republican) party officials, although COPE more frequently provides information to the latter. Some union PAC directors attend Democratic party breakfast briefings, and in the past few years the quality of party information at these briefings has improved. COPE also receives information from other PACs. In the 1992 election cycle, the Letter Carriers Union contributed to several other liberal PACs, including EMILY's List (whose name stands for Early Money Is Like Yeast) and Independent Action. They were then invited to attend the briefings of these other PACs and informally shared information with them. NCEC information on the newly drawn congressional districts was highly valued in 1992 by COPE officials.

Finally, some candidates appear before the committee and provide additional information. Candidates' PAC kits frequently contain polling information, and candidates will provide information on their positions on key issues, on other PAC endorsements, and on other matters.

The individual unions that nominate candidates for the COPE marginal lists generally follow a similar process in gathering information. COLCEP, the Letter Carriers' PAC, has five regional directors who coordinate with state legislative chairmen and legislative liaisons in every congressional district. Because postal employees are covered by Hatch Act restrictions, retirees and the spouses of union members play an active role in the districts. The regional directors meet weekly during the election season and recommend candidates for support. The committee staff gathers information on the voting records of incumbents and responses to questionnaires by nonincumbents, on the voting history and demographics of the district, on money raised from sources outside of labor, and on the professionalization of the campaign. COLCEP gets information directly from NCEC on the composition of the new districts, and interacts with the Democratic Congressional Campaign Committee (DCCC) and the Democratic Senatorial Campaign Committee (DSCC) frequently.

In many ways, the marginal committee meetings are more than a decision-making mechanism for COPE; they are an opportunity for various unions to share information. Some unions have strong presences in particular states. For example, the Garment Workers have special expertise in New York and Pennsylvania, while the Auto Workers are consulted on races in Michigan and Ohio. Although the Letter Carriers are a nationwide union, they appreciate the extra information that the Garment Workers have about New York campaigns. Similarly, the Auto Workers have special insight into races in Michigan, but they value information provided by other unions with strengths in other states.

Candidates whose names appear on COPE's marginal lists are involved in close but winnable elections: usually the victor will receive 55 percent of the vote or less. COPE considers the professionalization of the campaign and therefore looks more favorably on candidates with professional managers and consultants. The ability of the candidate to raise early money from sources other than labor is also important. COPE considers polling data that may be provided by the candidate or some other source. The PAC also considers the electoral history of the district, fundraising by the candidate, and for incumbents, the COPE legislative rating. Nonincumbents who seek labor funds will have completed a questionnaire for the State Federation of Labor, and this information is also considered by the committee.

COPE and its member unions also channel soft money (raised outside federal limits and restrictions) to state political parties. Initially this process was somewhat chaotic, with state party chairs approaching individual union PAC directors for hard- (federally allowable) and soft-money contributions. A few years ago John Perkins met with the House and Senate marginal committees and asked

PAC directors to withhold both hard and soft money from party committees until the party had provided a coherent plan to spend it. COPE worked with state party chairs to develop plans and helped them find appropriate political consultants. Today, soft-money decisions are contingent on well-defined state party programs for voter mobilization, as well as the importance and closeness of the races in the states. Although local and state labor organizations are critical to decisions to give hard money, soft-money decisions are primarily made by national leaders.

When a state plan is flawed but there is a need to make a strong effort in that state, COPE and its member unions occasionally work through the state federation of the AFL-CIO. They will give money to the state labor organization to help certain candidates with voter mobilization and other services.

One other COPE committee is influential in campaigns. The Political Works Committee, composed of the heads of fifteen unions, deals primarily with presidential campaigns. This committee determines the rules that will govern COPE activity in the presidential campaign, and it can endorse candidates.

The Benefits of a COPE Endorsement

The marginal lists for the House and Senate are distributed to all member unions. Many of the forty-eight PACS associated with member unions will contribute to candidates on the list, and between fifteen and twenty-five may contribute the legal maximum of $10,000 for the primary and general elections. A candidate endorsed by COPE and listed on a marginal list will receive substantial funds from member (and some nonmember) unions. Candidates who make it to the marginal list can expect to receive between $50,000 and $200,000 in direct labor contributions.

For some candidates, an early endorsement by COPE can be especially helpful. Labor can provide some of the important "seed money" that is especially helpful to nonincumbent candidates.[9] In some House races, labor unions supply up to $250,000 in early money to candidates, which enables them to professionalize their campaigns, establish an early media presence, and raise additional sums from other sources.

Candidates with strong COPE backing receive substantial benefits in addition to financial contributions. Most valuable are the communications that AFL-CIO unions make with their members. These communications come through telephone banks, direct mailings, and direct contact by union members walking the precinct. Union members are told of the endorsed candidate and encouraged to vote. Sometimes communications are coordinated with information provided by other sympathetic PACs. In the 1991 victory of Harris Wofford for the open Senate seat in Pennsylvania, COPE unions used targeting information provided by NCEC to identify counties where COPE efforts would have their greatest payoff. Although most unions focus on contacting their own members, union activists often volunteer for other campaign-related activities. In the 1992 elections, COPE voter mobilization efforts were especially valuable to Barbara Boxer in California and to Patty Murray in Washington.

This auxiliary activity is conducted by the member unions, not by COPE itself. COPE provides member unions with lists of registered members of that union, along with other information. It may appear that this is a minor benefit to unions that could maintain their own lists, but updating the lists is a major undertaking that COPE assumes for its member unions. In some unions the turnover in membership approaches 10 percent a month, so updated lists of registered union members are invaluable in mounting member-contact campaigns. The centralized COPE lists are shared only with member unions and their locals and are never provided directly to the candidate.

An endorsement by COPE and placement on a marginal list are very valuable to a candidate. But a candidate on the marginal list cannot count on contributions from all of the PACs from COPE member unions. Some labor PACs have separate issues and different politics. The Letter Carriers are more likely than other unions to give something to Republicans, but still the large majority of their funds goes to Democrats. Yet George Gould, director of COLCEP, notes that an endorsement by COPE is "very important" in inducing his committee to give, especially to a nonincumbent.

COPE in 1992

Early in the 1992 cycle, COPE did not foresee any great change in its strategy for the 1992 election. PAC officials anticipated that the House marginal list might grow from fifty to sixty in 1992 but doubted it would exceed that number. Although the poor economy would indicate an aggressive strategy of backing Democratic nonincumbent candidates, a variety of other factors, including redistricting and the House Bank scandal, lead COPE to support vulnerable Democratic incumbents early in the cycle.

As a parade of nonincumbents marched through the offices of COPE member unions' PACs, a majority stressed issues that were not especially germane to labor. George Gould of the Letter Carriers noted in late July 1992 that "two-thirds or so emphasized issues such as the House Bank and Post Office and wanted to end the perks of office. Only a few were interested in our issues. The women and minority candidates have been far more likely to talk about issues that we care about."[10]

As the election unfolded, COPE and many of its member unions had some trouble sorting through the large number of nonincumbent candidates running in possibly competitive districts. Yet COPE was better suited than many PACs to gather information in 1992 because of its strong grassroots organization. George Gould noted that his PAC relied more than ever on information from members in the local district and state. Of course, even with this generally reliable source of information, union PACs (like all PACs) were surprised by some outcomes.

The financial demands of a presidential campaign, two expensive Senate races in California, and many marginal House races meant that gifts to friendly incumbents who faced only token opposition were reduced. There was less money to invest in nonincumbent candidates who were running well ahead or well behind their opponents. Many gifts were reduced in magnitude.

Overall, COPE gifts to House and Senate candidates totaled just over $800,000, a substantial drop from the million dollars given in 1988. COPE contributed much less money to House candidates in 1992 than in the most recent election cycles, but increased its aggregate gifts to Senate challengers and especially open-seat candidates.

Conclusions: COPE in the Information Flow

In an uncertain election cycle, COPE benefited from a strong grassroots network of labor activists and from local and state union organizations in gathering information. This information was processed by committees composed of the heads of various labor PACs, and lists of important close races were developed and distributed. These lists influenced but did not determine the contribution strategies of member unions. They probably influenced the decisions of other PACs as well, for candidates on the COPE marginal list would make this information known to all other sympathetic PACs. This would signal that COPE's political operatives believed that the race was competitive, and this information would be helpful to other PACs with less widespread organizations to gather political information.

COPE was part of a larger network of information as well. COPE representatives and PAC directors from COPE member unions attended briefings by party organizations and informally shared information with party members. They consulted with state party chairs on the best ways to spend soft money. They attended briefings by other PACs to which they had contributed, and shared information at those meetings as well. They welcomed targeting information from NCEC, and that information helped state and local union activists to better use their resources in voter mobilization efforts.

Labor leaders were generally pleased with the outcome of the 1992 elections. For the first time in twelve years a Democrat was headed for the White House, Democrats held their own in the Senate although they had more seats to defend, and losses in the House were far smaller than had been feared a year before. This political lineup did not guarantee that labor's agenda would be fully enacted: indeed, the Clinton budget cuts and health care plan were certain to require modification before they could win labor endorsement. Yet labor leaders again had access to the White House, and Democrats controlled the major institutions that make national policy. This suggested the possibility that the 1990s would be a better decade for labor unions and their members.

Notes

The author is grateful to William Sweeney, Richard Murphy, and George Gould for interviews.

1. Arthur Schlesinger, Jr., "Labor's New Role: The 1936 Election," in Charles Rehmus, Doris McLaughlin, and Frederick Nesbitt, eds., *Labor and American Politics* (Ann Arbor: University of Michigan Press, 1976).

2. Rex Hardesty, "The Computer's Role in Getting Out the Vote," in C. Rehmus, D. McLaughlin, and F. Nesbitt, eds., *Labor and American Politics* (Ann Arbor: University of Michigan Press, 1976).

3. Edward Epstein, "Business and Labor under the Federal Election Campaign Act of 1971," in Michael Malbin, ed., *Parties, Interest Groups, and Campaign Finance Laws* (Washington, DC: AEI, 1980).

4. Since 1980, COPE has directed only $2,000 to Republican challengers. In 1982, however, the committee gave $5,000 to a House Republican open-seat candidate.

5. Some unions cannot use the payroll deduction system. Unions representing federal workers frequently do not use the checkoff because of Hatch Act restrictions. The Letter Carriers Union, for example, raises its funds by direct mail.

6. The executive board is composed of the representatives of the largest unions in the state.

7. Eventually the Senate marginal committee placed AuCoin on the marginal list, although this appears to have violated the norm that such a decision be made by consensus. One labor PAC director told me that this decision may have ultimately hurt AuCoin, for the divisive nature of the debate may have dried up some of the soft money that might otherwise have flowed to the state party.

8. Richard Murphy, "A Manual on How to Maximize Political and Logistical Assistance from the Trade Union Movement." Unpublished manuscript.

9. See Robert Biersack, Paul Herrnson, and Clyde Wilcox, "Seeds for Success: Early Money in Congressional Elections," *Legislative Studies Quarterly* 18 (1993), pp. 535–54.

10. Personal interview with George Gould, September 1992.

3

The Business–Industry PAC: Trying to Lead in an Uncertain Election Climate

Candice J. Nelson

The Business–Industry Political Action Committee (BIPAC) has been a lead PAC in the business community since its inception in 1963. Formed originally to give business a political voice, BIPAC was and still is a way for the business community to participate in elections. While BIPAC's role in the business community has changed, its importance has not. As more corporations and trade associations formed PACs during the 1970s, BIPAC's voice was joined by other voices representing the business community. BIPAC's importance today comes less from its contributions and more from the impact of its endorsements on the flow of money from other business-oriented PACs to political candidates.

BIPAC's contribution philosophy differs from that of other business PACs. While most PACs give to incumbents, the majority of BIPAC's support goes to challengers and candidates for open seats. In 1990, for example, 9 percent of all corporate PAC contributions went to challengers,[1] yet 36 percent of BIPAC's contributions went to challengers that year. BIPAC believes that electing a few new members of Congress each year makes a difference and perceives its role as promoting business interests.[2]

History

Though PACs have long been a vehicle for labor participation in politics, few business-oriented PACs existed prior to 1974. While most corporate money entered politics through individual contributions prior to the FECA, in the early

Table 3.1

BIPAC Contributions by Candidate Status, 1982–92 (percentage)

	1982	1984	1986	1988	1990	1992
Incumbent	36	33	43	44	22	29
Challenger	37	42	13	30	36	34
Open Seat	28	25	44	26	42	37

Source: Compiled from Federal Election Commission data.

1960s a group of individuals from the nonlabor private sector, including doctors, bankers, farmers, and insurance agents, began meeting on an informal basis to discuss ways in which the business community could more formally participate in politics. Both the American Medical Association's PAC and BIPAC were an outgrowth of these informal meetings.

Contrary to popular opinion, BIPAC was not formed by the National Association of Manufacturers (NAM), although NAM did provide some initial seed money for BIPAC, as well as the first staff director and the first five board members. BIPAC's independence from NAM has always been important because from its inception BIPAC has wanted to avoid being tied to any one organization's particular set of issues. BIPAC's mission has been to be involved in politics—political education and elections—not in lobbying. BIPAC's focus on challengers and nonincumbents also has existed from its inception (see Table 3.1). According to Bernadette Budde, BIPAC's Vice President for Public Relations, BIPAC expects to give to candidates who lose in about one-half the races it is involved in.[3]

When BIPAC was founded there were very few other business-oriented PACs. With the growth of corporate and trade association PACs during the 1970s the role of BIPAC changed. In its early years, BIPAC was important as much for the amount of money it contributed as it was for its choice of recipients. Today, though BIPAC contributes less money than it did in the 1960s, it has greater leverage because of the weight its endorsements carry within the PAC community. The evolution from the importance of dollar amounts to the importance of endorsements occurred as more corporations formed PACs during the early and mid-1970s and as campaigns became more expensive.

Organization

BIPAC is controlled by a board of directors that consists of between fifty-five and sixty-five people. Each state has one board member, and some states, such as California and Pennsylvania, have more than one. All members of the board have corporate titles, such as chairman of the board or chief executive officer. In addition to the board of directors, BIPAC also has a ten-person Washington office. From 1963 until 1970, BIPAC's headquarters was in New York, but it moved to the District of Columbia in September of 1970.

When it was founded, BIPAC's constituency consisted of traditional American-based, American-owned manufacturing firms, banks, and life insurance companies. As the business community has changed over the years, it has become harder to define BIPAC's constituency. Broadly speaking, BIPAC's constituency is "anyone who considers themselves part of the business community and identifies with what BIPAC does."[4] Yet as the business community has expanded, BIPAC's constituency has as well; it now includes businesses as potentially diverse as traditional manufacturing firms and the travel and entertainment industries. Consequently, BIPAC's criteria for evaluating candidates have changed to reflect changes in its membership.

BIPAC organizes its financial activity into two funds: the Action Fund and the Education Fund. Contributions to the Action Fund are used to advocate and support candidates. Contributions to the Education Fund are used to provide information about Congress and about congressional races, but not for advocacy of particular candidates. The Action Fund is supported by individual contributors and other PACs, while the Education Fund is supported by corporation and trade association treasury funds. Decisions about contributions from the Action Fund are made by the board of directors' Candidate Review Committee (CRC), while decisions about expenditures of the Education Fund are made by the staff of BIPAC's national office.

About 700 to 800 corporations and trade associations belong to the Education Fund. In return for their support they receive political information and opportunities to attend meetings. The Education Fund supports two publications, *BIPAC Politics*, published quarterly, and *Politikit*, published monthly. *BIPAC Politics* is a four-page newsletter that covers developments of interest to the business community, while *Politikit* is a longer, more detailed publication that provides details on House and Senate races and other electoral issues. The more money an organization contributes to the Education Fund, the more publications it receives from BIPAC. For example, for each $30 contribution to BIPAC a corporation gets one copy of *BIPAC Politics*. In addition to the publications, contributors to the Education Fund are invited to monthly briefings. BIPAC political director Bernadette Budde estimates that between forty and sixty people attend these briefings each month; of those, about one-third are regular attendees, one-third come occasionally, and one-third attend only when there is an issue of particular importance to their state.

Support for the Action Fund comes from two sources: other PACs and direct mail. According to Budde, BIPAC receives some money from PACs that want to contribute money to nonincumbents but cannot,[5] but most of the support for the Action Fund comes from very targeted direct mail. For example, BIPAC might do a mailing to a couple of hundred oil executives, or people in the energy industry, at the suggestion of a member of the board of directors. BIPAC has found that after an initial donation, its contributors give again, and thus much of the support for the Action Fund comes from old, not new, contributors.

While there has never been a scientific survey of BIPAC contributors, Budde says they are mostly business people—sophisticated political givers who contribute to other candidates, the political parties, and causes.[6] Budde suspects that the contribution to BIPAC is neither the largest nor the most salient one these individuals make. Most individual contributors to the Action Fund are not well-known or easily recognized political contributors, and those who are give more money to candidates and the political parties than to BIPAC. The average contribution to BIPAC is small, mostly under $100. Contributors receive a quarterly newsletter, which contains BIPAC's ratings of members of Congress, as well as fundraising appeals and thank you notes throughout the year.

Decisionmaking

Decisions about which candidates to support have always been made by BIPAC's Candidate Review Committee. The review committee consists of six members of the board of directors—three Republicans and three Democrats. Appointments to the CRC are made by the president of BIPAC and the chairman of the board of directors. In filling vacancies, an effort is made to keep a regional balance on the CRC, as well as to appoint members who have been on the board of directors, have good political judgment, understand BIPAC's goals, and do not have strong prejudices against members of the opposing political party. The most interesting thing about the CRC is that no one on the board of directors knows who the six members of the CRC are, nor does any of the six members know who the other five are. Anonymity is important to protect members of the CRC from being pressured to support particular candidates and to avoid horsetrading among CRC members. BIPAC wants members of the CRC to be equally comfortable supporting or denying support to a candidate, as well as postponing a decision on support. The review committee never meets; all communication is done by fax.

Candidates must meet three criteria to receive support from BIPAC: First, there must be a "preponderance" of support for business interests. Second, the candidate must be in a competitive race. Third, the candidate must need money. The requirement of preponderance of support for business interests reflects the changes in BIPAC's membership. The original criterion was a "clear choice" of support for business interests. This criterion assumed that everyone who supported business interests was on the same side of an issue. Yet as the business community has become more diverse, segments of that community may not always be on the same side of an issue. As a result, BIPAC changed its criterion for support from "clear choice" to a "preponderance" of support for business interests.

The other two criteria are also somewhat subjective. "Competitiveness" means that a candidate has a chance to "get in the ballpark," to do "better than expected," or to be well positioned to run next time. If a candidate has run and done fairly well but had lost in a previous election, BIPAC may support that candidate in a subsequent election if he or she meets the other criteria for BIPAC support. For example, in 1992 BIPAC supported Republican challenger Donna Peterson against Democrat incumbent Charles Wilson in the 2nd congressional district in Texas. Peterson had run against Wilson in 1990 and received 44 percent of the vote. BIPAC did not support her in 1990, but because BIPAC believes in "rewarding people who do well and try again," Peterson received BIPAC support in 1992.[7]

Budde thinks that to define "competitive" as 55 percent voter support or less may have made sense in the 1980s, but it is too rigid a criterion today.[8] Similarly, the need for money depends on how much money the candidate has in the bank and how much it costs to run in a particular district or state. BIPAC uses a candidate's budget and campaign plan to help assess need.

Recommendations for candidates to support come from both the board of directors and BIPAC constituents. Recommendations are processed by the staff in Washington and then periodically faxed to each of the six members of the CRC. CRC members are given information about the political and economic history of the candidate's district, his or her background, an evaluation of the race, what the candidates in the race are saying, and why the recommendation to support a candidate has been made. For incumbents, board members are also given information on the candidate's votes in Congress and congressional activities. Information on committee assignments is not included on the candidate review sheets, because whether or not a member is on a particular committee is not important to BIPAC. BIPAC is interested in an incumbent's position across a broad range of issues. For challengers, board members are given information about the candidate's relationship to industry and whether or not the PACs of business facilities in his or her district or state are making contributions.

Information about candidates and races comes from leaders in the district or state, people who have talked to residents of the district or state, candidate PAC kits, and anyone else who has heard about the candidates. This information is obviously easier to obtain about incumbents, about candidates in competitive districts, and in districts where large segments of the business community are active in politics.

Decisions on which candidates to support are made weekly, or sometimes more often. The CRC must unanimously agree to support a candidate before a contribution is given. While unanimity might seem virtually impossible given the bipartisan makeup of the CRC, the partisanship of the members is overshadowed by their business orientation. Moreover, directors are discouraged by the national office staff from making a recommendation that is not likely to be approved by

Table 3.2

BIPAC Contributions to House and Senate Candidates, 1982–92 (percentage)

	1982	1984	1986	1988	1990	1992
House	81	79	80	66	68	67
Senate	19	21	20	34	32	33

Source: Compiled from Federal Election Commission data.

the CRC. The national office staff encourages directors to make serious requests and to avoid making requests as favors to others. Consequently, about 90 to 95 percent of all requests for support are approved by the CRC. While the national office staff can help directors prepare recommendations, it encourages each director to make his or her own case, because if support is given to the candidate, it is the director who has to justify the decision. When support is denied it is usually because there is not support for the candidate among the business community in the district, the need for money is not yet clear, the opposition is not yet known, or support is requested too early.

BIPAC only recommends a candidate to other PACs after it has made a contribution to the candidate. Once BIPAC decides to support a candidate, it maintains an ongoing working relationship with him or her. While BIPAC does not force its help on candidates, it will make suggestions to the candidates it is supporting, talk to other people about the candidates, and make suggestions to the candidates about which other PACs they should talk to.

For challengers, particularly first-time candidates, BIPAC's support can be extremely important. For example, in 1992 BIPAC supported Republican Jim Greenwood, a challenger running against Peter Kostmayer in Pennsylvania's 8th congressional district. Because BIPAC had not supported any candidate against Kostmayer in recent elections, BIPAC's support of Greenwood told other PACs that Greenwood was a better candidate than others who had challenged Kostmayer in the recent past.[9] Similarly, BIPAC's support of Richard Pombo, who ran in an open-seat race in the 11th district of California, drew attention to the race—particularly important in a state where there was a lot of electoral activity occurring.[10]

BIPAC periodically sends a list of the candidates it is supporting, and their campaign addresses, to all business-related PACs that give $25,000 or more and give across state lines. Budde estimates that there are between 800 and 900 such PACs.[11] BIPAC does not give to both candidates in a single race. Normally, BIPAC does not get involved in primaries, but it helped Republican Senator John Seymour in his effort to retain his Senate seat in California in 1992. It also gives more money to House candidates than Senate candidates, because there are more of the former than the latter (see Table 3.2). When BIPAC does give money to a Senate candidate, it does so only during the election year. BIPAC does not make independent expenditures, nor does it get involved in presidential campaigns.

The 1992 Election Cycle

For BIPAC, 1992 presented a difficult election climate. First, there was an anti-incumbent mood in the country and, for a PAC with a history of supporting more challengers than incumbents, this posed an interesting dilemma. If BIPAC continued to give a majority of its support to nonincumbents, it might do so at the expense of incumbents in normally safe seats who needed help in 1992. Conversely, if BIPAC supported incumbents who were in trouble, its traditional support for nonincumbents would be compromised. Second, the delay in redistricting in some states prevented BIPAC from getting involved early in some races. By the end of March of 1992, BIPAC had made contributions to only five candidates, all of whom were incumbents.[12] In comparison, during the 1990 election cycle BIPAC began making contributions to general election candidates in July of 1989 and continued to make campaign contributions throughout the fall and early winter.[13]

While the slowness of the redistricting process frustrated BIPAC's early involvement in congressional races, redistricting also created opportunities for BIPAC to get involved in House elections in districts where it had not been involved during the 1980s. For BIPAC, the number of open seats in 1992 was less significant than the redistricting that created some of those seats. For example, both the 1st district in Oregon and the 8th district in New Jersey were open seats in 1992. The Republican candidate in Oregon, Tony Meeker, had run as a challenger against Congressman Les AuCoin in 1986, and BIPAC had supported him. BIPAC supported him again in 1992. In contrast, redistricting in New Jersey meant there was an opportunity for BIPAC to have influence in the 8th district, where there had been no opportunity before.

A year before the 1992 elections, Bernadette Budde said that she would not be surprised if over half of BIPAC's contributions went to incumbents, despite BIPAC's goal of supporting nonincumbents. Budde worried about the anti-incumbency mood and its effect on otherwise safe incumbents. She thought that for PACs predisposed to help incumbents, it was much easier in the 1992 election cycle to make the case that incumbents needed help.[14] For example, Congressman Dan Rostenkowski (D) asked PACs to contribute $5,000 to his primary campaign, despite having a million dollars in the bank. He spent hundreds of thousands of dollars in the primary and got 57 percent of the vote. Budde thought Rostenkowski made the case right there for incumbents.

Throughout the first quarter of 1992, requests for support from BIPAC were coming from incumbents. Budde worried about how much money would be left to support challengers when they did start to ask for money. At the end of 1991,

Budde had two conflicting concerns. First, she worried that PACs, particularly BIPAC, would pay less attention to the anti-incumbency mood than they should. As a consequence, in mid-October, when it became clear that many incumbents were going to lose, there would be nothing that could be done. Second, she worried that too much attention would be paid to the anti-incumbent mood, PACs would support incumbents, and then would have no impact on which challengers were elected.

At the end of March the latter scenario seemed more likely. Clearly a lot of attention was being paid to the anti-incumbency mood. BIPAC supported Republican John Seymour in the California Senate primary, even though BIPAC normally does not get involved in primaries, because of Senator Alan Dixon's (D) unexpected defeat in the Illinois primary. John McCain (R), a Senate incumbent, was one of only five candidates who had received support from BIPAC by the end of March, despite being a senator and an incumbent, because of the political situation in Arizona. While no one knew how the anti-incumbency mood would play in November, it was being taken very seriously by BIPAC in March.

The uncertain election climate continued over the summer and into the fall. As late as mid-October, BIPAC was still evaluating candidates and deciding whom to support. In contrast, in previous election cycles, BIPAC had given to everyone possible by mid-October and was making contributions to unusual races that nevertheless deserved support.[15] In 1992, as late as three weeks before the election it was still difficult for BIPAC to differentiate between candidates it was supporting and those it could support if it had unlimited resources.

The factors that inhibited early contributions in the beginning of 1992 continued to be important in October. Because of redistricting some candidates still did not have their campaigns fully up and running. Thus, BIPAC did not have the luxury in this election cycle, as it had in past cycles, of waiting to see how a race shaped up. Also, despite the fact that redistricting created opportunities for pro-business candidates in districts where there had not been opportunities before, with no voting history BIPAC could not judge how well a candidate would represent the business interests of the district.

The concern over incumbents continued to influence BIPAC's contribution decisions. Incumbent polls were shaky and incumbents were having trouble raising money; thus BIPAC was appealed to by, and supported, incumbents who would have easily been dismissed as not needing money in other election cycles.[16] For example, BIPAC supported Jay Rhodes, a Republican incumbent running for reelection in the 1st district of Arizona. This was normally a safe Republican seat and thus not a race BIPAC would participate in, but Rhodes only received one-third of the vote in the primary.[17]

The uncertain political climate meant that some open seats expected to be safe Republican seats were suddenly competitive, and Republican candidates in those races were suddenly scared and asking for BIPAC support. Budde cited Edward

Royce, running to succeed William Dannemeyer in California's 39th district, as an example of a candidate BIPAC supported but had not expected to have to support.[18] While some candidates who asked BIPAC for support expected, as challengers, to have tough races, it was the candidates who thought they had safe districts, and suddenly found out they did not, that seemed the most desperate in their requests for support.

In 1992, 30 of the 109 candidates BIPAC supported were incumbents (see Table A.2). While this is not as high a proportion as Budde had predicted a year earlier, BIPAC supported more incumbents and gave more money to them in 1992 than it did in 1990. In Senate races, BIPAC gave more money to both incumbents and open-seat candidates in 1992 than it did in 1990, but less money to challengers. In contests for the House, incumbents and challengers received more money from BIPAC in 1992 than in 1990, while open-seat candidates received less. Clearly the need to support incumbents reduced the amount of money available for nonincumbents.

In the end, BIPAC was able to support all the candidates it wanted in 1992, but its contributions at the end of the cycle were smaller than they were in other election cycles. During the last two weeks BIPAC was making contributions of $500 to candidates but would have made contributions of $1,000, and in some cases more, if there had been more money available.[19]

While all candidates BIPAC supported were equally important to the committee, it had three separate goals in 1992. One was to change the composition of the committee most important to the business community, namely, the House Committee on Energy and Commerce. To that end, BIPAC opposed Democratic Congressman Mike Synar of Oklahoma in both the primary and the runoff; opposed Democratic incumbent Gerry Sikorsky in the primary and supported his opponent, Rod Grams, in the general election; and opposed Democratic incumbent Peter Kostmayer. Synar was reelected, but both Sikorsky and Kostmayer were defeated. A second goal was to make an impact in the California delegation, thus the support for Republicans Richard Pombo and Edward Royce, both of whom won. Finally, BIPAC wanted to continue to support Jim Ross Lightfoot (R) in Iowa, because it had supported him for a long time. Lightfoot also won.[20]

Conclusions

Despite the concerns over the fate of incumbents expressed early in the 1992 election cycle, BIPAC continued its tradition of giving a majority of its support to nonincumbents. Because of its history of support for nonincumbents, BIPAC was ideally situated to identify qualified challengers and open-seat candidates; thus its role as a lead PAC became even more important in a year in which anti-incumbency and change were the dominant themes.

BIPAC was successful in just over 50 percent of the races in which it was involved, similar to its success rate in previous election cycles. Of the candidates who lost, most were within five percentage points of winning their elections.[21] Despite her concerns early in the election cycle about whether to support more incumbents than in previous years, in the end Bernadette Budde felt that BIPAC made sensible choices in the candidates it supported in 1992.[22]

BIPAC's role as a lead PAC remained intact in 1992. Despite the frustrations caused by the slowness of redistricting and the uncertainty over the fate of incumbents, BIPAC's decisionmaking procedures worked well, and there were few surprises for the PAC when the elections were over.

Notes

This chapter would not have been completed without the cooperation of Bernadette Budde, the political director of BIPAC. I am grateful to Ms. Budde for her willingness to share her thoughts on the 1992 election cycle with me. I also appreciate the help of my research assistant, Marni Ezra, in the compilation of some of the tables in this chapter.

1. Calculated from Federal Election Commission data.
2. Personal interview with Bernadette Budde, vice president, Public Relations, BIPAC, November 4, 1991.
3. Ibid.
4. Ibid.
5. Ibid.
6. Ibid.
7. Personal interview with Bernadette Budde, June 23, 1992.
8. Personal interview with Bernadette Budde, March 26, 1992.
9. Personal interview with Bernadette Budde, November 24, 1992.
10. Ibid.
11. Budde interview, March 26, 1992.
12. The five candidates were Congressman Jim Nussle (R-Iowa), a first-term incumbent supported by BIPAC in 1990, running against another incumbent, Congressman David Nagle (D-Iowa); Congressman Jim Ross Lightfoot (R-Iowa); Senator Dan Coats (R-Indiana); Senator John Seymour (R-California); and Senator John McCain (R-Arizona).
13. Budde interview, November 4, 1992.
14. Budde interview, March 26, 1992.
15. Personal interview with Bernadette Budde, October 12, 1992.
16. Ibid.
17. Ibid.
18. Ibid.
19. Budde interview, November 24, 1992.
20. Ibid.
21. Ibid.
22. Ibid.

4

The National Committee for an Effective Congress: Liberalism, Partisanship, and Electoral Innovation

Paul S. Herrnson

The National Committee for an Effective Congress (NCEC) is one of the oldest and most influential liberal PACs. Founded in 1948 to help liberal candidates get elected to, or remain in, the U.S. Senate, the committee has drastically altered its philosophy, mission, and election activities in recent years. It has changed from an independent bipartisan PAC to a staunchly pro-Democratic organization that works closely with Democratic candidates and party committees. It has broadened the scope of its mission to include the election of Democratic House candidates. It has greatly scaled back the amount of cash it contributes to candidates and has become one of the most important providers of "in-kind" technical assistance to Democratic candidates and party committees. Once heralded as one of the premier vehicles for translating ideology into electoral action, the NCEC has become a highly integrated and pragmatic player in Democratic campaign politics.[1]

The circumstances surrounding its formation and development alone make the NCEC one of the most interesting committees operating in the contemporary PAC community. Yet it is worthy of study for more important reasons. The NCEC's $2,016,935 budget made it the eighth largest nonconnected PAC participating in the 1992 elections.[2] The committee's informational resources, decisionmaking process, and technical services make it one of the most innovative organizations in electoral politics. Moreover, as a lead PAC, the NCEC affects the contributions of other PACs, individuals who make large contributions, and party committees. NCEC endorsements and campaign assistance are believed by many to be very important for Democratic candidates, especially those challenging incumbents or running for open seats.

Organizational Evolution and Strategic Adjustment

The NCEC was founded by Maurice Rosenblatt, Harry Louis Selden, Eleanor Roosevelt, and a number of other leading liberals to defend the domestic and foreign policy of the New Deal from attacks from conservatives, especially the radical right of the Republican party.[3] Its primary means for carrying out this mission were the distribution of campaign contributions and endorsements.[4] The PAC also engaged in related educational activities, such as the publication of newsletters and the formation of research organizations like the Fair Campaign Practices Committee and the "McCarthy Clearinghouse," which sought to educate the public about the unscrupulous activities of Republican Senator Joseph McCarthy of Wisconsin and his allies.

Historical circumstances had a significant impact on the NCEC's organizational structure. The Cold War and the threat of Communist infiltration led its founders to strictly limit its membership. Membership was, and continues to be, limited to the PAC's original cofounders, plus additional members who are invited to join the organization by the current membership. Total membership is limited to fifty. Membership terms are indefinite, ending when an individual dies, resigns, announces his or her candidacy for public office, or is expelled by a majority vote of the other members.[5]

The existence of rival political organizations—particularly the Congress of Industrial Organizations' Political Action Committee (the forerunner of the AFL-CIO's Committee on Political Education) and the Americans for Democratic Action (ADA)—also influenced the NCEC's development, encouraging it to search for a unique niche among liberal groups. The NCEC chose to differentiate its activities from those of the labor movement by limiting its role to the distribution of campaign contributions to general election candidates. Unlike many labor unions, the NCEC originally chose not to recruit candidates, carry out grassroots voter mobilization programs, or become integrated into the Democratic party apparatus.[6]

Unlike the ADA, the NCEC did not give the unions formal representation in its leadership. Yet labor provided roughly one-third of its income.[7] The NCEC also eschewed lobbying Congress in favor of an election-oriented approach. The ADA lobbied Congress, but it did not give campaign contributions to congressional candidates, although its statewide committees, local chapters, and affiliated student committees were free to do so.

Moreover, the NCEC differed from both the ADA and the labor movement in terms of its structure. While the latter two organizations were both decentralized and had state, local, or, in the case of labor, functional subdivisions, the NCEC remained a centralized PAC without subdivisions. Its bipartisanship, independence, centralized structure, and electoral orientation enabled the NCEC to carve out a unique role for itself in congressional election politics.

NCEC members have been and continue to be chosen on the basis of their liberal credentials, prominence in elite political and social circles, ability to raise money, and the potential impact that the presence of their names on the NCEC's letterhead could have on the PAC's ability to collect direct-mail contributions. Committee members are dispersed throughout the United States so as to promote the image of the NCEC as a fully national organization. The NCEC's bylaws require its members to select four officers—chairman, vice chairman, secretary, and treasurer—and an executive board composed of seven to fifteen members. The officers and board loosely oversee the NCEC's operations, approve its budget and recommendations for political activity, and play an important role in fundraising.[8]

The NCEC's development has been heavily affected by the political, technological, and legal changes that have taken place in American politics. During its early history, the committee mainly sought to assist in the election of liberal candidates to the U.S. Senate, regardless of their partisan identification. It originally focused on the Senate because the relatively small number of candidates running for that body at any one time made the identification of marginal races a manageable exercise.[9] It was also understood that Senate election victories had the potential to give the PAC more influence than a corresponding number of victories in House contests. The upper chamber's foreign policy prerogatives, its role in the confirmation of presidential appointees, and the more national orientation of its members made Senate elections a more attractive arena for NCEC involvement than the House contests.

The committee's early bipartisanship, though somewhat unusual for an ideological group, reflects the political conditions of the time and the group's pragmatism. After the 1948 election, in which the committee supported only Democrats, Roosevelt's Fair Deal coalition began to unravel in the Senate and it became apparent to NCEC board members that liberal Republican senators had the potential to make the difference between the passage and defeat of liberal legislation.[10] Many of these Republicans were becoming isolated from the core of their party and in need of outside electoral support. According to Harry Scoble, author of the definitive book on early NCEC activity, the PAC's bipartisanship grew out of ideological conviction and a belief "that if liberal groups did not aid liberal candidacies, no one else would."[11]

Bipartisanship, however, should not be confused with a lack of partisan preference. Throughout its history the NCEC has distributed most of its resources to Democratic candidates. This pattern reflects the ideological composition of the two parties, as well as the fact that Democratic candidates typically received substantially less national party support than did their Republican opponents.[12]

"Uneven bipartisanship" in contributing would persist through the 1986 election, when the committee would no longer be able to identify Republicans with the proper liberal credentials and changes in the composition of Congress would encourage the NCEC to experience a fundamental change in philosophy. The last Republican to receive an NCEC contribution was Representative Claudine Schneider of Rhode Island, who was given $1,000.

The 1980 Republican landslide victory had a catalytic effect on the NCEC that resulted in a major philosophical conversion. The emergence of a Republican majority in the Senate was devastating for the NCEC and other liberal groups. As the minority party in the Senate, the GOP had occasionally been able to coalesce with the southern Democrats in order to block liberal legislation; as the majority party, however, the GOP could block liberal policies far more effectively and much earlier in the legislative process. According to Mark Gersh, the NCEC's Washington director, the recognition that Democratic control of the chamber was critical to forwarding the PAC's liberal agenda prompted it to reject its previous bipartisan orientation and become a fully pro-Democratic partisan PAC. Following 1980, the NCEC began to support Democratic candidates of all ideological stripes and virtually stopped supporting liberal Republicans.[13]

Technological and legal changes in the political environment have provided the impetus for other changes at the NCEC. The PAC's first activities consisted of collecting contributions from roughly 400 individuals and distributing this money to liberal candidates. In 1952, it experimented with direct-mail fundraising, using a mailing list of 20,000 college faculty members, an appeal based on civil liberties issues, and the signatures of several prominent Harvard professors to generate a net profit of just under $13,000 (roughly 45 percent of its total disbursements that year).[14] Four years later, the direct-mail fundraising effort was supplemented by one-page advertisements in liberal magazines like the *Nation* and the *Progressive*. Its early success in raising small contributions made the NCEC one of the pioneers in direct-mail fundraising.

Personal meetings between candidates and potential backers, which are now commonly referred to as "meet and greets," were pioneered by the NCEC. These meetings were tremendously successful at helping candidates raise money from a large circle of wealthy individuals and interest groups.[15] They resulted in the PAC's becoming an important "middleman," or broker, in the campaign finance community. The fundraising meetings were so successful that they were soon imitated by the political parties and continue to be used by both parties' congressional and senatorial campaign committees and a number of PACs. The NCEC no longer uses this approach to help congressional candidates raise money, but it continues to play an important role as a cue-giver to many wealthy individual contributors and PACs.

Another NCEC innovation is the provision of campaign services to congressional candidates. During the early years of its existence, the PAC distributed cash contributions and did not try to influence how the candidates spent them. Within a few election cycles, however, it began to encourage candidates to spend their money on public opinion surveys and other specialized campaign functions. In 1956, it purchased a survey for a Democratic candidate for the Senate.[16]

The Federal Election Campaign Act (FECA) of 1974 and its amendments encouraged the NCEC to begin to distribute more of its campaign assistance in the form of campaign services. The PAC found that by obtaining blocs of services from pollsters, media specialists, and general consultants and then distributing them to candidates, it could purchase these services more cheaply and price them at below their true market value (and below the FECA's contribution limits) when distributing them to candidates. At first, this "in-kind" contribution strategy enabled the committee to increase its electoral influence.

Nevertheless, problems soon developed with this approach. The best consultants showed a preference for working directly for candidates so that they could earn bigger fees. Some refused to agree to advance contracts with the NCEC. Others gave short shrift to candidates whose services were purchased by the PAC, preferring to focus attention on their more traditional client-candidates. As a result, the NCEC began to develop its technical capacities so that it could directly provide candidates with "in-house" campaign services. It began to assemble statewide data bases, to hire technically skilled staff, and to train others in statistics and voting behavior research. It also sent generalists into the field to help recipients of NCEC data analysis make the most effective use of it. In 1991, the PAC had data bases that covered 80 percent of the election precincts in the United States and had gotten deeply involved in the redistricting process in thirty states.

The NCEC currently employs nineteen full-time staff. The New York office consists of the PAC's national director, Russell Hemenway, and three fundraising and administrative specialists. The Washington office has a staff of fifteen technical and political experts who analyze demographic and voting patterns, write reports, and help candidates plan their campaign strategies. The Washington staff includes several individuals who previously worked as political consultants, congressional aides, or for the Democratic party. Washington director Mark Gersh, for example, is a former employee of the Democratic Study Group.[17]

The PAC's constituency continues to be liberals with strong foreign policy concerns. Most are upper-middle-class residents of major metropolitan areas. Over half are male and live in the Northeast. Many are Jewish. Over 60 percent of the NCEC's members identify themselves as Democrats; 36 percent consider themselves Independents, and less than 2 percent are Republicans. By overwhelming margins, NCEC contributors favor the SALT Treaty, are for less defense spending, and support foreign aid. They are against the balanced budget amendment, prefer combating unemployment over controlling inflation, and believe in government regulation. The contributors also take predictably liberal stands on social issues. They are pro-choice on abortion and favor gay rights, the equal rights amendment, and gun control. Large majorities also believe in protecting Social Security and the environment, favor national health insurance, and are against allowing prayer in public schools. Their motives for contributing to the PAC are mainly ideological, although they also obtain information about candidates and their campaigns.[18]

Individual contributions have traditionally accounted for most of the NCEC's receipts (see Figure 4.1). In 1992, the PAC raised about 90 percent of the its money from individual contributors. Eighty percent of this was raised by direct mail, and approximately 79 percent was raised in amounts of under $500. In a good year, contributions are collected from about 20,000 people. The average supporter gives about $40 a year. Roughly 500 people give about $100. In 1992, 856 contributors gave contributions of between $200 and $999, and 158 gave between $1,000 and the legal maximum of $5,000.[19]

Over the years, the NCEC has developed a donor list of 40,000 individuals. It conducts all of its direct-mail fundraising in-house and acquires additional donor lists through brokers.[20] It frequently exchanges lists with the Democratic national, congressional, and senatorial campaign committees, as well as a few Democratic state committees in large states. Lists are also traded with the ADA, the National Abortion Rights Action League (NARAL), People for the American Way, Public Citizen, and a few large environmental groups.

PAC contributions to the NCEC grew significantly during the 1980s. In 1992, PACs accounted for roughly 10 percent of the committee's income. Fourteen labor PACs contributed $91,000 to the committee, while other PACs gave only $3,000.[21] Labor has developed a special relationship with the NCEC. Labor PACs provide the committee with financial support and receive reports on competitive districts in return. NCEC reports and briefings are one of several sources of information that labor PACs use when selecting candidates for endorsements and contributions.

In return for their contributions, individuals receive six newsletters per year that report on the NCEC's campaign activities, discuss the prospects of various congressional candidates, and analyze the implications of congressional elections for federal government activities. Additional reports that focus on Senate contests and marginal House races are mailed once or twice an election cycle to help NCEC supporters decide which candidates to support with their personal contributions. These reports are especially useful to contributors who give money to congressional candidates outside of their state.

PACs and individuals who make large contributions to the NCEC are also provided with more detailed information on marginal contests and relevant electoral developments. During the 1992 election cycle, the committee mailed these contributors booklets that described the impact of redistricting on all fifty states. They were also invited to attend PAC briefings at which the committee reported on the progress made by Democratic candidates competing in close elections.

Figure 4.1. **NCEC Receipts, 1980–92**

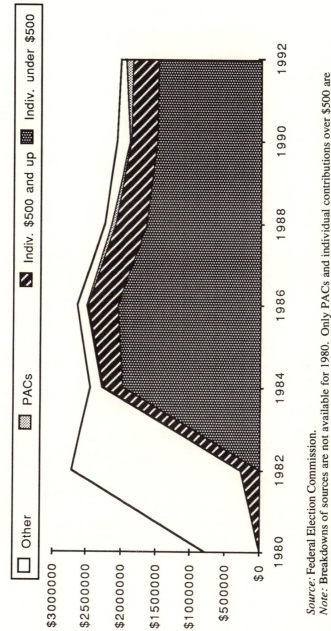

Source: Federal Election Commission.
Note: Breakdowns of sources are not available for 1980. Only PACs and individual contributions over $500 are available for 1982.

PAC Decisionmaking and Campaign Activity

NCEC supporters have virtually no influence over committee operations or campaign decisionmaking. This is consistent with the PAC's role as a disseminator of campaign information. As Mark Gersh explains,

> Most PACs and many individuals give to the NCEC because they value its information and the procedures it uses to target candidates. One of the reasons they support the NCEC is because they use its information to guide their own campaign contributions. They seek to benefit from committee targeting rather than influence it.

According to Gersh, the only direct impact that supporters have on the distribution of NCEC money occurs when they earmark the money they contribute to the committee for specific candidates. The PAC discourages this because it skews its contributions.[22]

The NCEC uses several criteria to select candidates for endorsement or campaign assistance. First, the candidates must be Democrats, reflecting the PAC's current goal of maximizing the number of Democratically controlled seats in Congress. Second, the closeness of the race is considered. All Democratic candidates in marginal districts receive NCEC assistance. Incumbents who are in jeopardy are automatically given priority status. Challenger and open-seat contestants in marginal or near-marginal districts also receive help. The PAC typically assists about sixty candidates: thirty in districts that are currently regarded as competitive and thirty in districts that were competitive in the previous election cycle.

The third criterion used to determine whether a candidate is given NCEC help is the campaign's ability to utilize the PAC's technical assistance and district analysis. Candidates who possess strong campaign organizations, replete with professional consultants, are more likely to get NCEC targeting assistance than candidates who wage amateur campaigns. NCEC staff learn about the quality of a candidate's campaign organization by visiting the candidate's campaign headquarters. These visits are also used to advise candidates on how they can improve their campaigns.

The impact of top-of-the-ticket races on congressional voting is also taken into consideration. House candidates running in states that are likely to be influenced by presidential or senatorial coattail effects typically receive extra help. In many cases, the NCEC does not need to go to great lengths to provide this assistance because it has already performed a detailed targeting study for Democratic candidates for the Senate. The PAC merely gives to the House candidates the portion of committee research that applies to the congressional districts in which they are running. During the 1990 election cycle, for example, the NCEC gave Representative Howard Wolpe of Michigan a detailed targeting study, even though his race was not considered a top priority, because it had completed the analysis as part of a larger study for Michigan Senator Carl Levin.

Ironically, ideology ranks near last among the criteria the NCEC uses to target races. In keeping with its present goal of increasing Democratic control of Congress, ideology—the PAC's original *raison d'être*—no longer plays a prominent role in committee decisionmaking. Liberal Democrats have only a slightly better chance than others of getting NCEC help. Roll call analyses, ADA scores, labor evaluations, and ratings published in *National Journal* are used to assess candidates' ideologies.

Unlike most PACs, the NCEC places little to no emphasis on agenda power when choosing candidates for support. Committee assignments, chairmanships, and party leadership positions have no impact on NCEC decisionmaking on House races. Only on very rare occasions do these factors influence decisions on Senate contests. This near total disregard for agenda power is consistent with the PAC's electoral goals. Because it is primarily concerned with maintaining and enlarging Democratic congressional majorities rather than advancing specific policy issues, the NCEC has no reason to seek access to members of the House or Senate who have the power to influence specific pieces of legislation. Similarly, it has no lobbyist and engages in no lobbying activities.

Finally, the NCEC continues to have a preference for individual Senate candidates. In the aggregate, however, more NCEC effort is typically made on behalf of House campaigns than Senate contests (see Table 4.1). This pattern persisted during the 1992 election cycle even though the committee assisted record numbers of House and Senate campaigns.

The NCEC has not become involved in many contested primaries in recent years. In the past, it sought to help liberal candidates defeat their conservative opponents, especially in the South. This type of activity could now be counterproductive to the achievement of the committee's goal of electing Democrats if the wrong candidate won the primary. Nevertheless, in some cases the defeat of a particular primary candidate has become a committee goal. In 1992, for example, the NCEC backed Mel Reynolds in his primary challenge in Illinois to incumbent Gus Savage—a confrontational, rebellious House Democrat who has been accused of a variety of indiscretions.

The NCEC relies on several sources of information to compile its target list. The most important source is the PAC's own precinct-level data. This is supplemented by polling data supplied by the Democratic Congressional Campaign Committee (DCCC). Next is information about candidates that is obtained by talking to Democratic party leaders and staffs in both Washington and the candidate's state, members of Congress from the candidate's state delegation, congressional staff who work in nearby district offices, veterans of previous campaigns in the area, and politically active NCEC supporters who reside in or near the candidate's district. Political aides to statewide officeholders are considered ideal sources of information because a major portion of their time is spent keeping tabs on the activities of politicians living in their state. They can inform the committee of a candidate's level of local support, ability to handle the press,

Table 4.1

NCEC Contributions to Democratic House and Senate Candidates, 1980–92[a]

	1980	1982	1984	1986	1988	1990	1992
House							
Incumbent	$186,071	$193,404	$341,801	$226,028	$231,914	$249,350	$270,900
	(59)[b, c]	(53)	(73)	(57)	(49)	(72)	(103)
Challenger	$54,097	$115,917	$216,393	$179,614	$175,717	$126,175	$119,050
	(29)	(43)	(48)	(40)	(34)	(43)	(44)
Open Seat	$73,379	$53,166	$70,944	$104,443	$107,338	$100,500	$120,800
	(28)	(17)	(11)	(22)	(16)	(24)	(42)
Subtotal	$313,547	$362,487	$629,138	$510,085	$514,969	$476,025	$510,750
	(116)	(113)	(132)	(119)	(99)	(139)	(189)
Senate							
Incumbent	$80,869	$24,528	$55,718	$38,319	$79,901	$84,050	$68,500
	(11)	(8)	(7)	(5)	(11)	(12)	(16)
Challenger	$13,003	$20,714	$70,796	$97,380	$59,993	$34,050	$42,000
	(5)	(6)	(7)	(5)	(11)	(5)	(10)
Open Seat	$7,000	$200	$38,470	$45,498	$29,753	$12,450	$29,500
	(1)	(1)	(4)	(6)	(4)	(3)	(7)
Subtotal	$100,872	$45,442	$164,984	$181,197	$169,647	$130,550	$140,000
	(17)	(15)	(18)	(16)	(26)	(20)	(33)
Total							
All Candidates[b]	$414,419	$407,929	$794,122	$691,282	$684,616	$606,575	$650,750
	(133)	(128)	(150)	(135)	(125)	(159)	(222)

Notes:
[a]The PAC gave $4,000 in contributions to Republican House candidate Claudine Schneider in the elections of 1980 through 1986. No other Republicans received NCEC money.

[b]The totals do not include the contributions to Claudine Schneider.

[c]Number of candidates is indicated in parentheses.

and other political skills. This information is especially useful in assessing the potential of nonincumbent House candidates. When they are available, polls are consulted to learn about candidates' levels of name recognition and general standing with voters. Some poll results are published in local newspapers, while others are circulated by party organizations and candidates themselves.

The NCEC assesses the quality of a candidate's campaign by learning which consultants are working on it and examining its budget, strategy, and fundraising records. Newsletters such as the *Rothenberg Political Report* and the *Cook Political Report* are consulted. NCEC staff use the information they collect to develop a list of targeting recommendations that is delivered to the committee's executive board for approval. The staff's recommendations are usually approved in toto. The committee's national director, Russell Hemenway, has enormous influence in both the selection of candidates and winning the board's approval. Once final approval is given, however, the Washington staff has virtually complete control over the kinds of assistance each candidate is given.

Unlike most PACs, the NCEC distributes the vast bulk of its assistance in the form of "in-kind" contributions of campaign services rather than cash. The committee provides two levels of candidate support. Good candidates who are considered likely winners or probable losers typically get district-level data analyses and small amounts of advice. Marginal and near-marginal candidates, on the other hand, get comprehensive assistance.

Precinct-level targeting data form the core of NCEC candidate support. Candidates get district profiles of the demographic composition and voting history of their districts and assistance in translating this information into campaign strategy. They also get advice about where to conduct their get-out-the-vote drives, drop campaign literature, and broadcast mass media advertisements. The NCEC helps with this last function by correlating its precinct-level target data with arbitron ratings of audiences for various radio and TV stations so candidates can make efficient media buys.[23] Other forms of assistance that are unrelated to the precinct data are given in the areas of fundraising, polling, image and message development, and campaign administration. The NCEC stopped providing issue and opposition research to candidates following the 1988 election, leaving the DCCC and DSCC to provide this assistance.

The NCEC fulfills its role as a lead PAC through the dissemination of large quantities of information to members of the PAC community and individuals who routinely give big campaign contributions. In addition to the booklets and newsletters described above, the committee organizes meetings to brief other PACs on upcoming congressional elections. Committee staff present an overview of the overall political climate and more detailed coverage of individual Senate elections and marginal House races. The primary goals of the PAC briefings are to review the findings of committee research on marginal contests and to encourage PACs to use this research when making their contribution decisions.

The committee typically holds three meetings during an election year and one in nonelection years. The meetings are open to any PAC manager who cares to attend, and roughly 100 show up per meeting. New attendees are invited to enroll on the NCEC's mailing list so they can receive notices about future briefings. Staff of the Democratic congressional and senatorial campaign committees also attend. The one group of individuals not invited to attend the meetings is congressional candidates or their representatives. They are discouraged from attending the briefings because their presence might influence PAC contributions in a way that is contrary to the NCEC's analysis. The NCEC leaves it to the Democratic congressional and senatorial campaign committees, and other PACs, to arrange meet-and-greet sessions for candidates.

The PAC mailings and briefings are supplemented by a steady stream of telephone calls and press releases that flows from the committee to PAC directors, journalists, and party staffs. This activity is designed to create an informational environment that will benefit the NCEC's endorsed candidates. It makes the committee one of the chief opinion leaders in the PAC community. It also helps the NCEC publicize its operations and attract more supporters.

The NCEC has enlarged the scope of its influence through the very close relationship it has forged with the Democratic party in recent years. It has provided the DCCC with demographic research and targeting assistance. The NCEC also advises Democratic party leaders on the impact that different campaign finance reform proposals could have on the fundraising prospects of Democratic party organizations and candidates.

The 1992 Election

The 1992 election cycle posed new challenges and opportunities for the NCEC and encouraged the PAC to broaden the scope of its campaign activities. Reapportionment provided the committee with the opportunity to make full use of its data analysis capabilities. Its demographic and behavioral research gave it the wherewithal to be a central player in the Democrats' redistricting program. Its precinct-level targeting data also made it possible for the PAC to figure prominently in the campaign strategies of dozens of candidates running in new or heavily redrawn districts. NCEC staff also expected the committee's endorsements to play a bigger role than usual in the contribution decisions of many PACs because of the uncertainties caused by redistricting.

The committee was prepared for the unique demands and possibilities of the 1992 cycle. Staff spent the earlier part of the cycle focusing on redistricting. They planned to delay providing candidates with the targeting assistance for which the PAC has become famous. Senior committee decisionmakers decided to respond to the uncertainties resulting from redistricting by getting involved in more races than usual, especially those being waged by Democratic non-incumbents. They also planned to work more closely with the DCCC and Democratic state party committees.

However, in politics, as in other areas of human activity where large numbers of individuals compete to accomplish divergent goals, the best-laid plans are often frustrated by unforeseeable complications. Court challenges over newly drawn districts and related incidents took up a tremendous amount of NCEC staff resources, delaying the committee's ability to begin other election activities. The House Post Office and Bank scandals further delayed the NCEC's ability to implement its election plans because they brought about last-minute retirements of a large number of House members. As a result of these events, the committee's first briefing on marginal races was postponed from its original date in early November 1991 until March 25, 1992. All later briefings were held jointly with the DCCC. Other campaign activities, such as the distribution of targeting assistance to candidates in marginal races, were also postponed. Pressure from nervous incumbents, who wanted help identifying the demographic composition of their redrawn constituencies, also caused the PAC to deviate from its original plan—it got involved in fewer open-seat and challenger campaigns than it would have liked.

The volatility of the electorate and complications arising from the uniqueness of 1992 resulted in the NCEC's making major revisions to its marginal list throughout the course of the election cycle. In September 1991, Mark Gersh predicted there could be about 150 close House races, 100 newly elected members, and that the Democrats would lose 30 to 40 seats. In July 1992, he revised these estimates to 100 close races, 135 new members, and a Democratic net loss of as few as 10 seats. The final estimates were extremely close to the eventual outcome.

In addition to its joint briefings with the DCCC, the NCEC mailed newsletters and election updates to keep its contributors and other PACs informed about developments occurring in close House and Senate races. Press releases, faxes, and telephone calls were used to keep journalists, PACs, and contributors abreast of fast-breaking events. These communications were used to help direct PAC contributions and large individual donations to 26 NCEC-endorsed Senate candidates and 140 committee-endorsed House contenders.

Besides its involvement in an increased number of congressional elections, the NCEC introduced some innovations during the 1992 election cycle. First, it worked more closely with the DCCC than it had in the past. The two organizations worked together to identify close races and held joint briefings to help other PACs identify marginal races. In advising PACs, the NCEC drew upon its knowledge of the demographic composition and voting patterns in congressional districts, and the DCCC presented candidate profiles and polling information.

Second, the PAC developed targeting data for California and Texas for the first time. In the past, the committee considered it too large a project to construct voter files for these states. In 1992, however, the addition of several new House seats and the prospect of influencing the boundaries of congressional districts convinced the committee that it was worth the effort. The fact that California would serve as the battleground for two competitive Senate campaigns, and the expectation that both states would host dozens of close House contests, also contributed to this decision.

Third, the NCEC made extensive use of demographic data in analyzing congressional districts, deriving its list of marginal races, and helping candidates with their targeting strategies. In the past, the committee had relied almost exclusively on geography and the partisanship of precincts as defined by previous election returns. Adding demographic information to its voter files enabled it to target districts more effectively.

Finally, as a result of the untimely death of Paul Tully, political director of the

Democratic National Committee, the NCEC became involved in the presidential election. Washington director Mark Gersh helped the Clinton–Gore campaign make some final strategic decisions and played an important role in the final phases of the campaign's targeting. This helped to further cement the PAC's ties to the Democratic party and the Clinton administration.

Unlike most PACs, the NCEC was not overwhelmed by redistricting or the other events connected with the 1992 congressional elections. Most of its planning and strategy, which are driven largely by its data bases, were conducted early in the election. The majority of its targeting assistance and strategic advice was given to candidates early or in the middle of the election cycle, despite delays imposed by redistricting-related court challenges. In fact, Gersh reports that the committee was more active early and midway through the election than at the end.

Of the 140 House candidates whom the NCEC endorsed, 75 were incumbents (including 4 who were pitted against other incumbents), 26 were challengers, and 39 ran for open seats. Three of these candidates were endorsed before their primaries took place. One hundred and four (74.3 percent) were involved in marginal races. Marginal candidates received the lion's share of the committee's campaign assistance. Others, including 49 candidates who were not formally endorsed by the committee, received lesser amounts. These unendorsed candidates were given targeting data that had already been prepared by the committee for the purposes of influencing their state's congressional redistricting process or assisting one of their state's Senate candidates. According to Gersh, the committee simply gave them the targeting information it had already assembled.

As was the case in the previous two election cycles, the NCEC concentrated over half of its resources on campaigns waged by incumbents. The next highest allocations were made to open-seat candidates for the House and challengers for the Senate (see the last column in Table 4.1). House Democrats involved in incumbent vs. incumbent match-ups were given extra assistance. The focus on two-incumbent races and House open seats was a response to the unique circumstances present in 1992. The NCEC sought to help defend House Democrats whose advantages of incumbency were offset by those of their incumbent Republican opponents and to exploit the opportunity to fill vacant House seats with Democrats.

Of the 26 Senate candidates who received NCEC endorsements, 9 were incumbents, 10 were challengers, and 7 ran for open seats. Nineteen (73 percent) were involved in marginal contests.[24] The candidates who were given committee endorsements got the vast majority of its campaign assistance. Seven others received some targeting assistance because the committee had already conducted targeting studies for the purposes of congressional redistricting or assisting Democratic candidates for the House in their states. The sharp fluctuations over time in the allocation of NCEC resources among Senate incumbent, challenger, and open-seat candidates reflects changes in the specific seats up for election in given election cycles, as well as the quality of the candidates who contested them. Republican control of the Senate from 1981 to 1986 and the need to rebuild a working Democratic majority in that chamber are responsible for the NCEC's increased focus on Democratic nonincumbent candidates between 1984 and 1988. In 1992, the committee split its resources fairly evenly among incumbents and nonincumbents, reflecting the levels of competitiveness of Democrat-controlled, open, and Republican-held seats.

The NCEC's win–loss record in 1992 was 92 to 48 for the House and 15 to 11 for the Senate, but committee decisionmakers prefer to assess the PAC's performance by its involvement in close races. According to Mark Gersh, the committee was a player in every close contest except New York Democratic House candidate Dennis Gorski's loss against Jack Quinn. Gersh also believed the NCEC's level of concentration in marginal contests was good, given the uncertainties of the 1992 election, its proclivity toward assisting incumbents it helped in previous elections, and a decision that was made some years ago to help all Democratic House candidates whose districts are located in states hosting marginal Senate races.

Overall, NCEC staff are very satisfied with the PAC's performance in 1992 and pleased with the election outcome. The committee had anticipated many of the events associated with the election and received few surprises. Georgia Democratic Senator Wyche Fowler's loss and Iowa House Republican Jim Ross Lightfoot's victory were unexpected. The number of House incumbents from both parties who lost was also slightly lower than the committee had predicted. The strong Democratic performance in Michigan and Illinois was somewhat of a surprise because the redistricting plans in those states were decidedly pro-Republican. In retrospect, Gersh wishes the committee had fought harder to persuade the Florida and Georgia state legislatures to pass redistricting plans that would have favored more Democratic House candidates, but he and the NCEC's staff have no plans to change their targeting system, their means for communicating with contributors or other PACs, or their candidate assistance programs.

The tremendous turnover in Congress is expected to have little impact on NCEC operations because the PAC does not lobby representatives or senators on issues. Any changes that occur in the laws governing campaign finance, on the other hand, would influence committee activity in future elections. The NCEC has not staked out an official position on campaign finance reform, but its Washington director will undoubtedly play a role in fashioning any legislation that is passed by Congress. Gersh has developed close relationships with many members of Congress as a result of the committee's involvement in congressional elections, and he expects that many members will seek his advice before approving any reform bills. He has formalized his ties to the Democratic party by serving as a consultant to the Democratic national and congressional campaign committees. By serving as a consultant to House Majority Leader Richard Gephardt's PAC, the Effective Government Committee, he has also strengthened his relationship with Gephardt, who will play a major role in fashioning any campaign finance legislation that comes to the House floor. Through these relationships, Gersh expects the NCEC to have an impact on campaign finance reform.

Conclusion

The NCEC has undergone major changes since its founding. Originally intended to be a funding organization for liberal candidates for the Senate, it has become a staunchly Democratic organization that works closely with Democratic candidates for both the House and the Senate and with Democratic party committees at the federal and state levels. In addition to abandoning its bipartisanship, the PAC has greatly reduced the level of cash it contributes and has become an important provider of campaign services to Democratic congressional candidates. It now works closely with Democratic party committees in formulating party strategy, identifying marginal districts, and helping to turn on the flow of PAC money to candidates involved in close races. In 1992, the NCEC was able to further expand its influence by playing a central role in the redistricting process. Just as ideology and campaign contributions once defined the NCEC, partisanship, pragmatism, and the provision of campaign services are its hallmarks today.

Notes

1. For an excellent discussion of the history of the NCEC and its activities into the mid-1960s, see Harry M. Scoble, *Ideology and Electoral Action: A Comparative Case Study of the National Committee for an Effective Congress* (San Francisco: Chandler Publishing, 1967).
2. Federal Election Commission, "PAC Activity Rebounds in 1992–92 Election Cycle—Unusual Nature of Contests Seen as Reason," Press Release, April 19, 1993.
3. Scoble, *Ideology and Electoral Action*, pp. 26–27, 36.
4. Some campaign contributions were given quietly, with no attendant endorsement, and some candidates received endorsements but no money.
5. To date, no members have ever been expelled from the committee.
6. Scoble, *Ideology and Electoral Action*, pp. 149–74.
7. Ibid., p. 174.
8. Ibid., pp. 28–89.
9. Ibid., p. 82.
10. Ibid., p. 87.
11. Ibid., p. 88.
12. Ibid., pp. 9, 51–57, 86.
13. Personal interview with Mark Gersh, Washington, D.C., October 10, 1991.
14. Scoble, *Ideology and Electoral Action*, p. 104.
15. Ibid., pp. 109–11.
16. Ibid., pp. 135–36.
17. Unless otherwise noted, the information in this section is drawn from personal interviews with Mark Gersh held on October 10, 1991, and January 14, 1992.
18. With the exception of the information about the religious affiliation of NCEC

contributors and their motives (which were provided by the NCEC's Washington director, Mark Gersh), these generalizations draw on figures from a survey of individuals who contributed over $200 to the NCEC. See John C. Green and James L. Guth, "Big Bucks and Petty Cash: Party and Interest Group Activists in American Politics," in Allan Cigler and Burdett Loomis, eds., *Interest Group Politics* (Washington, D.C.: CQ Press, 1986), pp. 91–113.

19. These figures were garnered from the Disclosure Data Base at the Federal Election Commission.

20. At one point the NCEC hired an outside direct-mail fundraising firm in an attempt to prospect for new donors. The PAC lost $100,000 and has not hired any outside fundraising firms since.

21. These figures were garnered from the Disclosure Database at the Federal Election Commission.

22. Personal interview with Mark Gersh, October 10, 1991.

23. Arbitron ratings record the number of persons who tune into radio and television programs.

24. Elections are defined as marginal if the candidate received between 40 percent and 60 percent of the vote.

5

The Demise of a Lead PAC: The Free Congress PAC

James G. Gimpel

Relatively few PACs have sought to exercise direct influence on political campaigns by sending consultants into the field to help assemble campaign organizations. Throughout its nearly twenty-year history, the Free Congress PAC (FCP), originally known as the Committee for the Survival of a Free Congress, has specialized in providing "in-kind" contributions to the campaigns of conservative candidates. The FCP has not been active in funding incumbents or in trying to influence legislation. Instead, it has focused on competitive conservative challengers. In the case of the FCP, the focus is on the soon-to-be-elected.

History

The FCP began as the Committee for the Survival of a Free Congress (CSFC) in 1973. It was and continues to be the brainchild of one man—political entrepreneur, conservative activist, and former Hill staffer Paul Weyrich. In the early 1970s, Weyrich, an employee of a Republican senator at the time, believed that the left had simply out-organized the right. Liberal scholars, journalists, union officials, and politicians appeared to have formed a cohesive bloc in opposition to President Nixon's efforts to roll back certain domestic programs. He created the CSFC to be a countervailing force to liberal groups that had formed in defense of government programs and regulations instituted in the 1960s.

As a parallel project, Weyrich immediately set about to help elect a more conservative Congress. The CSFC's most immediate goal was to provide direct support to conservative candidates. The issues most central to its mission were the right to life, the maintenance of a strong national defense, the preference for free-market economics, and the passage of right-to-work laws. The CSFC changed its name to the Free Congress PAC in 1986, but it continues to pursue its original goals.

A weaker consensus prevailed among PAC employees and supporters on other issues, such as opposition to gun-control legislation. Data from a survey of FCP donors show substantial ideological congruence between the FCP's leadership and its donor base.[1] About 90 percent of Free Congress donors were reported to be against government regulation, 76 percent for school prayer, 75 percent against a national health insurance plan, and 77 percent against the Equal Rights Amendment. Two-thirds of the PAC's donors were Republicans, 91 percent called themselves conservative, and 42 percent earned over $100,000 per year.

Ideological congruence between candidates and donors was largely ensured through careful candidate screening by FCP leadership. Candidates were required to pass an ideological litmus test to qualify for support. They were expected to answer a questionnaire that detailed their positions on key issues. In addition, each candidate would have to agree to run a grassroots-style campaign. This requirement was based on the supposition that electronic media campaigns seldom worked for challengers since they could rarely out-spend incumbents on television and radio. The candidate also had to be viable. There was no sense in providing support even for an extremely conservative candidate if that person stood no chance of winning. Finally, the candidate had to agree to heed the PAC's advice on campaign strategy and issue selection once the campaign was under way. In this manner, the PAC maintained some control over the candidate's organization throughout the race. Each campaign organization was audited throughout the election campaign to ensure that it had met established goals.

FCP insiders and former PAC directors declined to claim full credit for victorious candidacies. They did, however, claim that the organization's activity and support were crucial to the successful campaigns of Senators Charles Grassley (R-IA) and Don Nickels (R-OK), former senators Roger Jepsen (R-IA) and Dan Quayle (R-IN), and a significant list of House members, including John Kyl (R-AZ), Bill Dannemeyer (R-CA), Dan Lungren (R-CA), Jerry Lewis (R-CA), and Ralph Hall (D-TX).

Up to two-thirds of the FCP's campaign contributions have been given as in-kind services that are reported at under market-value rates. The FCP's contribution history indicates that the FCP's political activity has declined sharply since 1980 (see Table 5.1). The FCP was very influential in the late 1970s and in 1980 because it placed consultants into campaigns cheaply.

Organization

The FCP is an adjunct of a larger organization, the Free Congress Foundation, which is funded by contributions from larger donors and foundations, not

Table 5.1

**Total and In-Kind Contribution History of the Free Congress PAC,
1978–92** ($ thousands)

Year	1978	1980	1982	1984	1986	1988	1990	1992
$ to Republicans	203.0	122.2	127.3	32.5	57.4	12.2	8.7	11.3
$ to Democrats	37.0	12.0	27.9	1.6	2.7	0.1	0.0	0.0
Total $	241.8	140.6	131.6	33.7	60.1	12.3	8.7	11.3
In-kind $	134.4	36.3	33.9	24.5	16.3	4.8	2.9	0.0
% In-kind	55.6	25.8	25.8	66.8	27.2	39.4	33.4	0.0
N of Races	151	91	77	52	45	24	6	11

Source: Federal Election Commission.

through dues-paying members. Both the foundation and the PAC are headed by Weyrich. The foundation is a nonprofit organization that promotes conservative views on Weyrich's pet policy issues. An important recent activity of the foundation has been to train citizens of Eastern bloc nations in the principles of democracy. Staff regularly fly to Eastern Europe to run campaign schools that focus on Western electoral practices. Under Weyrich's direction, the foundation also publishes the *New Electric Railway Journal*, a magazine with no political content devoted to championing full-scale electric trains in the United States and abroad. There is no link between electric railways and conservative ideology; Weyrich is simply interested in both and uses his organization to promote these disparate interests.

The PAC is but one of the foundation's many branches. The daily operations of the PAC are run by an executive director and an assistant director. The executive director also serves as a vice president of the foundation. The executive director is staffed by an administrative assistant. There is a group of seven or eight loosely affiliated part-time field consultants spread around the country that provides expert advice on campaign organization to the candidates Weyrich designates.

The FCP's success as an ideological PAC can probably best be explained by a "commitment model," whereby participation is a function of the ideological commitments of its members. The FCP's campaign consultants, generally part-timers, are in pursuit of public goals consistent with their conservative ideology. Without ideologically motivated contributors and field staff, there would be no FCP.

Campaign Activity

From the beginning, the FCP has focused on providing in-kind contributions to nonincumbents, including technical assistance in organizing grassroots mobilization efforts and creating telephone banks, campaign training sessions for conservative activists, and the purchase of campaign advertising for candidates.

At its peak of influence, contributions flowed into the Washington office managed by Weyrich. The organization was highly decentralized when it came to the distribution of campaign assistance. Part-time field staff were located in Louisiana, New York, Colorado, Wisconsin, and California. The Washington office sent these field-workers out as consultants and paid them about $75 per day. The ideological nature of the FCP's business, coupled with the relatively low pay, ensured that only the most ideologically committed need apply. The consultants would spend considerable time with some campaigns. FCP operatives could put in as much as 15 to 20 days from July through November, running from campaign to campaign, sometimes traveling hundreds of miles.

Theoretically, to receive assistance, each campaign had to emphasize a strong grassroots organization component. In reality, some of the supported races never progressed far enough to meet this requirement. The strategy preferred and developed into a science by FCP consultants was the so-called Kasten plan.[2] This plan was used by campaign organizer J. Fritz Rench in several of former U.S. senator Robert Kasten's successful campaigns for public office in Wisconsin, including a state senate seat, a House seat, the Wisconsin governorship, and a U.S. Senate seat.

The Kasten plan is a system of establishing specific vote goals in each precinct. Well before the election, block captains identify and collect information about the candidate's supporters. A few weeks prior to the election, the block captains inform precinct captains about which individuals plan to support the candidate and identify those who are wavering. In the final days before the election, the candidate personally calls all of the precinct chairs to let them know how completely his success depends upon them. On election day, a warning system in midafternoon lets precinct chairs know how short of their goal they are so they can use the time before the polls close to turn out missing voters.

This plan for voter mobilization, which parallels that traditionally associated with local party organizations, is still taught by FCP consultants in campaign schools held periodically in the Washington office and in the field. Still, FCP consultants acknowledge that the Kasten plan does not work everywhere. Obviously, it pays off most clearly in low-turnout elections, where the mobilization of additional voters has the greatest marginal impact on the vote. The FCP has frequently acted to implement it in primaries to ensure conservative victories over liberal and mainstream opponents.

The Role of Ink: The FCP's *Political Report*

Campaign organizing was not the only activity provided to FCP's candidates during its peak in the late 1970s and early 1980s. Another major service provided by Weyrich's organization between 1978 and 1984 was the provision of favorable "ink" through the biweekly political newsletter the *Political Report*, circulated widely in the PAC community. The FCP's lead-PAC status was largely a function of the *Political Report*'s success. The *Report* was even widely read by PAC directors who did not share the FCP's conservative views. With FCP field staff located throughout the country, the *Report* could provide local insights and detail not available to an operative based in Washington, D.C. Political operatives in Washington looked to the *Report* for its biweekly update on the congressional races. Other PACS used the *Report* as an aid for targeting their funds.

The height of the *Report*'s distribution, and the FCP's lead-PAC status, was from 1980 to 1984. During this period, there were dozens of ideologically motivated small PACs that were looking for information. The *Report* was valued by the foundation and the PAC more for its political influence than its profitability. For each paid subscription, three free ones were mailed. In the early 1980s, 700 to 750 copies were mailed, but there were only 200 to 250 paid subscriptions. The *Report* was sold to its editor, Stuart Rothenberg, in 1989 and is now entitled the *Rothenberg Political Report*. It has severed its direct association with the foundation, and it remains a valuable source of campaign information for anyone wishing to purchase a subscription.

A Lead PAC in Decline

The FCP's political influence peaked in 1980, when it contributed to approximately 242 House and Senate campaigns. By 1982, however, the conservative movement's momentum had slowed. Paul Weyrich decided to lead his organization in a different direction, making it a nonprofit foundation to ease the burden of fundraising. Contributions to not-for-profits are tax deductible, while contributions to PACs are not, and FECA contribution limits do not apply to foundations.

Several factors contributed to the demise of the FCP's political activity in the 1980s. First, the liberal threat was no longer sufficient to mobilize the energies of conservative activists. Jimmy Carter had been defeated and the Republicans had captured the U.S. Senate. The Republican party's sustained minority status in the U.S. House was not enough to maintain the interest of conservative donors. Second, several of the FCP's biggest contributors were from southwestern states that had been severely hit by the depression in the oil economy. This made it difficult for Weyrich to raise money for both the nonprofit foundation and the PAC at the same time. Third, Weyrich himself lost interest in campaign politics and turned increasingly toward lobbying those already in office. Finally, the PAC was afflicted with management problems for several years after the 1982 elections. An expensive, high-tech, direct-mail fundraising drive lost money, and the PAC struggled for several years under a heavy load of debt.

Weyrich also decided to give up control of the *Political Report* to its editor,

Stu Rothenberg. According to Rothenberg, "Weyrich gave up the *Report* because he wanted to be more ideological."[3] The *Report* could not be ideological and at the same time be informative. To sustain credibility, it had to provide information on political races in an objective, balanced, factual way. Much of the FCP's status as a lead PAC disappeared when this important information source went independent.

Several years have gone by since these developments altered the scope and focus of the FCP's influence. The PAC has not recovered its full strength, although it was active in a number of races in 1986. It campaigned against the nomination of Republican Ed Zschau in the California U.S. Senate primary. Since 1986, the FCP has been moribund, although there may be plans for revival.

It is fair to say that Weyrich's organization changed the way Republicans thought about campaigns. Prior to the FCP's innovative training schools, most PACs were simply sending cash. Now, some other PACs have followed the FCP's example, offering training programs for public relations and grassroots organization.

The FCP and the 1992 Elections

There are signs that the winds of change may blow again in the halls of the Free Congress Foundation. With the Democrats in the White House, conservatives have a renewed cause, much as they did in the late 1970s. Still, the 1992 activity of the FCP was rather modest, reflecting Paul Weyrich's change in emphasis. During the closing months of the campaign, the PAC director and his assistant spent much of their time in the former Eastern bloc in their role as educators in the practice of democratic elections with the foundation's Kreible Institute.

Early on in the U.S. 1992 campaign cycle, PAC operatives had targeted about thirty races for possible support. In addition, during the spring and summer of 1992, three training schools for candidates and campaign staff were conducted in Washington, D.C., one in Connecticut, and another in Washington state. Over 100 campaign managers and aides attended these conferences, although the Connecticut conference was principally aimed at state legislative candidates. Each school was a three-day event, and PAC instructors emphasized the seven components of a sound campaign plan: research, strategy, tactics, management structure, expense budgeting, income budgeting, and adjustments. For staff, candidates, and managers in their first race, the lessons provided in the FCP's abbreviated campaign school are the only ones they receive on how to run. It is impossible to quantify precisely the dollar value of this training to each campaign. But if it provides a group of novices with the know-how to organize and field a competitive campaign organization, it could be the decisive factor in a race.

Another in-kind service provided to candidates in 1992 was an information hotline number. Throughout the election cycle, campaigns could call PAC phone operators and file requests for data and information to insert into advertising, stump speeches, fact sheets, and other campaign materials. Because candidates called the PAC rather than the other way around, this service did not require an expenditure report to the Federal Election Commission. Through the hotline, the Free Congress PAC provided information support to 125 different campaigns. Twenty of the hotline users, all of them freshmen Republicans, went on to win in November, and several others lost by slim margins. Was 1992 a success from the perspective of the FCP? On the one hand, considering how little they invested, the year could hardly be considered a failure. On the other hand, the cash contributions went mostly to losers, with northern Virginia's Kyle McSlarrow leading the group with $2,350 in FCP contributions in his loss to Democratic incumbent Jim Moran.

In conclusion, it is fairly clear that Paul Weyrich has lost interest in being a major player in the PAC community. Donations flowing into the Free Congress Foundation are going to his other ambitious enterprises, including the effort to democratize Eastern Europe. In addition, the foundation has increasingly turned its attention toward those already inside the Beltway, conducting research and issuing reports on various conservative policy initiatives. Many of the small conservative political action committees that burgeoned during the early and mid-1980s are no longer on the scene. For the first time in over a decade, a Republican is no longer in the White House. There is certainly ample opportunity now for the FCP to reassume a leadership role and recapture its lead-PAC status, or for another PAC to take its place.

Notes

Some of the information in this chapter was obtained in interviews with the following people: Dick Dingman, former PAC director, November 4, 1991; Stu Rothenberg, editor of the *Rothenberg Political Report*, November 11, 1991; Bob McAdam, former field worker and PAC director, November 25, 1991; and John Exnicious, current PAC director, December 9, 1991, and September 15, 1992.

1. Survey of PAC donors conducted by John C. Green and James L. Guth, 1982–84. See "Big Bucks and Petty Cash: Party and Interest Group Activists in American Politics," in Allan Cigler and Burdett Loomis, eds., *Interest Group Politics*, 2d ed. (Washington, D.C.: CQ Press, 1986), pp. 91–113.

2. Details on the Kasten plan are contained in the CSFC (FCP) publication, *Building for Victory*, no copyright.

3. Personal interview with Stu Rothenberg, November 11, 1991.

Part Two
Institutionalized PACs

The PACs discussed in this section share a number of characteristics—all have fairly substantial financial resources to invest in congressional elections, relatively stable organizational structures, several staff members who devote time to PAC activities, and a set of established rules and procedures for making contribution decisions. These characteristics provide them with the resources to react to political change, but also constrain them in their ability to adapt quickly.

Stable organizational structures and multi-member staffs allow these PACs to gather information from a variety of sources. Several of these PACs, including the Realtors, NARAL (National Abortion Rights Action League), and the NEA (National Education Association), are federated structures that gather information from state and local members. Many also consult with party committees, subscribe to newsletters, and otherwise seek out data from a variety of sources. In some cases, their size and prominence allow them to obtain specific information about candidates directly, either through questionnaires or through contacts initiated by the candidates themselves. The sizable budgets of these committees allow them to contribute to a large number of candidates and to perhaps invest some "venture capital" in promising nonincumbents.

The bureaucratic decisionmaking of these committees, however, may limit their flexibility. Many have regularly scheduled meetings of their boards, where contribution decisions are made. If the PAC board is scheduled to meet in June of the election year, the PAC may miss important opportunities that develop as the volatile election cycle progresses. If the PAC has a rigid set of criteria for contributions that favors incumbents, then it may be less able to respond to a large number of qualified nonincumbent candidates, as was the case in 1992.

Although these PACs share a number of characteristics, they also differ in important ways. The Realtors' PAC and ATT contribute to candidates in nearly all House and Senate elections, and the Realtors also reserve additional funds to make independent expenditures on behalf of their most preferred candidates. In contrast, Eaton Corporation's PAC has less money to spend and must pick and choose among potential legislative allies. In doing so, the political inclinations of the PAC's founder to support nonincumbent Republicans remains an important part of the decision calculus. NARAL and the National Right-to-Life PAC are both concerned with an issue that had special significance in the 1992 election cycle.

The PACs in this section represent a broader set of large, institutionalized committees. Although these PACs are small in number, they contribute a large majority of all PAC monies and an even greater proportion of contributions to nonincumbent candidates.

6

The Nationalization of Education Politics: The National Education Association PAC and the 1992 Elections

Denise L. Baer and Martha Bailey

National education policy was prominently debated in the 1992 presidential campaign, due in no small part to the sophisticated legislative and electoral strategies of the 2.1 million–member National Education Association (NEA). While the economy and health policy became *the* defining issues of the 1992 campaign, the partisan divide was just as deep and wide on education as it was on economic and health issues. What was different in 1992 is that both the embattled incumbent, "Education President" George Bush, as well as his ultimately successful challenger, "Education Governor" Bill Clinton, ran on the explicit platforms that there should be a national education policy, and that it is the president who should properly set the agenda. The prominence of educational issues in a presidential race was unparalleled in a policy area traditionally considered the province of state and local authorities. This marks the achievement of a major goal that NEA has pursued actively for two decades through a distinctive mix of coalition building, campaign field work, political education and training of its members, lobbying, and targeted campaign donations through its political action committee—NEA-PAC.

As one of the largest and oldest institutionally affiliated PACs, the NEA-PAC provides important insights into the goals, activity, and influence of PACs. This chapter discusses the history of NEA-PAC and its activities in the 1991–92 election cycle.[1]

The National Education Association

The NEA was founded in 1857 to "elevate the character and advance the interests of the profession of teaching and to promote the cause of education in the U.S."[2] The NEA began as a professionally based association comprising all ranks of education professionals, including administrators, principals, counselors, and educational support personnel, as well as elementary and secondary schoolteachers and college and university professors. By the 1920s, the NEA had emerged as the major professional organization of teachers. The NEA is the nation's largest employee organization, with fifty-two state-level affiliates and more than 13,000 local affiliates.[3] Currently, with 2.1 million members, NEA is also the largest trade union in the United States. The leadership of the NEA is drawn from its ranks. The national headquarters of NEA has a professional staff of about 400, of whom 70 percent to 80 percent are teachers.

The dilemma over professionalism versus trade unionism has created tensions and divisions among educators. For much of its institutional history, the NEA has suffered competition from its major rival, the American Federation of Teachers (AFT), founded in 1916. The NEA has traditionally been the more conservative, while the AFT has been much more closely allied with the labor movement.[4]

The Formation of NEA-PAC

Formed in 1972, NEA-PAC is a relatively old PAC predating the 1974 Federal Election Campaign Act (FECA). It has a fairly well developed structure of internal relationships. NEA-PAC represents the political interests of state and local NEA union affiliates. Long active in state and local elections, the NEA leadership realized that national, coordinated political action was necessary to advance the interests of teachers and education. In 1972, under the direction of president-elect Catherine Barrett, the NEA board of directors and staff launched the NEA-PAC fund with their personal contributions of $2,225 and an additional $28,000 from other NEA members. The association also authorized a $1 contribution to NEA-PAC expressly for political action (in addition to regular membership dues).[5]

Like its parent association, NEA-PAC is not allied with any political party. However, NEA-PAC *was* formed by a politically active organization with specific and well-defined electoral goals. Speaking of the formation of NEA-PAC, Helen Wise, president of the 1973 Representative Assembly, stressed that:

> Our first major objective, politically and legislatively, will be to reverse the national leadership in Washington and put a friend of education in the White House and more friends of education in Congress. . . .[6]

An internal NEA memo emphasized to its members that "politics is 'the art of the possible,' " and that NEA-PAC seeks to advocate and advance its "legislative program through the art of politics." The NEA recognizes that it needs support from both parties even as it asserts that "education, like justice and national defense, should be above partisan bickering." To maintain this stance, NEA-PAC encourages its members to participate in either party.

As an older PAC organized with broad goals, NEA-PAC has been better equipped than newer PACs to resist the power of incumbents and to adapt to changing circumstances. Since its founding, NEA-PAC has changed its tactics to reflect modern electoral politics. Joe Standa, a former teacher and principal from western Pennsylvania and senior professional associate for NEA's Government Relations, notes that he has seen enormous changes in NEA's political action since 1969, when he began working for NEA in Washington. For one thing, dollar contributions have grown. In 1972, NEA-PAC gave $30,000 to federal candidates. In 1992, NEA-PAC contributed more than $2 million to congressional candidates, plus another $2 million to state and national political parties for voter registration and get-out-the-vote activities.

The NEA-PAC also employs a more diverse mix of political communication techniques and a broader base of information. It uses television advertising and has commissioned public opinion polls. NEA-PAC's revised training booklets reflect changes in electoral strategy and campaigning techniques. The PAC focuses its activities on marginal races and races where incumbents have taken a leadership role either in support of or opposition to the NEA Legislative Program. In these races, the NEA and its PAC will the devote maximum resources, including:

- maximum PAC contributions allowable under the FECA;
- use of volunteer organizations;
- widespread use of media, polling, telephone banks, voter registration, get-out-the-vote efforts, and member contact programs;
- use of "soft money" wherever and whenever possible;
- possible use of independent expenditures.

During the 1989–90 election cycle, NEA-PAC made substantial independent expenditures on behalf of North Carolina Democratic Senate candidate Harvey Gantt and Florida Democratic House candidate Reid Hughes. Standa considers NEA-PAC's foray into independent expenditures to be in an "experimental mode." In addition to financial support, NEA-PAC believes that its strongest asset is its ability to conduct grassroots campaign activity. It has a large number of members who are willing to engage in person-to-person campaigning, organize and operate telephone banks, and perform other labor-intensive campaign tasks. NEA-PAC gives "in-kind" contributions of campaign services, such as polling, but most contributions are in cash.

There is no national PAC newsletter to inform contributors of PAC activity, but the NEA's publication *NEA Today* is sent to all NEA members. Most state and local affiliates also publish their own newsletters. NEA's Government Relations Department produces the *NEA Series in Practical Politics*, which is used to provide members with political skills beyond voting.[7] Members are also informed about PAC developments through national and affiliate meetings, where political activity is among the topics discussed. NEA-PAC and its state affiliates are also heavily involved in encouraging their members to become delegates to both national party conventions. Beginning in September preceding the presidential election year through March of the presidential primary and caucus season, NEA affiliates conduct statewide, regional, and local hearings to encourage NEA members to run for delegate slots. These meetings include a review of the NEA endorsement procedures, delegate selection procedures, identification of key federal and state issues, provision of candidate information, and discussion of candidate preferences. Since 1980, NEA delegates have regularly comprised one of the larger blocs of delegates at Democratic conventions, with 365 NEA members serving as delegates to the Democratic National Convention in 1992. The NEA has been far less successful in electing delegates to Republican conventions. In 1992 only twenty-five Republican delegates were NEA members, an increase from six who attended in 1988.

A major event in the history of NEA-PAC was the 1976 general election endorsement of Jimmy Carter for president. Carter was the first presidential candidate endorsed by NEA, and in 1984 they endorsed Walter Mondale during the Democratic primaries. During Carter's tenure, NEA realized its 100-year-old objective: the elevation of education to cabinet-level status—still considered by the NEA to be perhaps its most important achievement. The NEA is aware of its closer links with the Democratic party and has worked assiduously to increase its ties with the Republicans. Recently, the NEA hired a Republican political consultant to advise it on ways to improve its relationship with the GOP.[8]

Organization of NEA-PAC

NEA-PAC is governed by a council, established by the NEA, of approximately sixty-eight people. Voting on the council is based on proportional representation, with each member permitted at least one vote and additional votes allocated by a formula based on state contributions. Each state affiliate is represented by its president (or designee).[9] Two members of the NEA board of directors also serve on the council. In addition, the board includes representatives of NEA's minority caucuses, the Higher Education Caucus, the Women's Caucus, the Caucus of Education of Exceptional Children (CEEC), and the National Council of Urban Education Association (NCUEA), as well as students, support personnel, and retired members. The chair of NEA-PAC is the president of the NEA. The vice president and the secretary/treasurer of the NEA also hold corresponding offices in the national PAC. In addition to sharing staff with NEA-PAC, the NEA pays all of the PAC's administrative costs and overhead. NEA-PAC is administered by the NEA's Government Relations Department. Directed by Debra DeLee, the Government Relations Department has a total staff of forty-eight, including two regional field offices. The NEA political advocacy staff includes six professional staff and four support staff in Washington. All professional staff members hold the Senior Professional Associate title, though each performs a different function. Standa works as a political consultant with congressional and senatorial candidates, meeting with their campaign staffs and with groups supporting their candidacies. Other staffers work with governors and legislators at the state level. Still others are responsible for training members in political action and grassroots organization. The staffers have contacts with both the Democratic and Republican parties, though there is more extensive contact with the Democratic party.

NEA-PAC considers itself to be a "bottom-up" organization. State PACs make endorsement recommendations to the national PAC. The organization of state-level political activities varies by the state. In some cases, the president is the chair of the state PAC. In others, the state PAC is directed by someone else. Some affiliates are politically active; others are less so. Unlike many organizations, NEA-PAC has strong state and local representation, since, as Standa notes, "teachers and students are everywhere."

Local and state affiliates have more frequent communication with each other than they do with the national PAC. NEA-PAC meets four times in each election year and three times in a nonelection year. Speaking of the grassroots element in NEA-PAC endorsements, Standa says:

> All of our endorsements start at the local level. Our evaluation process always starts with incumbents. We look at his or her voting record—this is among the most important elements. The local affiliate's interview team will also send a questionnaire from the national office and ask the candidate to meet with them. If the candidate is highly supportive of us, we usually will not bother with the challenger.[10]

Fundraising and Contributors

NEA-PAC utilizes a variety of fundraising techniques, including person-to-person, telephone, and mail solicitation. Members can make a direct contribution or elect for payroll deduction. Of all of these, person-to-person fundraising is the most effective method of obtaining funds. All NEA-PAC contributors are also state and local members. Since the early 1970s, NEA members are invited to contribute to all three PACs—local, state, and national. In the early years, the NEA utilized a system in seven states in which an NEA-PAC donation was automatically deducted from all dues. The FEC, however, has ruled against systems such as these, requiring that all donations be made voluntarily. In 1980, the NEA was required to pay a $75,000 civil penalty and to refund $800,000 in contributions that it had collected through automatic deductions.[11]

This experience encouraged NEA-PAC to become more creative.

NEA-PAC's major fundraising event is held at its annual national convention. Like many PACs, NEA-PAC has used fundraising gimmicks, such as raffles, to encourage donations. In 1991, one-twelfth of all total receipts were obtained at the NEA-PAC Giveaway, which featured a lottery of three cars, a trip to Alaska, and color televisions. This event was a very effective fundraiser and a catalyst to involve the membership in political action. Besides the fundraising event, NEA-PAC organizes an annual fundraising drive that uses person-to-person contacts and telephone solicitations to raise money. As Standa notes, it is difficult to refuse to contribute if you meet with or are called by someone you know. NEA-PAC has also had some success with mail solicitations to prospect for new contributors but does not regard them as its most productive means of fundraising. NEA-PAC has occasionally relied on outside consultants for advice on fundraising.

State affiliates are responsible for collecting the PAC's contributions. All members are invited to make an annual NEA-PAC contribution of at least $10, and state affiliates generally also ask for an additional $5 to $10 for their PACs. Some states have Century Clubs to encourage higher contributions and offer buttons as incentives for joining them. Some state affiliates use payroll deductions to raise money. Some stage their own mini PAC Giveaways that mimic the national PAC fundraising event. To provide incentive to state PAC directors, states are ranked on how much they have given to NEA-PAC at the national meetings. This encourages competition among state affiliates to boost their fundraising efforts. Some states give out certificates or commendations for members who contribute time or effort to campaign work. All of this activity results in roughly 22 percent to 25 percent of all NEA members contributing to the PAC. In 1988, the average per-member contribution to NEA-PAC exceeded $1 for the first time. Standa believes most members give to NEA-PAC because they recognize that political action is necessary to ensure adequate appropriations for schools and education, to maintain support for collective bargaining, and to move forward on health care issues.

NEA-PAC Decisionmaking

The NEA-PAC makes two general decisions during elections: (1) whether to make an endorsement, and (2) how much and what type of support to give. Endorsements are issue driven. Candidates are evaluated on their level of support for the NEA Legislative Program, which is decided by delegates to the annual NEA Representative Assembly. The decision to support a candidate is made by the NEA-PAC council on the recommendation of the chair (the NEA president). Support for the NEA's legislative program is critical to a decision to contribute to a candidate.

The NEA's top priorities are pro-education incumbents in marginal districts.

The second priority is to support viable opponents of anti-education incumbents. Third, the PAC supports pro-education candidates running for open seats. Pro-education incumbents who do not face a difficult reelection are the PAC's fourth priority. Open-seat candidates who are considered long shots rank fifth, followed by long-shot challengers. Incumbents who have mixed records on education and whose endorsement is withheld pending additional evaluation are ranked last.

NEA-PAC has a major role in the presidential endorsement process, in contrast to the strong deference paid to local affiliates in initiating congressional endorsements. Presidential endorsements begin with the NEA president, who makes an initial recommendation to the NEA-PAC council. The NEA president may choose to recommend that one or more candidates for either or both of the two parties' nominations be endorsed. The president can also recommend that one candidate be endorsed in the general election or that no candidate receive the PAC's endorsement for president. Following a vote by the NEA-PAC council, the NEA board of directors would then vote on the recommendation. State affiliates are allowed to concur with one or more NEA-PAC primary endorsements. For the general election, the endorsement becomes official when locally elected delegates to the NEA Representative Assembly approve it.

Decisionmaking in NEA-PAC is governed by three major principles: bipartisanship, commitment to NEA programs, and grassroots endorsements. The "bottom-up" process starts with the local affiliates, who make their recommendations to state PACs. NEA-PAC has an endorsement kit to assist its local affiliates in making their decisions. The kit includes a survey questionnaire, information on how to interview candidates, and a profile sheet and lobby reports on incumbents from NEA's Federal Relations Unit, as well as a district profile and an overview of NEA issue positions. Issues in the NEA Legislative Program are not weighted, nor is a specific level of agreement needed. In cases where incumbents have voted against NEA's position, they are asked to explain why. Some information about incumbents is collected by Congressional Contact Teams, which are composed of two NEA members from each congressional district who go to Washington and collect information about (and usually meet with) the incumbent.

The state PACs then send their recommendations to the NEA-PAC in Washington. Standa notes that in 99 percent of cases, the national PAC will concur with state and local recommendations. Only rarely will the PAC board fail to support a state's recommendation. One scenario in which this could occur is if a candidate active in state politics who is a supporter of the local and state NEA affiliates decides to challenge the congressional incumbent who has been supportive of NEA at the national level. In this situation, the state PAC may recommend that the NEA-PAC support the challenger. The NEA-PAC may overrule the state PAC's recommendation and support the incumbent, following its philosophy of "not turning against your friends."[12]

Contribution decisions are made using staff and member reports compiled by the national office. The most important factor that influences the contribution decisions of NEA-PAC are incumbents' congressional voting records. If an incumbent has been highly supportive of NEA's positions, then he or she is likely to get NEA-PAC support. NEA-PAC tries to refrain from getting involved in contested, open-seat primaries where friends seek the same seat. It will give primary contributions to incumbents but prefers not to get involved when friends vie against friends.[13] Sources of information about political campaigns include briefings by the Democratic and Republican congressional campaign committees and communications with state party committees and state NEA affiliates. NEA-PAC staffers also attend meetings of the National Committee for an Effective Congress (NCEC). They used to attend briefings held by AFL-CIO's Committee on Political Education (COPE), but now have only informal telephone contacts with COPE. The national PAC relies on a number of political newsletters and specialized publications, such as *Roll Call*, *Hot Line*, *CQ News Clips*, and Kevin Phillips' *American Political Report*. Some information is collected through regional offices where staffers subscribe to local and regional reports.

Analysis: NEA-PAC Contribution Patterns

NEA-PAC contributions to congressional candidates are shown in Table A.5. NEA-PAC donations are overwhelmingly Democratic. Since 1978, they have ranged from a low of 82 percent Democratic for 1980 Senate candidates to a high of 99.6 percent in the 1992 Senate races. In House races, NEA-PAC contributions have ranged from a low of 93 percent Democratic in 1980 to a high of 97 percent Democratic in 1978.

Figures 6.1 and 6.2 compare of the amounts and relative proportions of donations given to incumbents, challengers, and open-seat races. PACs have been accused of an incumbent bias. Herbert Alexander reports that among all PAC contributions in 1989–90, 79.1 percent overall went to incumbents.[14] Against this benchmark, NEA-PAC is a risk-taker that contributes a fairly low proportion of its funds to incumbents. On average, the PAC gives only 61.3 percent of its contributions to incumbents in House races and 47.8 percent to incumbents in Senate races. In 1984 Senate races, only 30.7 percent of NEA-PAC funds was contributed to incumbents. In House races the low was in 1982, when only 42.4 percent of NEA-PAC contributions went to incumbents.

While the NEA-PAC's contribution patterns clearly demonstrate that incumbency, partisanship, and the chamber for which candidates are running are important, they reveal a striking level of support for Republican incumbents. From 1978 to 1992, an average of 78.2 percent of the PAC's contributions to Republican candidates for the Senate went to incumbents, and 64.8 percent of its contributions to Republicans running for the House went to incumbents. The averages for Democratic incumbents are lower: 44.9 percent of the PAC's contributions to Democratic candidates for the Senate went to incumbents, and just 60.9 per-

Figure 6.1. **NEA-PAC House Contributions, 1978–92**

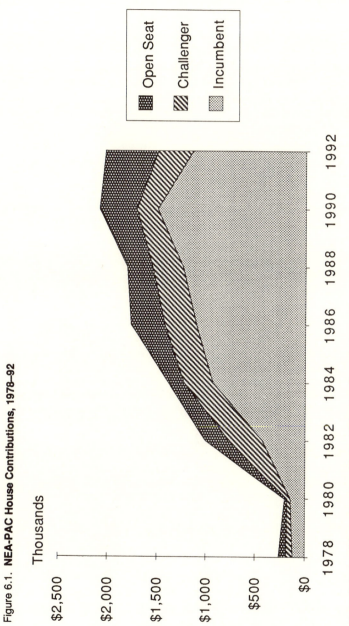

Thousands

Legend: Open Seat, Challenger, Incumbent

Note: Calculated by author from Federal Election Commission data.

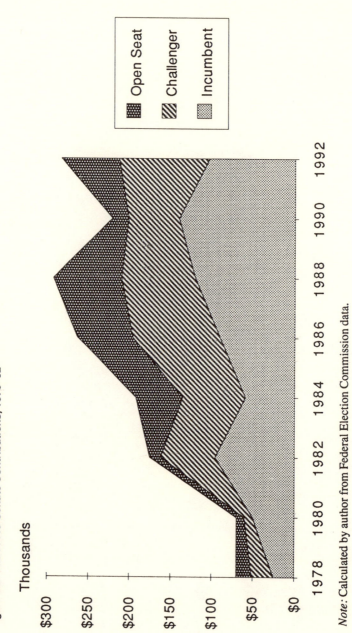

Figure 6.2. **NEA-PAC Senate Contributions, 1978–92**

Thousands

$300

$250

$200

$150

$100

$50

$0

1978 1980 1982 1984 1986 1988 1990 1992

Open Seat

Challenger

Incumbent

Note: Calculated by author from Federal Election Commission data.

cent of its contributions to Democrats campaigning for the House went to incumbents.

The emphasis on Republican incumbents, especially in the Senate, reflects that they are more likely than Republican challengers or open-seat candidates to be drawn from the party's moderate-to-progressive wing.

The 1992 Election

Early on, NEA-PAC saw the potential for great change in the 1992 elections. The NEA-PAC expected that the 1992 elections would be more highly contested because of redistricting. NEA was indirectly involved in the redistricting process. It provided some funds to IMPAC 2000, a Democratic party–affiliated group involved in the 1992 restricting, but did not actively work to help define the drawing of new districts. In planning for the 1992 cycle, Standa stressed that NEA-PAC would continue to back incumbents who supported the NEA legislative program. However, NEA-PAC would consider giving more money to non-incumbent candidates in 1992 because their contests were more likely to be competitive than in previous elections. No change was made in the long-established endorsement procedures in which the local NEA affiliates make the recommendations for endorsement to NEA-PAC. The NEA-PAC also cooperated with groups with similar agendas. It provided some funds to the National Committee for an Effective Congress, EMILY's List, and other liberal organizations.

Following established procedure, the NEA evaluated George Bush's record in 1991 as the first step in its presidential endorsement procedure. In October 1991, NEA decided that George Bush did not merit its support. Five of the Democratic primary contenders—Arkansas governor Bill Clinton, Senator Bob Kerrey of Nebraska, former senator Paul Tsongas of Massachusetts, Senator Tom Harkin of Iowa, and Virginia governor L. Douglas Wilder—answered the group's questionnaire and were interviewed by NEA president Keith Geiger about education issues. The resulting seventy-minute videotape of the interview sessions was sent to the state NEA affiliates. In addition, Clinton, Kerrey, and Tsongas appeared in person in December 1991 before NEA and NEA-PAC leadership. Former governor Jerry Brown of California was not invited to participate because he was determined by NEA not to be a viable candidate. Republican challenger Patrick J. Buchanan, a political commentator, was invited to participate in the endorsement process but declined to do so. In July, 80 percent of the 1992 Representative Assembly voted to endorse Bill Clinton, the highest level of support received by any nominee.

During the Democratic and Republican national conventions, NEA-PAC provided financial assistance to convention delegates. This bipartisan assistance also included round-trip coach airfare to the convention city; interest-free loans of up to $500; and a convention memorabilia kit (for those who completed an NEA delegate data survey), which could be auctioned off to offset expenses. A grant of $400 was also given to each delegate who attended the NEA delegate caucus meeting held at his or her party's convention.

Of the twenty-five NEA Republican delegates, almost half (44 percent) were alternate delegates. Only a bare majority—52 percent—identified themselves as Bush delegates. NEA delegates at the Democratic convention, on the other hand, overwhelmingly supported Bill Clinton; 72 percent identified themselves as Clinton delegates. Only 16 percent of the delegates had alternate status. NEA members were easily recognizable on the floor of the Democratic convention, wearing yellow vests emblazoned with "NEA." NEA members testified before the Democratic and Republican platform committees. Governor Roy Romer (Colorado), the leader of a 1991 panel on education goals, cochaired the Democratic party Platform Committee, signaling the Democratic party's commitment to education.

By July 1, 1992, the NEA-PAC had made 257 congressional endorsements, including 25 Senate candidates. Ultimately, a total of 316 House and 35 Senate candidates were endorsed. All 35 Senate endorsements were for Democrats. In House races, 15 Republicans, 299 Democrats, and 2 Independents received NEA-PAC endorsements. Republicans endorsed by NEA-PAC tended to be moderate or liberal, with a pro-choice and pro–civil rights voting record. They were largely from the Northeast and included representatives Christopher Shays (CT), Jim Leach (IA), Jim Ramstad (MN), Bill Green (NY), Hamilton Fish (NY), Benjamin Gilman (NY), and Constance Morella (MD).

The NEA-PAC devoted most of its resources in 1992 to the presidential election. NEA Government Relations Director Debra DeLee stressed the unparalleled nature of the effort for Clinton:

> We have, for the first time, released all of our resources—a tremendous amount of resources—both staff, as well as monetary, to do our member-to-member campaign on behalf of the Clinton–Gore team.[15]

About half of the resources went to soft-money contributions to state parties in targeted states for party-building and get-out-the-vote activities. Donations to state parties included $215,000 in hard money and $2,010,275 from nonfederal soft-money accounts. Consistent with its risk-taking strategy, no money was held back for post-election debt retirement or to assist in lobbying relationships with successful candidates the PAC had not previously supported at maximum levels.

The NEA's contribution patterns in the 1992 congressional elections did not change drastically from previous years. Even though the 1992 elections did provide a greater window of opportunity for NEA to act on its longstanding issue agenda, 47.8 percent of NEA-PAC Senate contributions went to incumbents, and 56.4 percent of House contributions went to incumbents.

The NEA-PAC was extremely active in attempting to persuade NEA members to support the Clinton–Gore ticket. It conducted extensive grassroots mobilization and voter education programs among its members. The national office sent out almost 16,000 campaign kits to local NEA affiliates, which included a videotape of Bill Clinton addressing the July 1992 Representative Assembly. A six-person "rapid response" team in the NEA's national office answered questions from field staff and set up a toll-free telephone number to provide daily updates on the campaign. Jerry Carruthers, an NEA government-relations specialist, was based in the Clinton campaign headquarters in Little Rock as a representative of NEA. Every targeted state was provided with an NEA staffer who helped persuade NEA members to vote for the Clinton–Gore ticket.[16]

The NEA was delighted with the victory of Bill Clinton and Al Gore. NEA-PAC was also rather successful with its congressional endorsements: 73 percent of House candidates it endorsed won, as did 60 percent of its Senate candidates. The PAC's success rate for House incumbents was 92 percent (177 incumbents reelected). Out of 51 House challenger races, only 5 endorsed challengers won—a success rate of only 10 percent. In House open seats, 50 endorsed candidates won, yielding a 68 percent success rate. In the Senate, 81 percent of NEA-PAC–endorsed incumbents won, while the success rates of NEA-PAC–endorsed challengers and open-seat–endorsed candidates amounted to 25 percent and 67 percent, respectively.

In addition to the presidential and congressional elections, state NEA-PAC affiliates were active in gubernatorial and state ballot measures. Eleven gubernatorial candidates were endorsed, including one Republican, as were eight candidates for open seats. Of these, eight won. State affiliates were active in sixteen state ballot initiatives, including defending choice on abortion, civil rights for gays and lesbians, campaign finance reform, term limits, and caps on sales and property taxes. State affiliates were successful in six of these ballot measures.

Overall, the NEA-PAC was very satisfied with the 1992 election results. Joe Standa says that the only surprise to NEA was that they "expected a lot more incumbents to lose because of redistricting and the pay raise issue."[17]

Conclusion

The National Education Association is a politically active organization that represents the average educator—not the stereotypical "special interest." Contrary to common views about PACs, the NEA-PAC takes risks. NEA-PAC's risk-taking behavior is strongly related to the type of organization it represents and its longevity as a PAC. Pre-FECA PACs, like the NEA-PAC, have generally been better able to maintain a "viable mix of legislative and electoral strategies" because they draw on "shared [long-term] goals" and a preexisting commitment to encouraging voter participation.[18]

The NEA-PAC endorsements are issue-driven and depend upon the particular incumbents and challengers as well as the number of open seats in any one election cycle. In this sense, NEA-PAC benefits American democracy—it works to increase voter information and political participation among its members. For the NEA, its 1992 campaign and PAC activities represent a continuation of long-standing, relatively institutionalized relationships with the Democratic party. These relationships may become even stronger as a result of the appointment of Debra DeLee, director of NEA's Government Relations, as an unpaid co–vice chair of the Democratic National Committee. Yet 1992 was also a success because NEA was able to make educational issues an important area of choice between the parties, even as both candidates stressed education's importance to their issue agendas.

Notes

1. The authors wish to thank Joe Standa for his graciousness, patience, and openness in answering questions about NEA and NEA-PAC in the 1992 cycle. The preliminary personal interviews in October 1991 and March 1992 were conducted by Martha Bailey; the pre- and post-election interviews in October 1992 and November 1992 were conducted by Denise Baer.

2. Allan M. West, *The National Education Association: The Power Base for Education* (New York: The Free Press, 1980), p. 193.

3. Includes the fifty state associations, the Overseas Education Association, and the Puerto Rican Association. "NEA Fact Sheet," National Education Association, Washington, D.C., March 1990.

4. Marjorie Murphy, *Blackboard Unions, The AFT and the NEA, 1900–1980* (Ithaca, NY: Cornell University Press, 1990).

5. West, *The National Education Association*, p. 193.

6. Ibid., 194.

7. Titles include: *You and Politics: A Workbook Introduction; How to Set Up and Operate a Local Association Political Action Program; How to Raise Money for NEA-PAC: Education's Defense Fund; How to Recruit, Organize and Manage Volunteers; How to Run Voter Contact Programs; How to Conduct Opinion Polls; How to Target for Elections (Including Campaign Research and Demographics), How to Participate in Party Politics; How to Prepare and Use Print Communications*; and *How to Conduct the NEA Congressional Contact Team Program.*

8. Personal interview with Joe Standa, October 1991.

9. Herbert Alexander, "The PAC Phenomenon," in Edward Zuckerman, ed., *Almanac of Federal PACS: 1992* (Washington, D.C.: Amward Publications, 1992), p. xiv.

10. Mary Jordan, "Education Chief Rebukes Biggest Teachers' Union," *Washington Post*, July 7, 1992, p. A4.

11. Personal interview with Joe Standa, October 1991.

12. Larry J. Sabato, *PAC Power: Inside the World of Political Action Committees* (New York: W.W. Norton, 1984), p. 62.

13. Personal interview with Joe Standa, October 1992.

14. Herbert Alexander, "The PAC Phenomenon," p. xiv.

15. Lynn Olson, "Unions Putting Time, Money, Energy to Task of Campaigning for Clinton," *Education Week*, October 14, 1992, p. 1.

16. Ibid.

17. Personal interview with Joe Standa, November 1992.

18. Frank J. Sorauf, *Inside Campaign Finance: Myths and Realities* (New Haven: Yale University Press, 1992), p. 108.

7

AT&T PAC: A Pragmatic Giant

Robert E. Mutch

AT&T PAC is the largest corporate PAC, having raised and spent more than other corporate funds since 1986. AT&T created its current PAC in 1984 after divesting itself, under federal court order, of its twenty-two operating companies. Divestiture was an event of massive proportions for the company, and the consequent reorganization of the PAC and reassessment of its purpose led directly to its rapid attainment of number-one status in 1986. AT&T has fully integrated the PAC with its lobbying arm, the Government Relations Division.

As would be expected of a PAC so closely linked to a lobbying operation, AT&T PAC supports more incumbents and Democrats than most other company PACs. It also is cautious and orthodox in its activities: it makes no in-kind contributions or independent expenditures, and the parent company makes very few soft-money contributions. It is because AT&T PAC is a model of the pragmatic corporate committee that its behavior in 1992 is of special interest. Because the development that determined the PAC's behavior was the very large number of House open seats in 1992, this chapter will concentrate on the PAC's activities in House elections.

Growth and Development

American Telephone and Telegraph Company engaged in little overt electoral activity before forming its first PACs in 1977 and 1979. The company had no organized political contribution program before creating its political funds, and few of its top officers are on record as having made contributions in or before the 1976 elections. Even after the Federal Election Campaign Act (FECA) explicitly legalized the creation of union and corporation PACs in 1971, AT&T did not

Table 7.1

AT&T PAC Receipts, 1978–92 (figures in thousands)

	1978	1980	1982	1984	1986	1988	1990	1992
AT&T HQ	65	163	136	78	—	—	—	—
W. Electric	25	76	73	55	—	—	—	—
Long Lines	—	59	68	43	—	—	—	—
AT&T PAC	—	—	—	215	1,821	3,044	2,836	2,757
Totals	90	298	277	391	1,821	3,044	2,836	2,757
(1992 $)	(194)	(507)	(403)	(528)	(2,331)	(3,610)	(3,044)	

Source: Federal Election Commission.

create a PAC because its management felt that "there was some cloud of controversy over the legality" of such committees.[1] This doubt stemmed from the federal prohibition against indirect contributions from government contractors, of which AT&T was one of the largest. Congress repealed that provision in the 1974 FECA amendments, but it was the Federal Election Commission (FEC) that set off the explosive growth of corporate PACs by its 1975 ruling on the Sun Company PAC.[2]

AT&T joined the movement, forming the Western Electric PAC and AT&T PAC in 1977, and a Long Lines PAC in 1979. By 1979 the regional operating companies also had formed their own committees. Had all these funds been treated as a single unit, AT&T would have ranked third among corporate PACs in receipts and expenditures in 1978; in 1980 it would have ranked first.

After divesting itself of its operating companies (now distributed among the seven regional Bell telephone companies, or "Baby Bells"), AT&T combined its three remaining committees, for the corporate headquarters, Western Electric, and Long Lines, into the current AT&T PAC. Financially, this was not as great a blow as it seems, as the three smaller PACs had been successful fundraisers (see Table 7.1). As early as 1980, the three by themselves would have been the seventh-ranked corporate committee in size of receipts. Judging only by the data in Table 7.1, the prospect of divestiture appears to have had a greater financial impact than the fact of it. Receipts dropped in 1982 but had recovered so well by 1984 that the elements of the current AT&T PAC would have ranked twelfth among corporate committees.

By 1984 the PAC's executive committee had decided to expand solicitations by reaching deeper into management ranks, seeking contributions from all administrative personnel except those with direct responsibility for nonmanagement employees. This move, plus the increasing number of white collar employees in the company—a product of reorganization—raised the number of people solicited to about 55,000. Expanded solicitation accounts for most of AT&T

PAC's nearly fivefold increase in receipts from 1984 to 1986. Since 1986 the committee has raised, spent, and contributed more than any other corporate PAC.

The PAC began the 1991–92 election cycle by confronting a fall in receipts that had begun in 1989–90. In January 1991, the national solicitation committee decided to try face-to-face solicitations as a way of reversing the decline. The committee was encouraged by initial results and continued the practice in 1992 with about 1,000 senior managers. Since personal solicitation is very time consuming, PAC officers have tentatively decided to do it only every other year for the entire 55,000-member solicitable class but every year for senior managers. To stay in more frequent touch with all donors, PAC officers also began issuing their newsletter quarterly rather than annually.[3]

AT&T divides its PAC and federal lobbying activities between its Washington office and its state and regional government affairs directors. Washington personnel are responsible for "issue management," that is, for lobbying congressional committee staff on behalf of the company's positions. State and regional directors lobby members of Congress and their personal staff on behalf of those same positions. These directors also are responsible for lobbying state legislatures, but their federal responsibilities require them to spend a great deal of time in Washington, up to thirty to forty weeks a year.[4] The frequent trips to Washington permit state directors to stay in touch with each other and with Washington staff, while their state activities allow them to monitor Congress members' electoral situations back home.

There are three committees at the national level: an executive committee and one each for the solicitation and disbursement of campaign money. The executive committee is responsible for overall administration of the PAC and makes appointments to the other two bodies. The company's senior vice president for government affairs, who also is general counsel, makes appointments to the executive committee.[5] It is unusual for a corporation's general counsel to be in charge of government affairs and take an active role in the PAC, but AT&T's case probably is explained by its heavily regulated environment.[6]

AT&T, like other corporations, tries to appoint PAC committees whose members represent each of its business units. Any PAC donor can volunteer to serve on a state or regional committee, and the company encourages them to do so. Few do, however.

Research on PAC donors suggests that giving is more a function of the donors' relationship to the PAC's sponsoring organization than of their interest in electoral politics. Employees contribute for the same reasons they give to United Way or buy savings bonds, not because they are, or have been persuaded to become, politically active.[7] The company thus finds it difficult to make its PAC committees broadly representative of its business units, and as a practical matter strives to prevent them from consisting entirely of government affairs personnel.[8]

Solicitation is centralized in the national committee, which solicits company managers all over the country. The money collected flows only one way, from the national to the state and regional disbursement committees. The only exceptions are ten states in which AT&T believes it is legally required to create separate federal PACs (called white card states for the color of the solicitation cards sent to them). Company managers in these states are still solicited nationally, but they send their contributions to state PACs, which in turn contribute only to federal candidates from that state.[9] Funds collected from AT&T managers nationwide then go to the national disbursement committee, which distributes the money to its state and regional counterparts. The PAC's financial transactions are the responsibility of corporate headquarters in New York, which keeps records for the FEC and issues the checks that the state committees give to candidates.

AT&T PAC collects nearly all of its funds by payroll deduction and has never used any other method. The average monthly contribution is roughly $10, the average annual contribution about $110. Year-end reports for 1989 and 1990 indicate that contributions under $200 made up 75 percent of PAC receipts for that election cycle. The few very large contributors in that cycle were all from top management.

PAC Decisionmaking

The first stage of deciding which candidates to support comes very early, in January or February of the first year in a two-year cycle. At that time the state and regional government affairs directors send their recommendations to the national disbursement committee. Since their requests usually total more than the PAC is likely to raise, the national committee then sends the state and regional committees its own recommendations for distributing the funds. Since the PAC gives a substantial portion of its total contributions in the first year of a cycle— 47 percent in 1989–90 and 1991–92—this first exchange greatly influences early contributions. At the annual meeting for the following year there is another exchange between state and regional government affairs directors and their counterparts at the national level.

According to Gregory Miller, AT&T's vice president for federal government affairs, the national committee's function is "to make sure there's some consistency across the regions. But it's really up to them [state and regional disbursement committees and government affairs directors] once they get the money."[10] The national disbursement committee makes the final decision on how much money will be allocated to the states and regions. State directors cannot increase the amount of money they get, but they have great latitude in distributing it to candidates.[11]

Every PAC wants to support candidates who are likely to win and who will support its objectives. AT&T PAC is one of the few that is large and decentral-

Table 7.2

Percentage of Contributions to House Democrats, 1978–92

	1978	1980	1982	1984	1986	1988	1990	1992
All Corporate PACs	43.4	39.2	36.8	44.2	47.8	51.6	52.8	n.a.
Top 10 Corporate PACS	49.6	42.8	35.3	(38.1)	46.6	(57.2)	(54.0)	n.a.
AT&T PAC	51.2	44.3	41.6	40.4	51.9	55.1	59.2	62.2

Source: Federal Election Commission.
Note: For 1978–84, "AT&T PAC" means the PACs that later merged to form the current PAC; for 1986–92, AT&T was omitted from the top ten corporate PACs when calculating percentages. In 1984, 1988, and 1990, FEC Reports on Financial Activity did not aggregate data by party by house, so percentages in parentheses are for all federal candidates.

ized enough to evaluate both of these factors for most candidates. Since most of the company's state directors are both state and federal lobbyists, their relations with senators and representatives often predate the members' congressional service. They also are likely to know, or at least know about, challengers and open-seat candidates in their states. Congressional nonincumbents supported by the federal PAC probably had earlier received backing from AT&T's state-level committees in state legislative races. This is why the PAC has never even considered giving questionnaires to candidates—the state directors already have the information such questionnaires are designed to elicit.

Patterns of Giving

Party and Candidate Status

Corporate PACs closely tied to lobbying operations typically select candidates on pragmatic rather than ideological grounds, and AT&T PAC offers no surprises here.[12] The selection process is "driven by the best assessment of what will minimize risk to the corporation and what will maximize our opportunities. . . . There is a disinclination to fall on our swords ideologically."[13]

One measure of pragmatism is the percentage of contributions given to Democratic House candidates. Democrats have exercised uninterrupted control of the House throughout the life of AT&T's PAC, so a pragmatic strategy would dictate a larger proportion of contributions to the majority party. As Table 7.2 shows, AT&T PAC generally has been more pragmatic than other corporate PACs, even more than the top ten corporate committees, which as a group tend to be less ideological than other business PACs.

Table 7.3

Percentage of Contributions to House Nonincumbents, 1978–92

	1978	1980	1982	1984	1986	1988	1990	1992
All Corporate PACs	37.0	31.0	24.1	19.6	14.8	9.4	13.1	n.a.
Percentage to Democrats	24.3	6.5	20.0	10.2	58.1	27.7	29.0	n.a.
AT&T PAC	20.7	19.5	12.9	12.4	11.8	7.9	7.1	14.2
Percentage to Democrats	32.8	10.2	25.6	28.2	44.7	47.8	58.1	62.0

Source: Data for all corporate PACs in 1978 and 1980 from Norman J. Ornstein, Thomas E. Mann, and Michael J. Malbin, eds., *Vital Statistics on Congress, 1991–1992* (Washington, D.C.: American Enterprise Institute, 1992), p. 98; all other data from the Federal Election Commission.

As the first and third rows in Table 7.3 show, AT&T PAC has also tended to give less money to challengers and open-seat candidates than other corporate PACs. The second and fourth rows in Table 7.3, which show the percentage of nonincumbent contributions going to Democrats, is even more revealing. In most years AT&T PAC shared business's preference for Republican nonincumbents, but it still gave more to Democrats, even in the crucial year 1980, when Republicans persuaded corporate committees to invest heavily in their attempt to achieve majority status in the House.

These figures reveal little about a long-running debate within the PAC over the tactical versus strategic importance of contributions to open-seat candidates. Gregory Millert referred to an "internal battle between those who say, 'What can a freshman do in terms of helping your issues? Why not give that money to someone who's likely to be able to help you?' But freshmen become senior members, and a contribution can be the beginning of a very good long-term relationship."[14] He added that several years ago the PAC gave $5,000 to an unidentified open-seat candidate who has "turned out to be very supportive of our issues. Maybe he would have been anyway. But there's a real open door there for us to talk about our issues. That's really what you have a PAC for—to help make sure that the member is willing to listen to your point of view."[15]

State directors also have other ways to build relationships with nonincumbents. "Pulling the steering committee together for the PAC fundraiser is more important than writing the check itself . . . picking up the phone and making introductions around town."[16] Any PAC can write a check, but AT&T's state directors can provide intangible benefits to open-seat candidates, as well as to the freshmen members of Congress the victors become. The PAC also has been tilting toward Democrats in its contributions to state and national party com-

Table 7.4

Percentage of Incumbent House Recipients on Three Key Committees

	1978	1980	1982	1984	1986	1988	1990	1992
All Incumbents	26.5	28.1	34.9	32.3	24.1	23.9	23.7	24.0
Incumbents Receiving More than Average	29.2	32.9	36.1	41.0	36.6	34.6	29.1	36.8

Source: Federal Election Commission.

mittees: in 1991–92 it gave $84,050 to Democratic committees and $81,000 to Republican ones. Preference for Republicans appears only in earmarked contributions from PAC donors of at least $200. In 1991–92, 81 percent of those contributions went to Republican candidates and party committees; in 1989–90 the figure was 75 percent.[17]

Committee Membership

Another measure of pragmatism is a PAC's concentration on key congressional committees. PAC officers said in interviews that the House committees most important to AT&T are Commerce, Way and Means, and Judiciary. The first row in Table 7.4 displays the percentage of House incumbents supported by AT&T PAC who sat on the three top committees. The second row displays the percentage of membership on those committees among House incumbents who received more than the average contribution for that cycle.

Since the combined membership of the three committees makes up about one-fourth of the House, the percentages in the first row of Table 7.4 are not much higher than AT&T PAC could have achieved by distributing its money at random. Since the PAC gives to 90 to 95 percent of House incumbents, looking at all recipients may reveal less than would a narrower focus on those who receive more than the average contribution. The percentages in the second row are higher, particularly after 1984, but on average they still show only that slightly more than one-third of incumbents favored with large gifts sat on the three top committees.[18] Either these committees are not as important as claimed, or there are other factors at work here.

Number of Recipients

The large number of candidates the PAC supports is not simply a function of the huge sums of money it raises. It has been giving to more candidates than other

PACs since before it became large enough to give the most money.[19] Indeed, for the last three election cycles, AT&T PAC has given to more federal candidates than any other PAC, including those of the Realtors and the American Medical Association, which raise and give much more money.

This unusual pattern is produced by familiar factors: AT&T is simply behaving like other corporations by using its PAC to support members from states and districts in which it does business.[20] Since the company provides long distance telephone service to every state in the country, this means giving to candidates from all those states. In AT&T's case, this pragmatic consideration is reinforced by a structural feature not usually associated with pragmatic PACs: the decentralized character of PAC decisionmaking, which reflects the geographically dispersed structure of the company's lobbying division.[21]

State directors and disbursement committees made up of employees who live and vote in that state make the final decisions on PAC contributions. This arrangement inevitably gives greater voice to local opinion than would be found in other large corporations.[22] This decentralization fosters pragmatism because state directors are also lobbyists who are held accountable for how members of Congress from their states vote. According to Millert, "Someone will say, 'Your member didn't vote the way we wanted.' They have the relationship responsibility, and PAC giving is one element of that."[23] That means giving to more members than just those who count company facilities and employees among their constituents. Financial support of a campaign creates its own constituency: "Contributions become a substitute for votes in a member's district—a surrogate."[24]

In addition to structural reasons for distributing contributions widely, there is the question of recent bills affecting the company. In any given Congress, members introduce bills that would benefit or harm some corporation; few of these bills attract much attention outside the committees that decide their fate. Most of the bills AT&T tracks fall into this category. The most important ones, though, are attempts to rewrite policy for the entire telecommunications industry, and these become the subjects of nationwide lobbying campaigns.

AT&T began its PAC during the most momentous of these policy changes—the first legislative moves in the long effort to break up the company.[25] In the late 1980s Congress began considering bills to amend the divestiture agreement by permitting the Baby Bells to compete with AT&T and others in the long distance and equipment manufacturing businesses, and to provide electronic information services over telephone lines and cable television. Billions of dollars are at stake here. The battle has spread beyond the telecommunications industry to involve publishers, newspapers, and a broad array of consumer groups. Gregory Millert states:

> One of the lobbying techniques we use to affect [these bills] before they get to the floor is cosponsorship drives. We want to get the whole House on a bill, or

keep them off a bill. So having a relationship with the entire Congress is more important to us than it might be to another company whose issues are decided in a specific committee.[26]

The percentages in Table 7.4 thus reflect a balance among different lobbying strategies. This particular balance raises the question of effectiveness: the more widely the PAC distributes its gifts, the more likely it is to support members who will not vote as it wishes.

The usual test of PAC effectiveness—roll-call votes—is unavailable in this case because the most important House telecommunications bill in the 102nd Congress never reached the floor.[27] What can be done is to measure AT&T's success in persuading members it backed in 1989–90 not to sign on as cosponsors of the bill, which the company opposed.[28] Of 405 House incumbents who won reelection in 1990, 256 opted not to back the bill. The mean 1989–90 AT&T PAC contribution to the majority who chose not to be cosponsors was $2,862, well above the $1,967 mean contribution to cosponsors. This evidence alone suggests that the centrifugal force of decentralized decisionmaking was more than adequately balanced by the lobbyists' common purpose of supporting members who would further corporate goals.

The 1992 Election

As the size of the 1992 turnover became clear, many observers assumed that PACs would take advantage of this once-in-a-lifetime opportunity to change the makeup of Congress. The expectation was that even pragmatic business PACs would respond to the unusually large number of open-seat races by giving stronger support to Republican candidates. AT&T PAC did give a larger proportion of money to nonincumbents than at any other time since 1980, but otherwise it did not act as expected.

One step PAC officers took to deal with the unprecedented situation was to decentralize decisionmaking even further. They did this "to give maximum discretionary authority to the people who are closest to the political situation in the states. . . . We anticipated upsets and surprises . . . the House bank scandal was really a wild card that was not anticipated . . . and decentralization provided the flexibility to deal with it on a case-by-case basis."[29] Since the final decision always had been up to the state and regional disbursement committees, the practical effect of this move was to reduce the amount of time the national committee spent discussing open-seat candidates.

Contributions to Nonincumbents

Open Seats

At the January 1992 meeting, the national disbursement committee set $1,000 as a suggested contribution limit to open-seat candidates. This was lower than the PAC's average 1989–90 open-seat gift ($1,355) and may have reflected uncertainty about the large number of open-seat decisions to be made about candidates, as well as budgetary restraints.

The PAC gave 11 percent of its contributions to House open-seat candidates, more than doubling the proportion it had allotted to such candidates in the previous two cycles. However, it gave nearly two-thirds of that money—66.1 percent—to Democrats, also an increase over the previous cycle.[30] The PAC's 1992 contributions did not depart from, but continued, the pattern of recent years. It gave more money in open-seat races, but there were more of those races; giving more money to Democrats continued a trend that dates back at least to 1986 (see Table 7.3). The PAC's behavior in 1992 contrasts most sharply not with that of recent years but with that of 1980, the last year in which it gave a comparably large sum of money to nonincumbents. In 1980 AT&T PAC did depart from previous behavior, not in the amount of money it gave to open-seat candidates but in the fact that it gave much more of it to Republicans (82.4 percent, up from 54.7 percent in 1978).

In retrospect, the PAC's continued support for Democratic nonincumbents in 1992 should have been expected. Expectations that PACs would depart from previous behavior were predicated on the absence of party, voting record, and other cues as crowds of political unknowns vied for the unusually large number of open House seats. Recall, though, that AT&T's state government affairs directors lobby state legislatures as well as Congress. State legislatures are fertile breeding grounds for congressional candidates, and Democrats have dominated most of those assemblies in the years since AT&T created its PAC. When state PAC disbursement committees debated the merits of open-seat candidates, they were not discussing nonincumbents or unknowns. As Gregory Millert put it, "Even candidates who are not current office holders typically don't come out of nowhere. They've been politically active, so their pros and cons are known."[31]

Just over half of the open-seat candidates the PAC supported (omitting post-general and year-end contributions) were members of state legislatures. Adding state executive officers and those serving in large city governments brings the total to just under two-thirds. Only a very few of the rest had held no political office. The company also has state-level PACs that give to state and local candidates, and it is likely that those committees had earlier backed the same congressional open-seat candidates who received federal backing in 1992. The 1992 election did not suddenly present AT&T PAC with the need to form new ties; rather, it offered a striking variation on the need to maintain existing ones.

Challengers

In the area of challengers, AT&T's PAC did better by Republicans, giving them 55 percent of its contributions. The PAC does not appear to have taken these contributions as seriously as those for open seats, though, for in all but four of the twenty races it also gave, usually more generously, to the incumbents. Two-thirds of the money the PAC gave to challengers went to thirteen primary candidates of the party to which the incumbent did not belong; nine of them lost. The PAC gave more money to challengers than to incumbents in only six races, and two of those incumbents lost. Only 9 percent of the PAC's contributions went to successful challengers. In nearly all of these races, the PAC's contribution decisions can be seen as a way to balance conflicting loyalties: it gave to friends on both sides, but gave more to those most likely to win. Here again, there is a sharp contrast with the PAC's behavior in 1980. In that year, the PAC gave 95 percent of its contributions to Republicans and 46.6 percent to winners. It gave to both incumbent and challenger in six of twenty-two races, but gave more to the incumbent in only three: two of those three incumbents were Republicans who defeated Democratic opponents. The only winning Democratic challenger to receive PAC gifts defeated an incumbent of his own party in a primary and ran unopposed in the general election. The PAC's support for challengers in 1980 was both more partisan and more serious than in 1992.

After the Election

Freshmen may find that one of the few familiar faces in Washington is that of the AT&T lobbyist—perhaps the same person with whom the new members had dealt in the state legislature. Those freshmen may draw on the lobbyist's Washington experience when trying to find their way around Congress. Donald Goff, AT&T's director for federal government affairs, said that freshmen had asked him, " 'How does this place work? How does it compare to the statehouse, where we were?' "[32] In large states where federal and state lobbying are handled by different people, state lobbyists "hand off" candidates to their federal counterparts after the PAC decides to support them. Not every new member won the PAC's backing, and some reached Congress by defeating candidates the PAC did support; in the House, AT&T lobbyists have access even to them.

AT&T provides telephone service to the House, which gives the company's lobbyists "a wonderful opportunity to either succeed or fail."[33] The chancy character of that opportunity was especially evident after the 1992 election, when the high turnover meant that the company had to install telephones, intercoms, and faxes not only for new members but also for senior members moving into more desirable quarters. Since this equipment has AT&T's logo on it, the company's credibility is intimately linked to the 435 members' daily activities. Company lobbyists can use this link to introduce themselves to representatives they don't know simply by calling to say, "As you go through this, here's my number in case anything goes wrong." The risk that something can go wrong is balanced by the opportunity to begin a relationship with a member on grounds other than PAC or policy concerns.

Conclusion

Those of us who expected AT&T PAC to act differently in 1992 underestimated the extent to which it had developed stable ties to state and congressional officeholders. The PAC has become an established organization with routinized operations. Such organizations are not remarkably agile because agility is unnecessary for survival, or even success. The PAC made no sharp departure from previous behavior because that is not how established organizations behave. When confronted with an unprecedented situation, it accommodated it within its operational precedents. To have used 1992 as a means of changing the composition of Congress would have meant an abrupt shift from pragmatic to ideological goals. It would have required PAC directors to sever many of the state-level ties they had established over the previous decade, a move that would have cast doubt on their commitment to all other ties. The spread of such doubt would in turn have jeopardized the success of the very lobbying function PAC contributions support. Such a dramatic shift in goals and methods would have constituted a revolution within the PAC, and we should never be surprised when revolutions do not occur.

Notes

1. Personal interviews with Gregory Millert, AT&T vice president for Federal Government Affairs and Federal Government Affairs Director Donald L. Goff, October 11, 1991.

2. The FECA specifically permitted corporations to have direct partisan communications with stockholders but did not mention employees. Nonetheless, all three Republican commissioners and one of the Democrats voted to permit SUNPAC to solicit hourly wage as well as managerial employees. Congress reacted to this move by defining executives and managers as the solicitable class for corporate PACs and explicitly excluding hourly-wage workers. See Robert E. Mutch, *Campaigns, Congress, and Courts: The Making of Federal Campaign Finance Law* (New York: Praeger, 1988), pp. 164–70.

3. Personal interviews with Donald Goff, June 23 and November 24, 1992, and AT&T PAC year-end reports. One factor in falling receipts that officers hope face-to-face solicitation will reduce is donor antagonism toward all PACs.

4. Personal interview with Donald Goff, October 11, 1991. Goff was once AT&T's Illinois state government affairs director.

5. Edward Handler and John R. Mulkern reported that in more than three-fourths of the corporate PACs in their sample, CEOs appointed all members of PAC committees. See their book, *Business in Politics* (Lexington, MA: Lexington Books, 1982), p. 75. Larry Sabato seconded this observation in *PAC Power* (New York: W.W. Norton, 1984), p. 34. See also Theodore J. Eismeier and Philip H. Pollock, *Business, Money, and the Rise of Corporate PACs in American Elections* (New York: Quorum Books, 1988), p. 16. On the other hand, a 1986 Conference Board study found that in 40 to 45 percent of large firms, "a senior corporate executive" made those selections. See Catherine Morrison, *Managing Corporate PACs* (New York: Conference Board, 1986), p. 13.

6. Handler and Mulkern also observed that in most corporations legal officers tended to restrain the enthusiasm of the public affairs people who ran the PACs. Exceptions were airline and railroad companies, which, like telecommunications firms, are heavily regulated. See *Business in Politics*, p. 67. The Conference Board's 1986 study found that in larger firms "it is almost certain that the company's general counsel . . . will be one of the officers of the PAC" (Morrison, *Managing Corporate PACs*, p. 11).

7. Ruth S. Jones and Warren E. Miller concluded that 1980 contributors to nonlabor PACs lacked political involvement and commitment. See "Financing Campaigns," *Western Political Quarterly* 38 (1985), p. 205. Frank Sorauf also found in his study of the Philip Morris PAC that donors were not politically active. "Who's in Charge? Accountability in Political Action Committees," *Political Science Quarterly* 99 (1984–85), p. 600.

8. Personal interviews, October 11, 1991, and June 23, 1992. This may be part of a broader trend. Early studies of corporate PACs reported that public affairs specialists influenced decisions by virtue of their expertise but were a minority presence on PAC boards (Handler and Mulkern, *Business in Politics*, p. 71; Sabato, *PAC Power*, pp. 38–41). By 1986 the Conference Board had found that in large firms, "about three in five of the PACs are positioned in the public affairs or government relations units" (Morrison, *Managing Corporate PACs*, p. 7).

9. In only a few of these states is it easy to tell why AT&T interprets the law as it does. New Jersey, for example, does not permit regulated public utilities to use treasury funds to establish PACs. AT&T's New Jersey federal PAC uses voluntary donations to pay administrative costs and to give to candidates. See Title 19:34–35 New Jersey Statutes Annotated.

10. Personal interview with Gregory Millert, October 11, 1991.

11. State and regional directors value this latitude. After PAC headquarters developed an equation that explained most of the variation in the PAC's contributions, some suggested that the equation be formally instituted as a decisionmaking guide. State directors saw the measure as a threat to their decisionmaking authority and got it shelved.

12. Students of PACs have long known that "[w]here major influence of a Washington representative is present, a pragmatic PAC appears" (Handler and Mulkern, *Business in Politics*, p. 27). See also Sabato, *PAC Power*, p. 78, n. 12; Frank Sorauf, *What Price PACs?* (New York: Twentieth Century Fund, 1984), pp. 48–49; and Eismeier and Pollock, *Business, Money*, pp. 53–54. Handler and Mulkern, *Business in Politics*, p. 29, and Eismeier and Pollock, *Business, Money*, pp. 43–47, also note that PACs formed by corporations subject to traditional, industry-specific regulations also tend to be pragmatic.

13. Personal interviews with Donald Goff, October 11, 1991, and June 23, 1992.

14. Personal interview with Gregory Millert, November 24, 1992.

15. Ibid.

16. Personal interviews with Donald Goff, October 11, 1991, and June 23, 1992.

17. The FEC collects data on earmarked contributions only for those who give more than $200. AT&T PAC donors did little earmarking before the 1989–90 cycle.

18. What does not show up in these figures is the fact that the PAC roughly calibrates its contributions according to a member's seniority on the committee. Telephone interview with Donald Goff, April 15, 1993.

19. This pattern has held in every cycle but two. In 1977–78, when only two of the funds that later merged to form the current PAC had been created, they gave to more federal candidates than all but one of that cycle's top ten corporate PACs. In 1983–84, the post-divestiture AT&T had four separate PACs, which raised more money than in the previous cycle but contributed only 39 percent of it to federal candidates, its lowest percentage ever. In 1990, the number of recipients of AT&T PAC money was more than three standard deviations above the mean number of recipients of the top fifty corporate PACs.

20. Eismeier and Pollock report that in 1984 corporate PACs gave 26 percent of their contributions to candidates from their home states. *Business, Money*, p. 67.

21. John R. Wright concluded from his analysis of five decentralized association PACs that the "dominance of local inputs emphasizes electoral considerations rather than

lobbying considerations." See his "PACs, Contributions, and Roll Calls," *American Political Science Review* 79 (1985), p. 406.

22. This point should not be taken too far. Members of the trade associations Wright studied measure their business success in local terms, not by rising within a national organization. By contrast, AT&T's government affairs directors and disbursement committee members are corporation employees and presumably look forward to rising within the company. More to the point, those directors are also lobbyists who spend perhaps a third of each year in Washington. In Wright's trade association PACs, it was decentralized fundraising by independent entrepreneurs that produced decentralized decisionmaking; in AT&T's case, it was decentralized lobbying by employees of a single corporation.

23. Personal interview with Gregory Millert, June 23, 1991.

24. Personal interview with Donald Goff, June 23, 1992.

25. The Department of Justice had sought some degree of divestiture since 1949. It intermittently pursued this goal, through Democratic and Republican administrations, until the 1982 agreement under which AT&T agreed to divest itself of its local operating companies. The company made the first legislative move itself in 1975, with a bill to confirm the legality of the company structure as it then existed. This bill failed, but other bills, on both sides of the issue, became the subjects of hearings and debate for the next seven years. See Donald L. Goff, "Congress and the Bell System Divestiture, 1981–1982" (Ph.D. dissertation, Northwestern University, 1991), chap. 3.

26. Personal interview with Gregory Millert, June 23, 1992. Some of the lobbying firms AT&T retained filed sufficiently informative reports with the Clerk of the House to indicate that in the 102nd Congress they did focus on attempts to amend the divestiture agreement. No reports from previous, postdivestiture Congresses indicate action on similarly far-reaching legislation (apart from the 1986 tax reform).

27. Roll-call votes probably are the wrong place to seek the influence of PAC contributions. Richard L. Hall and Frank W. Wayman argue persuasively that PAC money "matters most at that stage of the legislative process that matters most," i.e., in committee. It is there that the PAC most effectively "mobilizes support (or demobilizes opposition)" by, among other activities, persuading members to author legislation. See their "Buying Time: Moneyed Interests and the Mobilization of Bias in Congressional Committees," *American Political Science Review* 84 (September 1990), pp. 805, 814.

28. There were actually two House bills, a Republican and a Democratic version (H.R. 1523 and 1527) of a Senate-passed bill permitting the Baby Bells to provide long distance service and manufacture telecommunications equipment. AT&T opposed all of these.

29. Personal interviews with Donald Goff, June 23 and October 21, 1992.

30. Open-seat elections are defined here as the ninety-one general elections in which no incumbent ran. This definition thus includes those seats that became open due to an incumbent's defeat in the primary or by an incumbent's retirement or death following a primary victory.

31. Personal interview with Gregory Millert, June 23, 1992.

32. Personal interview with Donald Goff, October 21, 1992. Lobbyists might also have advice on setting up the congressional office: "For many of them, setting up an office from scratch is a totally new ball game, different from whatever they might have experienced in the state-house, or private business, or law practice."

33. Ibid.

8

The Eaton Corporation Public Policy Association: Ideology, Pragmatism, and Big Business

Joe Ferrara

The Eaton Corporation, an automotive and electronics firm ranked 112th in a recent Fortune 500 listing, founded its Eaton Corporation Public Policy Association (EPPA) in 1977 and has been an active and innovative player in the corporate PAC community ever since. Known for its stringent contribution standards and effective targeting of races, EPPA was formed "to help preserve and strengthen the American business system and the American tradition of economic and political freedom."[1] The company itself was founded in 1911 and got its start as a manufacturer of truck axles. Since then, Eaton has diversified broadly and now manufactures and markets over 5,000 products. Its principal business revolves around truck, power-train, and automobile components and electrical equipment. In the early 1980s, it was awarded a major defense contract to manufacture electronic countermeasures equipment for the Air Force's B-1 bomber.

EPPA is interesting to study for several reasons. First, unlike many corporate PACs, EPPA concentrates on challengers and open-seat races rather than incumbents. This characteristic alone makes EPPA a unique PAC in today's political environment.[2] Second, EPPA displays an interesting blend of pragmatism and ideology in the way it manages its political activity. Finally, EPPA presents a good case study of the American corporate PAC in action.

History

John Hushen, currently Eaton vice president for corporate affairs and former chairman of EPPA, was instrumental in the founding of EPPA. Hushen came to

93

Eaton after a career in journalism and government. His last government assignment had been deputy press secretary to President Gerald R. Ford, in which capacity he was called on to explain to the White House press corps Ford's decision to pardon former president Richard Nixon. Ford had served for years in the House Republican minority, and Hushen adopted Ford's concern for increasing the number of Republicans in the House. Hushen also brought from his career in government a conviction that corporate America needed to be involved in politics.[3]

Another aspect of Hushen's government experience that affected his later work at Eaton was his sense that labor interests were much better organized and more politically active. He was convinced that labor's organizational advantage led to substantive influence on the public policy process and to labor victories on substantive legislation, and that corporate America did not understand the relevance of business involvement in politics or simply did not want to involve itself in the nitty-gritty aspects of legislative politics.[4] Hushen arrived at the Eaton Corporation determined to change this mindset.

The Eaton Corporation provided an environment conducive to creating a PAC. The company's president was supportive when Hushen and fellow Eaton executives Marshall Wright and Jim Mason suggested the formation of an Eaton PAC. Wright went on to become the first PAC chairman, holding the same position that Hushen later occupied; Mason became secretary-treasurer of EPPA. Eaton had previously established a voluntary political contribution club, and after the Federal Election Commission's SUNPAC Advisory it joined other corporations in creating a PAC.[5] Eaton wanted to encourage its managers to participate in the political process but wanted to guide this involvement; establishing a PAC seemed to be the right solution.

Part of the later success of the Eaton Public Policy Association can be attributed to its getting a good start. Established in 1977, EPPA participated in the 1978 election cycle, raising approximately $100,000 through payroll deductions. This fundraising success resulted in EPPA finishing among the top twenty corporate PACs for the 1978 cycle.[6] Fully 55 percent of the targeted Eaton management population signed up for the payroll deduction program in EPPA's first election cycle. It is interesting to note that EPPA's win–loss ratio was quite favorable in the first election cycle: 61 of the 89 candidates receiving EPPA contributions won their races. Even more interesting to note, especially in light of EPPA's later contribution patterns, is the relatively even distribution of contributions among incumbents (30), challengers (30), and open seats (29).

Several factors have been important to EPPA's organizational evolution: (1) an organizational culture supportive of political participation; (2) a founding official with experience and high-level contacts in government who forcefully advocated the need for corporations to get involved in politics; and (3) the success of EPPA's inaugural campaign activities, which raised contributors' ex-

pectations and motivations and helped to convince Eaton leadership that forming
a PAC made good business sense.

Fundraising and Organization

Like many corporate PACs, Eaton targeted senior managers to be part of its
payroll deduction program. Decisions regarding membership and contribution
levels are strictly voluntary, although the company does suggest annual contribution amounts. The suggested scale is based on gross income and ranges from
one-fifth of 1 percent of income for gross incomes of up to $50,000 to three-
quarters of 1 percent of income for gross incomes of $125,000 and over. Under
this suggested schedule, a manager making $50,000 would contribute $100 annually while another manager making $150,000 would contribute $1,125 annually.[7] The actual annual contribution amount averages about $150.

EPPA raises its money almost entirely through a payroll deduction program,
although there are a few Eaton managers who contribute by personal check.
Since EPPA's founding in 1977, the total number of contributors has ranged
between 350 and 450 members, all of whom are Eaton managers. The managers
who join EPPA seem to be motivated by a number of factors. First, they tend to
find public affairs and politics interesting. Second, and perhaps more important,
EPPA members are career-oriented people in a competitive environment. Joining
the PAC is one highly visible way to become active in an important company
program, and some managers may have seen this as a way to help to advance
their own careers.[8]

The organization of EPPA is very closely linked to the overall Eaton corporate structure. EPPA's chairman, for example, serves simultaneously as its vice
president for corporate affairs.[9] EPPA is governed by a fifteen-member board of
trustees, who are selected by EPPA's management. The selection is based on a
number of criteria, some more tangible than others, such as reputation within the
company and a demonstrated interest in public affairs, including political activity
in the local community and within the Eaton Corporation. In addition, the EPPA
board of trustees is chosen to reflect the product mix and geographical diversity
within the company: Eaton makes a wide array of products and has plants in 26
states and 63 congressional districts. One-third of the membership of the board is
replaced before every election cycle. This policy allows a larger number of
Eaton managers to be board members.

The board of trustees meets three times during the election year to discuss
EPPA business. Board meetings often include briefings by various government
officials or political consultants. A meeting held during the 1990 election cycle,
for example, included a presentation by Senator Don Nickles (R-Oklahoma),
chairman of the National Republican Senatorial Committee, on major Senate
races, and the staff directors of the House Democratic and Republican congressional
campaign committees. During the 1992 election cycle, this practice continued as

the EPPA board heard from Republican congressional candidate Robert Gardner (who ultimately lost the race to represent Ohio's 19th District to Eric Fingerhut); Bernadette Budde, vice president for political education at the Business-Industry Political Action Committee (BIPAC); and Neil Newhouse, cofounder of the polling firm Public Opinion Strategies.

Most of the campaign research used by EPPA's board is generated by the Eaton Washington office.[10] The Washington office is staffed by three full-time professionals, all of whom have political or legislative backgrounds. There are no full-time Eaton employees who do only EPPA-related work.[11]

Contributions

EPPA clearly concentrates its contributions on challengers and open-seat races (see Table A.7). The proportion of EPPA contributions going to incumbent candidates in the last ten years exceeded 40 percent only in 1982, a year in which a large number of Republican incumbents were vulnerable because of the recession. More than 60 percent of EPPA's total contributions are routinely given to challengers and open-seat candidates. In the 1992 election cycle, EPPA contributed to 117 candidates in 38 states; only 23 were incumbents.

One exception to this general rule is illuminating. Examination of EPPA Senate contribution patterns shows that during the early to mid-1980s, when the Republicans controlled the Senate, the proportion of EPPA contributions going to incumbents increased. In 1986, for example, EPPA contributed to eleven Senate incumbents out of a total of twenty-one candidates, or 52 percent. In 1986 the Republicans lost control of the Senate, and the dynamics of that election year brought two of EPPA's major contribution objectives—supporting nonincumbents and supporting pro-business Republicans—into sharp relief. In 1986, the latter objective took priority in Senate contributions. Of course, another way of interpreting this pattern is that the EPPA objective of supporting nonincumbents is really instrumental and subsidiary to the primary objective of establishing a pro-business Congress.

EPPA contributes almost exclusively to Republican candidates (see Table A.7). Since 1982, the proportion of EPPA contributions going to Republican candidates has never dipped below 92 percent. For EPPA, creating a Congress sympathetic to business interests means creating a Congress with a Republican majority. Changing the party composition of Congress means that EPPA must support Republican challengers and open-seat candidates. But Hushen argues that EPPA's pattern of overwhelming support for Republican candidates does not mean that EPPA was a partisan organization:

> There are many Democratic senators and members of Congress who support business issues, but they are mainly located in the South and have only token opposition when they seek reelection. It is easy for them to raise money and

they do not need EPPA's help, so we look for the open-seat and challenger candidates who are usually desperate for money.[12]

EPPA focuses its contribution activity on House races, reflecting its goal of chipping away at the Democrats' large majority (see Table A.7). The jump in EPPA contributions to Senate candidates during the 1988 election cycle—the first cycle after the Democrats reclaimed the Senate—further supports this interpretation.

EPPA's win–loss ratio began favorably but has declined ever since. In the 1977–78 election cycle, 61 out of 89 EPPA candidates, or 69 percent, were victorious, but by 1992, only 58 out of 117, or 49 percent, won their races.

EPPA Decisionmaking

The Washington office meticulously screens congressional elections and prepares extensive reports that are used by the EPPA board to make contribution decisions. These reports focus on the candidates' support for business interests, broadly defined. The reports frequently focus on specific issues—positions on plant-closing notification legislation, for example, would be very important. Sources of information for these reports include consultations with the Business-Industry PAC (BIPAC) and others; perusal of legislative ratings produced by ADA, COPE, and the U.S. Chamber of Commerce; discussions with staffers from the Democratic and Republican national committees; newspaper accounts of campaign debates; and the *Almanac of American Politics*.[13] As we have seen, the EPPA board regularly receives information briefings from representatives of these various groups.

EPPA also gathers information from its members in the twenty-six states where Eaton has branches, although the PAC director and board lament that they do not get more input from the rank-and-file members. EPPA practice is to distribute to donors before each board meeting a list of candidates that the PAC is supporting, along with the reasons each candidate deserves an EPPA contribution. Usually these distributions do not elicit a sizable response from the membership, but there have been cases where membership input made a difference.[14] Probably the most dramatic example comes from the 1980 election year. The board had analyzed the North Carolina Senate race, where Senator Robert Morgan, a Democrat, was facing a challenge from Republican John East; the board decided that Morgan's pro-business conservative ideology should be rewarded with an EPPA contribution. After the list of candidates was distributed, the board began receiving numerous calls from members in Eaton's North Carolina facilities who complained that Morgan had been lackadaisical about constituency service and had often failed to follow up on even routine matters. After protracted discussions the board reversed itself, met with East, and contributed $2,000 to the East campaign. East ultimately won the election.

In the 1992 election, the EPPA board asked the PAC's staff to establish a rating scheme for candidates. They devised a four-point scale for rating candidates in their districts, with 1 being a "sure thing" and 4 being a "long shot, venture capital." Plant managers and other local staff applied these ratings to candidates in their districts. According to EPPA officials, the ratings proved to be fairly accurate. The board showed very little sympathy for House members who had bounced a large number of checks in 1992, although strong endorsements from plant representatives were a major factor in the relatively few EPPA board decisions to contribute to prolific check-bouncers in the 1992 House elections.[15]

Another less dramatic aspect of internal PAC democracy evident in EPPA operations is the practice of using PAC members to personally deliver checks to candidates.[16] Since Eaton has plants in twenty-six states, many checks can in fact be hand-delivered. EPPA management views this practice as serving two goals: first, it helps gets PAC members involved in EPPA operations, and second, it augments the impact of the contribution, hopefully making the candidate more likely to remember the Eaton donation than those he or she received by mail.

Contribution decisions are guided by the following questions: Is the candidate likely to support pro-business causes? Does the candidate have serious opposition and need EPPA's financial assistance? Given all relevant factors, does the candidate stand a reasonable chance of winning the election? These criteria are interesting because they reflect a mix of ideology and pragmatism. Clearly, EPPA is guided by a strong pro-business and largely pro-Republican ideology. However, it is not so ideologically zealous as to contribute scarce financial resources to an effort likely to go down in defeat.

The 1992 Election and Its Aftermath

The 1992 election year was noteworthy for EPPA for several reasons. First, there were an unusually high number of open seats. Second, the House check-bouncing scandal, as well as President Bush's unexpectedly poor performance, changed the dynamics of PAC decisionmaking. Third, EPPA's results were largely disappointing; indeed, in the aftermath of the 1992 cycle, Eaton decided to scale back EPPA to focus only on Ohio candidates.

EPPA began planning for the 1992 elections at least two years in advance. Several factors were important—the presidential election, post-census redistricting, and retirements. As Jack Hushen correctly predicted in a research memorandum to the EPPA board, these factors meant the likelihood of more open seats, more aggressive challengers, and greater opportunities to influence election outcomes. The board decided to withhold approximately $65,000 from the prior year's funds for disbursement in the 1992 cycle. This decision increased 1992 funding to nearly $220,000.[17]

Political developments during 1992 had important ramifications for EPPA decisionmaking. The House check-bouncing scandal, for example, caused the board to reconsider numerous contribution decisions. As Hushen explained, the board "really took the House scandal to heart." EPPA refrained from contributing to pro-business incumbents who might otherwise have benefited from EPPA largess because of their bounced-check totals. There seems to have been an informal scale: once an incumbent reached 75 to 100 bounced checks, the board essentially refused to make contributions, regardless of the candidate's pro-business record. No incumbent on the official list of the twenty-four worst offenders was recommended for an EPPA contribution.

An interesting aspect of the check scandal is the difference in the way it was perceived by the board and the Washington office. Contribution recommendations prepared by the Washington office downplayed the importance of the scandal and emphasized an incumbent's historical support for business. The board, however, elevated it to the top of the list of contribution criteria. The seriousness with which the board viewed the check scandal is perhaps best illustrated by their willingness to abandon traditional allies. In one particularly painful episode, EPPA declined to contribute to Republican incumbent Bob McEwen of Ohio's 6th district, who was locked in a very close race with Democratic challenger Ted Strickland. McEwen not only had an excellent pro-business voting record but was a close personal friend of several EPPA board members and staff. They were sorry to see him leave.

Another political development affecting PAC decisionmaking was the unexpectedly poor showing of President Bush in his reelection bid. The board perceived that Bush's coattails, if any, would be very short. In some cases EPPA contributed to Republican incumbents they felt were particularly threatened by the president's lack of popularity. EPPA contributed to Senator Kit Bond of Missouri, for example, because Bush was trailing Bill Clinton badly in that state.[18] With a stronger candidate at the top of the Republican ticket, EPPA might never have contributed to Bond's campaign.

Finally, in many ways, 1992 was a disappointing year for EPPA. Fifty-nine EPPA-supported candidates lost, while only fifty-eight won. The check-bouncing scandal and the Bush reelection debacle forced the PAC board to reconsider numerous contribution recommendations and hastily reformulate its overall strategy during the election season. The result often meant contributions to candidates who were never slated to receive EPPA donations. Still, EPPA was involved in several very close races and was able to target last-minute donations effectively. A good example of this tactic was EPPA's $3,500 donation to Republican challenger Paul Coverdell in the runoff election against then-Senator Wyche Fowler (D-Georgia).

After the election, the Eaton Corporation decided to close EPPA's Washington office and restructure EPPA into a regional PAC that would concentrate solely on federal, state, and local candidates in Ohio. Eaton management concluded that the expense of operating a Washington office and sponsoring a national PAC was no longer warranted. There are several possible reasons for this decision. One is purely economic. As Hushen and other company officials have argued, Eaton is not involved in a highly regulated industry such as the manufacture of drugs or chemicals, and thus its interest in specific legislative and regulatory issues is minor compared to firms dealing with more intensive government oversight. It may be that Eaton decided that its broad goal of fostering a more pro-business political environment was indulgent and not worth the expense of a national PAC with a Washington office operation.

Another possible explanation is that the EPPA strategy of focusing on non-incumbents may have finally proven to be too politically and practically difficult. EPPA's contribution approach clearly distinguished it from the majority of corporate PACs, although comments from observers in the PAC and candidate communities evidenced no overt ill effects.[19] Nonetheless, the extent of EPPA giving to challengers may have hurt Eaton interests with congressional incumbents over the long run. EPPA did not play the PAC game as it is normally played in Washington: the PAC board routinely "said no" to incumbents seeking contributions, did not make independent expenditures or debt retirement contributions, and did not attend fundraisers. The price of this nontraditional approach may have become prohibitive.

Practically, EPPA's nonincumbent focus meant a more arduous political research program. It is much easier to obtain salient political data on incumbents—through voting records, important policy positions, and the like—than on obscure challengers or new, untested candidates competing in open-seat races. Hushen acknowledges that this factor played a role in the decision to scale back EPPA.

Finally, EPPA management seems to have been somewhat ambivalent about the role of the PAC vis-à-vis the corporation. Hushen himself said many times that "the problems with most PACs is that they are run out of Washington." This comment may indicate not only a disillusionment with the "inside-the-Beltway" culture of PACs and other interest groups but also an uncertainty about whether the Eaton Corporation properly fit into this culture. Seen in this light, the postelection decision to concentrate on political activity close to company headquarters seems natural.

The Future of EPPA

Even in its new regional incarnation, EPPA plans to continue its nontraditional, nonincumbent approach. The PAC plans to encourage plant managers to become more acquainted with federal officials in their districts. Eaton will perforce have to rely much more heavily on trade associations, such as the National Association of Manufacturers and the Machinists' Alliance for Productivity and Innovation, to carry the corporate message to Congress.

Much of EPPA's activity in the coming months will be focused on reconfiguring the PAC's governing structure to reflect its new regional orientation. The former organization had been designed to reflect different geographical locations and product diversity across the corporation. What remains to be seen is whether former EPPA members maintain their interest in political affairs. Research has shown that most corporate PAC donors prefer to leave the political decisionmaking to PAC management and may even shy away from greater participation.[20] Without the stimulating presence of a company PAC soliciting input on upcoming races and faithfully distributing newsletters every several months, it is not clear whether EPPA's objective of keeping its managers politically active is viable.

Notes

1. Eaton Public Policy Association Statement of Purpose.

2. Recent data indicate that nearly 70 percent of all PAC contributions go to incumbents. The incumbent contribution rate for corporate PACs is approximately 75 percent. See Frank Sorauf, *Money in American Elections* (Glenview, IL: Scott, Foresman, 1988).

3. Hushen's belief that corporate America needed to be more involved in politics is well illustrated by the title of the EPPA newsletter, *GIPOGOOB*. "GIPOGOOB" is an acronym for "Get into politics or get out of business," a phrase the EPPA newsletter attributes to former Congressman Joe Waggonner (D-LA).

4. Indeed, recent surveys indicate that many corporations still hold this conception about political activity. See, for example, Catherine Morrison, *Managing Corporate Political Action Committees* (New York: The Conference Board, 1986).

5. The 1975 *SUNPAC* Advisory opinion handed down by the FEC was particularly influential in the development of corporate PACs. In a 4 to 2 decision, the FEC ruled that SUNPAC, Sun Oil's PAC, could use corporate funds to solicit voluntary political contributions from employees and stockholders. As scholars have noted, this decision reassured the business community about the legality of PACs. See, among others, Herbert Alexander, *Financing Politics: Money, Elections, and Political Reform*, 4th ed. (Washington, D.C.: Congressional Quarterly Press, 1992).

6. In 1978, the EPPA ranked 20th of 832 corporate PACs active in that cycle. In 1990 they were 128th of 1,972 corporate PACs.

7. Payroll information is derived from the EPPA information brochure that the PAC provides interested Eaton managers.

8. As compared with labor PACs, corporate PACs do not actively engage in much direct or voluntary political activity. In addition, there does not seem be a consensus on the question of whether to include stockholders in either funds-solicitation or public-awareness programs. See Morrison, *Managing Corporate Political Action Committees*, p. 9. Still, there is great potential to mobilize political constituencies (stockholders, employees, and their families). See Herbert Alexander, "Political Action Committees and Their Corporate Sponsors in the 1980s," *Public Affairs Review*, vol. 2 (Washington, D.C.: Public Affairs Council, 1981), quoted in Morrison, *Managing Corporate Political Action Committees*, p. 9.

9. This structure parallels that of many corporate PACs. See Morrison, *Managing Corporate Political Action Committees*, pp. 12–13.

10. The PAC director operates out of Eaton's headquarters in Cleveland, Ohio, and travels to Washington every several weeks.

11. Of course, all of this has recently changed with the closing of the Washington office and the reorganization of EPPA, which is discussed at the end of the chapter.

12. Personal interview with John Hushen.

13. EPPA officials rated various independent political reports, BIPAC analysis, and the *Almanac of American Politics* as particularly helpful information sources. Party committees were rated as the least helpful because their analysis was viewed as not really being independent.

14. Of course, most PACs are not "democracies." As Frank Sorauf has argued, "Donors often are sedulously informed about the PAC decisions, and their opinions and preferences are often solicited and even taken very seriously; but very, very few PACs take the further step to give donors any direct or representational role." See Sorauf, *Money in American Elections*, p. 92.

15. As Frank Sorauf has pointed out, donors to PACs with corporate sponsors hold the sanction of "exit" over the PAC if they disagree with PAC decisionmaking. This is one reason that corporate PACs such as EPPA are so willing to placate the strongly held views of their donors. In the end, most donors leave corporate PACs, not out of dissatisfaction over PAC policy, but for far more mundane reasons: death, moving away, leaving the company. See Sorauf, *Money in American Elections*, p. 96.

16. "Eaton's PAC Reflects Employees' Public Spirit," *PAC Manager*, November/December 1987, p. 3.

17. EPPA spent all of the 1992 monies, depleting their treasury to zero, with a $3,500 contribution to Republican challenger Paul Coverdell in his runoff race with (now former) Senator Wyche Fowler (D-GA).

18. Clinton ultimately won Missouri's eleven electoral votes in the general election.

19. Indeed, review of trade publications and discussions with PAC insiders demonstrate that many in the political community admired EPPA's contribution strategy as principled and innovative. Hushen and other EPPA leaders cited the nonincumbent strategy as a "net plus."

20. Sorauf, *Money in American Elections*, p. 95.

9

The National Association of Realtors PAC: Rules or Rationality?

Anne H. Bedlington

The key to understanding the behavior of the Realtors' Political Action Committee (RPAC) is the character of its contributors. As anyone who has bought a home knows, a realtor has an accountant's attention to economic and legal detail and a risk-taker's penchant for creating imaginative, nonlinear solutions. Realtors are smart, competent people who are economic activists. They understand the impact of public policy on their sector of the economy.

Since the late 1970s RPAC has pursued essentially the same goal—government policy that produces an economic climate favorable to real estate. The tactics used to achieve that goal, however, have varied. During the late 1970s and early 1980s, realtors assumed that the many detailed federal policies that benefited the real estate industry were secure. They felt free, therefore, to help candidates who supported more general economic policies that might lower mortgage interest rates, such as deficit reduction, tax cuts, and cuts in government spending. In 1986, their assumptions were shaken to the core by the Tax Reform Act, which eliminated many important real estate tax breaks. Since then, realtors have worked to reclaim their industry's special tax advantages and have shifted their campaign tactics accordingly. This tactical shift is consistent with their character as pragmatic yet creative activists.

Organizational Stability

RPAC's parent organization, the National Association of Realtors (NAR), was founded in 1908. The NAR, the major trade association for real estate brokers and agents, has a federated structure composed of a national organization, fifty-four state associations (the fifty states, plus the District of Columbia, Guam, Puerto Rico, and the Virgin Islands), and approximately 1,800 local boards of realtors. About 750,000 individuals belong to a local board: there are no organizational members in the NAR.

RPAC was formed in 1969. The PAC does not raise money directly from individuals but instead receives its funding from PACs sponsored by local realtors' boards or state associations, which, in turn, receive contributions from individual members. The local board or state association PACs give 35 percent of their contribution revenue to RPAC. In the seventeen states where it is legal, the local boards or state association PACs solicit by dues checkoff. A suggested contribution is included in the yearly NAR dues statement sent by the local board or state association. The dues checkoff is the most effective fundraising method available, generating two-thirds to three-quarters of total contributions in places where it is used. A more effective method is face-to-face solicitation—one politically active local realtor asking others for contributions. Other means include lunches, casino nights, and direct-mail requests sent to the local board's membership.[1]

In 1977, 44,000 NAR members (about 5 percent) contributed at the local or state level; this number has grown to roughly 200,000, or 25 percent per year.[2] The average annual contribution is $24, of which $8.40 is sent to RPAC, but nearly 500 realtors contribute at least $1,000.[3] In 1990, 65,000 people were active in the NAR's Opportunity Race Program, discussed in more detail below. A substantial number of realtors also volunteer their services on behalf of candidates supported by RPAC.

NAR membership surveys show that the typical PAC contributor has a yearly income of about $40,000 and works in a one- to three-person office. These surveys help NAR officials to understand its membership and also to identify important issues that are then used to select the roll-call votes that are included in candidate evaluations. Polling has confirmed that members supported a focus on partisan considerations during the early 1980s and also supported the shift toward more pragmatic considerations in later years. All NAR members receive political communications from their local and state associations, regular quarterly reports from RPAC, and articles concerning RPAC in the bimonthly NAR newspaper.

RPAC and the political wing of the NAR, including its lobbying and political education operation, are located in Washington, D.C. RPAC has four employees, who maintain accounting records, prepare FEC reports, and provide the trustees with political advice and technical support. The RPAC staff and the NAR's political education specialists are supervised by the vice president of the Political Affairs Division. These employees evaluate candidates' viability and consult with the lobbying division about issues and voting records.

The political education employees conduct the grassroots Opportunity Race

Program, which attempts to rally local realtors via mailings and phone banks to assist the campaigns of endorsed candidates. The Opportunity Race Program is a "partisan communications" effort by the NAR to get its members to support favored House or Senate candidates in competitive races. It is supervised by RPAC staff, conducted by field staff from NAR's political education office, and paid for by corporate contributions from real estate companies, which are put into the NAR's Political Administration Fund. During an election year a state association asks the NAR for funds for grassroots efforts to help a particular candidate. The NAR allocates money from the Political Administration Fund. The field people organize a mailing of a locally signed letter to all realtors in the district, suggesting how the realtor could assist the candidate in a number of ways. They also set up phone banks to call realtors with the same message.[4] In 1988, $85,819 was spent on two candidates, while in 1990, $209,144 was expended for twenty-five contestants.

Decisionmaking

RPAC supports federal candidates in two ways—contributions and independent expenditures—and has a separate decisionmaking structure for each. The structure for contributions puts a premium on local judgments, while that for independent expenditures emphasizes a national perspective. Contribution decisions are made at the local or state level by activist realtors who interview candidates, assess their voting records, and evaluate their probable electoral fortunes. These realtors sometimes ask NAR lobbyists for evaluations of incumbents. They also occasionally query NAR political field staff for assessments of nonincumbents. The state association then reviews the local- or state-level recommendations and sends requests to the RPAC trustees committee that certain candidates be given certain amounts of support.

The trustees committee has twenty-five members appointed by the president of the NAR: thirteen volunteer realtors from around the nation chosen to represent their region, six at-large trustees, a chairman and a vice chairman, the immediate past chairman, and three ex-officio/liaison members. The trustees committee meets three or four times during nonelection years and up to eight times in an election year to consider the contribution requests. They are given an analysis of each candidate's policy proclivities and an evaluation of the competitiveness of the race.[5] The trustees weigh a variety of factors when evaluating requests for incumbents: score on an NAR index of roll-call votes, electoral competitiveness, committee assignments, and agenda power. Party affiliation, ideology, and personal friendship are much less important.

The trustees begin by considering (and usually rejecting) requests for incumbents whose scores on the NAR roll-call index are 25 percent or less. The trustees then consider incumbent candidates with higher scores on the index in ascending order. For nonincumbents, the trustees assess a probable future voting record based on analysis done by the NAR field staff. They sometimes deny a local request for a challenger with a likely pro-realtor bent if that challenger is running against an incumbent with a strong record. In instances where the incumbent is unfriendly, the trustees will approve funding for a primary or general election challenger only if he or she favors real estate interests and is competitive. Since 1988 requests for dual contributions in a race (to the incumbent and the challenger, or to opposing open-seat candidates) have required a two-thirds vote of the trustees for approval. However, RPAC does not count contributions of less than $1,000 as involving a dual contribution and occasionally gives such small amounts in order to attend a fundraising reception.

Once a decision is made to support a candidate, the size of the contribution is determined. Candidates in close races generally receive more money than those in safe elections; those on important committees and in leadership positions are also usually given more generous amounts.

RPAC began to experiment with independent expenditures in 1980 and continued small-scale efforts in 1982 and 1984.[6] In 1986, RPAC spent $1,709,796 (representing 38 percent of all RPAC's candidate support) on behalf of just seven candidates. The amount of independent expenditures declined in the two subsequent elections as a result of savings achieved by producing more advertisements in-house (see Table A.8).

Decisions on independent expenditures are made by the NAR director of independent expenditures and an advisory board appointed by the NAR president.[7] The director and the board undertake an initial review of House and Senate elections, selecting twenty or so contests for further investigation. They then seek a block grant from RPAC's trustees to pay for polls but do not specify the races in which the polling will be done. The survey results are evaluated, and another grant to fund independent expenditures is requested. At this point, they reveal the candidates whom they intend to support but not the amount of the expenditure that will be made on behalf of each. The RPAC trustees can decide whether RPAC will make independent expenditures in each particular race.[8]

The director and the advisory board seek to concentrate their expenditures in a few close races.[9] Decisions to spend money on behalf of incumbents are based on NAR legislative ratings, while challengers and open-seat contestants must have a history of support for real estate interests and must be running against a candidate with an unsatisfactory record. The board also considers previous RPAC contributions as well as surveys of NAR members in the state or district when selecting races for independent activity.

The director of independent expenditures decides the amount and type of expenditure made in each race. The nature of each independent expenditure is based on the views of local realtors rather than on some perception of a candidate's electoral priorities. In 1990, for example, independent expenditures emphasized specific political themes, stressing the supported candidate's positions on topics like continuing the deductibility of mortgage interest and main-

taining other laws that promote home ownership. These policies were used because local realtors were concerned about pocketbook issues and thought that
voters were also.

The Evolution of Campaign Tactics

RPAC more than doubled its contributions to congressional candidates between
1978 and 1990, from $1,132,578 in 1978 to $3,094,228 in 1990 (see Table A.8).
It supported more than 500 candidates during a typical election cycle during this
period. Senate contestants received about 17 percent of RPAC money in 1978
and 1980 and about 10 percent since then. In 1978 and 1980 the PAC was
relatively supportive of nonincumbents, especially Republicans, but since 1982
incumbents have been receiving an increasing majority of RPAC money. RPAC
spending in the House has always favored incumbents. By 1990 RPAC was
giving over 80 percent of its contribution money to House incumbents, with 49
percent to Democrats and 34 percent to Republicans.

The 1980 election set the stage for the 1982 surge in RPAC support for House
Republican candidates. Ronald Reagan was elected president, the GOP had won
control of the Senate for the first time in decades, and a number of Republican
challengers and open-seat contestants had been swept into the House. The Realtors gave 41 percent of its contributions to House Republican incumbents in
1982 and increased the share of money going to Republican nonincumbents to an
all-time high of 28 percent because it thought the Republicans could win a
majority of seats in the House.

realtors soon discovered that GOP control of the Senate and White House did
not mean that their point of view would prevail. In 1984, the Senate Finance
Committee tried to alter the very favorable real estate depreciation rule that was
enacted as part of the 1981 tax bill. In 1985, the Treasury's plan for tax
simplification contained many provisions that the NAR found objectionable.
The final law, the Tax Reform Act of 1986, eliminated lucrative real estate tax
benefits.

Realtors were furious because they had been highly supportive of Republican
congressional candidates who played an important role in passing this legislation. As a result, they decided in 1987 to support any candidate who consistently
voted correctly on specific real estate issues, regardless of party. Contributions to
Democratic House incumbents jumped in 1988 and increased again in 1990,
after an analysis of voting records indicated that many House Democrats were
very supportive of real estate interests.[10]

The long-term decline in contributions given to nonincumbents is less a
function of disenchantment with nonincumbents per se than a more positive
evaluation of incumbents once the PAC trustees narrowed the range of legislative behavior they considered in their contribution decisions. Additionally,
the rigorous use of voting records as the initial determining factor in the

decisionmaking process discriminates against nonincumbents who have not held elective office because they lack a record on real estate issues.

The 1992 Election

During the last dozen years the NAR and its PAC have changed in several politically relevant ways. The membership of the NAR has become more diverse, the most notable change being that women now constitute a majority. RPAC has changed its policy goals from general to specific; it has modified its decisionmaking structure from one that emphasized state and local views to one that is now a mix of state, local, and national perspectives;[11] and it has altered its candidate-support behavior in response to changes in the political environment and variations in the quality of candidates. How, then, did RPAC respond to the opportunities and challenges of 1992?

The Realtors maintained its structured decisionmaking, with its primary emphasis on the roll-call index for contributions and its judgment by national staff on independent expenditures. During the 1992 cycle, RPAC made independent expenditures of $999,016 on behalf of ten candidates, representing 25 percent of all RPAC's candidate support. These figures are very close to those for 1988 and 1990 (see Table 9.1). As in 1990, the expenditures were for media and direct mail, both of which emphasized housing issues and were tailored for the particular group being addressed.

The realtors contributed $2,942,138 to candidates in 1992, and the distribution of these funds was quite similar to distribution in previous election cycles. Senate contestants received 9 percent, and these contributions were distributed by party and incumbency status in the usual fashion. House Democratic candidates received one-half of RPAC contributions, and House Republicans got 41 percent. The vast majority of these contributions in both parties went to incumbents, although approximately 7 percent of RPAC contributions went to House Democratic open-seat candidates, and an additional 10 percent went to Republican open-seat candidates. RPAC did increase its contributions to open-seat candidates in 1992, a predictable result of the large number of open seats.[12]

Another measure of behavior that shows surprising stability is the timing of contributions to House candidates. For 1991–92, RPAC advised the state associations not to make contribution requests to the trustees until after redistricting had been completed in a state. It also counseled waiting until adequate information was available for evaluating those running for open seats. PAC officials believed that they had made their 1992 contributions later than other PACs, but the actual timing of contributions was virtually identical to that in other recent elections. PAC officials may have consciously deferred decisions in 1992, but this would suggest that in earlier election cycles they also deferred their commitments for other reasons.

In 1992, as in the previous two election cycles, incumbent Democrats and

Table 9.1

Contributions to House Candidates Made during a Two-Year Cycle and by Quarters of the Election Year

	Cycle Total ($)	Election Year	Q1	Q2	Q3	Q4
			Percentage of Cycle Total			
Incumbents			Democrats			
1991–92	1,227,731	82.7	7.6	17.9	55.0	2.2
1989–90	1,509,772	86.8	11.1	21.8	21.5	32.3
1987–88	1,304,202	85.8	15.1	16.0	48.3	6.4
1981–82	282,885	83.9	4.1	17.8	38.6	23.5
1979–80	322,790	83.2	4.9	15.2	44.3	18.7
			Republicans			
1991–92	885,859	83.5	5.3	21.3	54.0	2.9
1989–90	1,039,390	86.7	9.5	28.3	17.4	31.4
1987–88	1,079,559	86.8	19.6	14.0	47,8	5.2
1981–82	860,799	90.2	3.7	14.4	52.1	20.0
1979–80	487,840	90.4	4.2	12.6	61.1	12.5
Open Seats			Democrats			
1991–92	218,500	96.1	9.6	24.7	55.7	6.0
1989–90	110,000	75.9	9.1	11.8	27.3	27.7
1987–88	131,125	86.6	15.2	7.3	52.6	11.4
1981–82	75,150	99.5	1.9	30.8	39.3	27.5
1979–80	40,900	95.1	0.1	29.9	45.8	19.2
			Republicans			
1991–92	284,440	87.7	—	21.4	44.6	21.6
1989–90	159,516	79.6	9.4	18.8	18.2	33.2
1987–88	144,800	99.8	10.8	8.6	58.6	21.7
1981–82	250,667	89.3	0.1	14.4	34.6	40.2
1979–80	138,800	82.3	2.9	18.4	43.6	17.4
Challengers			Democrats			
1991–92	39,000	100.0	12.8	7.7	66.7	12.8
1989–90	10,000	100.0	—	—	50.0	50.0
1987–88	26,350	77.8	26.6	—	3.8	47.4
1981–82	53,724	97.9	—	21.2	46.8	30.0
1979–80	33,025	98.8	18.2	36.3	29.1	15.1
			Republicans			
1991–92	35,300	99.1	1.4	35.4	22.7	39.7
1989–90	17,500	71.4	28.6	5.7	28.6	8.6
1987–88	46,800	100.0	7.5	10.3	37.4	44.9
1981–82	342,367	98.8	1.7	13.9	54.7	28.4
1979–80	258,825	99.0	0.8	7.5	53.1	37.7

Source: Federal Election Commission.

Republicans were given about 85 percent of their money during the election year. In 1991–92, Democrats received 57 percent of their RPAC contributions during the third and fourth quarters; in 1989–90 the figure for the two quarters was 54 percent, and in 1987–88 it was 55 percent. In 1991–92, Republicans also received 57 percent of their RPAC contributions during the latter half of 1992: in 1989–90 the corresponding figure was 49 percent, and in 1987–88 it was 53 percent. These figures show great stability. The same stability was true a decade ago, when the realtors behaved in the redistricting year of 1982 much the same as they had in 1980. In 1992, even open-seat contributions were not made unusually late in the cycle (see Table 9.1).

RPAC also did not alter the size of its contributions in 1992. Table 9.2 shows the percentage of candidates given a total amount of $4,999 or less, the percentage receiving a total amount between $5,000 and $6,999, and the percentage receiving larger gifts.[13] Only those candidates who were in the November 1992 general election or were on the final ballot for a special election during 1991 or 1992 are included in Table 9.2. When Senate and House candidates are combined, the percentages in each dollar range vary by less than 5 percent per election. Among Senate candidates, more Republicans received larger donations than Democrats, a pattern similar in all three cycles. For House incumbents there is a faint echo of the Republican advantage found among Senate candidates and the same stability of behavior over the six years. As is the case for Senate candidates, the number of House nonincumbents is small, making the percentages less stable. Remembering that caveat, it appears that RPAC reacted to the large number of open seats by giving somewhat smaller contributions to open-seat candidates than in previous election cycles. For both Democrats and Republicans there was a decrease in the percentage of candidates receiving contributions of $5,000 or more.

Table 9.2 also shows all Senate and House candidates ordered according to their percentage of the vote, admittedly an imperfect measure of their perceived competitiveness when the realtors actually made the contribution decision(s). The overall pattern in this data is again stable. Candidates who won easily with 60 percent or more of the vote were given fewer large contributions than their more harried counterparts and were given similar amounts in the three cycles. In 1992 more of the candidates supported by the realtors either lost or won against a serious competitor than in 1990 or 1988; these contenders were treated similarly to candidates in close elections in the two previous cycles, in terms of the percentages of small and large contributions.

Finally, Table 9.2 shows House Democratic and Republican incumbents, divided into those who were in contested elections and those who sailed to victory with 60 percent or more of the ballots. The tendency for easy winners to be given fewer large donations is the same here as for all Senate and House candidates combined. The "easy winners" percentages in each of the dollar ranges are similar in all three cycles. More Democrats than Republicans received small

Table 9.2

Contributions to General and Specific Election Candidates by Total Amount Given to a Candidate

		Percentage of Candidates in Each Range			
	Number	≤$4,999	$5,000–6,999	$7,000–8,999	$9,000+
All					
1991–92	480	28.3	33.5	16.3	22.0
1989–90	464	25.2	33.4	15.5	25.9
1987–88	480	30.2	31.5	17.1	21.3
Senate D					
1991–92	21	42.9	4.8	28.6	23.8
1989–90	15	46.7	13.3	13.3	26.7
1987–88	24	41.7	16.7	12.5	29.2
Senate R					
1991–92	16	12.5	25.0	25.0	37.5
1989–90	22	31.4	9.1	22.7	36.4
1987–88	19	36.8	5.3	15.8	42.1
House D Inc					
1991–92	207	33.8	31.4	16.4	18.4
1989–90	237	28.7	34.6	15.2	21.5
1987–88	229	38.0	28.8	18.8	14.4
House D NI					
1991–92	39	30.8	38.5	10.3	20.0
1989–90	16	18.8	56.3	—	25.0
1987–88	21	19.0	38.1	4.8	38.1
House R Inc					
1991–92	135	20.0	40.7	19.3	20.0
1989–90	151	18.6	35.8	18.5	27.2
1987–88	159	20.1	38.4	19.5	22.0
House R NI					
1991–92	42	23.8	33.3	2.4	40.5
1989–90	23	17.4	26.1	4.4	52.2
1987–88	28	17.9	39.3	3.6	39.3
All					
< 50% of vote					
1991–92	68	35.3	23.5	8.8	32.3
1989–90	35	20.0	28.6	14.3	40.0
1987–88	33	42.4	27.3	—	30.3
50–54% of vote					
1991–92	52	19.2	28.8	23.1	28.9
1989–90	42	19.0	28.6	14.3	38.1
1987–88	41	12.2	36.6	9.8	41.5
55–59% of vote					
1991–92	75	18.7	32.0	18.7	30.7
1989–90	74	20.3	29.7	16.2	33.8
1987–88	42	9.5	26.2	21.4	42.9

Table 9.2 *(continued)*

		Percentage of Candidates in Each Range			
	Number	≤$4,999	$5,000–6,999	$7,000–8,999	$9,000+
60%+					
1991–92	265	31.0	37.4	16.2	15.5
1989–90	313	27.8	35.5	16.0	20.8
1987–88	364	33.5	31.9	19.0	15.7
House D Inc					
< 60% of vote					
1991–92	74	24.3	23.0	21.6	31.1
1989–90	57	19.3	29.8	21.1	29.8
1987–88	25	16.0	36.0	8.0	40.0
60%+					
1991–92	133	39.1	36.1	13.5	11.3
1989–90	180	31.7	36.1	13.3	18.9
1987–88	204	40.7	27.9	20.1	11.3
House R Inc					
< 60% of vote					
1991–92	46	17.4	30.4	19.6	32.6
1989–90	48	12.5	27.1	14.6	45.8
1987–88	26	3.9	15.4	19.2	61.5
60%+					
1991–92	89	21.3	46.1	19.1	13.5
1989–90	103	21.4	39.8	20.4	18.4
1987–88	133	23.3	42.9	19.6	14.3

Source: Federal Election Commission. Included are candidates who were on the ballot for the November 1992 general election or on the final ballot for a special election during 1991 or 1992.

Note: D = Democrats; R = Republicans; Inc = Incumbents; NI = Nonincumbents.

sums, and more Republicans than Democrats were given $5,000 or more. The 1992 Democratic incumbents facing competitive challengers were given the same ranges of contributions as their peers in 1989–90 (the 1987–88 figures are suspect because of the small number of cases involved). The Republican advantage in the largest contributions that existed in 1989–90 disappeared in 1991–92; the decline in the percentage of candidates receiving $9,000 or more, 13.22 percent, runs counter to the overall pattern of stable contribution behavior but is based on a relatively small number of cases. Despite this decline in the largest contributions, more GOP candidates than Democrats benefited from larger donations.

The preceding discussion suggests that RPAC's 1992 strategy did not differ much from previous election cycles. There were, however, two areas of change. First, RPAC spent far more of its available funds in 1992 than in previous elections (see Table 9.3). It used 77.93 percent of its available money to support candidates, an all-time high. Only 2.34 percent of its available money was unspent as of December 31, 1992, an all-time low. At election time RPAC came

Table 9.3

How RPAC Did (or Did Not) Spend Its Funds

Year	Available $[a]	All Candidate Aid[b]	% of Available $ Spent on Candidates	% Unspent[c]
1978	$2,076,640	$1,132,578	54.5	13.1
1980	$3,034,631	$1,606,471	52.9	15.1
1982	$3,500,244	$2,295,247	65.6	10.2
1984	$4,647,343	$2,786,484	60.0	16.6
1986	$6,452,977	$4,461,384	69.1	6.9
1988	$6,620,083	$4,378,190	66.1	10.4
1990	$5,995,305	$4,193,813	70.0	9.6
1992	$5,057,412	$3,941,154	77.9	2.3

Source: Federal Election Commission's Reports on Financial Activity (and Disclosure Data Base for 1992).

Notes:

[a]Cash on hand at the beginning of a two-year cycle plus total receipts during the cycle.

[b]Contributions to and independent expenditures for Senate and House candidates, and token contributions to presidential aspirants.

[c]Unspent money is the cash on hand at the end of a two-year cycle.

dramatically close to its goal of having "not one red cent left in the bank."[14] RPAC began the 1991–92 cycle with unspent funds of $577,848, spent almost $4 million to help electoral contestants, and had only $23,000 left on election day. During October 1992, RPAC felt compelled to give smaller donations to potentially competitive open-seat candidates than it would have liked because of its nearly empty coffers. This constraint of limited funds, caused by the combination of less available money and more incumbents receiving large contributions because they were in tight races, was unfortunate because RPAC judged the 1992 open-seat class to be better than usual, with many experienced business people and elected officials running.

The second difference between 1992 and past elections was a substantial increase in the NAR's efforts to involve local realtors in the campaigns of endorsed candidates. The NAR Opportunity Race Program was expanded from twenty-five House races in 1990 to thirty-three House and four Senate contests in 1992. Spending for the mailings and phone banks suggesting ways to assist a candidate increased from $209,144 to $527,213.

Conclusions

What is the explanation for RPAC behavior in 1992? The realtors viewed 1992 as a watershed election because of the unusual number of open seats; they applauded the caliber of new candidates appearing on the electoral scene. In the face of the reduced amount of money they had to spend, why did they not, for example, reduce their contributions to $1,000 for those House incumbents who were electorally secure, in order to increase the donations to attractive people in tight open-seat races to $7,500 or $10,000? Why did the realtors, in large part, behave as if 1992 were just another election, like 1990 or 1988?

The explanation probably centers on the decisionmaking structure of the state and local Realtors. These realtors are aware, calculating, economic and political activists; they are the kind of people one would expect to take advantage of strategic opportunities because they so often create them in their professional activities. Yet their structure for making contribution decisions is formalized. The state and local PACs are given the task of evaluating opposing candidates for each House and Senate seat. This means that there will probably be a contribution request made for each House and Senate seat. The norms set the average contribution request at between $3,000 and $5,000 per election.

The candidate-evaluation rules emphasize using roll-call scores on a narrow range of policies affecting housing.[15] Since 1988 requests for dual contributions have been discouraged by requiring that two-thirds of the trustees approve these state recommendations. In a race involving an unacceptable incumbent, the challenger is given funding only if he or she is both pro-realtor and running a competitive campaign. The switching of support from an acceptable incumbent to a challenger is not encouraged. As a result, in many districts incumbents acceptable on a narrow range of issues have routinely received $3,000 to $5,000 per election in the past. These incumbents expected, and were given, contributions of a similar size in 1992. When all these rules and circumstances are combined, they greatly constrain the range of choices for state and local realtors. The result seems to be that people who are strategic actors become straitjacketed in a highly formalized decision structure.[16]

NAR and RPAC officials and the trustees committee worked at the margins of the decision structure to take advantage of 1992 opportunities. They continued funding for independent expenditures at previous levels; they increased NAR money for an expanded Opportunity Race Program; and they managed the PAC treasury to ensure that all money would be available for use by November 1992.

It is plausible to suggest that there was a conflict in 1992 between the realtors and their rules. The rules seem to have won. In late 1993, however, the PAC decided to change the rules. PAC officials announced that they would stop contributing to party committees and to the PACs of congressional party leaders, and would slash $1 million from their independent expenditure program. Instead, the Realtors has instituted new programs of local fundraising by realtors for candidates, bundling of contributions by individual realtors, recruiting of campaign volunteers, and increased use of soft money.

Notes

1. A decade ago face-to-face fundraising was the primary method used by all fifty-four state associations. Now that seventeen states use dues checkoff as the principal fundraising technique, RPAC may have less need to respect the candidate recommendations of local activists in those states. See John Wright, "PACs, Contributions, and Roll

Calls: An Organizational Perspective," *American Political Science Review* 79, no. 2 (June 1985), pp. 405–6.

2. Over the last twelve years, NAR membership has fluctuated between 600,000 and 800,000, while the number of contributors has grown steadily.

3. Personal interview with Douglas Thompson, NAR vice president for Government and Political Relations Administration, October 17, 1991.

4. Personal interviews with Desiree Anderson, RPAC director, August 11, 1992, and January 15, 1993. During the off-year, money from the Political Administration Fund is used for nonpartisan, non-candidate-specific grassroots training. The NAR field people go into a district and teach interested local realtors in a general way about how to get involved in a congressional campaign. Before 1988 the NAR's grassroots organizing was nonpartisan and non-candidate-specific in both years of an election cycle. In 1984, for example, the Opportunity Race Program registered 415,000 new voters and did an estimated $10,000,000 worth of volunteer work. See Peter Grier, "Lobbying in Washington," *Christian Science Monitor* (December 6, 1984), pp. 32–33.

5. Personal interview with Desiree Anderson, RPAC director, October 2, 1992.

6. The RPAC staff and the NAR political education employees use field reports, networking with other PACs, and political newsletters as their primary information sources.

7. The board is composed of thirteen regional representatives, three at-large members, a chairman, and a vice chairman.

8. In earlier years, the trustees were not told the identities of the candidates who would receive support from the block grant. Now the PAC tries to temper the judgment of the political professionals with input from the realtor trustees. All involved sign notarized affidavits certifying that they have had no contact with the favored candidates or their campaigns.

9. Wright argued that incumbents could ignore lobbyists and cultivate local realtors, since the latter made contribution decisions. NAR lobbyists now have two very large carrots to use for bargaining—selection as an RPAC independent expenditure candidate or as an NAR Opportunity Race. See Wright, "PACs, Contributions, and Roll Calls," p. 406.

10. The Tax Reform Act of 1986 may have focused the Realtors' attention on the importance of linking contributions to a candidate's stance on very specific real estate issues, but it cannot have been the sole cause of their shift from the general to the specific. In the last dozen years, the day-to-day work of a realtor has been increasingly regulated by federal laws, and these complex regulations require a good deal of record keeping and training. Just as doctors practice defensive medicine, since 1987 the Realtors may have been practicing defensive politics—giving contributions to incumbents, rather than to their challengers, in order to get an appointment to plead a case against additional federal regulation.

The NAR keeps confidential the exact pieces of legislation it uses for its roll-call index for a particular Congress. The NAR files quarterly lobbying reports with the secretary of the Senate and the clerk of the House of Representatives. These reports, however, do not list specific bills being lobbied or which bills might be inferred to be part of the roll-call index. Since the first quarterly report in 1979, these reports have contained an identical, very general statement of NAR legislative interests.

11. The independent expenditure program is the major source of the national perspective. RPAC also injects a very small amount of additional national judgment with its in-kind contributions. Based on RPAC staff recommendations, the trustees vote that a small number of candidates be given their contributions in the form of polls, conducted for RPAC by outside consultants. These dozen or so select candidates are very strong supporters of NAR positions judged to be in tight races. In 1992 RPAC's in-kind support was $43,619; in 1990 it was $50,538.

12. The definition of "open" is the one used in the Federal Election Commission's Reports on Financial Activity.

13. The normal RPAC contribution is $3,000, $4,000, or $5,000 per election, depending on perceived electoral circumstances and on committee/party-leadership position. Sometimes a contribution is given for just one election. The more usual pattern is a contribution for both the primary and the general, resulting in a doubling of the above-mentioned amounts. The dollar ranges in Table 9.2 were constructed to reflect the patterns of regularity in the ungrouped data.

14. Anderson interview, October 2, 1992.

15. The current use of roll-call scores on a narrow range of issues by the local and state realtors means that they are more likely than their counterparts studied by Wright a decade ago to view contribution decisions as devices for ensuring access for NAR lobbyists. See Wright, "PACs, Contributions, and Roll Calls," p. 406.

16. An alternative hypothesis, which would require survey research to test, is that these activists were in fact acting strategically when they chose not to alter their behavior. This explanation suggests that they decided in 1987 to practice defensive politics, created rules to assure this, and decided in 1992 that to discontinue defensive politics would be irrationally risky.

10

The National Abortion Rights Action League PAC: Reproductive Choice in the Spotlight

Sue Thomas

The National Abortion Rights Action League (NARAL) PAC was formed on August 5, 1977, to elect a pro-choice majority in Congress. NARAL (the national organization that formed the PAC) was concerned that abortion rights, guaranteed by the 1973 U.S. Supreme Court case *Roe* v. *Wade*, would be eroded by legislative action in Congress or the states. After *Roe*, pro-life activists had succeeded in passing legislation limiting abortion rights through spousal consent, twenty-four-hour waiting periods, and informed consent. Although almost all of these laws were subsequently struck down by the United States Supreme Court as antithetical to the spirit of *Roe*, leaders of NARAL realized that no guarantee existed to ensure that the Court would always protect this vital decision. Making contributions to supporters of reproductive choice was another avenue through which its preservation could be pursued.

NARAL PAC was formed to elect members of Congress who would protect women's reproductive rights in the event that the Supreme Court changed its view on the constitutionality of the right to privacy—the key to *Roe* v. *Wade*. During the early 1980s, the PAC concentrated on protecting pro-choice incumbents, but Supreme Court decisions in recent years have changed the dynamics of the abortion issue. Two cases—*Webster* v. *Reproductive Health Services* in 1989 and *Planned Parenthood of Southeastern Pennsylvania* v. *Casey* in 1992—allowed states to impose restrictions on access to abortion. The return of the abortion issue to the legislative arena had a dramatic impact on NARAL PAC's strategy in the 1992 congressional elections. Suddenly the PAC sought not to defend the status quo but to provide national protection for abortion rights through passage of the Freedom of Choice Act.

PAC Organization and Decisionmaking

NARAL PAC is affiliated with NARAL National, a C–4 tax-exempt organization. As a connected PAC, it may only solicit funds from members of NARAL National. Even though the majority of members do not contribute to the PAC (in 1990, for example, only 18 percent of NARAL members did so), it still had sufficient funds to contribute to many congressional candidates. According to a former PAC director, the PAC has had sufficient funds to contribute to all of its endorsed candidates in every election cycle. By 1990, NARAL ranked among the top twenty in receipts. This growth is evident from the figures provided in Table A.9.

Contribution decisions are made by the PAC's board of directors. The twelve-member board is headed by a chair and vice chair who are appointed by the elected board. The officers are required to be of opposite parties, and the full board is evenly divided in partisanship.

The national office, located in Washington, D.C., is part of the political division of NARAL National. It consists of the PAC director, the political director, the lobbyist, and an administrative staff of three. Fundraising is handled by staff outside of the political division. The PAC director meets with congressional candidates and makes initial decisions about who should receive contributions. The criteria for decisionmaking are viability of the candidate, whether or not choice is an issue in the race, and the position the candidate has taken on choice. These recommendations are reviewed by the executive director of NARAL and the political director before they are forwarded to the PAC board. Staff recommendations are rarely overridden by the board of directors. Occasionally, disagreements stem from the fact that the Washington staff, like the lobbying staff of most political organizations, tends to be more pragmatic than PAC members. Unlike many other PACs, controversy over decisionmaking is fairly low given the clear purpose of the organization and its PAC.

NARAL has about forty state affiliates. None of the state affiliates has a federal PAC, but most sponsor state-level PACs. Often, NARAL PAC will give grants to the states to assist them in supporting good candidates. For example, in the 1990 election cycle, the national PAC gave between $60,000 and $70,000 to various states. In 1989, NARAL PAC, in tandem with the state affiliates, also got involved in certain gubernatorial races, such as those in Virginia and New Jersey, as well as the Iowa gubernatorial primary.

The PAC has grown dramatically and now is one of the largest of its type. In 1978, it contributed $50,257 to congressional candidates. In 1992, that figure grew to $493,201. In addition to cash contributions, NARAL PAC has recently engaged in independent expenditures. In 1990, the PAC mounted mass media campaigns in seven states, sent 2 million pieces of election-related mail, distributed 500,000 pieces of literature door-to-door, trained 6,000 campaign workers, and mobilized students from more than 300 college campuses. NARAL claims to have contacted 1.5 million voters through these efforts.[1] These independent expenditures were primarily focused on state elections—especially the 1989 gubernatorial elections in New Jersey and Virginia.

A Controversial Issue?

At the inception of NARAL PAC, some congressional candidates were reluctant to accept endorsements and contributions. The fear was that abortion was an issue on which they could not win. Voters who favored reproductive choice believed that their abortion rights were guaranteed by *Roe* and were, therefore, less likely to base voting decisions on that issue. In contrast, voters who were on the pro-life side of the issue would use a NARAL PAC contribution as a major cue in choosing to vote against the candidate. From the candidate's point of view, therefore, contributions from the PAC had potentially high costs and few benefits. NARAL PAC worked to allay these fears by providing two compelling arguments. The first consisted of survey data showing that the majority of Americans, women and men alike, supported the basic right to abortion.[2] The second was to claim that no one had ever lost an election on the issue of choice.

The results of the 1980 presidential and congressional elections rendered the second argument somewhat ineffective. Several anti-choice and new right groups claimed credit for the victory of presidential candidate Ronald Reagan and the defeats of several prominent pro-choice senators, including Frank Church, Birch Bayh, and George McGovern.[3] This created an environment in which politicians questioned whether they should risk their careers over the issue of abortion. By 1982 some incumbent politicians were unwilling to accept NARAL PAC support.

On the other hand, with little to lose and a desperate need for campaign funds, House challengers were ready to accept endorsements and contributions. Several of these challengers won that year, including Bruce Morrison of Connecticut and John Bryant and Mike Andrews, both of Texas. In fact, the 1982 NARAL PAC director characterized that year as a very good one for pro-choice forces. After the 1982 election, candidates were not as leery of accepting pro-choice contributions. Although there were some candidates who sought to distance themselves from the issue, most pro-choice candidates welcomed the support. A notable example was Tom Harkin, who returned a NARAL PAC contribution to his 1984 senate campaign when it garnered negative press. By the time of his 1990 reelection campaign, however, he changed his mind and accepted the PAC's endorsement and contribution.

The United States Supreme Court case *Webster* v. *Reproductive Health Services*, handed down in July 1989, transformed the nature of abortion politics. In *Webster*, the Court stated that it would allow states to enact various kinds of restrictions on abortion as long as they did not prohibit it completely. The nature of the restrictions went unspecified, however.

The *Webster* decision had a galvanizing effect on pro-choice activists and citizens because its holding made clear that the Court was no longer a guarantor of reproductive freedom. Many pro-choice citizens shed their complacency and recognized that the right to abortion guaranteed in *Roe* was now in danger. The pro-choice plurality expressed their intentions to vote their policy preference on the abortion issue. Hence, NARAL PAC support was sought out rather than avoided, and candidates began to actively solicit the PAC's endorsement and contributions. This was particularly evident in state and local elections in 1989. The gubernatorial victories of Doug Wilder in Virginia and Jim Florio in New Jersey came with the highly active and public support of NARAL PAC. At the close of the 1990 election cycle, there were eight more pro-choice members in the House of Representatives, two more pro-choice Senators, five more pro-choice state legislative bodies, and four additional pro-choice governors. Three ballot measures across the nation were all won by the pro-choice side, including one in Oregon dealing with parental consent for minors.[4]

The victories by the pro-choice plurality became increasingly important as the personnel on the Supreme Court changed. The retirements of *Roe* supporters, justices William Brennan and Thurgood Marshall, and their replacement with two potential opponents, justices David Souter and Clarence Thomas, made the complete abandonment of *Roe* increasingly possible. Many, including NARAL's directors, believed that the Court's 1991 decision to hear *Planned Parenthood of Southeastern Pennsylvania* v. *Casey* was the vehicle through which that step would be taken. When the Court's ruling in *Casey* was handed down in June 1992, it did not overturn *Roe*, but it did reduce abortion from a fundamental right to one that may be restricted as long as the nature of those restrictions do not constitute an undue burden. Spousal consent was deemed an undue burden, but informed consent, parental consent for minors, and a twenty-four-hour waiting period were allowed. Court-watchers, including both pro-choice and pro-life activists, were aware, however, that the next appointment would determine the course of Court abortion policy for many years to come.

Membership Growth and Sophistication

The *Webster* decision and subsequent changes in membership of the Supreme Court led representatives from NARAL PAC to speak of its growth as an organization in terms of "pre- and post-*Webster*." Membership of the parent organization, NARAL, more than doubled, from 250,000 just after the decision to slightly more than half a million in 1992 (all of this was prior to the *Casey* ruling). The membership also became more politically active than it had been in the past. For example, NARAL managed to get 80 percent of its members to commit to calling or buttonholing their senators to advocate the rejection of U.S. Supreme

Court nominee Clarence Thomas. While it is difficult to tell how many of those who agreed to this request actually followed through, comments from Senate staffers indicate that the effort was widespread. This mobilization is also evident at the state level. Membership in NARAL's forty state affiliates has more than doubled since the critical events listed above. The number of local chapters has grown from 56 to 119.

The increase in membership led to the growth and professionalization of the staff at both the national and state levels. Members of Congress became increasingly responsive to NARAL lobbying efforts because they saw the results of grassroots mobilization efforts among their constituents. Telephone banks, door-to-door canvassing to distribute literature, direct mail efforts, and get-out-the-vote drives organized by national and state NARAL affiliates have resulted in national attention. A recent *Fortune* magazine article named NARAL's lobbyist as one of the ten best in the nation.

The 1992 Election

Although those who guide NARAL PAC believe it has been very successful in raising and distributing money, the officers and staff also recognized that 1992 presented special challenges and opportunities. In the wake of *Webster*, only a pro-choice Congress and a pro-choice president would ensure that women's reproductive rights continue to have national protection. NARAL and its PAC are intent upon passage of the Freedom of Choice Act, which will essentially codify *Roe*. To enact this legislation, both a pro-choice Congress and president or a veto-proof Congress is required. Representatives from NARAL PAC called the 1992 congressional election "perhaps the most important election of our generation." Between redistricting and a record number of congressional retirements, they predicted that no incumbent would be involved in as many as 100 races, and they were right. The year 1992 was, therefore, seen as a "once-in-a-lifetime opportunity to elect the pro-choice majority we need."

Fundraising

Direct contributions to pro-choice candidates and a mobilized electorate were the keys to achieving NARAL PAC's political goals in 1992. To raise the money for these efforts, NARAL needed to increase its membership. Only then could a larger set of PAC donors be tapped. Hence, the organization launched a more extensive membership drive than ever and solicited the wider political community with telemarketing and direct-mail appeals, as well as major donor events. One such gala was hosted in Washington on January 22 (the nineteenth anniversary of *Roe* v. *Wade*) and was attended by many of the major Democratic candidates for president. NARAL also ran four television advertisements to educate the public about the new threats to reproductive freedom. Two of these ads were personal stories about the tragedies connected with illegal abortion, and two focused on the consequences that reelecting George Bush would have for keeping abortion safe and legal.

Expanding NARAL's membership and its PAC's fundraising ability resulted in record contributions. By early June 1992, the PAC had already taken in twice the amount they raised for the entire 1990 cycle. At that point, 24 percent of NARAL members were donating to the PAC, a rise of 6 percent over 1990. PAC director Micque Glitman was optimistic about fundraising through the general election, but she also realized that a pre-election decision in *Casey* would alter the fundraising equation. If the ruling upheld *Roe*, fundraising would likely level off, since the threat to reproductive freedom would seem less imminent. If the decision reversed Roe, the political implication would be a dramatic escalation in giving. Contributors would want to ensure passage of the Freedom of Choice Act to restore a nationally enforced right to abortion.

As it turned out, *Casey* was decided on June 29. The Court upheld the right to abortion, although the basis on which abortion remained protected had changed and states were freer to enact certain restrictions on that right. Ms. Glitman was correct about how the decision affected fundraising—contributions were still much higher than they had been in 1990, but they leveled off from June through the end of the election cycle. Rather than tripling or quadrupling amounts raised in the previous cycle, as was initially expected, NARAL PAC's fundraising remaining at double the earlier level (see Table A.9 for specific levels).

Donation Strategy

The unique electoral climate also had a large effect on NARAL PAC's donation strategy. Because it was so crucial to create a veto-proof Congress or to elect a pro-choice president, the PAC focused the bulk of its attention on national races. State-level activity was reduced from the levels exhibited in earlier elections, though certain action was initiated (gubernatorial races in Montana and Missouri, for example).

Additionally, NARAL PAC spent its money later in the election cycle than was usual. Sophisticated political fundraisers and recipients know that early money is important in establishing viable candidacies; therefore, challengers, incumbents, and open-seat contestants clamor for donations well before primary season begins. In 1992, retirements were being announced continuously, and redistricting was ongoing in some states until very late in the electoral season, so NARAL PAC resisted the pressure to jump in too early. When they did get involved in congressional primaries, it was mostly in Republican races. The PAC wanted to ensure that pro-choice Republicans bested far-right opponents of abortion, especially those using graphic pro-life ads.[5]

A final reason NARAL PAC held off its spending was that it wanted to derive the maximum benefits from its independent expenditures. Television, radio, and newspaper advertising has the greatest impact closest to the election, so NARAL PAC planned to spend heavily in the last week of the general election. Similarly, get-out-the-vote drives must be conducted on election day, and NARAL PAC invested larger sums in this traditional activity than it had in previous years.

Following their successes in the 1990 election cycle, NARAL PAC spent sizable sums in independent expenditures in congressional elections in 1992. Although they had previously spent less than $3,000 in independent expenditures (i.e., PAC monies spent without coordination or communication with the candidate) on congressional elections in all past election cycles combined, in 1992 the total was more than $850,000. This was nearly twice the total that the PAC contributed directly to congressional candidates.

This sharp change in the expenditure patterns of the PAC was symbolic of an effort to concentrate resources in races where they might be most helpful. Rather than increasing the size of their contributions to candidates who appeared likely to win or lose by a wide margin, the PAC chose to spend large sums on behalf of pro-choice candidates in close races or to spend money against anti-choice candidates who might be defeated.

Although NARAL PAC did not greatly increase the proportion of its *contributions* going to nonincumbent candidates, the *independent expenditures* were generally targeted toward challengers and open-seat candidates. NARAL PAC gave approximately 56 percent of its contributions to nonincumbent candidates in 1992 (up from 51 percent in 1990), but fully 91 percent of its independent expenditures were either on behalf of a nonincumbent candidate or against an incumbent or open-seat candidate.

Standards for Giving

The timing of donations is only one decision related to an effective contribution strategy. Another is agreement on and clarity of the standards candidates must meet to receive contributions. Because NARAL PAC was established with the sole purpose of protecting women's reproductive freedom, there has been little controversy over the standards that should govern contribution decisions. From the beginning, viability of the candidate, the extent to which choice was an issue in the race, and the candidate's position on abortion rights were the three ingredients in decisionmaking.

In 1992, however, another stipulation was added. Because the Supreme Court might further limit reproductive freedom on the national level, NARAL PAC's bottom line for funding was support of the Freedom of Choice Act (FOCA). Challengers and candidates for open seats had to pledge to support FOCA. In the case of incumbents, the PAC board of directors decided that only those who had signed on as cosponsors of FOCA would be funded. This standard was much more rigid than the ones imposed in earlier elections, but it reflected what the board and staff of NARAL PAC perceived to be a greater threat than they had faced in previous elections.

Obtaining information about candidates' positions on abortion in general or the FOCA in particular was not as straightforward as might be expected. Representatives of NARAL PAC found that many candidates saw the electoral advantage of a pro-choice position and wanted to reap its benefits. Many cited Florio's and Wilder's gubernatorial successes as models. Hence, candidates who supported abortion with some restrictions, such as parental consent or opposition to public funding, claimed to be pro-choice, as did some politicians who supported abortion only in circumstances of life endangerment for the woman involved or cases of rape or incest. It was important for NARAL PAC to sort out the candidates it considered to be true supporters of reproductive freedom from those who were trying to gain electoral benefit from a blurred stand. Not only was this the key to decisionmaking on funding, it was crucial to helping voters discern who were the "true" pro-choice candidates.

To obtain accurate portrayals of congressional candidates across the country, NARAL PAC relied on an extensive array of sources, including questionnaires sent to candidates, published information in *Roll Call* and *Congressional Quarterly Weekly Report*, meetings with candidates, communications from affiliates and board members, and information from Washington-based advocacy groups. PAC director Micque Glitman noted that no one source of information was sufficient by itself; it was only by mining every possible avenue that accurate information about candidates could be compiled.

Despite the need for extensive information, NARAL PAC forfeited the benefits of meeting or trading information with other pro-choice groups or campaign representatives. The PAC officials believed that federal law governing independent expenditures on behalf of candidates prohibited coordination with candidates or with groups working on behalf of candidates.

Funding Amounts and Allocations

Because maximizing the number of pro-choice legislators was NARAL PAC's goal for Congress, there was no room in funding decisions for questions about partisanship, race, gender, or incumbency status. Only support for the FOCA and viability of the candidate were considerations in decisions for support. In the final analysis, the funding distribution favored incumbents over challengers or open-seat candidates, with money for challengers coming in second (see Table A.9). Indeed, despite the large number of open seats, NARAL PAC allocated a smaller portion of its funds to open-seat candidates in 1992 than it had in 1990. NARAL PAC spent more than $3 million in the 1992 election, including independent expenditures and assistance to state affiliates. It also endorsed over 200 candidates, from the presidential race (with the endorsement of Bill Clinton) to a variety of state-level races.

Mobilizing the Grassroots

The last crucial component of NARAL PAC's 1992 campaign strategy was to engage in an "unprecedented grassroots program to identify more than a million pro-choice voters in key districts and states across the nation." In October, the PAC launched a campaign called "Thirty Days to Save Choice." Its symbol was a single, flickering flame meant to illustrate that the replacement of one more Supreme Court justice could end women's right to abortion. Actor Dustin Hoffman narrated a fifteen-second advertisement aired on Cable News Network emphasizing this message. Telephone banks, leaflet drops, neighborhood canvasses, targeted mailings, and get-out-the-vote rallies were organized in all fifty states to educate and mobilize pro-choice voters, especially Republican and Independent women. The key organizing tool of the campaign, the Choice Action Leader Program, trained more than 5,000 activists to coordinate these activities and recruit additional volunteers. The goal was to demonstrate to politicians that a candidate's position on abortion would weigh heavily on voters' ballot decisions when reproductive freedom faced a fundamental threat.

Results

According to NARAL PAC's postelection tallies, 2.4 million pro-choice voters were identified, 1.12 million get-out-the-vote calls were made, 6 million pieces of mail were sent, 58,000 activists were mobilized, and more than 1 million pieces of literature were distributed in leafleting or door-to-door canvassing. The results of these substantial efforts were gratifying to those affiliated with NARAL PAC. After November 3, pro-choice forces enjoyed a net gain of eleven seats in the House of Representatives and one in the Senate.[6]

Further, all of the new members of the Senate—Dianne Feinstein, Barbara Boxer, Patty Murray, Russ Feingold, Carol Moseley-Braun, and Ben Nighthorse Campbell—are pro-choice. The House of Representatives convened with 215 clear pro-choice votes, 47 mixed votes, 172 pro-life, and 1 unknown vote. Before, pro-choice forces could count on only 204 sure votes, 49 mixed votes and 182 pro-life votes. These figures are still short of those needed for a veto-proof Congress. With the election of Bill Clinton to the presidency, however, the majority status of pro-choice legislators should be sufficient. Furthermore, according to PAC tallies, supporters of reproductive freedom are numerous enough in the Senate to invoke cloture to end filibuster attempts.

A different view of the NARAL PAC tally shows that 153 of the 238 candidates it endorsed (64 percent) won on election day. This list includes 12 of 22 people running for the U.S. Senate (55 percent); 142 of 205 candidates for the U.S. House of Representatives (69 percent), and 4 of 7 gubernatorial candidates (57 percent). NARAL PAC's coordinated campaigns supported the Senate candidacies of Russ Feingold in Wisconsin, Carol Moseley-Braun in

Illinois, Barbara Boxer and Dianne Feinstein in California, and the House candidacy of Pat Williams for Montana's only seat. Independent spending campaigns were launched for Ben Nighthorse Campbell in Colorado, where NARAL PAC reached 42,500 pro-choice Independent and Republican women through targeted mail and telephone mobilization efforts.

Additionally, two abortion-related ballot measures were decided in favor of reproductive freedom. Maryland's Question 6, which repealed pre–*Roe* v. *Wade* laws and codified the principles of *Roe*, was successful, winning 61 percent of the vote. Sixty-nine percent of Arizona's voters rejected Proposition 110, which would have banned the vast majority of abortions in that state.

Another result of the 1992 elections is that pro-choice forces can now count on the support of thirty governors, a net gain of one. That one additional supporter is Mel Carnahan in Missouri—a victory that was symbolic as well as practical. Carnahan was the victor over Attorney General William Webster, who brought Missouri's abortion law to the U.S. Supreme Court in *Webster* v. *Reproductive Health Services*. NARAL PAC, in coordination with Missouri NARAL and Missourians for Choice, conducted voter identification and voter education campaigns with the use of direct mail and phone banks to support Carnahan. Electing pro-choice governors is important in fighting restrictions on abortion rights that may be imposed by states under the *Casey* ruling.

Judging Success

It is difficult to render judgment on how important NARAL PAC's efforts were in the 1992 elections. Standards for assessing success vary considerably, and it is impossible to say how much of an individual candidate's victory can be attributed to any one source of support. Despite these constraints, it seems fair to say that NARAL PAC was successful in meeting its goals of increased fundraising and widespread voter education and mobilization. The PAC's record in these areas was greatly increased from previous election cycles. Moreover, NARAL PAC met its goals of electing a pro-choice president and augmenting pro-choice supporters in the House and the Senate. The ratios of wins to loses is impressive enough to judge the PAC's efforts as successful.

It is true that the abortion issue had a higher profile in this election season than in previous cycles, and it goes without saying that it would have been a factor in a number of races whether or not NARAL PAC had been pressing its case. It is also true that most people do not vote on the basis of any one issue (including abortion) and that the dynamic of each individual campaign is the primary determinant of its outcome. Nevertheless, without concerted efforts to keep abortion rights in the public eye and to educate voters about the fuzzy stands of many candidates, some contests might have been decided differently. NARAL PAC and other pro-choice organizations were responsible for making sure information was accurate, accessible, and abundant. Combined with the donations the PAC provided to candidates, it is safe to say that they had an important impact on the 1992 election results. Even Bush campaign spokespeople acknowledged that the loss of suburban Republican women who were disillusioned with the president's abortion stand factored significantly into his defeat. These voters were heavily targeted by NARAL PAC.

Postelection Plans

Now that NARAL PAC has achieved its goals of contributing to the election victories of pro-choice candidates to the Congress and the presidency, its sights are set on a series of policy reversals, the enactment of the Freedom of Choice Act, and legislation to protect abortion clinics. It also plans to conduct more educational efforts geared toward making abortion less necessary.

The first set of NARAL's goals concerned executive orders issued by former Presidents Reagan and Bush and previous legislative decisions on public funding of abortion. For the past twelve years, executive orders have imposed a "gag" rule on abortion counseling in federally funded family planning clinics, barred abortions in overseas military bases regardless of whether the woman paid for the procedure herself, banned federally funded medical research using fetal tissue from elective abortions, and banned the abortion pill RU–486 from importation into the United States. Executive orders also prohibited aid to international organizations that perform or promote abortions.

Pro-choice advocates did not have to wait long after Bill Clinton took office for the reversal of these policies. On January 22, 1993, the twentieth anniversary of *Roe* v. *Wade*, President Clinton overturned all five of these directives. Although President Clinton supports legislative action to overturn the sixteen-year prohibition of public funding for abortion except in cases of rape, incest, and life endangerment, this will be more difficult to achieve. Some legislators who support the right to abortion are ambivalent about federal funding for the procedure. The exact number of swing votes, however, is unknown. A related action to allow the District of Columbia to spend its own taxes on such funding is much more likely to garner the support necessary for passage.

NARAL's top priority is, of course, passage of an unamended Freedom of Choice Act. Without this legislation, states may restrict abortion by imposing twenty-four-hour waiting periods, informed consent requirements, or parental consent for minors seeking abortion. The Freedom of Choice Act would reinstitute a uniform national right to abortion free of patchwork restrictions. The current bills (S 25 and HR 25) were stymied in both chambers of Congress in 1992, in part because former president Bush promised a veto. This year, with the support of President Clinton, the bills are moving in both chambers. Still, a pro-choice majority in Congress and a supportive president do not guarantee FOCA's passage. Legislators are divided about whether the bill ought to contain any amendments (provisions for parental consent seem to have the most support), and deadlock over whether any restrictions ought to be included in the legislation may yet halt its progress. NARAL and other pro-choice advocates insist on a clean bill, but it is presently unclear whether that strategy will prevail.

Another goal, intended to ensure that the right to abortion can be exercised without interference, concerns threats to clinic access. After more than ten years of violence against abortion clinics, including bombings, the release of noxious chemicals, and clinic blockades, Congress has introduced a bill to criminalize obstruction of abortion clinics. The bill has taken on increased momentum after the March 10, 1993, murder of Dr. David Gunn, a physician who performed abortions, by an anti-abortion protester. The first protest-related death in the United States has highlighted the need for federal law to protect those who perform or assist in abortions and those who seek them. The legislation, if passed, would hold blockade participants and organizers responsible for up to triple the monetary damage they cause, including awards for pain and suffering. Additionally, a fine of up to $100,000 and a year in prison could be imposed.

Equally important to protecting women's reproductive freedoms, NARAL says, is educating citizens on how to avoid unplanned pregnancies, supporting the development of safe contraceptives, and making adoption a better option. As NARAL has repeatedly asserted, its mission goes beyond keeping abortion legal. It includes creating an environment where the procedure is relied upon less often. The 1992 elections increased NARAL's leeway to concentrate on this mission. As the organization's postelection blueprint notes:

> Among the most dramatic changes certain to result from this presidential election is a fundamental shift in the federal government's approach to issues of reproductive rights and health. The election of Bill Clinton promises an end to the extreme anti-choice policies of the last 12 years.

Conclusion

Since its inception in 1977, NARAL PAC's fundraising and campaign contributions have grown dramatically. Because the majority of citizens support some form of reproductive choice, and because the abortion issue has been pivotal in more than one recent election, candidates' receptiveness to the PAC's support has also grown. This receptivity was evident in the 1992 elections, as were the unprecedented challenges and opportunities NARAL PAC faced. Another four years of George Bush in the White House could have led to additional Supreme Court appointments that might have resulted in a complete reversal of *Roe* v. *Wade*. That would have been compounded by a certain veto of the Freedom of Choice Act. To foreclose this possibility, NARAL PAC heavily supported the presidential candidacy of Bill Clinton.

The events of 1992 also gave NARAL PAC an unprecedented opportunity to influence the shape of the 103rd Congress. Because this was the first election cycle after the latest round of redistricting, and because of scandal, frustration with gridlock, and the final opportunity for incumbents to keep previously raised campaign contributions, a record number of incumbents retired. Groups like NARAL and its PAC had an opportunity to reach voters who would be unaffected by the lure of incumbency. NARAL PAC made use of this rare circumstance to endorse and contribute to a record number of candidates, all of whom supported the Freedom of Choice Act.

NARAL PAC worked toward victory by raising and spending more money than ever before, engaging in greater coordinated campaigns with its state affiliates, and relying more on independent spending than it had in the past. It also concentrated almost exclusively on federal elections and focused its message on only one issue—whether voters wanted to lose the right to choose abortion and allow the government to decide their reproductive choices. The message appeared to have been successful. While a veto-proof Congress was not achieved, pro-choice forces gained seats in the House and Senate and, most important for the selection of Supreme Court justices and the overturning of previous restrictive executive orders, Bill Clinton won the presidency. While none of this can be attributed directly or solely to NARAL PAC or other pro-choice advocates, it is not clear whether the outcomes would have been the same without them.

Notes

1. This information comes from a January 11, 1991, memo from NARAL political director James Wagoner to the NARAL Board of Directors.

2. In fact, the most recent Hickman-Brown poll has the support level at 68 percent (January 21, 1992, media packet from NARAL executive director Kate Michelman).

3. However, many analysts discount the effect of the evangelical right on voter decisions. See Michael Corbett, *American Public Opinion: Trends, Processes, and Patterns* (New York: Longman, 1991).

4. This information was culled from a January 11, 1991, memo from NARAL political director James Wagoner to the NARAL board of directors.

5. As it turns out, most of the pro-choice Republicans lost, and the general election contests were mostly between pro-choice Democrats and anti-choice Republicans. The NARAL PAC director noted that the right-wing evangelical Republicans who were so prominent later on at the Republican National Convention were extremely active and had dominated these primary races.

6. Now that President Clinton has selected members from the House and Senate for cabinet and other positions, final figures on the level of pro-choice support are pending.

11

A New Political Pragmatism? The National Right to Life PAC

Roland Gunn

The National Right to Life PAC (NRLPAC) is the seventeenth largest ideological PAC and the largest of all the pro-life PACs. It accounted for 75 percent of the $722,353 spent by pro-life PACs during the 1989–90 election cycle. NRLPAC's expenditures have historically favored Republicans and incumbents. In its membership recruitment materials, however, politicians from both parties are featured.

When the ruling in *Roe* v. *Wade* was issued on January 22, 1973, abortion became a major national issue.[1] There was a rapid response by opponents of this decision. Within a week, Representative Lawrence J. Hogan (R-MD) had introduced a right-to-life amendment in the House. Opponents of *Roe* were not unified as to the best way to reverse its impact. This led to open conflict in their ranks. The National Right to Life Committee (NRLC) was founded in 1973 as a part of an effort "to resolve the movement's incessant internecine battles."[2] It quickly became a leading and highly visible group with the pro-life movement.

Prior to 1980, there was no direct NRLC activity in electoral politics. There were, however, "close informal connections" between the NRLC and the Life Amendment Political Action Committee.[3] The formation of the NRLPAC in 1980 coincided with the closer alignment of the NRLC with the new right; but ironically, the single-issue focus of the NRLC prevented it from being taken over by the new right.[4] The formation at the PAC was also in line with the redefinition of the NRLC's goals:

> The NRLC meanwhile is increasingly articulating its goals in political terms. In its 1978 annual convention, it announced it would step up its campaign for a

human-life amendment by actively enlisting votes, establishing a "citizens lobbying arm" in voting and campaigning in state and congressional elections against its enemies.[5]

The NRLPAC was founded in 1980 as a result of the efforts of state NRLC chapters who perceived the need for a formal structure to raise and distribute campaign contributions. The existence of a national PAC allows individuals who live in areas where there are no current pro-life candidates to contribute to the cause. The fact that the impulse for the formation of the PAC came from the state level reflected both the pre-*Roe* political situation and the grassroots character of the organization.

PAC Leadership

Since the early 1980s, both the NRLC and its PAC have had stable leadership. The NRLC has had only two presidents: John C. Willke, M.D. (1981 to 1991), and Wanda Franz, Ph.D. (1991 to the present). Before her election as president, Franz had been an organization vice president. David O'Steen, Ph.D., has been the executive director since 1984. He, too, had prior experience as a state executive director before assuming a position of national leadership. Sandra Faucher, the PAC director from 1980 until 1991, performed her duties from Maine. Carol Long, who had been the executive director of the North Dakota Right to Life, is Faucher's successor. The PAC director and the executive director play an important part in decisions about the funding of candidates. The third decisionmaker is the state director for each candidate's state. The state director, who also serves on the NLRC's board of directors, is chosen by the state organization. The role of state officials in the decisionmaking process highlights the grassroots character of the NRLPAC. Although the executive director has veto power over funding decisions, this power has never been exercised.

Contribution Decisions

The NRLPAC has developed an elaborate set of criteria to select candidates for endorsement. Candidates are evaluated in terms of ideology (using their past voting records in the case of incumbents and other officeholders), relationships with local pro-lifers, ability to attract the support of other pro-life PACs, and willingness to cosponsor NRLC's version of the Human Life Amendment. Electability, qualifications for office, and the overlap of their electorate with those in other "pro-life races" form a second, pragmatic set of criteria. The PAC has a built-in bias toward pro-life incumbents, as reflected in the NRLP Committee's internal publication, *Criteria for Selection of Candidates*: "In general, in both the primary and general elections, the pro-life incumbent should get the endorsement if all other criteria are equal." This bias is reflected by PAC expenditures in the

1989–90 congressional election cycle: incumbents received 58 percent of the NRLPAC contributions and independent expenditures.

During the six election cycles between 1980 and 1990, the PAC has strongly favored Republicans, giving them approximately 80 percent of its contributions. Nevertheless, the PAC seeks to endorse candidates in both parties' primaries, further revealing its bipartisanship and pragmatism.

From its inception, the PAC has been concerned with presidential politics. In the 1980 presidential campaign, Ronald Reagan actively worked to gain the support of various groups that compose the religious right. He was endorsed by the NRLPAC after agreeing to appoint pro-life judges.[6] However, the endorsement did not directly translate into the expenditure of resources. In spite of Reagan's support for pro-life positions as part of his 1984 campaign strategy,[7] there was less support from the PAC in 1984 than in 1980. In light of the fundraising success of Reagan's 1984 campaign, the NRLPAC's allocations of its resources made sense.

The 1988 election cycle marked a major change in the allocation of funds. The PAC spent $1,091,872 (69 percent of its total expenditure) on the presidential campaign. Most of the money was not, however, given directly to the candidates. In fact, the PAC's total presidential contributions amounted to $1,000 each to Bush and Kemp. The vast majority of the money went to independent expenditures in support of Bush ($851,915) and against Dukakis ($167,216).

The preference for Republicans and independent expenditures over Democrats and direct contributions held true in the 1992 election as well. However, the percentage of the PAC's resources devoted to the presidential election fell from 69 percent in 1988 to 41 percent in 1992. With the exception of a small independent expenditure against General Haig in 1988, Republican candidates have been the beneficiaries of all the PAC's presidential spending.

Fundraising Techniques

The NRLPAC is sponsored by a membership organization and can therefore only solicit contributions from members of its parent organization, the NRLC. The NRLC recruits these members in several ways. In addition to the publicity generated by its normal lobbying and campaign activities, it uses a wide range of media to get its message out to prospective members. It sponsored the controversial videotape *The Silent Scream*; produced a radio program, "Pro-Life Perspectives," which is aired on 264 stations five days a week; and advertised in newspapers. In addition, it sends a biweekly newspaper to its 3,000 local chapters and general membership and publishes books that provide members information about the pro-life cause. The NRLC recruits its membership through a fully multimedia effort. There is also an NRL Educational Trust Fund that is eligible for support from the Combined Federal Campaign. The proceeds of the

Table 11.1

PAC Receipts and Contributions, 1979–92

Cycle	Receipts ($)	Contributions ($)	Percentage of Receipts Given to Candidates
1979–80	126,767	72,837	57.5
1981–82	394,767	194,667	49.3
1983–84	866,513	390,869	45.1
1985–86	1,775,060	695,641	39.2
1987–88	1,660,936	256,104	15.4
1989–90	1,528,187	112,177	7.3
1991–92	2,153,435	229,841	10.7

trust fund are divided equally between the national and state chapters. Fundraising for the educational trust fund does not appear to be as high a priority as other aspects of the NRLC work.

The NRLPAC leadership believes that FEC rules limit them as a membership PAC to soliciting for NRLC members twice per year. The PAC's primary means of fundraising is direct mail. Although it has a self-selected mailing list, NRLPAC experienced a sharp decline in its revenues through the 1990 elections, and the proportion of receipts that is contributed to or spent for candidates has also declined: in 1987–88 the figure was 15 percent, and in 1989–1990 it was only 7 percent (see Table 11.1). Darla St. Martin, an associate executive director of NRLC, described the funding situation in the 1988 election:

> Through the generosity and sacrifice of many pro-lifers, National Right to Life was able to get the funds to do the job. It wasn't easy! Other important projects were cut back. Funds were diverted from the Senate and House races, and we ended up $250,000.00 in debt.[8]

From St. Martin's perspective, the presidential election was NRLC's major concern. But it is clear that a shortage of funds prevented it from accomplishing all that it wanted.

In spite of the shortage of campaign funds, the NRLC was pleased with the results of the 1988 elections. In *The Triumph of Hope*, a NRLC publication, it claimed that about 5 percent of Bush's total support came from the pro-life movement. The NRLC also performed a peace-keeping function within the anti-abortion movement during the 1988 Republican presidential primaries by asking members to support their favorite pro-life candidate but refrain from spreading criticism of the abortion positions of the other pro-life candidates. This would allow the movement to unite around any of the eventual Republican nominees.

The 1992 Election

The 1989 *Webster* decision energized pro-choice activists, and pro-life candidates lost important gubernatorial elections in New Jersey and Virginia. Pro-choice PACs and other groups experienced a sharp increase in fundraising, as abortion policy returned to the legislative arena. In 1992, NRLPAC also experienced a sharp increase in receipts, and it contributed a somewhat higher proportion of those funds than it had in 1990.

In the 1992 election cycle, the NRLPAC's fraction of total pro-life PAC expenditures increased from 75 percent to 80 percent of pro-life PAC expenditures. This figure underestimated the relative size of the NRLPAC among pro-life PACS for two reasons. First, the second largest pro-life PAC, the Minnesota Citizens Concerned for Life Committee for a Pro-Life Congress, is affiliated with NRLPAC. The Minnesota group was the only other pro-life PAC to spend more than $100,000 on federal candidates in this cycle. Second, although there are sixty-four pro-life PACs registered with the FEC, only thirty-one made contributions this cycle. Most of them spent less than $1,000.

In light of the size of the NRLPAC, one would expect that it would serve as a cue giver for the smaller pro-life PACs, especially in an election cycle such as 1992, where information was at a premium. There is some evidence to support this assumption. For example, the director of JustLife Action said that NRLPAC endorsement was an important factor in his group's decisionmaking process. Many of the candidates endorsed by the NLRPAC are also endorsed by one or more of the other pro-life PACs. This is not in itself sufficient evidence of cue giving, however. It may be that other pro-life PACs are merely responding to the same information as the NRLPAC and therefore give to the same candidates. Indeed, when the timing of endorsements by other PACs is compared to the activity of the NRLPAC, there is little evidence that NRLPAC is consistently the first to give to promising candidates. For example, the Republican National Coalition for Life Political Action Committee (third largest of the pro-life PACs in the 1992 cycle) contributed a total of $3,000 to the campaign of Ralph T. Hudgens (R-GA 10th) in July, September, and October. Neither the NRLPAC nor its affiliated Georgia Right to Life National PAC became active in this race until the end of October. In this race both the NRLPAC and its Georgia affiliate made contributions on the same day. Sometimes the affiliated PAC moved before the national PAC. In the Georgia senate race, the Minnesota Citizens Concerned for Life Committee for a Pro-Life Congress made its first contribution to the Coverdell campaign eleven days before the NRLPAC became active in the race. This suggests that NRLPAC is not a major source of cues in pro-life contributions but rather that all pro-life PACs respond together to the same set of political circumstances.

Goals and Objectives

NLRPAC's major objective for the 1992 election was to keep "our pro-life president in the White House."[9] The PAC's point of view was neatly captured by an article in the *National Right To Life News* entitled "A Horror Story for 1992:

Bush Loses." The story detailed the effect of the election of a pro-choice president. The importance the presidential election had for the NRLC was reflected in its allocation of resources. At the end of July, the PAC informed its membership that it wanted to raise $1,881,000 for the 1992 campaign budget. The money was to be divided three ways: 50 percent for the presidential race and 25 percent each for Senate and House races. These goals were not fully realized. In fact, the PAC only spent 41 percent of its funds on the presidential campaign and made only a token direct contribution to the Bush campaign ($773).

A large amount of NRLPAC's spending was in independent expenditures on behalf of President Bush ($739,139). The PAC also spent $18,884 against the candidacy of Bill Clinton.[10] The independent expenditures went for a wide variety of activities, including advertising, printing, postage, and campaign staff expenses. In addition to placing ads in mainstream publications, the PAC also reprinted ads in their own publications. Yet a careful inspection of the FEC microfilm records of NRLPAC reports suggests that most of the independent expenditure funds were probably spent in direct fundraising. In other words, the PAC claimed to have spent nearly three-quarters of a million dollars on behalf of Bush and against Clinton, but most of this consisted of endorsing Bush or denouncing Clinton in fundraising letters to PAC supporters. PAC officials defend this type of expenditure as communications designed to inspire political mobilization, although it is likely that most of those who give to NRLPAC were already ardent Bush supporters.

The most significant action by the NRLPAC in the 1992 presidential race was the decision in late February to endorse President Bush. This endorsement, which came before Super Tuesday, was important to the Bush campaign because it helped Bush among Southern conservative voters who might otherwise have been attracted by the message of the Buchanan campaign. The mid-June annual meeting of NRLC focused on the upcoming election. It featured an address by then–vice president Quayle and a videotaped message from then-president Bush. Because Ross Perot was still in the race, the positions of both Perot and Clinton were scrutinized and found to be unacceptable because of their views on the abortion issue.[11]

The apparent strength of Perot created the possibility that the presidential election would be thrown into the House. This fact was used to highlight the importance of House contests. The NRLC also used its newspaper to encourage political activity among its members. It regularly published records of congressional votes on issues that were important to members. During the general election, it also provided detailed information on the scope of permissible activities that local churches and their leaders could use to keep within the limits of the federal campaign finance and tax laws. The paper also had charts that compared the positions of the three major candidates on abortion. Readers were encouraged to copy and distribute these charts. Each issue of the newspaper also had an article by the voter identification coordinator.

The other goal in the national election was the building of a "solid pro-life majority in the U.S. House." In keeping with the grassroots character of the organization, there was also a well-developed general strategy for involvement in state and local races. Local PAC members were encouraged to become active in local campaigns of pro-life candidates or to support activities of state PACs that are associated with NRLPAC. The PAC's newspaper also included articles encouraging participation in its voter identification project. Some were also asked to get involved in screening candidates for the PAC.

NRLPAC responded to the opportunities of the 1992 elections by more than doubling its contributions to congressional campaigns. Contributions to nonincumbents increased dramatically. While in 1990 only 25 percent of NRLPAC's contributions had gone to nonincumbent Republicans in the House, in 1992 this figure was fully 46 percent.

In addition, NRLPAC nearly doubled the amount of money it spent independently on behalf of congressional candidates, from $418,436 in 1990 to $783,518 in 1992. These independent expenditures were made primarily on behalf of nonincumbent candidates: 69 percent of the PAC's congressional independent expenditures in 1992 were on behalf of nonincumbents, compared with only 41 percent in 1990. Once again, most of these expenditures were on behalf of Republicans, although the PAC did spend more than $100,000 on behalf of House Democratic incumbents and challengers.

Two aspects of the behavior of the NRLPAC in 1992 congressional races are of particular interest. First, the committee chose for the first time to endorse independent pro-life candidates. This willingness to move outside the two-party system indicated a commitment to ideological purity at the expense of electoral outcomes, since none of these independent candidates came close to winning.

In addition, however, the committee endorsed for the first time major-party candidates who did not take strict pro-life positions, as long as they opposed the passage of the Freedom of Choice Act (FOCA), which would codify *Roe*. The reason for this newfound pragmatism might be the importance that the NRLC placed on FOCA. In almost every issue of *National Right to Life News*, one of the two front-page articles was devoted to some aspect of this legislation. FOCA was also the subject of an April 1992 PAC fundraising effort. Indeed, opposition to FOCA was a major rationale for NRLPAC activity in House and Senate campaigns. For example, the May issue of the PAC's newspaper listed FOCA's sponsors. Among those listed was then-senator Weyche Fowler (D-GA).

NRLPAC activity in the Georgia Senate race among Fowler, Paul Coverdell (R), and Jim Hudson (I) demonstrates the PAC's ability to act pragmatically under some circumstances. Georgia law requires that candidates for the Senate win 50 percent of the vote or face a run-off between the top two. In this first round, Hudson received enough votes to prevent either Fowler (with 49 percent) or Coverdell (with 48 percent) from being elected. Coverdell, who views abortion as a state issue, was opposed to FOCA but did not meet the criteria for endorsement. During the general election there was no NRLPAC activity in the race. But a combination of the PAC's adamant opposition to FOCA and Coverdell's likely votes on cloture overcame their disagreements on the Right-To-Life Amendment and other issues.

During the run-off the PAC contributed $2,500 to Coverdell's campaign and spent $15,327 on independent ads in behalf of his candidacy. Minnesota Citizens Concerned for Life Committee for a Pro-Life Congress was the only other pro-life PAC active in the race. It also made a $2,500 direct contribution to Coverdell and spent $8,585 in independent expenditures. NRLPAC behavior is typical of other groups within the religious right in this race. Although Coverdell was not its ideal candidate, he was seen as a vast improvement over Fowler. The PAC worked with other pro-life groups and the Georgia Republican party to elect Coverdell by a narrow margin. PAC director Carol Long said that their support for Coverdell was dictated by the special conditions of the 1992 election and that it did not mark the beginning of a new policy.

When then-senator Lloyd Bentsen (D-TX) resigned his Senate seat to become secretary of the Treasury, a special election for the remainder of his term became necessary. The May 1 primary was narrowly won by Kay Baily Hutchison, a pro-choice Republican who, like Coverdell, is opposed to FOCA. Because she failed to win 50 percent of the vote, a June run-off between Hutchison and Governor Ann Richard's appointee, Senator Bob Krueger (D-TX), was neces-sary. Krueger is a strong supporter of FOCA. The similarity between the two contests is striking; however, the Hutchison campaign and the NRLPAC were not able to come to terms over the form her opposition would take. This pre-vented the PAC from supporting her candidacy.

In a departure from its past practice, the PAC also backed two Independents and one Right-to-Life party candidate. None of these candidates won, although Stephen Grote (OH–1st) an Independent endorsed by Republicans, ran a credible race, finishing with 43 percent of the vote.

David O'Steen described the activity of the NLRC in the 1992 congressional races as taking place "in essentially every closely contested pro-life versus pro-abortion House and Senate contest across the country."[12] The PAC distributed 14 million pieces of mail and ran pro-life radio ads. In some congressional races graphic ads were used, which featured pictures of aborted fetuses. Only two candidates who used this type of ad won in the primaries: Michael Bailey, a Republican (IN–9th), and Daniel Becker, a Republican (GA–9th).[13] Both re-ceived small direct contributions ($250) and indirect contributions. Neither pre-vailed in November.

Other Issues

Abortion was not the focal point of every candidate backed by the NRLC. One of the races in which it was active was the contest in the 4th district of Georgia between John Linder (R) and Cathey Steinberg (D). The PAC contributed $4,000 directly to Linder and spent another $9,080 on behalf of his successful effort. Linder did not stress abortion as an issue: "Abortion was not the focus of my campaign, but my position had been strong and consistent."[14] The use Linder made of abortion in his campaign was typical of the eight new Republicans interviewed by *Policy Review*.

Although it might seem that an ideological PAC would welcome the opportunities that come from redistricting, the NRLPAC viewed redistricting in negative terms for two reasons. First, it thought that pro-life incumbents were treated unfairly either by being forced to run in new districts or by having their districts combined. O'Steen elaborates: "An example of this was Illinois, which had four pro-life incumbents redistricted into two districts."[15] The second negative impact on the NRLC's goals was the creation of minority districts. O'Steen described the situation: "Of the seventeen new minority districts, fifteen went to pro-abortion candidates, including all eleven new black majority districts which backed Democratic nominees, each of whom was pro-abortion."[16]

Conclusion

From the perspective of the NRLC, the results of the 1992 election were mixed. The right-to-life movement lost its major objective: President Bush was defeated. For the first time since the end of the Carter administration, it faces a hostile White House. The other major goal, electing enough members of Congress to prevent FOCA from being enacted, met with greater success. In his article on the 1992 elections, O'Steen tried to maximize popular support for the pro-life position. The failure of some of the successful pro-life Republican candidates to emphasize abortion is a cause for concern. If the PAC continues to endorse candidates like Coverdell, this will mark the beginning of a new, more pragmatic type of political activity. It also holds out a way to reconcile factions within the Republican party.

Notes

1. Gerald N. Rosenberg, *The Hollow Hope: Can the Courts Bring About Social Change?* (Chicago: University of Chicago Press, 1991).
2. Frederick S. Jaffe, Barbara L. Lindheim, and Philip R. Lee, *Abortion Politics: Private Morality and Public Policy* (New York: McGraw-Hill, 1981), p. 77.
3. Eve R. Rubin, *Abortion, Politics, and the Courts* (Westport, CT: Greenwood Press, 1987), p. 110.
4. See Michele McKeegan, *Abortion Politics: Mutiny in the Ranks of the Right* (New York: Free Press, 1992), p. 25.
5. Jaffe et al., *Abortion Politics*, p. 121.
6. McKeegan, *Abortion Politics*, p. 31.
7. Ibid., p. 95.
8. Darla St. Martin, "The Poll that Really Counts: Abortion and the 1988 Election,"

in David Andruko, ed., *The Triumph of Hope* (Washington, D.C.: National Right to Life Committee, 1989), p. 25.

9. Carol Long, "The Challenge of 1992: Everyone Is Responsible, Everyone Is Needed," *National Right To Life News* 19:1–2 (January 1992) p. 1.

10. This figure does not agree with the D Index for the NRLPAC at the Federal Election Commission. The D Index indicates an expenditure of $1,884 on behalf of the Clinton candidacy. Carol Long is certain that all money in regard to Clinton was spent against his candidacy.

11. Although sixteen of the thirty-one pro-life PACs devoted some of their resources to support the Bush campaign, only Wisconsin spent money against the Perot campaign.

12. David N. O'Steen, "Bush Defeat Spurs Pro-Life Movement to Renewed Effort on Behalf of Unborn Babies," *National Right To Life News* 19:16 (November 16, 1992), p. 12.

13. Keith Glover, "Aborted Fetus TV Ads Work for Two Candidates, Create Furor," *Wall Street Journal*, October 3, 1992, p. A4.

14. John Linder, "How I Won," *Policy Review* no. 64, p. 55.

15. O'Steen, "Bush Defeat Spurs Pro-Life Movements," p. 13. The NRLC was part of a wide range of groups opposed to the 1982 revisions to the Voting Rights Act, which created minority districts.

16. O'Steen, "Bush Defeat Spurs Pro-Life Movements," p. 13. It should be noted that the NRLPAC did support the only candidate endorsed by the Black Americans for Life PAC, Lonzy F. Edwards, Sr. (D-GA 2nd).

Part Three

"Mom and Pop" PACs

The PACs discussed in this section are primarily one-person operations that rely on the ingenuity of their PAC directors to give them a presence on Capitol Hill. Unlike the institutionalized PACs in the previous section, these organizations lack the staff and resources to gather information on many candidates. They also lack the financial resources to contribute to large numbers of candidates and usually develop a short list of candidates to whom they regularly contribute. For these reasons, these small PACs may have been limited in their ability to respond to the unique opportunities of the 1992 election cycle.

However, the PAC managers for these small committees often have considerable latitude in selecting candidates for this list. Unlike the institutionalized committees, the directors of these PACs are generally not constrained by an established set of procedures and criteria for contribution decisions. If a manager of a "Mom and Pop" PAC decides to support a set of nonincumbent candidates, he or she usually need not seek approval from a board of directors at a later meeting. In a few cases, such as that of the American Association of Publishers PAC (AAP-PAC), the PAC manager formally consults with a board, which almost always approves the contributions. For other PACs, there is no formal consultation.

The influence of these small PACs is often a function of the creativity and political skills of their directors. AAP-PAC contributes little money to political candidates, but its manager uses high-visibility political and social activities such as fundraising events and networking to enhance the PAC's influence. Similarly, the National Federation of Federal Employees (NFFE) is a small union PAC that is limited by Hatch Act restrictions in its fundraising. NFFE has formed a coalition with other small union PACs, and together these committees evaluate the voting records and electoral prospects of congressional incumbents and host fundraising breakfasts to maximize the group's contact with those to whom they give. The Conservative Victory Committee, faced with the decline in direct-mail returns of conservative PACs, has focused instead on raising money from a small number of wealthy individuals who share its ideology.

Despite these innovative strategies, all of these PACs must limit the number of candidates to whom they contribute. Some focus on candidates in a particular geographical area. Prior to the 1992 elections, FHP-PAC gave to candidates in western states and in Guam, where the corporation operates. Others concentrate on incumbents who serve on particular committees. The AAP-PAC, for example, directs most of its money to members of particular committees, such as the House Judiciary Committee. Still others limit their contributions to candidates that take a narrowly defined ideological position. JustLife gave to pro-life candidates who supported spending on social welfare programs.

Although each of these small PACs is unique, they represent the majority of all committees. Most PACs have small staffs and limited financial resources. Their contribution behavior is less predictable than that of large, institutionalized committees, both because of the latitude accorded to the PAC director and because of the idiosyncratic nature of the factors that shape their contributions.

12

The National Federation of Federal Employees: Big Little Man?

William A. Pierce

With an average annual budget of only $29,118, the National Federation of Federal Employees PAC (NFFE) could easily be classified as a small PAC with little influence in the political process. However, looks can be deceiving. Through its relationship with the Fund for Assuring a Fair Retirement (FAIR) and the Federal Postal Coalition, NFFE is able to achieve far greater access and wield far greater influence in Congress than the mere examination of its contribution records would indicate.

In the Beginning

NFFE began its life in 1917 as a charter member of the American Federation of Labor (AFL), representing workers from several federal government agencies regardless of craft. This makes it different from most AFL unions. NFFE membership was originally composed of mostly professional employees. Its membership now includes mostly blue collar workers in over 400 locals, representing 150,000 members in 42 federal agencies. Membership is concentrated in the Departments of Defense and Interior, especially the Bureau of Land Management.

NFFE split from the AFL in December of 1931 over the issue of the Classification Act, which established the system of pay grades. The AFL rejected this system because it interfered with collective bargaining. NFFE leadership disagreed, however, arguing the system to be in the best interests of its membership because it provided a more stable bargaining system. Even now, there is little formal contact between the two groups, although informal contact does occur.

A PAC Is Born

NFFE leadership saw the Federal Election Campaign Act (FECA) as providing a potential channel of access to Congress. On March 20, 1978, the Executive Committee formally sanctioned the Public Affairs Council as an official PAC intended to supplement its legislative department. Another reason for establishing the PAC was the Hatch Act,[1] which restricts all federal employees from engaging in direct political activity, including fundraising. The act prevents NFFE members and officers from directly participating in raising money for the union's PAC.

NFFE and its PAC are two separate organizational entities because of the Hatch Act's ban on political activity by federal employees. According to its charter, NFFE's president can be on the PAC committee only if he or she is a retired federal employee. The immediate past president retired from government service and became a member of the PAC's executive committee. National presidents cannot sign any fundraising letters and are barred from having prior knowledge of their contents. Regional vice presidents are also prohibited from engaging in fundraising. Only the PAC director and secretary/treasurer, who are not NFFE members, can make fundraising appeals to the union's membership.

The Hatch Act represents a major impediment to NFFE fundraising efforts because the PAC staff are not well known to the national membership. The PAC director during the 1992 cycle, Josh Neiman, believes that the PAC's fundraising is hindered by the inability of the union's president to sign fundraising appeals. Another Hatch Act restriction prohibits NFFE from using payroll deductions as a fundraising tool. This method is the principle fundraising mechanism of nearly all nonfederal unions.

The PAC has an executive committee composed of three members. NFFE's legislative director serves as the PAC director. The PAC's secretary/treasurer is NFFE's legislative liaison. Each spends only one-third of his or her time on PAC duties. The third board member is NFFE's executive director. Although none of these staffers is a union member, they are not barred from communicating with union members. Therefore, the shared responsibilities result in those most familiar with NFFE's legislative goals working to accomplish its electoral objectives.

The PAC director and secretary/treasurer both have backgrounds in labor movement politics. The director, Josh Neiman, previously worked as a legislative assistant at the AFL-CIO, and immediately before coming to NFFE, he worked for the Subcommittee on Civil Service of the House Committee on Post Office and Civil Service. The secretary/treasurer, Claire Renner Hassett, previously worked on labor issues in the Texas State Senate.

Who and What Is NFFE PAC?

Several recent legislative actions have threatened the collective benefits for which NFFE has fought. They have energized the PAC. These include the 1978 Civil Service Reform Act, the 1983 reauthorization of the federal retirement system, and the Social Security Reform Act of 1983.[2] Other contemporary issues include the downsizing of the defense budget, the base closure plan, Social Security cost-of-living adjustments (COLAs), the federal deficit, and the growth of the bureaucracy. These issues threaten collective benefits as well as federal employment.

NFFE has members in nearly all fifty states who perform jobs varying from janitorial duties to the maintenance of some of the military's most sophisticated weapons systems. Only 4,500 to 7,500 of its members, or 3 to 5 percent, contribute annually to the PAC. NFFE conducts several membership surveys a year, none of which is directed specifically at PAC members. A recent survey focused on the issue of temporary workers, which NFFE represents. Other topics included health care issues, Lobby Week activities (which will be discussed later), and a survey of Department of Defense (DOD) employees' views on downsizing defense. The results are published in NFFE's two primary publications, *Federal Employees*, which is sent to all members of the union, and *NFFE 91*, which is sent to all local presidents and secretary/treasurers. The survey's findings are used to set NFFE's agenda, to inform members of Congress about what NFFE members think, and to tailor the PAC's contribution appeals.

NFFE's contribution decisions are made by the PAC director and secretary/treasurer. In the rare event of a disagreement, the executive director acts as arbitrator. NFFE staff members may make suggestions, which are communicated to all committee members. Although cash contributions are the major form of help NFFE can provide candidates, the PAC can also highlight the records of incumbents who have been supportive of the union's issues. The Hatch Act bars NFFE from becoming involved in presidential elections beyond communicating the candidates' issue positions in its publications.

The PAC has recently begun to use some new technologies and strategies. It now uses Legislate, an on-line computerized legislative tracking system, to follow Congress's agenda. The PAC and the legislative department use coordinated mailings to increase membership awareness of the PAC and to solicit donations. In addition, the PAC is conducting its first pledge drive, with one well-known and longtime NFFE member promising to shave off his beard at the national convention if the PAC raises at least $20,000. The PAC's staff are continuously searching for creative ways to raise money within the constraints imposed by the Hatch Act.

Sixty percent of the PAC's money is raised through face-to-face solicitations either at the national convention or during Lobby Week, when NFFE members come to Washington, D.C., to lobby members of Congress on union issues. At this time, the PAC staff directly solicit contributions from its members. This is the PAC's biggest single fundraising activity, accounting for 60 percent of its revenue. The remaining 40 percent is raised through direct-mail solicitations. The PAC has three categories of givers: the Congressional Club, whose members each give $25 annually; the Capital Club, whose members each give $50 annually, and the Presidential Club, whose members each give at least $100 annually.

Although the PAC has never surveyed its contributors, anecdotal evidence suggests that most are DOD employees, women, or retirees who are interested in politics and public policy issues. The only selective benefit they receive are club pins and PAC coffee cups. PAC officials try to provide PAC members with a sense of efficacy by encouraging them to become active in politics beyond their activities during Lobby Week.

NFFE does all its direct mail in house. The typical contribution to the PAC is between $15 and $20, with only a few members giving over $100 dollars annually. Some retirees try to raise money at the local level, holding events that typically raise anywhere from several hundred to several thousand dollars. Other PAC communication with contributors is limited to information conveyed through the general union newsletter.

Who Gets What?

PAC staff occasionally receive contributions earmarked for individual candidates and recommendations from members suggesting whom the PAC should support. By law, earmarks must always be followed, even if the national staff disagrees with them. Recommendations are seriously considered when setting PAC priorities. The PAC has some "friends" who receive contributions every cycle (see Table 12.1). "Friends" are defined as members of Congress who support NFFE when it counts most. Many of these "friends" serve on the House Post Office and Civil Service Committee, including the committee chair, William Clay (D) of Missouri, and Democratic Representative Gary Ackerman of New York. Overall, the PAC gave to seven members of the committee, including five of the fourteen Democrats on the panel. In addition, Democratic Senators John Glenn of Ohio and Tom Daschle of South Dakota are considered among the chief "friends" of NFFE (see Tables 12.1 and 12.2).

The PAC was no less conspicuous in its contributions to relevant senators. Senate "friend" Glenn is chairman of the Committee on Governmental Affairs. In the Senate, the NFFE contributed to twelve key senators, spreading its limited resources rather well (see Table 12.2).

Although NFFE does not officially take ideology or incumbency into consideration in its decisions, such considerations do matter. Historically, 95 percent of NFFE's contributions have gone to Democrats, with the proportions nearly equal in the Senate (94 percent) and the House (96 percent). PAC staff explain that Democratic incumbents are heavily favored because they control the House and

Table 12.1

House "Friends," Scores, Contributions, and Key Committees

Democrats			Republicans		
House Representative	Score	Contribution	House Representative	Score	Contribution
Ackerman (NY)[a,b]	100	$1,250	Gilman (NY)[b]	100	$500
Sikorski (MN)[b]	86	$1,550	Morella (MD)[b]	71	$250
Fazio (CA)[a,c]	100	$ 800	Schuster (PA)[f]	29	$300
Clay (MO)[a,b]	86	$ 800			
Hoyer (MD)[a,c]	100	$ 750			
Schroeder (CO)[a,b]	57	$ 750			
Andrews (ME)[a,e]	100	$ 500			
McClosky (IN)[a,b]	100	$ 500			
Horn (MO)[a,f]	100	$ 500			
Kostmayer (PA)[a,d]	86	$ 450			

Sources: Federal Election Commission; NFFE Voting Guide (1991).
Notes:
[a]NFFE "friend"
[b]Civil Service and Post Office Committee member
[c]Appropriations Committee member
[d]Interior and Insular Affairs Committee member
[e]Armed Services Committee member
[f]Public Works and Transportation Committee member

Senate. The PAC staff considers challengers only potentially influential and claim that the PAC only rarely supports them. This is especially true in the House, where between 1978 and 1992 incumbents received 84 percent of all NFFE contributions. In the Senate, incumbents received slightly less than half of contributions during this period, with challengers receiving 36 percent and open-seat candidates 15 percent. Because NFFE directed 70 percent of all contributions to House candidates during this period, overall a substantial majority of NFFE contributions went to House Democratic incumbents.

The reason NFFE gives to Senate challengers more frequently may come from the PAC's perception that Senate challengers are more substantial, credible candidates with a better opportunity of unseating incumbents. Historical trends show Senate races to be much more competitive. For the period 1980–92, the reelection rate was 93.5 percent for House members and only 83 percent for Senators.[3]

The Big Little Man

NFFE PAC is a member of both the Federal Postal Coalition and its related policy group, the Fund for Assuring an Independent Retirement (FAIR). FAIR

Table 12.2

Senate "Friends," Scores, Contributions, and Key Committees

Democrats			Republicans		
Senator	Score	Contribution	Senator	Score	Contribution
Glenn (OH)[a,b,f]	100	$800	McCain (AZ)[f,g]	50	$250
Daschle (SD)[a,g]	83	$500	Bond (MO)[c]	83	$250
Dodd (CT)[a,f]	100	$250			
Hollings (SC)[c]	83	$250			
Graham (FL)[a,d,h]	100	$250			
Fowler (GA)[a,c,e]	100	$250			
Mikulski (MD)[a,c]	100	$250			
Sanford (NC)[a]	100	$250			
Conrad (ND)[e]	83	$250			
Adams (WA)[a,c]	100	$250			

Sources: Federal Election Commission; NFFE Voting Guide (1990).
Notes:
[a]NFFE "friend"
[b]Government Affairs Committee member
[c]Appropriations Committee member
[d]Environment and Public Works Committee member
[e]Energy and Natural Resource Committee member
[f]Armed Services Committee member
[g]Select Committee on Indian Affairs
[h]Veterans' Committee member

was established to lobby Congress and share tactics and strategies with other members. The Federal Postal Coalition acts as a conduit for its members to contribute to candidates. Members of the coalition are PAC directors from participating groups.

FAIR meets weekly to discuss legislative activities. Several times per year, FAIR formally adjourns its meeting and the Federal Postal Coalition begins deliberations. Coalition members are encouraged to compile lists of candidates for whom they believe the Federal Postal Coalition should host a fundraising event. Two rules govern fundraising decisions: any group member can veto any other's suggestion, and fundraisers cannot be held for members of Congress who sit on relevant committees. The coalition follows the latter rule because its members believe that as individual PACs they already reach members on relevant committees; they see the coalition's goal as increasing the reach of its members. The goal is to have as many organizations show up for the events as is possible.

As the fundraiser nears, attending Federal Postal Coalition members cut their own checks, linking the contribution to the event and sending it to the candidate being feted. In doing so, Federal Postal Coalition members are careful not to give the appearance of bundling (the collection of separate checks from individuals and delivering them as a bundle). In a calculated decision, 60 percent of NFFE's contributions are made through Federal Postal Coalition fundraisers, with the remaining 40 percent simply sent to NFFE "friends" with no link to FAIR or the Federal Postal Coalition. The 60 percent contributed through FAIR fundraisers is given to candidates with whom NFFE has less contact and to whom it wants to raise its level of access. Through the FAIR association, NFFE is able to wield more influence than it can acting through its own small PAC.

In addition to committee membership, the PAC also uses its official voting guide in its decision criteria. The voting guide is a rating prepared by NFFE using the votes on issues it believes to be most important to its membership. The rating is derived by comparing how often individual congressmen agree with NFFE's established position (see Tables 12.1 and 12.2). Although the PAC does not base its decisions on party or ideology, Democrats are its primary beneficiaries. In 1992, only five out of seventy-one contributions (or 7 percent) were given to Republicans. Of the total, 65 percent of donations went to incumbents, 17 percent to challengers, and 18 percent to open-seat races. House members received 65 percent of all contributions, with House Republicans getting 6 percent of the House total and incumbents 84 percent. Senate Republicans received 6 percent of Senate contributions, and Senate incumbents received 46 percent.

For NFFE, 1992 represented somewhat of a change. Due to a high number of retirements and vulnerable incumbents attracting credible challengers, NFFE contributed to a near record percentage of open-seat and challenger races (35 percent). Only in 1986, when 48 percent of the PAC's contributions went to open-seat and challengers races, had it given more. This shift caused NFFE's giving to incumbents to drop from 89 percent in 1990 to 65 percent in 1992 in the House, and from 83 percent to 46 percent in the Senate. Overall contributions remained steady in 1992 at $25,200, up only slightly from $24,775 in 1990, but below the average of $29,118.

FAIR and the Federal Postal Coalition are the chief sources of the information NFFE PAC uses to learn about political campaigns. NFFE PAC staffers also attend forums sponsored by the Democratic national, congressional, and senatorial committees. On rare occasions they have attended Republican-sponsored events. The PAC does not have the resources to subscribe to outside publications, such as the *Cook Political Report* or the *Political Report*, and believes it can gain any information it requires through informal contacts within the general Washington community.

The 1992 Cycle

The primary issues NFFE used to guide its decisions in the 1992 cycle were the economy and quality of life, the federal budget and job security, the Civil Service Reform Act, the Civil Rights Act, the Thomas nomination to the Supreme Court, striker replacement legislation, unemployment compensation benefits extension, and the family medical leave bill. The most interesting changes in NFFE's giving patterns—its increase in giving to challengers and open-seat races—stem from the large number of competitive races and the uncertainty this created for the PAC director. Winners were not as easy to predict. The 1992 cycle also saw an increase in the number of FAIR/Federal Postal Coalition fundraisers and in the direct solicitations for money by members. They continued asking right up until the end.

According to the PAC's own officials, the size of NFFE's PAC is limited primarily by the constraints placed on it by the Hatch Act. With a liberalizing reauthorization working its way through Congress, it will be interesting to see whether NFFE's ability to raise money improves. However, there may also be other reasons for NFFE's inability to raise substantial money: reliance on the FAIR/Federal Postal Coalition relationship and union leadership's lack of emphasis on the value of the PAC. The union leadership's reluctance/inability to provide more operating funds to the PAC, and the dual role of the PAC director as legislative director and the lower priority given PAC activity, lead me to believe that a liberalization of the Hatch Act will not necessarily increase member contributions to NFFE's PAC.

Notes

1. For a more detailed discussion of the Hatch Act, see Congressional Research Service briefs IB87153 and 91-544 Gov.

2. This was a complete reorganization of federal benefits.

3. Norman J. Ornstein, Thomas E. Mann, and Michael J. Malbin, eds., *1991–1992 Vital Statistics on Congress* (Washington, D.C.: Congressional Quarterly & American Enterprise Institute, 1993).

13

The FHP Health Care PAC

John J. Pitney, Jr.

Issues have life-cycles.[1] A problem may fester quietly for years until it reaches the national political agenda as the result of either a crisis or the gradual buildup of concern from citizens and policymakers. Then comes a burst of public debate that culminates in new laws and rules. As policy implementation unfolds, the general public loses interest while groups with a special stake in the issue come to dominate the field. The policy eventually causes, aggravates, or fails to stop new problems that plague the issue area. At this point, the cycle may start again. The politics of health care provides a clear example of the life-cycle of issues.

In the 1950s and early 1960s, concern with the health problems of the elderly and the poor gradually mounted and eventually resulted in the Medicare and Medicaid programs. Two decades later, the nation's medical needs appeared to be outstripping the capacity of these programs: problems of cost and access were vexing all segments of society, not just senior citizens and welfare clients.

In the late 1980s and early 1990s, health issues were again rising to the top of the political agenda. This changing political environment affected all the players in health policy, especially the providers of medical care. One such provider was a California-based corporation, FHP, Inc. (Family Health Program). An analysis of the FHP Health Care Political Action Committee provides a case study of how a corporate PAC adapts to the life-cycle of its issue area.

Corporate History

In traditional medical care, patients pay for each individual service, a practice that may encourage physicians and hospitals to carry out needless services in order to generate more income. One alternative in this practice is the health maintenance organization (HMO), which directly provides or arranges for health services in exchange for a monthly premium. HMOs engage in "managed care," for their fixed income encourages them to curb costs by avoiding needless procedures and practicing preventive medicine. (Critics argue that they pinch too tightly and deny necessary treatment.[2]) HMOs have played an increasingly important role in American health care: between 1976 and 1991, total national enrollment grew from 6 million to 34 million.[3]

Dr. Robert Gumbiner was an HMO pioneer. In 1961, he converted his Long Beach, California, medical practice to the nonprofit Family Health Program, providing prepaid health services to 2,000 patients.[4] The organization later changed its name to FHP, Inc., because some people mistakenly thought that the company engaged in family planning.[5]

From its earliest years, FHP had a strong interest in public policy. In the 1960s, Dr. Gumbiner lobbied for the passage of Medicare and decided that FHP would be the first California health maintenance organization to contract with Medicaid (the means-tested health program for the needy, called Medi-Cal in California). In 1973, Congress passed the HMO Act, which required large employers to add an HMO option to employee benefits packages wherever HMOs were available.[6] Four years later, FHP became a federally qualified HMO.[7] In 1983, FHP launched its Senior Plan, thus becoming the first HMO on the West Coast to contract with the federal government to provide prepaid health services to Medicare beneficiaries. The company converted from nonprofit to for-profit status in 1985 and became publicly held the following year. When the company celebrated its thirtieth anniversary in 1991, it had annual revenues of more than a billion dollars and served 640,000 members—one-third of whom were Medicare beneficiaries.[8]

Origins of the FHP Health Care Political Action Committee

Once FHP became subject to federal regulation under the HMO Act, the company's management decided to establish a presence on Capitol Hill. FHP opened its Washington office in 1977 and shortly thereafter started a political action committee. Originally called the Health Services Political Action Committee (or HESPAC), it was a relatively modest operation in its early days. In the 1980 cycle, it gave a little over $10,000 to federal candidates, a figure that rose only to $12,300 in 1982 (see Table A.12).

According to Stuart Byer, who served as PAC treasurer for much of the 1980s, the PAC did not need to spend much because the company still covered only a limited geographic territory: southern California, Utah, and Guam. "We weren't an ideological PAC, we were an access PAC," he explained. "We contributed to maintain some profile with the delegation that covered the areas in which we operated. We tried to pop out of the business community as a politically active company that would become known to members and staff."[9] The

PAC also gave to lawmakers who served on subcommittees dealing with HMO issues.

For much of the 1980s, health care occupied a relatively low place on the national political agenda, so the PAC focused not on participating in grand debates but on "tweaking the regulatory structure."[10] The PAC worked with the Washington office to gain access to the Hill and to educate lawmakers and regulators about the fine points of the managed-care industry. Overall, FHP and other HMOs stirred little controversy because policymakers tended to see them as a "white-hat industry" (that is, a nonpolluting industry that provides important and valuable services to people).[11]

Organizational Response to Political Change

FHP's world began to change in the late 1980s. The deregulatory fervor of the early Reagan years was giving way to renewed calls for government intervention in the marketplace.[12] In the field of health care, years of medical price inflation were taking their toll. During the 1980s, real spending on health care grew at an annual rate of 3.4 percent. Between 1988 and 1989, constant-dollar health spending rose by 4.3 percent, the largest increase in nearly a decade. In 1989, total expenditures reached $603 billion, or $2,346 for every American.[13] In 1990, the Census Bureau reported that more than a quarter of the population had lacked health insurance for at least a month between 1985 and 1987.[14] Medicaid, the health insurance of last resort, was straining many state budgets.[15] And federal outlays for medical care went from 12 percent of total federal spending in fiscal 1980 to 16 percent in fiscal 1990.[16]

Proposed solutions ranged from a Canadian-style national health insurance system to a tax-credit plan to help individuals buy their own insurance. One concept that gained increasing support was "managed competition," in which health care consumers would join large purchasing cooperatives that could bargain down prices.[17]

For good or ill, all of these plans promised to have a major impact on the managed-care industry, and FHP responded with renewed attention to the policy arena. In 1988, Christobel Selecky, regional vice president for California and chair of the PAC board, worked to increase PAC fundraising. In 1990, the company hired its first-ever vice president for government affairs, Nick Franklin, a political heavyweight who had formerly chaired the New Mexico Democratic party and run for the United States Senate. Franklin believed that the PAC was integral to the company's public affairs efforts and that it had to expand its base of support.[18] "It's important now, especially as the national health care debate intensifies," he said in 1991, "that the PAC become more important in the process and that employees protect not only the livelihood of the corporation but the livelihood of their own families by getting involved in the political process."[19]

The PAC embarked on a two-part effort at reinvigoration. The first step was structural reorganization (see below) to ensure broader representation on the PAC board. The second step was an employee education program: an ongoing effort to get employees involved in the political process. Its message would be that because FHP is in a highly regulated industry, its people must understand the impact of Washington politics.[20]

In March 1991, the FHP PAC board approved the plan. With Stephen Gaskill of the Wexler Group, Herb Schultz of the company's Washington office then drafted the education program, including the assignment of PAC captains in each company facility. The PAC also produced a videotape, "You're in Good Company," designed to persuade employees to join the PAC because it promoted their own interests. A new PAC director came aboard in July, and over the summer, PAC membership went from 500 to 800. According to the PAC director, Lisa Minshew Pitney, many of the new members contribute only one dollar per pay period, "but it is important to get members as well as dollars. By making even a small contribution, people get the feeling that they have a stake in the political process. And they 'back up their bets' by getting politically involved in other ways."[21]

Organization

In general, a corporate PAC board serves to make sure that the PAC and the government relations unit know, and respond to, the needs of the entire corporation.[22] At FHP, the PAC's board of directors has the final say over PAC activities. Its revised organization chart provides for regional representation by apportioning one member each from Arizona, New Mexico, Nevada, Utah, and Guam. Each of the company's six California regions is to have a representative, as is FHP Life Insurance and the FHP corporate headquarters. (The board itself may choose additional members.) The members of the PAC board are chosen by regional PAC committees, whose members are in turn chosen by regional PAC members. At each FHP workplace, center coordinators run grassroots PAC activity.

The corporation pays the overhead costs of the PAC, which is run from the corporate headquarters in Fountain Valley, California.[23] The vice president for government affairs serves as PAC treasurer, while day-to-day management is the responsibility of the PAC director, who is a manager in the government affairs department.

Fundraising and Membership

The PAC enjoys a good deal of support from the corporation. The chief executive officer is personally committed to the PAC, and all senior managers belong. According to Stuart Byer: "What's important is the vision and awareness of the

CEO. The PAC gets you a place at the table, but you have to know which fork to use."[24] The FHP Health Care PAC is unusual among corporate PACs in that its members come not only from management but from other levels of the company. About 10 percent of FHP employees (including nonsupervisory workers) contribute to the PAC, with the usual contribution ranging from one to five dollars per pay period. The PAC solicits memberships from corporate supervisors on a one-to-one basis, and other employees receive mailings twice yearly.

The PAC's promotional video, "You're in Good Company," is used to recruit new members by stressing the employee's personal stake. In the narrator's words, "Right now federal legislators are making decisions about laws and regulations that will determine the future of the managed care industry—your future." The video features testimonials from current PAC members and from Representatives Bill Richardson (D-NM) and Christopher Cox (R-CA), who attest to the PAC's effectiveness in educating lawmakers about the managed-care industry. The PAC publishes a quarterly newsletter, *Voices*, which informs members about PAC activities and developments in the politics of health care. The fall 1991 edition included an interview with the chair of the New Mexico Regional PAC Committee, who reiterated the point made in the video: "I tell employees that the PAC is an investment in their future, and that their contributions allow them to participate in shaping the future of health care policy in the United States."[25]

In February 1992, the PAC director mounted "government awareness week," a series of presentations in every region to demonstrate the importance of political action. The goal was not simply to generate more PAC contributions but to persuade FHP employees to engage in other forms of political participation as well. Observed Herb Schultz of the Washington office:

> I would much rather send a contribution to a candidate who realizes that 1,200 of his constituents are employed by FHP. Note that our PAC newsletter is called *Voices*—as opposed to the PAC having a single voice. We want members of Congress to understand health maintenance organizations and to understand that they have constituents who work for or use HMOs.[26]

Decisionmaking

In its early days, the PAC gave to state and local candidates as well as federal ones. Today, however, state and local contributions come from the corporate treasury, so that the PAC can concentrate on federal races.[27] In consultation with the Washington office, the PAC treasurer and director draft the proposed budget, which outlines proposed contributions to federal candidates. The board members then take these proposals to the regional PAC committees, which may suggest changes. After these suggestions are in, the PAC board approves the budget. The PAC board meets on a quarterly basis, and when last-minute decisions are necessary, the staff will either conduct a telephone poll or send information by mail and ask the board members to make a decision on a particular contribution. PAC members may make candidate recommendations directly to officials or board members, who take these preferences very seriously. The PAC has also sent out candidate evaluation forms to solicit members' views.

In addition to member preferences, the PAC takes several other items into account when making contribution decisions:[28]

1. Region. The PAC focuses most of its support on candidates who represent FHP service areas: California, Utah, Arizona, Guam (which elects a delegate to the House), and Nevada (whose first FHP facility opened in 1992). In the 1990 cycle, the PAC gave nearly 80 percent of its contributions to candidates from these places.
2. Knowledge of managed health care issues. In 1990, for instance, the PAC gave $3,000 to Senator Jay Rockefeller (D-WV), who chaired the bipartisan Pepper Commission on health policy and has emerged as a leading congressional expert in the field.[29]
3. Position on a relevant committee or in party leadership. Among other 1990 recipients were: House majority leader Richard Gephardt (D-MO), House Ways and Means Chairman Dan Rostenkowski (D-IL), House Energy and Commerce Chairman John Dingell (D-MI), and House Energy and Commerce ranking Republican Norman Lent (R-NY). As Table A.12 indicates, the FHP PAC has always given most of its contributions to incumbents. It has no explicit policy on partisan support: it gave more to Republicans in 1986 and 1988, and more to Democrats in 1990.

No one is guaranteed automatic support: candidates are reevaluated every cycle. Unlike most other corporate committees, this PAC does contribute to candidates in contested primaries. In the 1992 California Republican Senate races, for instance, it contributed early in both Republican and Democratic primary campaigns. It has no policy against giving to opposing candidates, provided that they have similar stands on managed care. Because the PAC deals with a relatively small universe of candidates (i.e., those from its regions and incumbents in health-related posts), it has less extensive information needs than PACs of larger corporations.

Nevertheless, the PAC does require a substantial amount of political intelligence, for which it relies upon several sources: First, it encourages its members to supply it with political news about their home states. The PAC director explains, "They are usually following the races closely, reading the local papers, talking to people who are involved in the campaigns. The PAC relies heavily on them."[30] And those who sit on the PAC board have strong influence over contributions to candidates in their states. Second, the FHP Washington office supplies current information about national politics and health care policy. Headed by

Janet Newport, associate vice president of federal affairs, the Washington office monitors regulatory and legislative activity that could affect FHP's interests.[31] Third, the PAC gets information from all national party committees. According to the PAC director, "In general, the party committees won't tell you their candidates will win if they have absolutely no chance. Where they will shade the information is a case in which their candidate might have a chance and they want to funnel money into that race."[32] Fourth, both the Washington office and the corporate headquarters receive various trade journals and publications from groups such as the National Association of Business PACs (NABPAC). In June of 1992, NABPAC held a pre-election conference where PAC directors received briefings from political consultants, journalists, and lawmakers.[33]

Health Care Politics in 1992

The 1992 election season really started with the 1991 special election for a Pennsylvania Senate seat. Appointed Democratic Senator Harris Wofford beat former governor and attorney general Richard Thornburgh—and most observers attributed his upset victory to his support for national health insurance. "If criminals have the right to a lawyer," said Wofford in his television commercials, "I think working Americans should have the right to a doctor."[34]

Although one subsequent survey showed that the condition of Pennsylvania's economy was really the top issue of the race,[35] politicians concluded that medical care would affect the 1992 campaign at all levels. According to FHP's Nick Franklin:

> The Thornburgh–Wofford race was a flashpoint. In 1991, there was interest but it had not yet reached the candidate agenda. The Wofford election gave it focus. Since then, people have realized that other issues influenced the Pennsylvania race—but health care was one of them.[36]

Health care had now shifted from the low-visibility politics of regulatory marginalia to the high politics of nationwide concern. Such political arenas attract a huge array of interest groups.[37] As of 1992, 741 national health organizations had offices or representatives in Washington, compared with just 117 in 1979.[38] In July, the consumer group Citizen Action reported that health-related PACs had increased their contributions to congressional candidates by 22 percent, from $7.9 million during the first fifteen months of the 1990 election cycle to $9.6 million during the same period of the 1992 cycle.[39]

Although some accounts depict the "health care industry" as a monolith, health groups have diverse and competing interests. FHP and other HMOs could gain from "managed competition" proposals that would favor relatively low-cost providers. By contrast, some fee-for-service providers fear that such reforms could put them out of business.[40] And according to Nick Franklin,

You also have an interesting internal struggle. As the insurance industry recognizes that managed care is growing, the insurance industry is trying to define managed care broadly. The trade associations, by contrast, have tried to keep the definition narrow. So one source of confusion is the industry's own definition of itself.[41]

The Campaign Season

FHP faced high stakes in a contentious field. The PAC's challenge was further complicated by economic woes. The recession cut into FHP's growth, so in November 1991 the company had to trim its corporate staff.[42] There were now fewer employees for the PAC to solicit, and those who remained were skittish about donating their money. Still, membership did edge up, so the PAC was able to increase its contributions over 1990 levels (see Table A.12).

The FHP PAC had to target these resources with great care. On the one hand, it could not afford to give the legal maximum ($5,000 per election) to every candidate it supported. On the other hand, it strove not to give too little, lest it get lost amid the tumult of conflicting voices. Most of its contributions, therefore, ranged between $500 and $1,000.

In sharp contrast to previous years, open-seat candidates got a large share of these contributions. Indeed, during the 1992 cycle, the FHP PAC gave more money to candidates for open House seats than in the previous seven cycles put together. This change largely reflected the unusual character of the 1992 election: not only did the year see a historic level of retirements, but redistricting boosted competitiveness in a number of the newly open districts.[43] The PAC was receiving more and more requests from candidates, and it now had to scrutinize their views more than ever before. During the campaign, PAC director Lisa Minshew Pitney explained:

> In evaluating open-seat candidates, we try to see if they support managed care. We consider geographic location: we're giving to two candidates in San Diego, where the company is expanding. We'll also look at the candidates' potential for advancement to health-related committee assignment.[44]

She added, however, that some open-seat candidates showed far less persistence than incumbents in seeking PAC support. Whereas some PACs wait until late in the season to make decisions, the FHP PAC intentionally gave early. In some cases, it made contributions to candidates who then lost primaries. For instance, the PAC supported two unsuccessful candidates—Representative Tom Campbell (R-CA) for the Senate and Representative Marty Russo (D-IL) for reelection to the House. Both contributions made sense, however, because Campbell and Russo were major figures in the health care debate who appeared to have a good chance of success.

California had two U.S. Senate races in 1992. In the general election for the seat of retiring Democratic Senator Alan Cranston, the PAC contributed to Democratic Representative Barbara Boxer but not to Bruce Herschensohn, the conservative commentator who had bested Tom Campbell in the GOP primary. Until the last days of the campaign, Boxer seemed to hold a big lead, though her final margin of victory was quite modest. The state's other Senate seat had belonged to Pete Wilson, who won the governorship in 1990. As his replacement, he appointed Republican John Seymour, who then had to seek election for the final two years of the term. The FHP PAC gave both to Seymour and to his Democratic challenger, Dianne Feinstein. Although the PAC had seldom contributed to challengers, Feinstein's advantage was so wide and durable as to warrant an exception.[45]

The PAC did not make gender or ethnicity a criterion for contributions. It backed Feinstein and Boxer not because they were women but because they were strong candidates who supported managed care. Similar considerations prompted the PAC to support the Senate candidacy of Representative Ben Nighthorse Campbell (D-CO), whose victory made him the only Native American in the United States Senate.[46]

Results

How did the FHP PAC fare in the 1992 campaign? One measure consists of the number of races in which it supported winners (whether or not it also gave to candidates in those races who lost primaries or general elections). During the cycle, it made contributions to candidates running in ten Senate races, backing eight winners, for a success rate of 80 percent. In the House, it backed thirty-three winners in thirty-nine races, for a success rate of 85 percent.[47] A slightly different measure consists of the total share of contributions that went to winners. Of $96,000 it gave to congressional candidates during the cycle, $66,000 went to contenders who ultimately won, for an overall success rate of 69 percent. The PAC also gave more than $30,000 to national party committees; meanwhile the corporation and its chairman gave $80,000 in "soft money."[48] Accordingly, FHP's political presence is greater than the individual contributions might suggest.

The bulk of the PAC's contributions went to incumbents, most of whom won. Still, there were some surprises. It gave to Republican representative John Rhodes of Arizona, who was upset by Democrat Sam Coppersmith. The outcome was not a drastic defeat for FHP interests, however, because Coppersmith had argued against total government control of health care and instead supported managed competition.[49]

In the race for the White House, both George Bush and Bill Clinton took stands that heartened the managed care industry. President Bush's comprehensive reform program put great emphasis on "coordinated care" (e.g., HMOs).[50] Bill Clinton, after tentatively embracing different proposals, spoke of encouraging companies to enroll their workers in large, privately managed insurance networks.[51] "It's a very pro-managed care concept," said Nick Franklin after Clinton's election, "We're positioned very well to respond and to be very proactive in the new Administration."[52]

The Future

Soon after taking office, President Clinton underscored the health care issue by naming his wife, Hillary Rodham Clinton, as head of a task force to plan comprehensive reform of the health care system. Together with the presence of 110 new House members and 13 new senators, the prospect of radical change created a fluid environment for interest groups. The managed-care industry was particularly engaged, because some of the reforms under study by the task force would reportedly work to its advantage. "It won't be business as usual, but HMOs can better adapt compared with the standard fee-for-service part of the industry," said FHP's Nick Franklin.[53]

Although many of the congressional newcomers had supported the general concept of managed competition, many balked at taking specific stands. This vagueness made it difficult to foretell what they would do in office, but it also gave FHP and other HMOs an opportunity to influence their views. The FHP Washington staff worked hard to make contact with new members and to provide the relevant committees with policy information.

During the 1992 campaign, Franklin described a problem facing the managed-care industry: some policymakers disdained the concept.

> Bob Squier did focus groups with Hill staffers, whose definition of "managed care" was "compromised care." They saw it as cutting quality to cut cost. They incorrectly thought that managed care eliminates choice: in fact, choice exists within the managed-care system. But the learning curve is accelerating. All the sophisticated reforms have included managed care as an element.[54]

In 1993, the industry's climate appeared to grow warmer. Policymakers increasingly spoke about managed care, and the general public began to embrace the idea. In a New York Times/CBS poll, 54 percent of respondents said they would opt for a fixed-fee system (as practiced by HMOs) if given the chance, compared with 36 percent who preferred fee-for-service medicine.[55] FHP in particular gained some political points from a generally favorable profile in *Newsweek*: "FHP's experience presents grounds for optimism, and a close look at the way the company operates suggests that managed care could be a major plus in health reform."[56]

No one could be sure of which reforms would ultimately become law. But the 1992 election and its immediate aftermath provided some favorable signs for FHP. And by helping maintain the company's presence in the political community, the PAC played a role in improving the chances for success.

As the health issue gathered momentum, the PAC got back to work. As planned, it had practically emptied its coffers during 1992. But with payroll deductions supplying its main source of funds, it already had money coming in. In this early stage of the next election season, the PAC director reflected on options for change. Although the PAC appeared to have a good formula for the early identification of candidates, it seemed prudent to consider a larger contingency fund, so that it could make last-minute contributions where conditions warranted.[57]

The PAC's future depended in part on the state of campaign finance law; here, too, the Clinton administration offered a favorable omen. Currently, PACs may give up to $5,000 per candidate per election (primary and general), whereas individuals may only give $1,000. During the campaign, President Clinton proposed limiting PAC contributions to the $1,000 level.[58] As we have seen, the FHP PAC seldom topped this level during the 1992 election cycle—and its experience was quite typical.[59] The limit proposed by President Clinton would instead affect the AMA and other interests with rich PACs, thereby producing a more level playing field within the interest-group community. But in the early days of the Clinton administration, campaign finance reform would have to wait a while. Health care was leading the national agenda.

Notes

1. Anthony Downs, "Up and Down with Ecology—The 'Issue-Attention' Cycle," *Public Interest* 28 (Summer 1972), pp. 38–50; John W. Kingdon, *Agendas, Alternatives and Public Policies* (Boston: Little, Brown, 1984); Rogene A. Buchholz, William D. Evans, and Robert A. Wagley, *Management Response to Public Issues* (Englewood Cliffs, NJ: Prentice-Hall, 1985), ch. 1.

2. Robert Kuttner, "Sick Joke: The Failings of 'Managed Care,' " *New Republic*, December 2, 1991, pp. 20–22.

3. U.S. Department of Commerce, Bureau of the Census, *Statistical Abstract of the United States 1992* (Washington, D.C.: Government Printing Office, 1992), p. 106.

4. FHP, Inc., "Fact Sheet," Fountain Valley, California, October 1991.

5. Leslie Berkman, "HMO Iron Man Leaves Quite a Healthy Legacy," *Los Angeles Times*, November 4, 1990, p. D3.

6. For a history of the HMO Act, see Joseph L. Falkson, *HMOs and the Politics of Health System Reform* (Chicago: American Hospital Association, 1980).

7. The four-year gap stemmed from bureaucratic delay: it took the Department of Health, Education and Welfare a long time to develop rules governing how HMOs would qualify under the 1973 act. See Lawrence D. Brown, *Politics and Health Care Organization: HMOs as Federal Policy* (Washington, D.C.: Brookings Institute, 1983), pp. 276–344.

8. FHP, "Historical Highlights," October 1991.

9. Personal interview with Stuart Byer, associate vice president for government and public affairs, FHP Inc. Cerritos, California, November 22, 1991.

10. Ibid.

11. Ibid.

12. David Vogel, *Fluctuating Fortunes: The Political Power of Business in America* (New York: Basic Books, 1989), pp. 290–300.

13. Kathleen M. King and Richard V. Rimkunas, "National Health Expenditures: Trends from 1960–1989," *Congressional Research Service Report* 91–588 EPW, July 29, 1991; Kathleen King and Richard Rimkunas, "National Health Spending 1990: A Description of Spending by Services and Players," *Congressional Research Service Report* 91–814 EPW, November 18, 1991.

14. U.S. Department of Commerce, Bureau of the Census, "More than One-Quarter of Population Had Health Gaps, Census Bureau Survey Shows," Press release CB90–71, April 12, 1990.

15. Julie Rovner, "Cost of Medicaid Puts States in Tightening Budget Vise," *Congressional Quarterly Weekly Report*, May 18, 1991, pp. 1277–84.

16. Calculated from U.S. Office of Management and Budget, *Budget of the United States Government Fiscal Year 1992* (Washington, D.C.: Government Printing Office, 1991), pp. 7–129.

17. John B. Judis, "Whose Managed Competition?" *New Republic*, March 29, 1993, pp. 20–24.

18. Personal interview with Nick Franklin, Fountain Valley, California, June 26, 1992.

19. FHP Health Care PAC, "You're in Good Company," videotape, March 1991.

20. Personal interview with Herb K. Schultz, Washington, D.C., October 22, 1991.

21. Personal interview with Lisa Minshew Pitney (the author's wife), Anaheim, California, January 5, 1992.

22. Dan Clawson, Alan Neustadtl, and Denise Scott, *Money Talks: Corporate PACs and Political Influence* (New York: Basic Books, 1992), p. 45.

23. It is common practice for business corporations to pay PAC administrative costs. See Sara Fritz, "GE Spent Nearly as Much on Its PAC As Its Employees Gave," *Los Angeles Times*, March 27, 1993, p. A8.

24. Byer interview.

25. *Voices* (FHP Health Care PAC newsletter), Fall 1991, pp. 4–5.

26. Schultz interview.

27. Schultz interview. The one exception is Arizona, which forbids corporate contributions.

28. *Voices*, Summer 1992, p. 4.

29. Phil Duncan, ed. *Politics in America 1992* (Washington, D.C.: CQ Press, 1991), pp. 1593–94.

30. Personal interview with Lisa Minshew Pitney, San Diego, California, October 24, 1992.

31. *Voices*, Winter 1993, p. 1.

32. Minshew Pitney interview, October 24, 1992.

33. Personal interview with Lisa Minshew Pitney, Anaheim, California, June 28, 1992.

34. Dale Russakoff, "How Wofford Rode Health Care to Washington," *Washington Post National Weekly Edition*, November 25–December 1, 1991, pp. 14–15.

35. Pennsylvania postelection study, conducted November 6–7, 1991, for the Health Insurance Association of America by Public Opinion Strategies and Mellman & Lazarus.

36. Franklin interview.

37. A similar intensity surrounded the original passage of Medicare in 1965. See Theodore R. Marmor, *The Politics of Medicare* (Chicago: Aldine, 1973).

38. Robert Pear, "Conflicting Aims in Booming Health Care Lobby Help Stall Congress," *New York Times* (national edition), March 18, 1992, p. A17.

39. Citizen Action, "Unhealthy Money: The Growth in Health PACs' Congressional Campaign Contributions" (Washington, D.C., July 22, 1992, photocopy).

40. Marlene Cimons, "Managed-Care Issue Divides U.S. Doctors," *Los Angeles Times*, March 23, 1993, pp. A3, A16.

41. Franklin interview.

42. Anne Michaud, "FHP to Cut Its Corporate Staff as Growth Slows," *Los Angeles Times*, November 18, 1991.

43. Gary C. Jacobson, "Congress: Unusual Year, Unusual Election," in Michael Nelson, ed., *The Elections of 1992* (Washington, D.C.: CQ Press, 1993), pp. 153–82.

44. Minshew Pitney interview, October 24, 1992.

45. Kathryn L. Pearson, "California's 1992 United States Senate Races: Myth and Reality Surrounding the 'Year of the Woman'" (Senior thesis, Claremont McKenna College, 1993).

46. Minshew Pitney interview, October 24, 1992.

47. *Voices*, Winter 1993, p. 4.

48. Liz Pulliam, "New Sources of 'Soft Money' Develop in OC," *Orange County Register*, February 1, 1993, p. A14.

49. "The New Congress," *Congressional Quarterly Weekly Report* special supplement, January 16, 1993, p. 38.

50. The President of the United States, *The President's Comprehensive Health Reform Program* (Washington, D.C.: Government Printing Office, February 6, 1992).

51. David Lauter and Robert Rosenblatt, "Clinton Spells Out His Plan to Curb Health Care Costs," *Los Angeles Times*, September 25, 1992, pp. A1, A25.

52. Ted Johnson and James M. Gomez, "O.C. Firms Sense Opportunity Knocking in Clinton Victory," *Los Angeles Times* (Orange County edition), November 5, 1992, p. D1.

53. Jerry Hirsch, "A Dose of Reform," *Orange County Register*, April 4, 1993, pp. K1, K4.

54. Franklin interview.

55. Robin Toner, "Support Is Found for Broad Change in Health Policy," *New York Times* (national), April 6, 1993, pp. A1–A10.

56. Tom Morganthau and Andrew Murr, "Inside the World of an HMO," *Newsweek*, April 5, 1993, pp. 34–40, at p. 40.

57. Personal interview with Lisa Minshew Pitney, Orange, California, December 6, 1992.

58. Bill Clinton and Al Gore, *Putting People First* (New York: Times Books, 1992), p. 46.

59. David G. Magleby and Candice J. Nelson, *The Money Chase: Congressional Campaign Finance Reform* (Washington, D.C.: Brookings Institute, 1990), pp. 85–89.

14

The American Association of Publishers PAC

Julia K. Stronks

In 1973 the American Association of Publishers (AAP), headquartered in New York City, opened a Washington office and hired its first lobbyist. Months later the AAP Political Action Committee (AAP-PAC) was formed to develop a "visual presence" on Capitol Hill.[1] Over the past nineteen years, the AAP's lobbying efforts and PAC contributions have been integrated and directed by one woman, Diane Rennert. Although the influence of a small trade/membership PAC may be limited in scope, the organization of the AAP-PAC sheds light on the ability of a small number of people to use pooled contributions in a way that effects policy change for an organization's benefit.

Organizational Development and Fundraising

The American Association of Publishers is made up of over 200 book publishing corporations. In past years the book publishing industry was run by "families and men of literature."[2] The AAP catered to the publishers' interests in an informal way. However, twenty years ago the national growth of the publishing industry led the AAP to consider the need for a legislative issues office in Washington. Diane Rennert, a former political aide to Senator Hubert Humphrey, was hired to lobby Congress on issues of interest to publishers such as taxes, postal rates, copyright law, and First Amendment protections.

Rennert's prior Capitol Hill experience had led her to believe that although organizations could not purchase votes or influence legislators directly, the contributions of even a small PAC could give an organization a "presence" in

Washington politics. When a PAC gives a token "thank you" to a legislator, the PAC's parent organization and its lobbyists are considered part of the Washington game. When Rennert came to the AAP, one of her primary goals was to raise $25,000 to spend on developing the capital to play the game. As part of her job as a lobbyist Rennert organized the AAP-PAC; it took five years to raise the first $25,000. Although nine people work in the Washington AAP office, most of these are researchers. Diane Rennert is the sole lobbyist, and she is the PAC manager. She has one assistant, and together they accomplish all of the tasks associated with the two roles. Of all the office members, only the director of the AAP has any direct contact with the PAC. His involvement is limited to informal discussions with Rennert and to his position on the executive committee of the PAC.

The PAC's executive committee is charged with making decisions regarding PAC contributions. It is made up of Rennert, the AAP director, and three chief executive officers (CEOs) of member book publishing corporations. The committee members keep in touch with each other by telephone and make their decisions through Rennert. The committee has never met in person.

The AAP pays for the costs of running the PAC, including Rennert's salary and office overhead. The PAC raises its own contribution funds, but because Rennert is both the PAC director and the lobbyist, the PAC budget seems to do double duty. For example, as a lobbyist, Rennert believes her most effective role is to take a seat on the fundraising committees for key senators or representatives. The legislators will recognize her on their fundraising steering committee and will remember her in the future. Therefore, when invitations to fundraising events come in, Rennert decides which ones to accept based on who the legislator is and how much the ticket costs. Sometimes political friends will give her a ticket to the event so she does not need to use PAC funds to pay for it. At the event, Rennert tries to get on the spearheading committee for raising further campaign funds. As a lobbyist Rennert creates a presence by raising funds for legislators; as a PAC manager she creates a presence by offering token thank-yous to legislators for their positions on particular issues.

The PAC budget is generated by an annual direct-mail effort. Each year Rennert mails one PAC fundraising letter to the CEO of each of the 230 book publishers that are members of the AAP. This letter requests permission to solicit funds from the employees of the publishers and asks the CEO to support the request by writing letters to the employees.

Approximately twenty CEOs give permission immediately. Rennert follows up on the others with telephone calls; in the final count about twenty to thirty publishers will ultimately allow solicitation of PAC contributions. Of those giving permission, approximately 75 percent of the CEOs will write a letter to their employees. Money is received from about 75 percent of the publishing companies that allow solicitation.

According to Rennert, there is a strong relationship between the amount of money gathered from any one publishing company and the willingness of the CEO to get behind the request and write a personal fundraising letter. The CEOs generally solicit money from their top executives, not from all employees. Rennert believes that although the contributions come directly to the PAC, and the PAC assures contributor confidentiality, the greatest incentive for an executive to give money is to please the CEO. Fifty percent of the checks are for less than $100, and the average check is for $20. The most any one individual has ever given is $500.

The PAC offers no material or solidary benefits to its contributors. The AAP publishes a newsletter, but all member corporations receive it whether or not they contribute to the PAC. Each contributor receives a thank-you letter from Rennert, but that is the extent of contact between the contributors and the PAC office. There are no other fundraising activities or meetings. The PAC raises on average about $20,000 per year, making it very near the median for trade or membership PACs who were active in recent election cycles.

AAP-PAC has attempted to raise money in other ways. For example, members of the AAP board of directors have been asked to contribute. These requests were unsuccessful. Fewer than 50 percent of the board gives contributions. Groups of five or six CEOs have also been invited to gather together to discuss the necessity of PACs. Rennert believes that these meetings have been unsuccessful because publishers in general disassociate their business from politics, and they do not want to get involved in the fundraising process. Moreover, they do not want to acknowledge the importance of money in generating a "presence" on Capitol Hill. Even when Rennert tries to educate them with respect to "reality"— that is, the need to bind together to bring about policy change in areas that affect them, such as copyright law, piracy, pornography issues, postal rates—publishers "refuse to be galvanized as a group."[3] Some scholars have argued that groups are reluctant to form PACs because they have "an aversion to politics" and because the general public perceives a "vague scent of corruption" surrounding corporate contributions.[4] Rennert agrees and attributes the difficulty in getting the PAC off the ground to the book publishers' belief that politics "is dirty and doesn't really involve them."[5]

Another reason for the difficulty in raising significant amounts of PAC money is that several PACs compete for the same funds. The book publishers are also contacted by lobbyists and PACs that raise funds for distribution by the Direct Marketing Association, the Magazine Association, and so forth. Rennert has no formal contact with the lobbyists or PAC managers of these organizations, but they are her friends and she socializes with them. Although they do not meet together as a group to discuss strategy or public policy initiative, they do influence each other in informal ways. For example, Rennert helped the PAC manager of the Direct Marketing Association in organizing that PAC, and the lobbyists for these organizations do share information about legislators, other lobbyists, and fundraising opportunities.

Distributing Money: The Decisionmaking Process

The AAP-PAC gives almost all of its money to incumbents.[6] In 1990, incumbents received all of the PAC's contributions during that election cycle, and in 1992 incumbents received all but 5 percent (see Table A.13). Rennert says the PAC contributions are so small that they function not as a "financier of elections" or an "influence peddler" but rather as a "thank you for work done in the past."[7]

Concern for important committees makes up 98 percent of the PAC's decisionmaking process. For example, the Judiciary Committee is important because it deals with legal issues such as copyright. Although agenda power and committee assignment are key, Rennert also keeps an eye on new people who seem to be sponsored by powerful legislators, banking on the belief that these people will be powerful in years to come.

More money goes to House members than to Senate members simply because there are more representatives than senators. The PAC limits contributions to approximately $500 for House and $1,000 for Senate elections because of its limited financial resources.

The PAC responds to contribution requests as they come in. It gives money only during the last year of a senator's election cycle. It never responds to letters requesting contributions. Rather, it responds to invitations for fundraising breakfasts or other meetings. Rennert believes that these meetings give the PAC more for its dollars because they allow it to develop greater presence. The executive committee does not meet in person, but its members are contacted by telephone or fax. Committee members are given funding recommendations, which are generally accepted. Occasionally, an executive committee member will make a suggestion during the year regarding a particular candidate; such suggestions are usually accommodated. The PAC director occasionally responds to personal appeals, including those from senators and representatives who request funds for another candidate.

Contributors have no formal means to influence the decisionmaking process. At the end of the year, the PAC publishes a list of contributions in the AAP newsletter. This is the only information the PAC gives to its constituents or contributors about its work. The AAP-PAC example raises serious questions about the claims that some people make for the existence of PAC democracy. Although the PAC may encourage constituent activity in the form of contributions, donors are not participators in the democratic process. As Frank Sorauf has said, the PAC's relationship to the donors is, at most, one of responsiveness: "Intrinsic to the decision to contribute to a PAC is the decision to leave effective political decisions to others. . . . Ironically, at least in a democracy, that limited involvement is a major source of [the PAC's] political effectiveness."[8]

1992 Election

The political environment of the 1992 election year was one of "desperation" and "emotional gridlock," according to Rennert. Redistricting, the public's reaction to the savings and loan crisis, and the House banking scandal created a frenzy among the incumbent candidates as their efforts to raise campaign funds intensified. Capitol Hill analysts expected the 1992 political environment to have an impact on the way individuals and political institutions like PACs made election choices. However, although 1992 did bring change to Capitol Hill, it had little effect on the decisionmaking process of the AAP-PAC. The PAC's decisions regarding its money were made, as usual, by its executive committee. Although the peculiarities of this election year may have caused the executive committee to discuss the candidates more thoroughly, there were no conflicts among the decisionmakers regarding recipients. Candidates were more tenacious than ever in their bids to receive financing, but the PAC's constituents, the publishers, did not increase their contributions. Moreover, the publishers were not more involved in the decisionmaking process— the PAC received no requests from its constituents for more information about its activities. The only difference that the 1992 election year made to the AAP-PAC financing decisions is that the PAC broke with tradition and gave more money than usual to some of its most important candidates if those candidates were particularly threatened in their election bids. The PAC funded the same number of candidates as in the past with the same number of total dollars, but in some instances individuals received a little more money than in past years, making the pie smaller for other candidates. The money was distributed throughout the year as it came into the PAC office; because the PAC works with limited funds, there was nothing reserved for the end of the election cycle.

Once again, nearly all of the PAC's contributions went to incumbents. Because more House incumbents were involved in close races in 1992, the PAC increased its share of contributions going to House Democratic incumbents from 40 percent to 52 percent. Senate Democratic incumbents, in contrast, received a smaller share of total PAC contributions than in 1990.

In general, the election results were viewed favorably by the AAP-PAC. However, the PAC does anticipate some problems in the areas of copyright, computer technology, and the recycling issues as the new administration develops its own perspective on the tension between government involvement and private-sector initiative. After an election, the PAC always introduces itself to the new members of Congress by using the informal social circuit. Courtesy calls are one method of informal introduction, and the AAP holds parties of introduction for new senators and representatives as well as "old friends." The AAP will hold educational seminars to discuss difficult or technological aspects of legislative proposals with the new members. In addition, the AAP hosts a "Freedom to Read" party for all members. The party is an informal opportunity to encourage continued sensitivity to First Amendment issues.

Conclusion

The 1992 election brought more than 100 new members of Congress to Washington, D.C., but as the AAP-PAC looks to the future it sees few changes in store for the way in which it operates. In recent years, some scholars have spoken of the need for campaign finance reform or term limitations to restore public confidence in Congress. According to Rennert, one of the most significant aspects of the recent election is that it proved that term limitations are unnecessary. The power of incumbents is easily checked by the will of the electorate. Rennert does believe, however, that campaign finance reform is both necessary and inevitable, but that the reform package should emphasize total spending limits rather than limits on individual contributions. She points out that although the public may believe PACs are involved in "influence peddling," this suspicion holds no merit for the activities of the AAP-PAC. No one buys votes for the sum of $500 to $1,000, and the PAC is a mechanism by which even a small contributor can be heard.

Although the democratic character of a PAC that does not involve constituents in its decisionmaking could be called into question, Rennert emphasizes that in a PAC structured like the AAP-PAC the publishers have the opportunity to become more involved. The PAC's constituents are kept fully informed of its activities, and although they are not specifically involved in the funding choices, the constituents' preferences, if expressed, are taken into account.

Notes

1. Personal interview with Diane Rennert, Washington, D.C., November 12, 1991.
2. Ibid.
3. Ibid.
4. Larry J. Sabato, *PAC Power: Inside the World of Political Action Committees* (New York: W.W. Norton, 1984); and Edward Handler and John R. Mulkern, *Business and Politics* (Lexington, MA: Lexington Books, 1982).
5. Rennert interview.
6. According to Federal Election Commission statistics, throughout the past decade the AAP-PAC has contributed to only two challengers running against an incumbent.
7. Rennert interview.
8. Frank Sorauf, *Money in American Elections* (Glenview, IL: Scott, Foresman, 1988), p. 98.

15

Grassroots Organization in Defense of Mother Nature: The Clean Water Action Vote Environment PAC

Robyn Hicks

Clean Water Action describes itself as "a national citizens' organization working for clean and safe water at an affordable cost, control of toxic chemicals, and protection of our nation's natural resources."[1] Created in 1970, the organization's primary activities are in grassroots organizing. The goals of the group are to bring environmental issues home to the average American and to influence environmental policies through the governmental process. As an environmental group, the organization wants to protect the environment. As an interest group, it wants to see people get elected who will be favorable to their interests.

Through the formation, in 1986, of its PAC, Clean Water Action Vote Environment (CWAVE), the organization has succeeded in combining both goals. Clean Water Action's activities are premised on the belief that because governmental officials make environmental policy, the PAC's primary focus should be electing environmentalists. Unlike most PACs in Washington, whose goals are often only the short-term influence with specific legislators, CWAVE has a broader, more long-term goal of influencing policy agendas by gradually filling national, state, and local legislatures with environmentalists.

Organizational Structure and Evolution

Clean Water Action's grassroots structure begins in the living rooms of America. Every day, environmental activists, many of whom are students, conduct what they term "field canvasses" across the country. The job of the canvassers is to go door to door talking to people about environmental issues. During their visits, canvassers attempt to mobilize people to write letters to their members of Congress about environmental issues affecting their communities. They may attempt to get their listeners to help conduct telephone polls on environmental issues, attend rallies to stop environmentally detrimental actions in their communities, or simply consider the impact of their actions on the environment. One activity that canvassers always encourage is giving money to become a member of Clean Water Action.

In addition to field canvassing, Clean Water Action does a fair amount of direct election work. Originally, they worked only indirectly with environmental PACs, including the League of Conservation Voters. The growth of Clean Water Action's campaign work, however, persuaded the organization to form its own political action committee. The PAC makes endorsements, gives funds to candidates, and communicates to its members about elections.

Over the past five years, the organization has grown dramatically. In 1986, the PAC contributed about $10,000 to all candidates. In 1990, it raised and spent approximately $100,000, including that spent by its state affiliates. This growth in fundraising has given the PAC the opportunity to expand its involvement to include more state and local races, furthering the grassroots goals of the organization.

The structure of Clean Water Action is quite complex. At the national level (represented by the Washington office), the organization is broken down into three branches (see Figure 15.1). The first, and primary, part of the organization is the Clean Water Action Project.[2] This is the membership branch of the organization. Its distinction from the other branches is primarily centered around the Internal Revenue Code and the Federal Election Campaign Act (FECA). Its classification as a 501(c)(4)—"a nonprofit corporation or association designed to develop and implement programs for the promotion of 'social welfare,' "[3]— gives it a tax-exempt status,[4] while allowing a broader range of political activities. The 501(c)(4) organization is allowed unlimited lobbying activities[5] and limited election activity.[6] It is this branch of the organization that conducts canvassing operations and membership drives.

The 501(c)(4) organization is the parent organization for the other branches and is by far the largest unit. It is run by a national board of directors. Various aspects of administration are handled by several standing committees devoted to such activities as development and budgeting. However, the bulk of this branch of the organization lies in its core of grassroots workers. Hundreds of canvassers work nationwide to bring environmental issues into the living rooms of Americans, encouraging them to become more environmentally conscious and to become members of Clean Water Action. The success of this solicitation is evidenced by the current nationwide membership of over 1 million.

The second branch, Clean Water Action Fund, is the education and research side of the organization. Under IRS regulations, this branch of the organization is classified as a 501(c)(3) organization. A 501(c)(3) organization is "a nonprofit

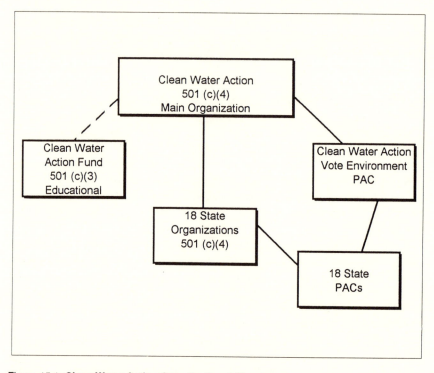

Figure 15.1. **Clean Water Action Organizational Structure**

corporation . . . or trust which engages in educational, religious, scientific or other charitable activities and is exempt from federal income tax under Internal Revenue Code section 501(c)(3)."[7] Because these regulations restrict lobbying activities and prohibit political campaign activity, Clean Water Action uses this branch for what its director terms "moms and apple pie kind of stuff," such as training environmentalists, staff, volunteers, and members to get involved in elections and to deal with environmental issues. This is not a membership organization. Instead, its funds come from pro-environment foundations or individuals who may be looking for tax deductions. Because this branch of the organization is prohibited from engaging in campaign work, it has almost no association with the PAC and refrains from sharing employees as much as possible.

The third branch of the organization, Clean Water Action Vote Environment, the PAC, is considered the real political arm of the group. While the PAC is controlled by the 501(c)(4), it is considered a separate political organization under the tax code and FECA reporting requirements and as such must keep a separate bank account. The 501(c)(4) pays for administrative and fundraising costs for the PAC, including rent, telephones, printing, and staff, but it has no part in any direct or in-kind contributions to candidates. In addition, all direct campaign work must take place through the PAC and be financed by the PAC.

For example, when the PAC holds press conferences related to particular campaigns, the organizers of the conference, as well as any overhead costs directly associated with the conference (such as copying, advertising, long-distance calls) are paid for by the PAC.

The director of the PAC is the only full-time permanent CWAVE employee at the national level. During presidential election years, the director often hires a full-time assistant. In 1991, as the organization became more involved in electoral activity, it formed a national PAC committee of eight members, distinct from the national board of directors.

PAC funds can only be solicited from members of Clean Water Action—the 501(c)(4). Thus, the larger the membership of the parent organization, the greater the PAC's fundraising potential. This has encouraged the organization to use a door-to-door grassroots strategy for both expanding membership and fundraising.

In asking for money, the group uses very specific appeals. Telephone-bank callers might inform members which candidates are supporting the Clean Water Act, the competitiveness of their elections, and other environmental issues. They then indicate that in order to get specific legislation passed, they need "your" money this year. Because all funds come from grassroots efforts, 90 percent are in denominations of between $25 and $35. However, a few big contributors give up to $5,000 a year. The organization offers no special incentives for giving, and the PAC surmises that most contributors are "armchair activists."[8] They are interested in the issues but lack the motivation to get actively involved. By writing a check to an environmental group, they feel that they have done their part for the environment.

Clean Water Action is also tied to twenty-two separate offices in approximately eighteen states.[9] All of these offices are run by separate 501(c)(4) organizations and have their own PACs. While the practical relationship between the national and the state PACs is very close, the distinctions between these organizations are very important. To meet FEC reporting requirements, each state PAC has its own account, from which it must make its expenditures. Due to differences in federal and state law, some state PACs can contribute general membership funds to candidates for state or local office. Federal law, however, prohibits PACs from contributing general membership funds to candidates for federal office. Instead, they must receive contributions specifically designated to the PAC and given within the limits established by the FECA. If California Clean Water Action Vote Environment wants to participate in the California gubernatorial race, it must do so from its own funds or may use funds from the national PAC. However, when the director of the California PAC decided to hold a press conference for Diane Feinstein, who was running for a U.S. Senate seat in California, he had to clear this activity with the national office and go on the national PAC payroll for the length of time required to organize and hold the press conference. Thus, the legitimate transfer of funds works like a one-way valve. The state PAC may not make contributions to or expenditures on behalf of any federal election, nor may it transfer funds to the federal PAC. Transfers from the federal PAC to the state PACs, on the other hand, are permissible.[10] Therefore, the employees of the state PAC must temporarily become employees of the national PAC before being permitted to work on any federal races.

Only one state organization, New Jersey Environmental Federation, retains a year-round election staffer. Due to limited funding, all other state PACs dissolve their staffs when they are not involved with elections. Typically, the PAC directors merely shift into another function within the state 501(c)(4) organization. State directors, for example, often become involved in lobbying when the legislature is in session; conduct election work during an election year; and focus on fundraising, membership drives, and canvassing at other times.

During election years, each state PAC sets up a steering committee made up of members and other environmental activists. The committees recruit and evaluate candidates and make endorsement recommendations to the federal PAC committee. Each state committee operates differently. For example, in Virginia, where election work within the organization is relatively new, there is a very small, six-member, informal committee. In New Jersey, the oldest election organization, there is a very formalized system in which the state organization parallels the national organization, including a state steering committee, development committees, and a PAC.

Decisionmaking within the Federated PAC

The PAC's endorsement and contribution processes are quite complex and reflect the relationships between the state- and federal-level PACs. It is the highly structured nature of this system that serves to inhibit conflicts between the different levels of the organization. Additionally, this structure creates a great deal of stability, which remains even during what could be unsettling personnel changes.

At the start of each election cycle, the federal PAC designs a questionnaire containing questions on issues of concern to its members. The questionnaires are then distributed to the state offices, where they are often modified to fit the issues of greatest concern to the local community. In Colorado, dams and wilderness are important, while in Virginia, coastal issues are significant. The state offices will then give the questionnaire to all candidates in a particular race.

Candidates with strong environmental records are more likely to return the surveys. In a recent special election for a congressional seat in Virginia, the candidates were diametrically opposed on environmental issues. Kay Slaughter was an environmental activist before she became involved in politics. George Allen, on the other hand, had a very poor voting record on environmental issues as a Virginia state delegate. Slaughter promptly returned her questionnaire, while Allen did not even bother to reply. It was obvious to him that he would never get the support of an environmental group.

Once the questionnaires are completed, they, along with any other information gathered about the campaign, are reviewed by that state PAC's steering committee. Because there is generally a clear difference between the candidates, funding decisions in state committees are almost always made by consensus. A number of other factors are also considered. Only candidates with reasonable chances of winning are given funds because the PAC has limited resources. The actions of other environmental groups are also taken into consideration. If a group such as the Sierra Club endorses a different candidate, CWAVE confers with the other group(s) to gather additional information. Once the research on the candidates and the election is completed, the state committee addresses the following questions: Can we make a difference in this contest? Is there much of a difference between the two candidates on environmental issues? How great an impact would the outcome of this election have on environmental policy? If the state PAC decides favorably for a candidate, it then turns the information over to the federal PAC with a recommendation for endorsement.

The federal office has a designated form to be completed by the state PAC for each candidate it endorses. The form, attached to the questionnaire, includes all the basic information about the election: candidates, parties, current polling data, activities of other environmental groups, and major issues. Sometimes state PACs include letters of recommendation or literature in which the candidate talks about the environment.

Candidate information is gathered from a variety of sources. CWAVE's director reports that the PAC has frequent contact with the Democratic Congressional Campaign Committee (DCCC). Former CWAVE director Sandra Ledbetter reports that she had a very difficult time extracting information of any type from the various Republican committees, even when the PAC was endorsing a Republican candidate. She explained in a personal interview, "There is not much of a history of a relationship between the Republican party and environmental groups." The Maryland state PAC director indicates that she receives most of her information from the candidates themselves. Because of the smaller, community atmosphere in state legislatures and legislative races, the PAC will often have a longstanding relationship with the candidates and therefore know them and their records very well.

Once the information is complete, the federal PAC director sends the candidate information to the national PAC committee for perusal. Because committee members are spread around the country, no discussion takes place before each member is polled by telephone. This is generally not a problem, however, as the information about each candidate is quite comprehensive by the time it reaches committee members, and it is therefore quite clear which candidates will and will not be chosen for endorsement.

Determinants of Campaign Support

CWAVE estimates that roughly half of its campaign funds go to federal races and half are spent on state and local races. On the national level, House races are preferred over Senate races simply because it is easier to make an impact in them. Because Senate candidates often raise and spend several million dollars, a single contribution has less effect than in House races involving hundreds of thousands. Additionally, since environmental issues are more generally handled on the local, rather than the national, level, House candidates, with their more narrow constituencies, are preferred over Senate candidates, who may serve a state of many millions. Since 1988, CWAVE has designated only 26 percent ($11,220) of its federal campaign contributions to Senate candidates, while 74 percent went to candidates for the House of Representatives (see Table A.14).

Because of the need for local environmental influence, the PAC supports many state and local candidates. Ledbetter points out that many environmental problems for which an immediate difference can be made occur at the local level. Local issues may include whether or not to build an incinerator or landfill or how to determine what is an acceptable level of industrial dumping into a river. By becoming involved in these races, the PAC has an opportunity to influence both how the issues are discussed in the campaign and the election outcome itself. For these reasons, the organization strongly prefers the smaller state, local, and U.S. House contests to presidential or U.S. Senate campaigns.

Another reason for becoming involved at the local level is that local candidates have often not formulated concrete positions on environmental issues. Therefore, CWAVE has the opportunity to help shape the issue agendas for what Ledbetter terms "knee-jerk" environmentalist candidates. These are candidates who want to take strong stands on environmental issues but do not know what to say. The PAC can have its greatest influence with these candidates because it can educate them on the environmental issues in their districts, help them formulate policy positions, and even assist with press releases or speeches. By the time candidates run for the U.S. Senate, in contrast, they typically have been working on environmental issues for a long time, have a staff doing research for them, possess well-established policy stands, and are typically less receptive to suggestions by the PAC.

A candidate's party identification is not a crucial factor in determining whether a contribution will be given. While the overwhelming majority of federal contributions go to Democratic candidates, the PAC claims it would prefer to be more equally bipartisan in its giving. Since 1988, only one out of thirty federal candidates who received contributions from the PAC was a Republican. It is interesting to note that the candidate, Trudy Coxe of Rhode Island, currently serves on the national board of directors for Clean Water Action. "Actually," says Ledbetter, "we go out of our way to look for good Republicans." What they have found thus far is that Republicans have not been very focused on the environment.

On the state level, the endorsement of Republicans and Democrats is much more evenly balanced. Younger Republicans moving up through the ranks are more likely to support environmental issues than are those who have long been a part of the party establishment. Says Ledbetter, "I am optimistic that as those Republicans run for state legislatures, and state legislators run for national offices, we will see more good Republicans. But, for right now, there are always going to be more [good] Democrats."

The PAC directors indicate that CWAVE is more likely to give to challengers than to incumbents. As a progressive PAC with state affiliates, CWAVE is less likely to get close to incumbents than is a nonfederated Washington-based PAC whose staff may work with members of Congress on a daily basis. However, campaign finance records indicate that over the past three elections, the organization has actually given slightly more to incumbents than to challengers. During this same period, open-seat candidates have received more than twice the support received by incumbent candidates. Open-seat candidates are favored over challengers because they have a better chance of victory.

The competitiveness of a race is also a critical factor in determining support. If an environmental candidate has no viable opponent, the PAC will refrain from spending money in that contest. While ideology or issues beyond the environment are not often direct factors in deciding on a candidate, they do sometimes play a role. Ledbetter cites Republican Senator Jesse Helms of North Carolina as an example of a candidate who could never receive an endorsement from the group.

Looking only at the relatively small contribution levels of the PAC does not accurately capture the campaign influence of the organization. CWAVE estimates that 90 to 95 percent of the support it gives to candidates is in the form of in-kind contributions. The Maryland state director indicates that the Maryland PAC almost never gives money to candidates; most of its campaign activity comes through endorsements. This emphasis on endorsements has an impact on campaign strategies. For example, both Maryland PAC directors indicated that CWAVE does not think of its contributions as buying access to candidates. For this reason, the organization does not give money for debt retirement and would almost never support both candidates in a race. When situations do arise in which they are forced to choose between two very good candidates, they almost invariably decide to stay out of the race, holding to their belief that supporting both candidates sends a "mixed message." The PAC does not feel as if this decreases its access to the winning candidate, because ultimately this access is gained by the PAC's political base, that is, the support it has in the district and in the state for the environmental issues. Ken Brown, the most recent CWAVE director, states that while it might make sense for some PACs to contribute to both candidates, that is not how CWAVE operates. Unlike most PACs, there is a great value for candidates in just getting Clean Water's endorsement. Says Brown, "Our name is worth a lot of votes . . . because there is so much publicity and good will connected to our name, it is harder to [support both candidates]."

The 1992 Election

One of the PAC's major goals for the 1992 election cycle was to persuade good candidates to run for office. While the work currently being done to help existing candidates formulate environmental strategies and get elected is very effective, there is need for improvement in the candidate recruitment phase. The PAC director feels that this is the most difficult part of the process. Some of this difficulty lies in the "purist" attitudes of environmentalists. They feel that they are cleaning up the world and fighting for a safer environment and future. Yet, as Ledbetter points out, the fact that politics is perceived as a "dirty, nasty business" makes it very hard to convince these activists that they must be a part of the governmental process in order to change it. The strategy is, then, to educate and convince potential candidates that the best hope for influencing policy lies with having environmental activists in office.

The PAC had anticipated that redistricting would help in its election efforts. The creation of many new open seats was expected to give CWAVE many opportunities for candidate recruitment and training on environmental issues. CWAVE did anticipate some drawbacks caused by the redistricting process. First, the creation of so many open seats was expected to cause an administrative burden on state offices as they attempted to sort out what races would be most worthy of their efforts. Second, CWAVE might find itself choosing between two pro-environmental incumbents running against each other in a newly drawn district. A third expected consequence was the increased aggressiveness in fundraising by nervous incumbents whose district boundaries had been redrawn. Most incumbents will say they are in a tough race in an effort to gain campaign funds, because everyone else is saying the same thing. This was expected to make objective decisions about limited resources even more difficult. As a result, Ledbetter anticipated that endorsements and contributions would come later in the election cycle than usual.

The group found that most of its predictions did not come to pass. The multitude of open-seat races did increase the number of potential races for the PAC to become involved in, but CWAVE did not respond with increased spending. In fact, CWAVE's total congressional contributions for 1992 came to about two-thirds the amount they gave in 1990 (see Table A.14). The director during the 1992 election cycle, Ken Brown, indicated that elevated spending in 1990 was an outcome of the nationwide emphasis on congressional races in non-presidential election years. Almost half of CWAVE's disbursements in 1990 went to Senate candidates. In 1992, however, the PAC did not contribute any money to candidates for the U.S. Senate. Again, it should be noted that most of the organization's support comes in the form of in-kind contributions. Therefore, decreased cash contributions do not necessarily indicate decreased participation in campaigns.

As a result of redistricting, CWAVE did find itself confronted with hard choices between two very good candidates. In Maryland, for example, Wayne Gilchrest (R) and Tom McMillan (D), both candidates who had received CWAVE support in the past, were pitted against each other. While the Sierra Club endorsed Gilchrest, CWAVE opted to stay out of the race. Because of favorable ongoing relationships between the organization and both candidates, Brown did not believe that their choice would decrease their influence with the victor.

Finally, the PAC found that the requests for contributions were not very different from those in previous election years. While there may have been slightly more requests, the appeals were not made any later in the campaign than usual and they were not significantly different in content.

Doing well in an election year is not just about winning elections for CWAVE. While the group does look at who wins and who loses, CWAVE often measures success in terms of whether or not the environment became a central issue in the campaign. In this sense, 1992 was a successful year for the organization. From the perspective of the PAC's director, the selection of environmentalist Al Gore, Jr., as vice president made an enormous difference in bringing environmental issues to the forefront.

With an administration strongly supportive of environmental interests, CWAVE anticipates that it will now have to fight fewer defensive battles for the environment than in the past twelve years. Ken Brown states that in the past, polluters and developers have had very good relations with the administration, resulting in perpetual proposals to weaken regulations and extend compliance deadlines. With the arrival of the Clinton administration, Brown anticipates that CWAVE will now be able to turn its attention to more positive initiatives on the environment and less "rear-guard" defensive action.

Looking toward the Future

In looking toward the future, CWAVE anticipates the passage of campaign finance reform legislation. When asked what recommendations he would have for finance reform, Director Ken Brown adamantly declares, "Public financing!" From CWAVE's perspective, anything short of public financing will only hurt the organization more than it does its larger opponents. Brown indicates that because CWAVE's resources are fairly small compared to most of the PACs that support opposing viewpoints, public financing would "level the playing field a little more." Brown believes that those with more resources will find loopholes and other creative ways to get their money into elections. Therefore, he feels that anything short of public financing is a waste of time.

In planning for the next election, CWAVE does not intend to make any significant changes in its decisionmaking structure. There has been some discussion about doing more polling and focus groups, particularly in races in which the PAC is uncertain if it should give its support. Brown states that the most valuable activities it can focus on are raising more resources and providing training and technical assistance to chapters so that they can be more effective in performing their campaign work.

In the near future, there is little anticipation of changes in the decisionmaking structure of the organization. This highly structured system has created a stability in the organization that allowed for efficient decisionmaking even amidst what could have been tumultuous personnel changes. The PAC's director through the 1990 election, Sandra Ledbetter, left Clean Water Action early in 1992 to work on the staff of a congressional campaign. Ledbetter was replaced by former New Jersey director Ken Brown. During what might be considered the busiest time of the year for most election-centered organizations, the last three weeks prior to a major election, Director Ken Brown was away on his honeymoon. Just after the election Brown informed Clean Water Action that he would be leaving in January 1993 to begin his own environmental consulting firm. The position of CWAVE director was filled by Sue Sergent later that year.

Clean Water Action does plan on continuing its election work through its national PAC and its state affiliates. State organizations began preparing in 1993 for the gubernatorial and state legislative races held in November of that year. Even while the national PAC temporarily lies dormant, grassroots activities continue throughout the country in attempts to defend Mother Nature.

Notes

1. *Clean Water Action News*, Winter 1991.
2. Considered the "parent organization," this branch is referred to as Clean Water Action or the 501(c)(4) organization.
3. Perkins Coie, "Non Profit Organizations, Public Policy, and the Political Process: A Guide to the Internal Revenue Code and Federal Election Campaign Act" (Washington, D.C.: Citizens Vote, Inc., 1990), p. 23.
4. Membership dues and contributions, however, are not tax deductible.
5. This is true as long as the lobbying is directly related to the primary purpose of the organization.
6. Currently, Clean Water Action employs a full-time congressional lobbyist.
7. Coie, "Non Profit Organizations," p. 3.
8. In fact, former PAC director Sandra Ledbetter admits that contributors generally have very little influence on the PAC's activities and that members who do get involved do so only after the decisions have been made.
9. It is interesting to note that neither PAC director I spoke with could tell me exactly how many state organizations were in existence. Sandra Ledbetter estimated eighteen, while one year later Ken Brown suggested that there were about fourteen.
10. Coie, "Non Profit Organizations," p. 45.

16

Le PAC C'est Moi: Brent Bozell and the Conservative Victory Committee

Ronald G. Shaiko

Throughout the last decade, the world of nonconnected ideological PACs has changed significantly. This change has had a disproportionate effect on conservative ideological committees. Today, conservative PACs are feeling the pinch of the economy like most political enterprises. However, there is an additional burden felt by many organizations that are heavily dependent on direct mail as a means of organizational maintenance.

Perhaps the best example of the volatility of the conservative political market dependent upon direct mail is the rise and fall of the National Security PAC (NSPAC). At first glance one might expect this organization to represent pro-defense interests. In this case, the name is a bit of a misnomer. While the names of several retired military officers are featured prominently on the PAC's letterhead, the organization's major project in the 1988 presidential election was known as "Americans for Bush." This PAC was responsible for the most controversial aspect of the 1988 campaign—the Willie Horton advertisement.

NSPAC was founded in April of 1986. During its first twenty months of operation, it raised and spent approximately $800,000. Then the direct-mail explosion hit. While most conservative PACs had experienced their peak direct-mail fundraising efforts in the early 1980s, NSPAC was quite successful in mobilizing conservative support on the issue of the Strategic Defense Initiative (SDI). The Reagan message of "Peace through Strength" continued to be a marketable idea. In the election year 1988, NSPAC generated $9.5 million, largely through massive direct-mail expenditures. Unfortunately for the PAC, by

181

the end of 1988 it was more than one million dollars in debt. Today, the PAC is dead for all intents and purposes. However, the Federal Election Commission requires that PACs showing outstanding debts continue filing financial reports. As of January 1993, NSPAC has debts and obligations totaling more than $1.25 million. Of this debt, more than $800,000 is owed to the firms responsible for the PAC's direct-mail and telemarketing efforts.

At least one individual in the conservative political industry views this meteoric rise and subsequent demise as an important object lesson for the 1990s. L. Brent Bozell III has been involved in conservative political activity since the late 1970s when he came to Washington looking for a job in the movement. Upon his arrival he quickly met with several of the more prominent activists, his entree being his uncle, William F. Buckley, Jr. One of the activists he met was Terry Dolan, then chairman of the National Conservative Political Action Committee (NCPAC). In early 1980, Dolan hired Bozell as a researcher. Within seven years Bozell rose to become finance director, president, and chairman of the board, following Dolan's death.

The NCPAC experience, like NSPAC's rise and fall, also taught Bozell a great deal about the organization and maintenance of a political enterprise. In his seven years at NCPAC, he saw the organization grow from six full-time employees to almost forty. According to Bozell:

> You had all sorts of researchers, political directors, assistants, administrators; there were all sorts of things going on. As a result, a lot of money was being raised, but a lot of money wasn't going out [to candidates]. In 1978 and 1980 you could sneeze and raise money from the conservative element; that has changed also. There was attrition with the lists that were being used. It was becoming more and more expensive to use direct mail; there was a complacency factor, and there was a proliferation of conservative groups. Everything was making it more and more difficult. So while you had a larger bureaucracy, you had less money to play with. What happened? Some groups went out of business; some groups should have gone out of business; some still should go out of business; and other groups that are really trying to do something were just limping along.[1]

As a result, in October of 1987, Bozell organized the Conservative Victory Committee (CVC), having resigned as head of NCPAC a month earlier. At approximately the same time, he and several others created the Media Research Center, a 501(c)(3) tax-exempt foundation aimed at putting together "the most exhaustive research facility ever to document and expose the leftist bias in our national media in order to advance the cause for political balance." Bozell is perhaps most widely known for his role as chairman of the Media Research Center. He regularly appears on network news, CNN, and C-SPAN as well as various political talk shows. His articles on the media are often found in the *Washington Times*, the *Wall Street Journal*, and in conservative opinion journals such as the *National Review*. In 1990 the Media Research Center published an edited volume that seeks to identify a liberal bias in the various media outlets.[2]

Structure

Due to his concerns about the financial struggles evident in other conservative political organizations, Bozell was committed to making the CVC a low-cost enterprise, with little reliance on direct mail for fundraising. As a result, the relationship between the CVC and the Media Research Center is an important one. Technically (and legally), the two organizations are separate and distinct. In reality, they are inextricably linked. Or, perhaps more accurately, the Center is a reality, a physical presence, and the CVC is an idea, an inanimate object. At most, the CVC exists as a single telephone line on the Center switchboard. When one visits the CVC, one visits the Center.

In addition to sharing the same office space, the two organizations share virtually the same leadership staff. Bozell is chairman of the Center and executive director of the CVC. Leif Noren holds the titles of administrator for the Center and chairman for the CVC. Richard Kimble and Lawrence Gourley are finance directors and assistant finance directors, respectively, of both organizations. Only Juanita Sholes appears to be solely affiliated with the CVC, as treasurer. Interestingly, only the names of Juanita Sholes and Leif Noren appear on the payroll of the CVC, according to FEC reports. In the entire FEC file on the Conservative Victory Committee, from 1987 to present, Brent Bozell's name never appears. This is one of the most serious shortcomings of the FEC reporting process. The FEC requires that only the name of the treasurer of the PAC as well as payrolled employees be reported. Consequently, for most PACs, one is able to identify the treasurers, the clerical staff, and little more.

In addition to the overlap at the management level, one finds an interesting financial connection between the members of the Media Research Center board of trustees and the major donor base of the CVC. Currently there are forty-four members of the Center board, including several husbands and wives. Analyzing the FEC donor records for contributors giving at least $1,000 to CVC, one finds the names of thirty board members. Between 1987 and 1992, these individuals contributed more than one-quarter million dollars to the Conservative Victory Committee.

This pattern of big-dollar donations is consistent with Bozell's philosophy of organizational maintenance:

> When we started the CVC it was my thought that this organization would never have a large staff. . . . The second point I made is that we will never go into debt. Where the second point is concerned, we have been very hesitant or reluctant to go into direct mail. . . . This organization began small and has stayed small. As a result, in 1990 we raised about $400,000 to $500,000, but

Table 16.1

Receipts: Conservative Victory Committee

	1987–88	1989–90	1991–92
Total receipts	$1,142,157	$675,831	$387,625
Receipts from $1,000+ donors	$465,000	$337,250	$285,350
Percentage of total receipts from $1,000+ donors	40.7	49.9	73.6
Number of $1,000+ donors	123	59	70
Average contribution of $1,000+ donor households	$3,780	$5,716	$4,076

Source: FEC Political Action Committee Reports.

when you look at all the conservative PACs as far as dollars given out, we've given out more money than any [conservative] PAC in the country; we were number one. . . . So, that has been our philosophy. We have no full-time employees. We have four part-time employees, but that is all we need to fulfill this organization.[3]

While the CVC utilized direct mail in 1987, 1988, and 1989 to a limited extent, the bulk of the fundraising activity involves one-on-one contacts with big-dollar donors by Bozell. Fewer than 10,000 individuals have given money to the CVC in the past six years. In the first two election cycles, almost half of all the funds raised by the CVC were received in checks of $1,000 or more. In 1991–92 individual donations of $1,000 or more constituted almost three-quarters of all CVC contributions (see Table 16.1).

Obviously there is nothing random about the distribution of wealthy conservative donors in the United States, as the linkage between the Media Research Center and the CVC demonstrates. In addition to the substantive or ideological connection, one finds a geographical connection as well. Bozell was born and raised in Texas. Not coincidentally, the CVC donor base offers evidence of a Lone Star connection. In each of the election cycles reported in Table 16.1, donors from Texas who contributed $1,000 or more accounted for more than 10 percent of all contributors, and Texans supplied approximately one-quarter of the big-dollar donations (e.g., $121,000 of $465,000 in the 1987–88 cycle). Consistent with the old adage that "everything is big in Texas," the average contributions from Texans are larger than those given by Americans nationwide. In 1991–92, for example, eleven Texan big-dollar donor households gave an average of $5,227, whereas the remaining fifty-nine big-dollar donor households from across the nation gave an average of $3,862.

While the strategy of one-on-one solicitation, combined with an occasional major fundraising event, has left the CVC in solid financial shape and comparatively debt-free, it has limited the organization's ability to capitalize on fortuitous political events and issues, namely the CVC/Citizens United effort during the Clarence Thomas Senate confirmation hearings. Bozell and Floyd Brown, executive director of the 80,000-member nouveau conservative interest group Citizens United, were jointly responsible for what Ron Brown, in his former role as Democratic National Committee chairman, referred to as "ad hominem character assassinations of the most vicious and reprehensible kind"—the Kennedy–Biden–Cranston commercial aired during the Thomas hearings. Just three years earlier, as political director of NSPAC, Floyd Brown crafted the Willie Horton advertisement.

The Bozell–Brown joint effort was equally provocative. The Kennedy–Biden–Cranston ad received more free air time than any political commercial in television history. Yet the two organizations combined invested only $100,000, including only $40,000 spent on air time. In the span of two weeks, the ad ran free on virtually all major media outlets, providing several million dollars of media exposure. Clearly the ad was viewed by millions of Americans, but neither the CVC nor Citizens United was prepared to capitalize on the media coverage of this ad. Neither organization had the mailing lists necessary for an immediate direct-mail effort. It is indeed ironic that such a potentially lucrative opportunity for direct-mail fundraising was orchestrated by two organizations whose leaders do not utilize this method of fundraising.

Decisionmaking: A One-Man Show

Due to the streamlined nature of the CVC, the bulk of the political decisionmaking is done solely by Bozell. With his connections throughout the conservative political community, he has developed a consultative approach to selecting candidates for funding. Rather than hire several researchers to analyze the field of potential candidates as well as imperiled incumbents, Bozell relies on the expertise of a few political operatives on the staffs of other conservative organizations. For example, he contacts Ed Seal at Paul Weyrich's Free Congress organization and Karl Gallant from the National Right to Work PAC. According to Bozell,

> Ed Seal is a walking encyclopedia on the politics of this country. Instead of hiring a half-a-dozen staff members to research congressional races, I would call Ed Seal. I would give Ed a list of fifty races and he would patiently brief me on all fifty races. Another fellow named Karl Gallant would do the same thing. Between the two of them, in several hours' time, I received all the information I needed to know.[4]

Like most conservative PACs, the CVC tends to give the bulk of its contributions to nonincumbents. Given the Democratic majorities in Congress, this is to be expected. Further, during its first two campaign cycles, the majority of its candidate-related spending had taken the form of independent expenditures. For example, during the 1987–88 election cycle, the CVC spent more than $400,000 on congressional races; of this amount only $84,000 went directly to candidates (with $50,000 going to challengers or open-seat candidates). When it comes to independent expenditures, CVC spending patterns have varied. In the 1987–88 cycle, almost $300,000 was targeted independently against Democratic Senate candidates; whereas in the 1989–90 cycle, the vast majority of independent expenditures were conducted on behalf of Republican House candidates. Obviously the 1987–88 cycle also included the presidential election. The CVC spent an additional $250,000 on independent expenditures in this race, largely against Democratic nominee Michael Dukakis. However, in the 1991–92 cycle, CVC contributed nearly all of its funds directly to candidates (see Table A.15).

Bozell looks for four basic criteria when deciding to support a particular candidate:

> First, the ideological bent of the candidate. Second, the winnability of the race—and on that one I am willing to go way out on a limb because criterion three is: Does he need the money? We rarely give to incumbents—they don't need it. We are not the kind of PAC that shows an 80 percent success rate. We have a 10 percent success record and that is three times better than the national average for challengers, and that's what we're here for. Fourth, we look at how much of a fighter is this person going to be. A red flag for me is when a candidate says this will be a great campaign; we've got everything but the money. This tells me that it will be a lousy campaign. We try to see how much money they can raise on their own first. However, I do believe in getting in the race early.[5]

When the time comes to attach a dollar value to each candidate, Bozell and Leif Noren, the chairman, sit down and make the choices. As chairman, Noren controls the day-to-day operations of the PAC. Bozell controls the political aspect of the PAC: candidates and causes to support (or oppose), campaigns to be launched (e.g., the Thomas hearing ad), and major fundraising strategies. Noren's decision to support a candidate or a cause is not determined by the "viability of the candidate but, internally, by how much money we have. He will say, 'Let's not send $5,000. Let's send $2,500 now and another $2,500 later in the campaign.' "[6] While Bozell may rely on an informal network of contacts to help formulate his candidate agenda, the decisionmaking process in the CVC is, for all intents and purposes, a one-man show.

Accountability of the CVC

Unlike many of the PACs discussed in this volume, the CVC is closely linked to its donor base, not only for financial support but for substantive input as well. With Bozell's one-on-one approach it is difficult, if not impossible, to extricate the fundraising aspect of organizational maintenance from the mission of supporting conservative candidates. And, while the ultimate decisionmaking process regarding the allocation of funds centers on Bozell, donors are involved throughout the process. Supporters are free to offer suggestions to Bozell, which are often incorporated into the allocation of funds. Whatever the method, Bozell tries to get as much for the buck as possible:

> Donors want to know what they get for their money. Our donors do not have to ask that question because they know what we do. For instance, you can give to a candidate or you can invest that money for a candidate. One of the things I have done with this one fellow [donor], and I have used this approach for several candidates including Steve Symms, Orrin Hatch, Jeremiah Denton, and Chic Hecht, is to invest in his services. He will host a fundraiser for a campaign. We will pay up to $10,000 for the expenses ($5,000 for the primary and $5,000 for the general). He will charge $1,000 a head to attend. He will have 100 people come to his house. It is cosponsored by him and by us. All the checks are made out to the candidate. So when the dust settles, what happens? The candidate walks away with $100,000. The host feels like a million dollars, and we can go back to our people who invested the $10,000 with us and say we raised $100,000.[7]

Bozell stresses a system of checks and balances in his relations with his donor base. Ideas percolate up from supporters and are pursued by Bozell. Sometimes a connection is made with a candidate, sometimes not. When an agreement cannot be reached regarding support, the donor may withdraw his or her support from the CVC. Bozell has little problem with this relationship with his donors:

> We had a case two years ago, the donor was a bit conservative, but he was adamantly pro-abortion and I am adamantly pro-life. And we said that we would not give his candidate money because he, too, was adamantly pro-abortion. So, he said he should give his money to someone else and I encouraged him to do that.[8]

Beyond the individual level of informal contacts between donors and Bozell, the CVC communicates with its donor base on a formal basis through monthly updates. Federal Election Commission (FEC) reports are also available to donors through the PAC. For Bozell, communication with supporters is critically important. It is surprising that in many PACs, particularly the ideological organizations, the communications between leaders and supporters are limited to direct-mail solicitations for financial support and little more; this is not the case with CVC.

CVC and the 1991–92 Election Cycle: The "Squish" Factor

For Brent Bozell and the CVC, as well as for the larger conservative political community, the 1991–92 election cycle was quite different from the two previous electoral efforts in 1988 and 1990. While the beginning of the end for George Bush, at least in the minds of the conservative activists, occurred immediately prior to the 1990 midterm elections, the full impact of his broken pledge of "Read my lips; no new taxes" was not felt until the 1991–92 election cycle. This singular act did more to disengage the Republican party and, particularly, the conservative movement, than any political event since Watergate. According to CVC chairman Leif Noren, George Bush not only sealed his fate but also wounded the conservative movement on a most fundamental level: "I think we need to look at the top of the ticket, at the kind of damage he did. When George Bush caved in on taxes, he did more to hurt the Republican party in one year than the Democrats could have done in two decades."[9]

The most demonstrable impact of the damage was felt in conservative fundraising. Bozell summed up the views of CVC supporters regarding the Bush campaign in two words: "utter apathy." Interviewed in late July, prior to the Republican Convention, Bozell expressed concern that this apathy was being transferred to other Republican conservative candidates:

> I was on the road last week, around the country. I met with a number of people, all of whom were Bush supporters in 1988, and I asked every single one if he was going to the convention. And every single one said no, with a look like you've got to be kidding. What Bush is doing is screwing up the whole campaign; he's just killing Republicans, just killing them. There is no sense that our time is coming, and the great irony is that it has on the House side.[10]

George Bush had become what conservatives loathe the most, a "squish." In the conservative political jargon of the 1990s, virtually all Democrats are squishes; however, the label is far more damning when attributed to a Republican. Generally speaking, as a Republican, being pro-choice, against a balanced budget amendment, against a line-item veto, or in favor of raising taxes, is grounds for being labeled a squish. By 1992 George Bush had become the poster child for the squish movement.

Clearly, conservatives were always somewhat suspicious of Bush's conservative credentials. However, by November 1992, the movement had abandoned ship, at least financially. Noren argues that the impact of the Bush pronouncement reached far beyond the presidential level:

> There was just a tremendous amount of dissatisfaction with Bush. I think it dragged down candidates at various levels. He dragged down fundraising. I don't think he had an ideological bent to him. He didn't have Ronald Reagan's perseverance. He wasn't the kind of leader Reagan was. We certainly got some feedback. We know that people were disillusioned. I mean that people were less inclined to give.[11]

The Conservative Victory Committee as well as many other conservative PACs felt the financial pinch of both the slow-moving economy and the widespread disaffection among conservative donors. As shown in Table 16.1, CVC receipts were down more than 40 percent from the 1989–90 cycle. More significantly, CVC managed to raise only one-third the amount that it had raised four years earlier when George Bush was elected. While fundraising was clearly a problem distinct to this cycle, the actions of Brent Bozell and the CVC in 1991–92 were quite similar to CVC activism in the 1987–88 cycle in one important respect. During the primary season in 1987–1988, Bozell had not chosen Bush as his horse in the race for the presidency; Jack Kemp received Bozell's political and financial support (see Table A.15). Similarly, in the 1991–92 primaries, Bozell backed another Republican, someone more closely linked to his conservative ideals—Pat Buchanan.

Bozell's support for Bush was never strong, but following the broken tax pledge, his personal dissatisfaction was palpable. Within three months of the economic summit that resulted in the Bush compromise, Bozell had picked his horse and began the effort to mobilize the candidate-to-be:

> I had urged Pat to run in December of 1990, and at that time Bush's favorable ratings were 70 percent. And Pat said, "I've thought about it, but look at his favorable ratings." And I said, "Look, don't worry, Pat, it can't go any higher." And about three weeks later I was on "Crossfire" with him and before he said hello and how are you doing, he looked at me and said, "Ninety-one percent." Later, he calls me up and he said he was going to do it and he asked me to help.[12]

Bozell did help the Buchanan effort get started, although much of his advice was not heeded by the new candidate, particularly in the area of direct mail. Buchanan had a house list of 30,000 subscribers to his newsletter at the time of his announcement. Beyond that, he gathered another 40,000 new names from various conservative list sources. Bozell, along with Buchanan's sister and campaign manager, Bay Buchanan, was not pleased with the candidate's drafting of the fundraising letter. According to Bozell, "Pat broke all the rules in the letter he wrote. It was a very nice letter, but it wasn't a fundraising letter. It was a very poor fundraising letter, and if he grossed $100,000 he would be doing very, very well."[13]

Proving Bozell and his sister wrong, candidate Buchanan grossed $600,000 off the initial mailing and quickly qualified for matching funds. Bozell compared the efforts of Buchanan with those of Kemp four years earlier:

> It took Kemp four-and-a-half months [to receive matching funds] with all of his organization behind him; he started with a PAC, a foundation, a congressional list, everything, and the top consultants in the business, and it took him four-and-a-half months. It took Pat nineteen days to do it when the president had ratings in the eighties.[14]

As a result of this rapid outpouring of financial support, Bozell took a leave of absence from the CVC and the Media Research Center and worked on the Buchanan campaign from the end of December 1991 until the end of March

1992. The CVC was marginally involved in the Buchanan effort, as FEC records show a total of $817 received by Buchanan as in-kind contributions from the organization. However, Bozell's time away from the Center and CVC limited his ability to maintain his fundraising schedule during a crucial time in the election cycle. As a result, the CVC allocated less than $100,000 to congressional candidates in the 1991–92 cycle.

CVC Congressional Allocations in 1991–92

Following the lead of other conservative interest groups, the CVC employed a fundraising tactic that is becoming increasingly commonplace—the pledge. In recent years, organizations such as The National Taxpayers' Union and Americans for Tax Reform have garnered more than 200 signatures from members of Congress pledging support for "no new taxes." The CVC pledge is similar in its focus on fiscal responsibility. What is different about Bozell's pledge is there is a stick attached along with the financial carrot.

> The pledge is very innocuous; no conservative will have a problem signing off on it: balanced budget, line-item veto, don't raise taxes, that kind of stuff. Should a candidate receive support from us . . . and break his word on any one of these things, no matter who he is, he will become our number one target in 1994. . . . We are not putting up with these election-year conservatives.[15]

Fifty candidates in the 1991–92 cycle signed the CVC pledge and received financial support. Consistent with their methods of giving discussed earlier, the CVC supported only five incumbents; all won reelection (see Table 16.2). Twenty-eight challengers were supported (twenty-three in House races, five in Senate races), while the remaining seventeen candidates receiving support were involved in open-seat races, including three for the Senate. Of these forty-five nonincumbent candidates supported by the CVC, eleven were victorious in 1992. Compared with earlier election cycles, the CVC sharply increased its contributions to Republican House challengers and to open-seat candidates but gave relatively little to Senate candidates (see Table A.15).

The Texas and Beltway Electoral Connections

Similar to the pattern of CVC donor giving discussed earlier, there is a Texas connection in the allocation of funds to congressional candidates. Of the fifty races in which CVC supported candidates, forty-one were House races. Candidates for Texas House seats represented eleven of the forty-one races, or more than one-quarter of funded candidates.[16] When one focuses on the actual dollars allocated, Texas candidates received a disproportionate amount of CVC funding. Of the $76,205 allocated to House candidates, $32,955, or more than 40 percent of all contributions, were given to Texas candidates.

Table 16.2

Successful CVC Candidates, 1991–92

Incumbents		Nonincumbents	
Senate	Amount of donation ($)	Senate	Amount of donation ($)
Dan Coats (R-IN)	1,000	Lauch Faircloth (R-NC)	5,000
		Dirk Kempthorne (R-ID)*	1,000
House		House	
Robert Dornan (R-CA-46)	2,000	Spencer Bachus (R-AL-6)	1,000
Sam Johnson (R-TX-3)	5,000	Roscoe Bartlett (R-MD-6)*	1,000
James Nussle (R-IA-2)	250	Henry Bonilla (R-TX-23)	695
Toby Roth (R-WI-8)	5,000	Robert Goodlatte (R-VA-6)	1,000
		John Linder (R-GA-4)*	1,000
		Donald Manzullo (R-IL-16)	500
		Richard Pombo (R-CA-11)*	1,000
		Edward Royce (R-CA-39)*	500
		James Talent (R-MO-2)	2,500

Note:
*Open-seat races.

As demonstrated in Table 16.2, $5,000 in Texas spending is accounted for in one race, the successful race of Sam Johnson in the 3rd district. Interestingly, this was not the totality of CVC spending in this district during the 1991–92 election cycle. Included in this cycle was the 1991 special election to replace Steve Bartlett, who was elected mayor of Dallas. In this overwhelmingly Republican district, which includes the North Dallas area, twelve candidates emerged to contest the special election. Bozell and the CVC chose to support Thomas Pauken, the top choice in the special election, with 28 percent of the votes cast. Johnson, with the second largest vote total, 20 percent, joined Pauken in the run-off election. The CVC supported Pauken in both elections with a total of $7,000. Johnson won the special election. One year later he received maximum support of $5,000 in the general election and won with 86 percent of the votes cast.

Two additional House races in 1992 accounted for the bulk of Texas spending by the CVC. For the CVC, the "one that got away" was the race in the east Texas 2nd District. Democratic incumbent Charles Wilson was challenged in 1990 by a very recent West Point graduate, Donna Peterson. In that race, the political novice garnered 44 percent of the vote and, as a result, attracted a significant amount of attention in Republican and conservative financial circles. With Wilson's check-bouncing record, even more interest was generated in Peterson's efforts. Bozell and the CVC climbed on board wholeheartedly, as FEC records show contributions in the primary and general elections totaling $9,895. Unfortunately for Peterson and the CVC, the outcome of the 1992 race mirrored the previous contest, with Peterson again receiving 44 percent.

The other Texas race that generated significant CVC support was in the 9th district for the seat held by senior Democrat Jack Brooks, chairman of the House Judiciary Committee. Coming off a 1990 election in which he received only 58 percent of the vote, Brooks was identified as potentially vulnerable. The CVC supported Republican challenger Stephen Stockman in the primary and general election cycles with $5,695. However, like the outcome in the 2nd District, Brooks was reelected with 56 percent of the vote.

Beyond the Texas connection, one additional pattern of CVC support emerges from the FEC reports. Candidates running in districts immediately outside the Capital Beltway in neighboring Maryland and Virginia attracted the support of CVC. Of the nineteen House candidates contested in these two states, CVC was active in five races. Two candidates, Bartlett in Maryland's 6th district and Goodlatte in Virginia's 6th district (identified in Table 16.2) were successful in their electoral efforts. Of the remaining three races, two were contested in the northern Virginia district closest to Washington, the 8th district, held by Democrat Jim Moran, and the newly created 11th district. Republican challenger Kyle McSlarrow in the 8th district received $2,500 from CVC but lost with 43 percent of the vote. In a bitter battle for the new 11th district seat, CVC supported Republican Henry Butler with $1,000, but he, too, lost—to Democrat Leslie Byrne in a tight race, 52 percent to 48 percent.

The final Beltway House race that attracted CVC attention was a Republican challenge to House Democratic Caucus chair Steny Hoyer in Maryland's 5th district. In this redrawn district, Hoyer, who had won his three previous elections with no less than 79 percent of the vote, withstood the challenge of Lawrence Hogan but won with only 55 percent of the vote. CVC gave Hogan $500 in support of his challenge. Finally, in the Maryland Senate race, the CVC supported the unsuccessful challenge of Republican Alan Keyes with $1,000. Incumbent senator Barbara Mikulski won easily with 79 percent of the vote. In total, more than half of CVC contributions to House races in the 1991–92 cycle had either a Texas or a Beltway connection. The remaining CVC funds were spent in congressional races identified by Bozell through his informal information network within the conservative political community.

Prospects for 1994 and 1996:
Recharging the Conservative Batteries

While the 1991–92 election cycle will not be looked upon by conservatives as one of their more memorable political campaigns, there is a growing sense of excitement in the conservative Republican ranks as the 1994 midterm elections approach. In a very significant way, losing the White House has had an energizing effect on the conservative movement. In February of 1993, the conservative political network met formally in Washington for CPAC, the Conservative Political Action Conference. At these meetings, attended by virtually all of the major conservative activists as well as conservative members of Congress, the common ground shaped by conservatives was mapped out. Keynote speakers included many of the likely Republican presidential candidates. Bozell participated formally as he provided the introductory speech for keynote speaker Pat Buchanan. Since the February meetings, various game plans for the 1994 elections have surfaced within the network.

According to CVC chair Leif Noren, the conservative political network will be activated at a higher level in 1994:

> I think what is going to be happening is that there will be a lot of networking going on, and, by design, that's the way we do it. We'll just do a lot more networking, a lot more reading of political newsletters, and based on what we see unfolding in terms of where the best opportunities lie, that's where we'll start focusing attention. Just as the cream rises to the top, these races start becoming known to the Washington political community. There are people who do have large structures that can identify these candidates and share that information.[17]

Bozell also foresees the possibility of significant Republican gains in the 1994 midterm elections but worries whether 1994 might be a bit too early to challenge the Democrats for control:

> Will the conservative batteries be recharged enough to mount such a change? In '94, it's going to be interesting to see what speaks more—the tremendous money the left has—oh God! do they have money—or the Joe Six-Pack out there that is not motivated anymore by campaign commercials. . . . I don't think money can buy as much as it used to buy.[18]

As for the 1996 presidential election, a free-for-all on the Republican side is not out of the question. Bozell concurs, and identifies the potential pitfalls of such a campaign.

> All hell's gonna break loose. It's gonna be fun. I think all hell's gonna break loose in both parties. I think there is going to be another third-party phenomenon arising. My guess is there'll be another Ross Perot. I think within the Republican party, my fear is that it will be the California 1986 Senate primary all over again. Remember when Ed Zschau won against six conservatives.[19]

It is indeed ironic that in just four years the conservative movement will have transformed itself from the ugly stepchild of the Republican party to a state of an embarrassment of riches in the form of a full stable of strong presidential candidates, and that this large number of competitive conservative aspirants may lead to the choice of a Republican presidential nominee from outside the conservative stable. Regardless of the outcome, Bozell argues that the 1996 presidential campaign will be one worth watching. Stay tuned.

Notes

1. Personal interview with L. Brent Bozell III.
2. L. Brent Bozell III and Brent H. Baker, eds., *And That's the Way It Isn't: A Reference Guide to Media Bias* (Alexandria, VA: Media Research Center, 1990).
3. Bozell interview.
4. Ibid.
5. Ibid.
6. Ibid.
7. Ibid.
8. Ibid.
9. Ibid.
10. Ibid.
11. Ibid.
12. Ibid.
13. Ibid.
14. Ibid.
15. Ibid.
16. There were no Texas Senate seats contested in the 1991–92 cycle.
17. Bozell interview.
18. Ibid.
19. Ibid.

17

JustLife Action

Mary E. Bendyna, R.S.M.

JustLife Action is a small ideological PAC that defines itself as "pro-justice," "pro-life," and "pro-peace."[1] Unlike most ideological groups or groups committed either to a pro-life stance or to issues of justice and peace, JustLife Action advocates a "consistent ethic of life" that seeks to protect and promote human life "from womb to tomb." This consistent ethic of life, which is also referred to as the "seamless garment," calls for moral consistency in addressing the many threats to human life in the world today.[2]

At present, JustLife Action focuses on the issues of poverty, abortion, and the arms race, which it views as posing the most immediate threats to justice and life. In particular, JustLife Action advocates policies that support the economic and social needs of women and children, that provide equal access to education and health care for all, that protect the unborn, that reduce the production and distribution of weapons of mass destruction, and that reallocate human and financial resources to meet basic human needs and provide equal opportunity for all. Although JustLife Action has chosen for the present to focus its efforts on these issues, it emphasizes that all life issues, including euthanasia, capital punishment, drug addiction, sexism, and racism, must be seen as interwoven in the seamless garment.

Organization and History

JustLife Action was founded as JustLife PAC in 1985 by David Medema, Stephen Monsma, Ronald Sider, Juli Loesch Wiley, and others who shared a commitment to a consistent pro-life stance. The immediate impetus for the creation of JustLife PAC was the unsuccessful congressional campaign of Stephen Monsma. Monsma, a pro-life liberal Democrat, believed it was necessary not only to oppose abortion but also to advocate policies that provide alternatives to abortion and offer assistance to women with children. While Monsma's positions may have been morally consistent, they were not politically consistent. He was too liberal on many issues for most right-to-life supporters and too conservative on abortion for most liberals. Monsma, therefore, had difficulty raising money from traditional funding sources. JustLife PAC was founded to support candidates like Stephen Monsma. In 1987, JustLife Education Fund was founded as a separate nonprofit, tax-exempt 501(c)(3) corporation to educate on JustLife issues and to promote the consistent life ethic. In 1992, the name of the PAC was changed from JustLife PAC to JustLife Action, and the JustLife Education Fund became known simply as JustLife.

JustLife and JustLife Action are headed by separate, overlapping boards of directors. Board members are responsible for making all decisions about PAC contributions and for recruiting and appointing new members. The national office, which relocated from Philadelphia to Grand Rapids, Michigan, in 1991, has a permanent staff of two that reports to the board of directors. JustLife, which attracts far greater donor support, provides administrative services for JustLife Action at cost on a contract basis. David Medema, a founding member of JustLife, served as the executive director of both organizations during the 1992 election cycle. In December 1992 he was replaced by Jill Mann, who had previously served as the executive assistant. In addition to the national organization, JustLife also has a few local chapters and is in the process of organizing several new ones. JustLife chapters, which are based largely in the Midwest, serve as a source of information and advice for the national organization. These chapters also engage in educational activities, including the training of volunteers for political campaigns.

JustLife, which identifies itself as "an ecumenical gathering of Christians," works closely with a variety of religious groups, as well as with pro-life groups and justice and peace groups. JustLife and JustLife Action are part of the Seamless Garment Network, a coalition of about eighty-five organizations that share a commitment to the consistent life ethic. This network includes groups such as Evangelicals for Social Action, Pax Christi, Sojourners, Feminists for Life, Common Ground, Catholic Worker Houses, and a number of religious orders. JustLife Action is the only PAC in the network. JustLife also consults regularly with a number of other interest groups and PACs that share some of JustLife's concerns.

A recent survey of members provides a great deal of information about JustLife's constituency.[3] JustLife currently has a national membership of approximately 6,000. Almost all of its members are Christian, although they come from a wide range of religious preferences and denominational affiliations. Just over half of the members are Catholic, approximately one-sixth of whom identify themselves as charismatic. Evangelical and mainline Protestants make up 27 percent and 19 percent of the membership, respectively. Fewer than 2 percent of the members are affiliated with Pentecostal denominations.[4] The variety of religious preferences represented in JustLife's membership reflects the ecumenical focus of the organization.

One of the most striking characteristics of JustLife members is their high level of education. Nearly 90 percent are college graduates, and fully 58 percent hold graduate degrees. Although political contributors tend to be well educated, the education levels reported by JustLife members are significantly higher than those of other political contributors.[5] Most JustLife members are professional or white collar workers. However, because many are academics, members of the clergy, or religious workers, their income levels are relatively low. JustLife members are also fairly young, particularly when compared to members of other religious interest groups. Nearly half of the members are under the age of forty. Geographically, membership is concentrated in the Midwest, although there is also a large contingent on the East Coast. Members of JustLife are very interested in politics and highly involved in political activity. Majorities identify themselves as Democrats and as liberal. Only 18 percent identify themselves as Republican or as conservative. JustLife members are generally very supportive of the organization's positions on issues.

Most of JustLife and JustLife Action's funding comes from individual contributors and from religious organizations, such as churches and religious orders. The average contribution to JustLife from individual donors is $30. Most of JustLife's fundraising is done through a pledge program and through regular mailings to individuals. The average contribution to JustLife Action is $50. Most members of JustLife do not contribute financially to JustLife Action.

JustLife communicates with and mobilizes its contributors in a variety of ways. It sends regular mailings to contributors, publishes a bimonthly newsletter, and produces a variety of educational materials, including a study guide with articles and updates on JustLife issues. JustLife also publishes the voting records of members of Congress on issues that are within its realm of interest. Contributors are encouraged to contact members of Congress, to sign petitions, and to be directly involved in campaign activities. They also have the opportunity to participate in national and local conferences.

All decisions about JustLife Action endorsements and campaign contributions are made by its board of directors. JustLife Action supports only those candidates who are clearly in agreement with its positions on all three of its main issues—economic justice, abortion, and the arms race. It does not endorse or contribute to candidates who are "the lesser of two evils." JustLife Action determines candidate positions through the voting records of incumbents and through responses to a questionnaire that it distributes to challengers and candidates for open seats. These questionnaires query nonincumbents on how they would have voted on key issues had they been in Congress. In making its decisions, the board also consults with groups that share JustLife's interests, such as the United States Catholic Conference, the National Right-to-Life Committee, Bread for the World, SANE/Freeze, and Peace PAC.

In addition to direct monetary contributions to candidates, JustLife Action supports candidates through in-kind contributions. These contributions are generally in the form of radio or newspaper ads, often in religious publications. JustLife Action also supplies volunteers to work on campaigns. The PAC does not make independent expenditures.

JustLife Action targets elections that meet several criteria. JustLife Action looks for elections in which there is a clear contrast between the candidates. It also considers whether the candidate has the ability to wage a viable campaign and whether support from JustLife Action could make a difference in the outcome. Finally, it looks at whether there is a support base in or near the district for which the endorsed candidate is running.

In 1986 and 1988, the first two election cycles after the founding of JustLife Action, the PAC concentrated its efforts on supporting just a few congressional candidates. During these two election cycles, JustLife Action contributed a total of nearly $11,000. Although JustLife Action gave significant contributions to a few incumbents, the bulk of its contributions went to challengers. All but one of the candidates JustLife Action supported in these elections were Democrats.

JustLife Action's endorsements and contributions increased significantly in the 1990 election cycle. In that election, JustLife Action contributed nearly $22,000 to fifty-six candidates. Most of the contributions were very small—many for only $16, which represented each candidate's share of the cost of in-kind advertising. Although JustLife Action contributed to Democrats and Republicans, to incumbents and nonincumbents, and to candidates for the House and for the Senate, two-thirds of its endorsees were incumbent House Democrats. Many of JustLife Action's largest contributions, however, again went to challengers, most of whom were from the Midwest, where JustLife's national office, most of its local chapters, and many of its members are located. In a year of extremely low incumbent turnover, three of the challengers who received targeted assistance from JustLife Action won election. In all, forty-nine of the fifty-four candidates supported by JustLife Action in the general elections were victorious.

The 1992 Election

Neither the process nor the criteria JustLife Action used to select candidates to support changed in any significant way for the 1992 elections. According to the *JustLife Action 1992 Pre-Election Update*, candidates who merited JustLife Action's support voted or promised to vote in a pattern that is clearly in agreement with its stands on justice, life, and peace. These candidates were also viewed in generally favorable terms by various congressional staff and organizations that focus on issues of concern to JustLife Action; demonstrated the ability to wage viable, credible campaigns; and had not been disciplined for any ethics violation and were not facing punishment for violation of any civil or criminal law.

On the basis of these criteria, JustLife Action endorsed thirty-seven candidates for Congress in 1992. This was significantly fewer than it had supported in

1990. One of the factors that accounted for the lower number of endorsements in 1992 is the fact that twenty-four of the candidates JustLife Action supported in 1990 were not endorsed in 1992. Nine of the endorsees from 1990 retired, and another four lost primary elections to other incumbents after they were combined into the same district by redistricting. In addition, JustLife Action withdrew support from eleven previously endorsed incumbents because they either reversed their positions or voted in ambiguous patterns on JustLife issues. However, four incumbents who were not previously endorsed by JustLife Action were endorsed for the first time in 1992. JustLife Action also endorsed seven challengers and four candidates for open seats.

As was the case in 1990, nearly two-thirds of the candidates JustLife Action supported in 1992 were incumbent House Democrats. Again, most of JustLife Action's contributions were very small—many for $23, which again represented each candidate's share of the cost of in-kind advertising. As in previous elections, JustLife Action targeted several key races where its support might have had a significant impact on the outcome. Most of these races involved challengers or candidates for open seats. However, unlike previous elections, JustLife Action was not able to give large contributions to these candidates. Only one challenger, who lost the primary, received a large contribution from JustLife Action. Although twenty-three of the twenty-five incumbents JustLife supported in 1992 were returned to office, not one of the nonincumbents it supported was successful.

JustLife Action's relative lack of success in the 1992 elections was due in part to financial difficulties. According to David Medema, the executive director of JustLife Action during the 1992 election cycle, fundraising was much more difficult in 1992 than it had been in 1990. Medema attributed this in large part to the poor economy. Because of financial constraints, JustLife Action contributed less than $6,000 to candidates in 1992.

Medema also suggested that partisanship played a much greater role in the 1992 elections than it had in the past. In Medema's view, the Democrats placed greater emphasis on the party's pro-choice stance in this election and exerted pressure on both incumbent and nonincumbent candidates to follow suit. Moreover, the Democratic party committees, which had previously been helpful in directing JustLife Action toward Democratic candidates who fit JustLife criteria, were much less cooperative in this election. The party's refusal to allow William Casey, the pro-life liberal Democratic governor of Pennsylvania, to speak at the Democratic National Convention is also indicative of the Democratic approach to the abortion issue in the 1992 election.

Medema felt that partisanship and politics also played a significant role among Republicans. In his view, a number of moderate Republicans, who tended to cross party lines on economic and defense issues, were pressured to support the positions of President Bush and the Republican party on these issues. Medema also noted that there was a cadre of moderate Republicans whose views were close to those of JustLife Action on economic and military policy but who favored abortion rights and, therefore, did not merit endorsement.

Conclusion

Despite its limited success in the 1992 elections, JustLife Action remained firmly committed to its consistent pro-life position. Initially, Justlife and JustLife Action intended to focus their educational and legislative activities on the application of the consistent life ethic to children. Among other things, they planned to emphasize what they view as the inconsistencies between defending the rights of children and the proposed Freedom of Choice Act. Both organizations hired Jill Mann as their new director after the 1992 election. Mann emphasized that if JustLife Action was to remain viable as a PAC, it must have sufficient funds and other forms of support to give to candidates. In a post-election interview, Mann suggested that in the 1992 elections, JustLife Action could have focused on fundraising earlier in the election cycle. She also suggested that JustLife might have identified potentially credible candidates earlier and given more support to these candidates in the primaries. For future elections, Mann hoped to inform JustLife supporters about ways to become more active as well as to provide opportunities for greater participation.

After careful consideration of their financial situation, however, JustLife and JustLife Action terminated their national organizations in 1993. Although membership in JustLife had grown steadily, contributions to JustLife Action had sharply declined. Both organizations were in debt, and fundraising efforts in 1993 had been largely unsuccessful. It appears that in the polarized world of abortion politics, there was not a sufficiently sizable constituency for a PAC that endorsed a consistent ethic of life.

Notes

1. Unless otherwise noted, all information on JustLife and JustLife Action was obtained through publications provided by the organizations or through telephone interviews with David Medema, the executive director of JustLife and JustLife Action during the 1992 election cycle, or Jill Mann, the most recent executive director of the organizations. The author would like to thank Mr. Medena and Ms. Mann for their assistance in providing information on JustLife and JustLife Action and for their helpful comments on earlier drafts of this chapter.

2. The principal proponent of the consistent ethic of life has been Cardinal Joseph L. Bernardin, the Roman Catholic archbishop of Chicago. For a collection of addresses and commentaries on the consistent ethic of life by Bernardin and others, see Thomas G. Fuechtmann, ed., *Consistent Ethic of Life* (Kansas City, MO: Sheed and Ward, 1988).

3. The survey of JustLife members is part of the Religious Interest Group Survey Project directed by Lyman A. Kellstedt of Wheaton College. A summary of the findings on JustLife respondents can be found in Chris Fastnow, "Seismic Activity—The Faultlines Within JustLife," Paper presented at the 1991 Meeting of the Association for the Scientific Study of Religion.

4. Evangelicals are generally characterized by a belief in the "born-again" experience of accepting Jesus Christ as the only way of attaining eternal salvation and by a belief in the inerrancy of the Bible. In addition to sharing the doctrinal beliefs of Evangelicals, Pentecostals, and charismatics emphasize the gifts of the Holy Spirit, such as speaking in tongues and faith healing, and are characterized by enthusiastic and emotional worship.

5. For an analysis of the education levels of political contributors, see Frank J. Sorauf, *Money in American Elections* (Glenview, IL: Scott, Foresman/Little, Brown, 1988); and James L. Guth and John C. Green, "Politics in a New Key: Religiosity and Participation among Political Activists," *Western Political Quarterly* 43 (1989), pp. 153–79. Sorauf found that 42.6 percent of all political contributors had completed college. Guth and Green found that among contributors to party, ideological, and interest-group PACs, 28 percent were college graduates and 43 percent had done postgraduate studies.

18

The Washington PAC: One Man Can Make a Difference

Barbara Levick-Segnatelli

Founded in 1980 to ensure "a secure Israel in the best interests of the United States," the Washington Political Action Committee, (WASHPAC) has become a respected leader among the well-funded and highly organized groups in the pro-Israeli lobby.[1] WASHPAC began as a "hobby" for the former executive director of the American Israeli Public Affairs Committee (AIPAC), Morris J. Amitay. Federal law forbids lobbying organizations such as AIPAC to contribute to campaigns or to establish or direct the activities and contributions of "pro-Israeli" political action committees. Amitay established WASHPAC so that he would no longer be prohibited from collecting contributions for congressional candidates. Under his leadership, WASHPAC continues to rank second among pro-Israeli PACs in overall contributions to congressional candidates.

In the 1992 election cycle, Washington PAC, in its twelfth year of operation, carefully distributed $235,000 to 150 U.S. Senate and House candidates. While the number of races that WASHPAC contributed to in 1992 is slightly less than the two previous cycles, it may be explained by money being diverted to the presidential candidates and to the number of WASHPAC members who started pro-Israel PACs in their own communities.[2]

Like other pro-Israeli PACs, WASHPAC bases its contribution decisions on senators' and representatives' "commitment to the principle of a secure Israel in the best interests of the United States as evidenced by voting records, public and private statements, sponsorship and cosponsorship of bills, actions, letters to constituents and ability to influence policy."[3] WASHPAC is unique among the pro-Israeli PACs and lobbying organizations in that it does not have an elaborate

organizational structure or formal membership obligations. This PAC is a literally a one-man show there are no by-laws governing its fundraising or
decisionmaking processes. As Amitay puts it, "I raise the money, I give out
the money."[4]

The perception is widespread that the seventy or so pro-Israel PACs cooperate
formally or informally in their decisionmaking. Ed Zuckerman writes in the
Almanac of Federal PACs,

> With near universality, the pro-Israel PACs share a tendency to contribute
> heavily to liberal Democrats and to adopt names which do not convey their
> true political purpose. . . . There is little doubt that contribution decisions are
> centralized, either through a formal or informal arrangement.[5]

Morris Amitay disagrees that such an arrangement exists and comments
that such an arrangement would be illegal. It is true that pro-Israeli PACs
give overwhelmingly to the same candidates, but this is due to the nature of the
issue—Israel—not to the directed decisionmaking processes of the PACs. Issues
that concern the pro-Israel community, namely American foreign policy toward
Israel and the Middle East, are very narrow. Foreign policy issues are also
generally bipartisan. Amitay refers continually to the obvious paper trail that
candidates leave behind indicating their level of support for a strong Israel.
Candidates publicly and privately speak, write, and vote on various foreign aid
and arms sales bills, and these speeches, papers, and votes are duly noted by
pro-Israeli PACS. There are no surprises.

The seventy pro-Israel PACs share the same basic goal and use the same set
of candidate speeches, papers, and votes to make their contribution decisions.
For instance, National PAC, the largest of the pro-Israel PACs, told its contributors in a recent newsletter that National PAC "supports those candidates who
believe . . . that Israel is a great strategic asset to the United States and our only
reliable ally in the Middle East."[6] The similarity to Amitay's statement that
WASHPAC bases its contribution decisions on senators' and representatives'
"commitment to the principle of a secure Israel in the best interests of the United
States" is no coincidence. All pro-Israel PACs share the same basic strategy and
goals. Amitay knows National PAC's executive director, Richard Altman, formerly AIPAC's political director. The two PACs do not collaborate on contribution decisions. Amitay receives the newsletters of National PAC and other
pro-Israeli PACs but does not use them as the basis for WASHPAC's contribution decisions.

In January 1989, acting with assistance from the Arab-American Anti-
Discrimination Committee, six persons filed a formal complaint with the Federal
Election Commission (FEC) alleging that AIPAC violated federal election laws
by spending its corporate treasury funds on election-related activities and failing
to register as a political action committee. The complaint asked the FEC to

investigate whether AIPAC's relationship with twenty-seven PACs constituted "affiliation." If the FEC found for the complaint, the PACs would be considered a single political unit that could contribute up to $5,000 to a candidate's election under current campaign finance laws, not as twenty-seven separate PACs, each with its own $5,000 contribution limit.

Under federal election law, PACs are deemed to be "affiliated" if they are established, directed, or controlled by a common organization or if they have the same officers, vendors, or contributors. However, making contributions to the same candidates is not a factor in determining "affiliation." Recently, the FEC voted against the complaint, finding that AIPAC has not violated federal election laws and that the pro-Israel PACs can continue to contribute to candidates as twenty-seven separate committees. If it wanted to, AIPAC could provide its own endorsements for the pro-Israel PACs to follow or disregard at their own discretion. Such recommendations would be no different than the practice followed by dozens of corporate PACs that base their contribution decisions on advice by such groups as the U.S. Chamber of Commerce and the National Association of Manufacturers.

Amitay points out that the pro-Israel community is small, cohesive, and similarly committed to a strong, secure Israel. It is necessary that members of the community maintain personal relationships with one another. Conventional wisdom may be that the decisionmaking processes of these pro-Israeli PACs are somehow centralized, or directed by AIPAC, but the truth is that the seventy PACs and AIPAC are committed to the same goals and therefore attract similar contributors and give to the same candidates. It is the issue of a secure Israel that unites them, not some grand, deliberate, and illegal design.

Because of the sensitive nature of American-Israeli relations and the negative public perception of the role of PACs in the election process, the majority of pro-Israeli organizations are reluctant to expose their decisionmaking processes and organizational activities to public scrutiny. WASHPAC consented to do so because of its unique organization and fundraising tactics and Morris Amitay's personal desire to address the misperceptions about PACs in general and pro-Israeli PACs in particular.

Organization and Decisionmaking

WASHPAC was formed following the election of 1980. Amitay left his job as executive director of AIPAC in October 1980, started his own law practice, and, "as a hobby," registered and organized WASHPAC. WASHPAC is literally and figuratively a one-man phenomenon. Amitay is the founder, sole organizer, and sole staff member of the Washington Political Action Committee. There is one assistant. The single office, on North Capital Street in Washington, D.C., offers easy access and proximity to legislators and committee hearings. Amitay sees legislators frequently in Washington restaurants and at the Capitol; and as he so aptly puts it, "Candidates aren't shy, they ask for money."[7] Amitay had been a leader in the pro-Israeli community for over twenty years, but it was his time at AIPAC that allowed him to make the political and social connections to begin WASHPAC with a strongly committed contributor base and assured access to congressional candidates.

All contributors who give WASHPAC $1,000 or more are eligible to serve on its advisory board, but few have the inclination to do so. The advisory board, which has eighty-three members, exists solely as a solidary benefit for major donors. It is not a decisionmaking arm of the PAC. It serves social and informational purposes, holding luncheons about once a month during the congressional session. These gatherings provide board members with the opportunity to meet congressional candidates and give a contribution. The meetings also give Amitay the opportunity to keep the board informed of the status of the campaigns in which the PAC is involved.

Roughly 99 percent of the PAC's contributions are distributed at its luncheons. This approach allows WASHPAC to "show its gratitude while at the same time reminding the candidate of the reason for it."[8] Amitay maximizes the effectiveness of the luncheons for everyone involved. Members of Congress are invited, allowing them and Amitay to work the room. Advisory board members depend on the WASHPAC luncheons to make decisions regarding their own individual contributions to candidates.

The approximately 700 members of WASHPAC represent a wide variety of business, academic, and professional interests, but they all share the common desire of ensuring a secure Israel. They are predominantly from the Washington area. Amitay knows more than half of them personally or through AIPAC or other organizations. Members are also concentrated in Florida, New York, and Los Angeles. Many other cities and regions have begun their own PACs through the contacts they have made at WASHPAC luncheons. These smaller, regional pro-Israel PACs, such as the Delaware Valley PAC, which serves Pennsylavania and Delaware, or the Heartland PAC, which serves the northeastern Ohio area, are formed, and make contribution decisions, independent of WASHPAC.

Ninety-nine percent of WASHPAC's contributions are raised through frequent personal letters. This is done without the assistance of outside political consultants or direct-mail fundraising companies. As Amitay states, "The larger PACs use advanced fundraising efforts, but that takes planning, it takes overhead and it takes time, and their average contribution is only $25 or $30. I do it myself and I get the expenses back."[9] While a significant number contribute over $1,000, most WASHPAC members contribute between $200 and $300. WASHPAC considers all contributors to be members, even though only those who contribute $1,000 or more are eligible to serve on the advisory board. Amitay's letters are friendly, informative, and personal. His handwritten notes assure the contributor that all contributions are sincerely appreciated. While most of the larger PACs enjoy the advantage of a professional marketing company's experience and creativity in fundraising, Amitay's style lends itself to the community it serves—Jews who feel emotionally and personally involved with the issues of concern to the PAC.

WASHPAC communicates with contributors through a newsletter published four times a year. The newsletter profiles the elections in which the PAC is involved and keeps the membership informed of any changes in contribution decisions. Amitay reports on the activities of the other side by writing commentary for newspapers and magazines on issues of interest to WASHPAC. Recently, Amitay's commentary for the *Broward Jewish World* addressed the issue of "Just How Powerful Is the Arab-American Lobby?" by stating that

> while the Arab-Lobby is better organized, funded and more vocal than it was a decade ago, it still suffers from a lack of popular support among the American public and in the Congress. . . . Access in political terms has to be earned, not demanded. The American Jewish community has earned its access by its many years of active and consistent support to the Democratic Party and its candidates—its participation in the political process.[10]

Contributors are both consumers and providers of information for the PAC. Sometimes they call Amitay with questions about a particular election or a candidate. They frequently send newspaper clippings from out-of-state newspapers. When Amitay needs information about an election or candidate, he utilizes his network of contributors, candidates, polling organizations, other PACs, lobbying organizations, and clipping services. Amitay receives the publications of AIPAC and other pro-Israeli PACs but does not rely on them in his decisionmaking. He uses the *Cook Political Report* for information about obscure House races, saying, "It's pretty reliable—he plays it down the middle. . . . But when you are talking about Israel-related issues, we have the records of all of the incumbents, so they speak for themselves."[11] He finds that his personal communication network is a far superior source of accurate and timely information.

Contributor input into WASHPAC's decisionmaking process is very limited, except in a few rare instances. For the most part, contributors do not earmark their contributions for particular candidates. Some contributors make suggestions for backing certain candidates, but Amitay ultimately has a free hand in distributing WASHPAC money. Amitay admits, "Some House races we get involved in mainly because a large contributor to the PAC has a pet race, and the guy is good on Israel, and it's an open seat. We'll kick in $250 or $500, we don't mind losing that." For example, the election of freshman representative Sam Coppersmith "was recommended to us by a PAC member, really a shot in the dark, but this woman's judgment is pretty good and she told me he had a real shot. I looked into it, spoke to the candidate, and basically, on her recommendation, we helped him and he won." Amitay only values advice from people he considers "pretty sophisticated," people whose "judgment is based on knowledge and experience."[12]

The competitiveness and the cost of the race are of particular interest to Amitay when he makes contribution decisions for WASHPAC. The PAC tries to give money where it will make the biggest difference. Amitay says he "would rather make an impact on a $2 million dollar race than a $12 million race. We try to put more of the money in a state where they aren't raising that much money and we have more of an impact." Amitay relates an incident that illustrates his views on the issue:

> The only example of a challenger being more pro-Israel than an incumbent would be Bruce Herschensohn verses Barbara Boxer, but we didn't get involved in California at all. It's not a good buy. I'd rather get involved in North or South Dakota where a $1,000 or $5,000 contribution goes further than a $10,000 [the maximum allowed] would in California where they are spending $6 to $8 million in a race.[13]

Whether an incumbent serves on a committee that can influence legislation of importance to Israel is of primary consideration. Friendly members serving on foreign relations or appropriations committees are the most desirable, and therefore deserving of the most consistent WASHPAC support. When asked in October and early November about how he planned to prepare for the 103rd Congress, Amitay agreed that WASHPAC had to "watch for key committee appointments, and then we'll know who to focus on—it's fairly obvious—look to see who are the new subcommittee chairmen and who is moving up."[14]

Amitay denies that certain issues or pivotal events may determine which candidates receive help from WASHPAC. Congressional action on the loan guarantees to Israel was watched closely in 1992, although the results of the debate did not cause the PAC to support, or to withhold support from, any of the candidates. Amitay relates another incident when "we were surprised—there was a pretty lopsided vote on a foreign aid bill in the House, and a few people we had contributed to voted no. I think we had already helped them, but I don't recall any of them ever coming back and asking for more."[15]

To maximize WASHPAC influence, Amitay is a real believer in the adage "Early money SHOUTS!!" He says,

> We tend to try to get in money early in the cycle and give it out early in the cycle. The rationale here is that not only is it appreciated more but in the case of a senator you have six, and in the case of a congressman, you have another close to two years that they are still going to be in office.[16]

This propensity to give early in the election cycle also may lead to trouble. Amitay admitted that the PAC has a column in its books labeled "PA," or "Pissed Away"—early contributions to House members or senators who decided to retire. The PAC received almost 20 percent of these early contribution "mistakes" back from the retiring candidates.[17]

Dollars and Common Cents

Over the last five years, WASHPAC has reported contributions to congressional candidates totaling over $860,000, ranking it consistently as the second largest pro-Israel PAC. WASHPAC's fundraising success is mainly a result of Amitay's ability to personalize communication with American Jews and with congressional candidates. In 1982, its first full election cycle, WASHPAC distributed $88,925 to 120 House races and 33 Senate races. Certainly an admirable beginning for a "hobby"! Ten years later, in 1992, WASHPAC distributed $235,000 to 118 House races and 39 Senate races (see Table A.17). Amitay explains that the decrease from the PAC's 1986 and 1988 spending levels was a result of "the economic recession, funds solicited by the presidential candidates and the growth in the number of pro-Israel PACs."[18] In 1992 WASHPAC contributed to 23 Senate winners and to more than 80 victorious incumbents and new members in the House. The problem, as Amitay sees it, is having too many friends in Congress and not enough PAC money to go around.

Although in previous cycles WASHPAC has supported three times as many Democrats as Republicans, Amitay said he had expected the ratio to decline to about two to one in the 1992 election because many of WASHPAC's staunchest Republican allies were involved in contested races and in need of financial support. Amitay's prediction turned out to be off the mark; WASHPAC actually supported 130 Democrats and 42 Republicans in 1992, closer to the three-to-one ratio consistent with earlier election cycles. It has been established that the majority of the Jewish community's support goes to Democrats, but many Republicans who serve on strategic committees also receive WASHPAC money. The average contribution to Senate Democrats totals about $125,000 per election cycle, compared to $45,000 given to Senate Republicans (see Table A.17). In 1992, over 72 percent of total contributions were given to Democrats. In 1990, 75 percent, and in 1988, 77 percent, went to Democrats (see Table A.17). Amitay insists that the lopsided support does not mean that the PAC is ideologically allied with the Democrats, merely that more Democrats than Republicans hold pro-Israeli opinions and records and serve on key committees in Congress. If an incumbent Republican is friendly to the cause and serves on a strategic committee or subcommittee, WASHPAC contributes.

Incumbents in both the House and the Senate, from both sides of the aisle, receive the greatest support. In 1992, 83 percent of overall contributions, or $165,000, went to incumbents. The amount of contributions to Democratic incumbents in both the Senate and the House is far greater than the amount given to Republicans, challengers, or members of either party running for open seats. Democratic incumbents received over $113,580, or 57 percent of total contributions. Republican incumbents received $51,340, or 26 percent of total contributions.

WASHPAC reluctantly helps challengers and candidates for open seats if they are supporters of Israel and their opponents are not and if the election is close enough for WASHPAC contributions to have an impact on the outcome. In 1992, WASHPAC gave only 2.4 percent of total contributions to challengers, while about 15 percent went to open seats. Twenty-two percent of contributions to all Senate races went to open seats. The three open-seat races in the Senate led WASHPAC to make some unusual and some unlucky contribution decisions this election cycle. In California, WASHPAC supported Representative Mel Levine in the race for the seat vacated by Alan Cranston. WASHPAC does not usually support a candidate in the primaries, but in this case an exception was made because of Levine's strong record of support for Israel. Levine lost. In Idaho, WASHPAC supported Democratic representative Richard Stallings, who had no primary opponent but lost in a predominantly Republican state. In Utah, WASH-PAC supported Democratic representative Wayne Owens in a race that promised to be a mad scramble but resulted in a relatively easy Republican victory. In 1992, contributions to twenty-one open-seat races totaled almost $30,000, a very small proportion of the total. This illustrates a trend that Ed Zuckerman notes in *The Almanac of Federal PACs: 1990*: "They [pro-Israel PACs] would rather support the reelection of an incumbent with a decent record for supporting Israel without regard to other issues, even at the expense of challengers whose devotion to Israel may be equally passionate or sincere."[19]

An Insider's View of the 1992 Elections

The election of 1992 was a strange one according to Amitay. He acknowledges that the PAC usually gives more to incumbents, but this time the redistricting process, the recession, and the political climate created after the House Bank and other scandals left incumbents particularly needy. In late October, Amitay predicted that there would be about 130 new members in the House and 12 in the Senate. Incumbents were so persistent that Amitay had his assistant speak to many of them because he finds it difficult to say no to longtime friends. The number of retirements and resignations led to an unprecedented number of open-seat races. As a result, Amitay knew much less about the candidates than he did in 1990. Despite repeated attempts by challengers, or candidates in open-seat races, to meet Amitay, he refused to meet with those he did not plan to give a check to. Amitay says:

> We get loads of [position papers] in here. Normally, in the past, I would try and meet with more of these people, and if they have a good position paper, and if I thought they had a shot, we'd help them, but it's just that the incumbents . . . it's such a weird political year, some of the incumbents see that they're in trouble and they're frightened . . . and we have to continue giving to incumbents, mainly because of location. I'm right here, I know these guys, they call, I run into them. I'd rather say no to someone I don't know than to someone I know.[20]

The PAC labeled three hotly contested 1992 Senate races as high priorities for the pro-Israel community. In Oregon, WASHPAC supported victorious Republican Bob Packwood, who was involved in a very close race. In Pennsylvania, WASHPAC supported victorious Republican Arlen Specter, who faced both strong primary and general election challenges. Amitay called Specter " 'a vital Republican friend' who sits on the critical Defense and Foreign Operations subcommittees of the Senate Appropriations Committee."[21] WASHPAC usually avoids contested primaries unless there is a real difference in the candidates on the issue of a secure Israel. In Wisconsin, WASHPAC supported another Republican, Bob Kasten, a ranking member of two key subcommittees and a leader in the fight for Israeli loan guarantees in the Senate. According to Amitay, "Everyone was writing his [Kasten's] political obituary for the longest time, and given his slender margins of victory in the past, as soon as Feingold got his astounding 70 percent in the primaries, everyone said Kasten's dead. But if someone has been down the line with you on your issue, you have to show support."[22]

In evaluating the results of the election on the Senate side in a memorandum to WASHPAC's advisory board entitled "Election Day: So What Does it All Mean?" Amitay wrote, "Overall, the results were excellent for our side. The only glaring exception was the defeat of Sen. Bob Kasten in Wisconsin. Kasten, seeking a third term, was the ranking Republican member on the Foreign Operations Appropriations Subcommittee."[23]

Amitay also measures the pro-Israel community's victory by keeping track of the number of Jewish Senators elected. After the 1992 election, he had the pleasure of informing his membership that a "minyan," the Hebrew word referring to the minimum number of people needed in temple to pray, had been achieved in the Senate—there are now ten Jewish Senators, as compared with only two twenty years ago. He noted that Jewish Senate candidates Abrams (vs. D'Amato) in New York, Rauh (vs. Gregg) in New Hampshire, Rothman-Serot (vs. Bond) in Missouri, and Herschensohn (vs. Boxer) in California were not successful.[24] Despite the defeat of these four, all pro-Israel incumbents won.

In terms of beating the bad guys, Amitay reported that in one key race matching a strong pro-Israel incumbent, Jim McCrery (R-LA), against "a much less preferable incumbent foe"—McCrery won. A leading spokesperson for the pro-Arab side, veteran Democrat Mary Rose Oakar (D-OH), was also defeated.

In the House of Representatives, the huge turnover resulted in fewer than ten new GOP seats but brought an unprecedented number of new faces to the 103rd Congress. Many incumbents lost. WASHPAC noted the losses of such pro-Israel friends as Tom Downey (D-NY), Peter Kostmayer (D-PA), David Nagle (D-IA), Gerry Sikorski (D-MN), Ben Erdreich (D-AL), Al Bustamante (D-TX), Tom McMillen (D-MD) Bill Green (R-NY), Nicholas Mavroules (D-MA), and John Cox (D-IL).[25]

Members holding key positions, such as Representative Les Aspin (D-WI), chairman of the Armed Services Committee; Representative Sam Gejdenson (D-CT), the new ranking Democrat on Foreign Affairs; and Charlie Wilson (D-TX), on Defense Appropriations, survived late strong challenges. It is safe to assume that the pro-Israel community as a whole was pleased with Les Aspin's confirmation as Bill Clinton's secretary of Defense. Regarding the numerous freshman Representatives due to take on strategic positions on House committees, Amitay writes, "Given the number of pro-Israel position papers received by the PAC from winners in many of the open and new seats, a significant number of entering freshman representatives have already focused in on the key issues of interest to us."[26] WASHPAC contributed to seven House freshman in the 1992 election. When asked how he was going to introduce himself to the new members of the 103rd Congress, Amitay smiled and said "with a check."[27]

Pleased with the overall performance of WASHPAC in the 1992 elections, Amitay reports that he is "very optimistic" that the legislative agenda under the Clinton administration will be much more friendly toward Israel than that of George Bush. Amitay maintains contact with friends in the Clinton transition team and with newly appointed committee chairmen. Now that there is a president and Congress of the same political party, Amitay comments, "There will be more legislation sent over by the administration that isn't tossed in the wastebasket."[28]

Plans for the Future

WASHPAC has no formal decisionmaking review process, nor meetings to gauge the success of the PAC following the election. Its director is satisfied with its operation and sees no reason to change it. He does not plan to incorporate more contributor input into deciding who gets WASHPAC money. There are no plans to employ professional direct-mail or consulting companies to help make decisions in the 1994 election cycle. In 1994, Amitay would like to hold back money to see how things develop, so as to avoid getting surprised by scandals or retirements, but, "if you're asked early, and you have it, it's very difficult—there's really no reason—to say no."[29] Other than attracting larger contributors to "cut down on thank-you letters and solicitations," the "One-Man PAC" will continue to operate as it has for the last twelve years—with Amitay personally contacting PAC members for contributions and distributing money to candidates at advisory board luncheons held once a month.

A major issue of concern to all PACs is the possibility of campaign finance reform. Currently, PACs can contribute up to $5,000 in the primaries and $5,000 in the general election. A campaign reform bill that eliminates PACs or cuts the amount of money PACs can give will reduce their influence. Amitay does not seem worried. He is an avid believer in the rational self-interest theory of politics: if most of the recipients of PAC money are Democrats, why would the Democrats bite the hand that feeds them? Amitay does not buy the argument that PACs have undue influence on the political process and need to be controlled. He states,

> PACs are just about everything, just about everyone is represented. And a PAC contribution is not that much more than an individual. PACs don't give

$10,000 shots to a lot of people. Yet individual fundraisers are people who come in . . . a husband and wife can come in with a $4,000 check. I don't see what the big difference really is; it seems to me that PACs are for everyone.[30]

WASHPAC is getting ready for 1994. A mailing sent out a week before the 1992 elections yielded contributions for debt retirement and help for a few people that the PAC was unable to help before the election. The reelection campaigns of Frank Lautenberg (D) in New Jersey, and Kent Conrad (D) in North Dakota have also been identified as priority races. WASHPAC had already contributed to twenty-two of the thirty-four Senate races.

Conclusion

WASHPAC was created by one person to pursue one goal. Begun by Morris J. Amitay for the purpose of ensuring a safe Israel, it grew from a mere hobby to the second largest pro-Israel PAC. The 1992 election offered WASHPAC the opportunity to alter drastically its pattern of contributions to congressional candidates. Nevertheless, WASHPAC, like most other political action committees, gave most of its contributions to incumbents and showed a strong tendency to favor Democrats. This pattern of giving reflects its desire to help ensure the presence of many friends of Israel in Congress. The election results demonstrate the wisdom of this strategy. This, and the experience of WASHPAC in general, shows that one man can make a difference in American politics.

Notes

1. Personal interview with Morris J. Amitay, treasurer, Washington Political Action Committee, Washington, D.C., November 26, 1991.
2. Memorandum from Morris Amitay to Advisory Board and Key Members, "Election Day: So What Does It All Mean?" November 4, 1992.
3. Ibid.
4. Ibid.
5. Ed Zuckerman, *The Almanac of Federal PACs: 1990* (Washington, D.C.: Amward Publishing, 1990), p. 547.
6. Ibid, p. 554.
7. Amitay interview, November 26, 1991.
8. Ibid.
9. Ibid.
10. *Broward Jewish World*, October 16–22, 1992.
11. Personal interview with Morris J. Amitay, Washington, D.C., October 27, 1992.
12. Personal interview with Morris J. Amitay, Washington, D.C., November 30, 1992.
13. Amitay interview, October 27, 1992.
14. Amitay interview, November 30, 1992.
15. Ibid.
16. Ibid.
17. Ibid.

18. Memorandum from Morris Amitay to Advisory Board and Key Members, "Election Day: So What Does It All Mean?" November 4, 1992.

19. Zuckerman, *The Almanac of Federal PACs: 1990*, p. 547

20. Amitay interview, October 27, 1992

21. WASHPAC Newsletter, Winter 1992.

22. Amitay interview, November 30, 1992.

23. Memorandum from Morris Amitay to Advisory Board and Key Members, "Election Day: So What Does It All Mean?" November 4, 1992.

24. Ibid.

25. Ibid.

26. Amitay interview, November 30, 1992.

27. Ibid.

28. Ibid.

29. Ibid.

30. Ibid.

19

New Kids on the Block: The WISH List and the Gay and Lesbian Victory Fund in the 1992 Elections

Craig A. Rimmerman

The 1992 elections offered both women and gay and lesbian voters an opportunity to flex their electoral muscles at all levels of government. Never before had women or gays and lesbians mobilized in ways that highlighted their electoral power. The October 1991 Clarence Thomas/Anita Hill senatorial hearings and the impending threat that the Supreme Court might well invalidate the 1973 *Roe* v. *Wade* abortion decision surely helped awaken women to the power of their numbers. For gay and lesbian voters, the 1992 presidential election was the first in which a major party candidate, Bill Clinton, courted them by promising sustained federal government attention to AIDS and an overturning of the statute banning openly gay and lesbian people from serving in the military.

For women's and gay and lesbian PACs, the 1992 electoral landscape offered opportunities for important electoral gains, given the record numbers of open seats created at all levels of government. This trend was rooted in three major factors: the surge in anti-incumbency reflected in the popularity of term limitations, redistricting, and retirements. This chapter places an evaluation of the WISH List's (which stands for Women in the Senate and House) and the Gay and Lesbian Victory Fund's 1992 political strategies within the context of this turbulent electoral scene. Both these political action committees are nascent organizations, and as a result, this was the first election in which they endorsed candidates and made campaign contributions.

Organizational Histories

The WISH List

The success of EMILY's List (which stands for Early Money Is Like Yeast) played an important role in the creation of the WISH List and the Gay and Lesbian Victory Fund in 1993. Glenda Greenwald, the founder and president of the WISH List, had long admired the electoral success of EMILY's List and its ability to recruit pro-choice Democratic women to run for public office. She contacted Ellen Malcolm, EMILY's List founder and president, and solicited her support and advice in creating a Republican organization for pro-choice women candidates running for Congress and in gubernatorial races. After receiving encouragement and advice from Malcolm, Greenwald gathered eight women together and secured financial commitments of $5,000 to $10,000 from each of them. In essence, this marked the creation of the WISH List. Malcolm was supportive from the word go and was particularly helpful in sharing advice on what strategies had worked well for EMILY's List and what approaches were less than successful.

From its inception, the WISH List has been committed to raising money for pro-choice, Republican women candidates running in House, Senate, and gubernatorial elections. State and local elections have been ignored because as a new organization, the WISH List simply does not have the resources needed to have a meaningful and tangible impact everywhere. The WISH List founders recognized that over time, men have had the financial resources needed to wage competitive campaigns, while female candidates have been grossly outspent. As a result, organizations such as the WISH List and EMILY's List are needed to help more women get elected to public office.

The Gay and Lesbian Victory Fund

The efforts of EMILY's List in helping Ann Richards defeat Clayton Williams in the 1990 Texas gubernatorial election were not lost on William Waybourn, the founder and current director of the Gay and Lesbian Victory Fund. When analyzing her own victory, Richards pointed to the integral role played by EMILY's List at a vital, early point in her campaign. Waybourn thought that such an organization needed to exist for openly gay and lesbian candidates at all levels of government as well. With this in mind, he contacted Vic Basile, former executive director of the Washington, D.C.–based political action committee the Human Rights Campaign Fund (HRCF). Basile responded enthusiastically and joined Waybourn in securing the support of gay and lesbian donors throughout the country. They found individuals who had considerable fundraising and political experience, and who were committed to giving or receiving $10,000 each initially to fund the newly created organization; these individuals ultimately comprised the organization's board of directors.

From its inception, the central goal of the Gay and Lesbian Victory Fund has been to elect qualified openly gay and lesbian candidates to public office. The Victory Fund joins fellow PAC HRCF, and a policy institute, the National Gay and Lesbian Task Force (NGLTF), as important political organizations representing the interests of gays and lesbians nationally. The Victory Fund is, however, the only national organization that exists solely to recruit and elect openly gay and lesbian candidates to public office at all levels of government. Unlike the Victory Fund, HRCF only supports candidates at the federal level and mostly endorses candidates who are not gay or lesbian but who have demonstrated a lasting commitment to promoting gay and lesbian rights. In addition, HRCF is a connected PAC and as a result is limited by law to federal campaign limitations on contributions. NGLTF does little work in the electoral arena; it engages in the lobbying of Congress, advocacy, grassroots organizing, and policy research relating to gay and lesbian concerns.

The Victory Fund has received support from both organizations. For example, all three organizations held a joint event at the 1992 Democratic National Convention. But HRCF has been particularly helpful in assisting the Victory Fund in its formative years. In the words of William Waybourn, "We [the Victory Fund] wouldn't be here without HRCF. They have given us advice, support, and assistance in every way."[1]

Organization and Decisionmaking

Both the WISH List and the Victory Fund are characterized by strong boards of directors that play integral roles in determining which candidates the respective organizations will endorse. Each also has a strong but small support staff that handles the day-to-day office operations.

WISH List president Glenda Greenwald is largely responsible for raising money and hosting fundraisers throughout the country. Her efforts, as well as those of her staff, have paid off: the WISH List raised close to $400,000 from their formation through November 3, 1992 election. Lynn Shapiro, the executive director, runs the Red Bank, New Jersey, headquarters, whose staff includes Shapiro, an office manager, a full-time clerical person, and a summer intern. Shapiro's long involvement in Republican party politics has given her the needed political expertise to provide leadership in that area as well.

In a very short period of time, the WISH List has been successful in securing the required financial commitment from some 1,500 members across the United States. All members are required to give an annual $100 membership contribution, which entitles them to the annual WISH List newsletter, regular member updates, and current candidate profiles. In addition, members agree to contribute $100 each election cycle to at least two candidates recommended by the WISH List. The average contribution to individual candidates' campaigns has been $100. Members have very little influence on whom the WISH List ultimately decides to endorse in a given election.

It is the board of directors that makes the final decisions over which candidates the WISH List will support financially. The board is composed of founding organizational members and others who have expressed an interest and made a financial commitment. The board sets policy at its quarterly meetings and has charged the executive director to implement that policy.

After conducting extensive research, a five-person candidate selection committee presents its findings and makes recommendations to the board of directors in time for its quarterly meeting. The chair of the selection committee, Candy Straight, is also a board member. She has an extensive political background from working in the Women's Campaign Fund and has been an important WISH List fundraiser. The candidate selection committee plays an integral role in choosing the candidates that the WISH List ultimately endorses. It is important to note, however, that the board's favor is hardly a rubber stamp. The board engages in spirited discussion of the selection committee's recommendations.

The WISH List adheres to the following criteria in making decisions about whom to support:

1. whether the WISH List's campaign contributions can affect the outcome of the race;
2. the ability of the candidate to raise money in her district;
3. the viability of the race;
4. the quality of the campaign organization;
5. whether the candidate in question is running in a newly created district;
6. the candidate's party, gender, and position on abortion (the WISH List only supports pro-choice Republican women);
7. whether the candidate is an incumbent;
8. what congressional committees the candidate sits on if she is an incumbent.

The WISH List prefers to support candidates running in open-seat races because it is in this situation that new women candidates for the office have the best chance of winning. Open-seat races also afford WISH List the best opportunity to affect election outcomes because contributions can have their greatest impact.

Unlike EMILY's List, the WISH List did not recruit candidates to run for office in the 1992 elections. Instead, candidates generally contacted the WISH List about securing its financial and organizational support after hearing about the newly formed organization through the news media. This will likely change in future elections, as the WISH List, with one election under its belt, intends to follow the lead of EMILY's list in going to the grass roots and encouraging pro-choice Republican women candidates to run for office at the national level.

Twenty-five candidates sought WISH List support for the 1992 elections, and the board concluded that only nine met their criteria. Members then chose from among the nine candidates and wrote checks of $100 for at least two. In general, if a member wishes to support a particular candidate financially, she then writes a check, for example, to "Susan Stokes for Congress." This allows the WISH List to engage in earmarking and bundling. Earmarking enables "the individual PAC contributor to name specifically the candidate(s) or party to receive the money."[2] Political scientist Larry Sabato contends that earmarking is "a marvelous way to enhance a PAC's influence . . . because most earmarked contributions are counted as individual gifts, not PAC donations, and thus the amount earmarked does not count against the $5,000 PAC contribution limit; at the same time the PAC gets most of the credit for the gift in the candidate's eyes."[3] Bundling permits the WISH List to " 'bundle' all individual gifts for each candidate and to transmit them with a cover letter from the PAC identifying the donors as PAC members."[4] By law, the WISH List must send individual contributions to candidates within ten days of receiving them.

The bulk of the WISH List's initial funding came from a handful of individuals who contributed $10,000 each. The WISH List has found that local events in people's homes, in restaurants, at country clubs, and on boats have been the most successful fundraising events. For the most part, these are relatively small gatherings of forty to sixty people. Direct mail has also been a lucrative fundraising strategy. Lists of potential contributors have been gathered from magazines and from a Washington, D.C., direct-mail firm that was recently hired to assist in direct-mail fundraising. While EMILY's List has been supportive in a variety of ways, it has not shared its fundraising lists.

Any candidate that receives the support of the WISH List must sign the same legal contract used by EMILY's List. This contract basically states that when the election is over, the candidate must allow the WISH List to use her donor list. These lists are yet other important sources of names used in direct-mail fundraising.

Like the WISH List, the Gay and Lesbian Victory Fund has a small office staff, albeit one that has been most successful in raising a considerable amount of money in a short period of time. As executive director, William Waybourn is responsible for the day-to-day running of the Washington-based organization and coordinates its political and fundraising strategies. Vic Basile is responsible for development. The Victory Fund has one staff person responsible for membership services, a financial services coordinator, and an administrative assistant, all of whom work out of the Washington, D.C., office.

From its founding in May 1991 through the November 1992 elections, the Victory Fund raised $233,000 from 1,313 members. Waybourn estimates that 95 percent of the membership is gay. All members contribute at least a $100 yearly organizational fee as well as pledge another $200 over a one-year period to any two candidates recommended by the Victory Fund. The average contribution to candidates has been $252.21. Waybourn attributes this high figure to the 1992 Republican National Convention, which showcased several speakers, most notably Pat Buchanan and Pat Robertson, who singled out gays and lesbians as objects of hatred and scorn. The Victory Fund welcomes input from its members regarding potential candidates that the organization might support.

It is the board of directors, however, that plays the central role in determining who will receive Victory Fund support in a given election. The board, which meets quarterly, is also responsible for hiring the executive director and for serving as the organization's eyes and ears on the political world. Board members are located throughout the country and made significant financial contributions when the Victory Fund was founded.

The process of choosing potential candidates for support is a thorough one. The Victory Fund uses an outside consulting firm to make an independent analysis of races in question. Then the Victory Fund staff makes a recommendation about a particular candidate to the board of directors. After lengthy and often spirited discussion, the board then votes to decide which candidates the Victory Fund will support. Some seventy-two candidates contacted the Victory Fund asking for its support in the 1992 elections. The Fund decided to support thirteen candidates at all levels of government. Candidates who hope to receive Victory Fund support must meet the following published criteria:

1. openly gay or lesbian;
2. endorsement of Federal Gay/Lesbian Civil Rights Bill;
3. aggressive positions on AIDS funding and antidiscrimination issues;
4. pro-choice; and
5. viable candidacy.[5]

Unlike the WISH List, the Victory Fund does not require that a candidate be a member of a particular party. Like the WISH List, however, the Victory Fund prefers open seats, especially at the congressional level. Races without incumbents afford a greater opportunity for the Victory Fund's electoral efforts to have a visible impact.

The Victory Fund has encouraged gay and lesbian candidates to seek Victory Fund support and to run for office. In addition, publicity regarding the organization has been so favorable that potential candidates have sought the endorsement of the organization. Both the Victory Fund and WISH List anticipate that they will become even more aggressive over time in recruiting potentially viable candidates to run for office. In this way, then, they will be following the kind of electoral strategy used by EMILY's List.

Like the WISH List, the Victory Fund earmarks and bundles funds in order to have the maximum possible impact on the outcome of races. Nonconnected ideological PACs are able to avoid the $5,000 spending limitation by requiring their members to earmark their contributions to specific candidates. Victory Fund members write their checks, for example, to "Gerry Studds for Congress," and the checks are then bundled every two days so that the Studds campaign has a constant flow of cash at every stage of the electoral season.

During its brief history, the Victory Fund has found that direct mail is the most successful form of fundraising. William Waybourn estimates that 85 percent of the organization's funds have come through direct-mail efforts. The

Victory Fund shares lists of potential contributors with other groups, most notably the HRCF and the NGLTF. The lists of HRCF and NGLTF supporters have been particularly useful to the Victory Fund in its efforts to recruit new members. In addition, the Victory Fund belongs to Pro-Net, a Washington, D.C., coalition that runs seminars for progressive PACs on how to build a successful fundraising strategy and to discuss candidates. Some of the groups belonging to Pro-Net are Clean Water Action, EMILY's List, the Human Rights Campaign Fund, the National Abortion Rights Action League, Handgun Control, Planned Parenthood, the Sierra Club, the National Organization for Women, and SANE/ FREEZE. The Victory Fund has also hired the New York City–based consulting firm Eidolon Communications for advice in designing a successful direct-mail fundraising strategy. It is interesting to note that Eidolon Communications has also assisted HRCF and EMILY's List in their fundraising efforts.

The Victory Fund also conducts an aggressive mail campaign to recruit new supporters by requesting that all those who join the organization send in a list of people who might be interested in contributing. The more a member contributes financially, the more the Victory Fund will contact that individual through direct-mail solicitation.

Waybourn estimates that telephone solicitation has been the second most successful fundraising form, accounting for some 10 percent of the Victory Fund's overall contributions. Major donors have often made their financial commitments after being contacted by telephone. The Victory Fund anticipates acquiring an 800 number soon, which will allow individuals to join by phone with their credit cards.

Receptions are the third form of fundraising. They account for roughly 5 percent of the Victory Fund's overall contributions and are generally held in major urban areas where there is a large gay and lesbian population. The Victory Fund relies on advertising in local gay and lesbian newspapers as well as letters to Victory Fund members in specific communities to guarantee that any given reception will be well attended. An August Washington, D.C., Victory Fund fundraiser was advertised in the gay/lesbian newspaper *The Blade* and had some one hundred people in attendance.

All candidates who receive Victory Fund support must sign a written contract. The Victory Fund requires candidates to make the following concessions after a campaign:

1. provide the Victory Fund with access to their mailing lists;
2. sign Victory Fund fundraising appeals;
3. make appearances on behalf of the Victory Fund.

In this way, the Victory Fund adds to its list of possible direct-mail contributors and secures the support of openly gay and lesbian candidates to tout the organization's efforts in the important fundraising game.

The Benefits of WISH List and Victory Fund Endorsements

Both WISH List and Victory Fund endorsements offer candidates important resources that will surely enable them to run more competitive races. Each provides candidates with financial support and technical assistance. Technical assistance includes the following:

1. advice on how a candidate can better market himself/herself to the electorate;
2. hands-on campaign management;
3. advice on how to raise money from potential contributors;
4. advice on dealing with the media;
5. crisis management.

The Victory Fund offers a campaigning skills program consultation for the openly gay and lesbian candidates it endorses, while the WISH List hopes to conduct candidate training workshops prior to the next election cycle.

The WISH List funnels individual donations from a national network of citizens who wish to see pro-choice Republican women elected to office, while the Victory Fund does the same for openly gay and lesbian candidates. This has allowed candidates to secure support that simply was not available prior to the creation of the two organizations.

The 1992 Elections and Implications for the Future

The 1992 elections afforded both the WISH List and the Victory Fund unique opportunities to have an impact, given the number of open seats. In addition, conventional wisdom had it as well that the WISH List would benefit from the so-called year of the woman, and the Victory Fund would garner support from a gay and lesbian community that was recognizing the power of its numbers. Lynn Shapiro pointed to the Clarence Thomas/Anita Hill hearings as a catalyzing force in mobilizing women. She contends that many of the WISH List contributors were galvanized by the fact that twelve white men sat on the Senate Judiciary Committee in judgment of Bush Supreme Court nominee Clarence Thomas.

The 1992 electoral results offered the WISH List encouraging news. Four out of the twelve women who had received WISH List financial support were elected to the U.S. House of Representatives. This is a particularly impressive accomplishment given that the WISH List is in its first election cycle. Shapiro believes that this augurs well for the future, especially when one considers that the entire organization will be more experienced in electoral politics during the 1994 elections. Looking ahead to 1994, the WISH List hopes to provide more technical assistance and training to candidates early in the electoral season in addition to much-needed financial contributions. In this way, the WISH List can have a demonstrated impact throughout the electoral cycle.

William Waybourn believes that mobilization in the gay and lesbian community can be attributed to the Reagan and Bush twelve-year record in neglecting

gay and lesbian concerns, especially in their failure to offer a forceful governmental response to the AIDS crisis. The 1992 Republican convention highlighted
the morally conservative element of the Republican party's hostility toward gays
and lesbians. The result, according to Waybourn, is that "George Bush engi-
neered the first gay voting bloc in the history of this country. And it was not for
him."[6] Indeed, most surveys released in the aftermath of the election reveal that
close to 90 percent of all gays and lesbians who voted supported the Clinton/
Gore ticket.

Like the WISH List, the Victory Fund also had reason to cheer the results of
the 1992 elections. The Victory Fund supported twelve openly gay or lesbian
candidates, and six of those candidates won. When asked to reflect on the 1992
election outcomes, Waybourn says he feels "very good about what we did in our
first year."[7] The Victory Fund intends to recruit gay and lesbian candidates to run for
open seats in the future. It is here that Waybourn believes the organization can
have its greatest impact. The Victory Fund does not like to support candidates
challenging incumbents because incumbents win 96 percent of the time.

The Federal Election Commission's 1992 data show that the WISH List and
Victory Fund supported candidates in different ways. As Table A.18 suggests,
the Wish List gave most of its contributions directly to candidates, often in the
form of in-kind contributions of services. In contrast, the Victory Fund made few
direct contributions of cash or service but instead concentrated on encouraging
their members to give directly to the candidates. Waybourn explained this strategy by concluding that "the goal of the Victory Fund is for our members to give
money directly to our candidates."[8] Bundling allows Victory Fund members to
accomplish that goal.

Conclusion

Both WISH List and the Victory Fund are structured in ways that allow small
donors to have an impact on electoral outcomes. Shapiro and Waybourn believe
that their respective organizational strategies enable them to educate citizens
about candidates running for public office and to afford them a more meaningful
impact in the electoral arena. In the end, the results of the 1992 elections and
the ability of both organizations to raise an impressive amount of money from
many small donors in a short period of time suggest that WISH List and the
Victory Fund are most successful given current campaign finance laws. As President Clinton and Congress begin to tackle campaign finance reform, it will be
interesting to see whether the reformers view the campaign finance strategies
practiced by WISH List and the Victory Fund as consistent with democratic
principles. To the extent that they do, these two organizations will serve as
models for other PACs that wish to have a meaningful influence on electoral
outcomes.

Notes

The author would like to thank Lynn Shapiro and William Waybourn for their patience and support in answering three sets of questions during the 1992 elections.

1. Personal interview with William Waybourn.

2. Larry J. Sabato, *PAC Power: Inside the World of Political Action Committees* (New York: W.W. Norton, 1990), p. 63.

3. Ibid., pp. 63–64.

4. Ibid., p. 64.

5. The following is the set of questions that the Victory Fund uses in determining the viability of a candidate. Candidates who wish to secure Victory Fund support must answer all of these questions satisfactorily:

1. What do demographics and past voting behavior say about your ability to win?
2. What is your campaign plan?
3. What demographic groups will you target?
4. What is your theme or message? What issues will you emphasize?
5. What are your greatest strengths *and* weaknesses as a candidate?
6. Have you ever held elected or appointed office? Please list offices and dates.
7. Who is (are) your opponent(s)? If your opponent is an incumbent, how is s/he vulnerable?
8. What is your campaign structure? What staff do you plan to hire?
9. Who is your campaign manager? What is his/her campaign experience?
10. What consultants have been hired for media, polling, and fundraising?
11. What is your budget for both the primary and general elections? How much do you anticipate spending on fundraising, media, field, and administration?
12. What is your fundraising plan? How much can you raise from individual donors?
13. How much money have you raised in past campaigns? How much have you raised to date? How much cash do you have on hand?
14. What are the individual and corporate spending limits for this race? What are the maximum individual and corporate campaign contributions allowed?
15. What endorsements have you received or do you expect to receive? What endorsements has (have) your opponent(s) received?

6. Waybourn interview.

7. Ibid.

8. Ibid.

20

How the Little People Choose: PAC Decisionmaking in the PHH Group, Inc., and the National Air Traffic Controllers' Association

Jack E. Rossotti

In the 1991–92 election cycle, approximately 75 percent of all PAC contributions came from only 8 percent of the 4,729 PACs registered with the Federal Election Commission.[1] While most scholarly and popular attention has been focused on these few, there are also a large number of political action committees that raise and contribute small amounts. They can be found among all PAC types—corporate, labor, membership, and ideological—and they have widely diverse organizational forms and political strategies.

Given the dominance of large PACs in terms of dollars contributed to candidates, the very existence and continued activity of these small committees warrants some consideration. What benefits do these organizations derive from their modest involvement in campaign finance? How do their procedures for making decisions differ from those of the larger PACs with which we are more familiar? How are these "little guys" affected by the actions of their larger contemporaries? Do they simply follow the lead of big organizations with similar interests, or are they more likely to go their own way, unincumbered by the demands imposed on more important players?

This chapter examines two small PACs that give modest amounts to federal candidates:[2] one corporation, the PHH Group, Inc., and one labor organization, the National Air Traffic Controllers' Association. While similar in size during the 1990 election cycle, they represent two very different stages in the life-cycle of PACs, with one shrinking and the other growing, and they have different approaches to the political process.

PHH Group, Inc.

The PHH Group, Inc.,[3] a publicly held corporation, was founded in 1946 and engages in two types of business activities: commercial vehicle leasing and the relocation of business personnel. PHH has offices in four locations in the United States employing about 4,400 people and is headquartered in Hunt Valley, Maryland.

The PHH political action committee was formed in the mid-1980s, a time when proposed changes in the tax code might have had a major impact on the company's primary businesses. The first PAC contributions were given to candidates who supported certain types of federal tax legislation. In particular, the company was interested in depreciation and investment tax credit provisions in legislation enacted in 1982 and 1984. This legislation determined whether the company would be entitled to tax benefits for many of its activities, especially regarding equipment leasing. The company received tax benefits for its investment in large and expensive equipment, which it then leased to other companies. Proposals to eliminate or reduce the deductability of these activities might have significantly affected PHH's financial position.

PAC Organization

The PAC director since 1988 has been Samuel H. Wright, the company's vice president and general counsel. Before becoming the PAC director, Wright was involved in the PAC's contribution decisions on a less formal basis. Since 1988 Wright has been chair of the PAC committee, which consists of five company employees. One employee is chosen from each of the company's two operating divisions (relocation and leasing), along with one representative of the human resources division and one from financial operations. This committee makes the PAC's contribution decisions.

At one time, the committee had one additional part-time staff employee, but today the administration of the PAC rests exclusively with the chair.[4] Overhead costs are paid entirely by the corporation so that member contributions can be used exclusively for campaign activity.

The PAC collects contributions in two ways: annual lump-sum contributions; and payroll deduction, in which management employees have contributions to the PAC automatically deducted from their paychecks. Initially, the payroll deduction system increased the PAC's treasury and the size of its contributor base. Receipts grew from about $19,000 in 1986 to more than $31,000 in 1988, but they then began to decline, falling to $20,000 in 1990 and to only $12,000 in 1992. Most observers agree that payroll deduction is the most efficient way to finance PAC activity, but in this case other factors seem to have driven fundraising in the opposite direction. The limited corporate resources used to support the

PAC may account for the decline in financial support. The company has reacted to the decline by providing one half-time staff member devoted to more effective communication with management employees.

The PHH PAC holds biannual informational meetings with its contributors that are attended by as many as 800 employees. The PAC's governing committee provides information about candidates the PAC is supporting as well as about relevant legislative issues. These meetings have been contentious at times, with members questioning the PAC's decision not to participate in presidential primary campaigns and sometimes criticizing the PAC's support for Democratic members of Congress. PHH's largely Republican contributor base often objects to PAC contributions to Democrats, but Wright believes the company benefits from contributions to chairs of congressional committees and subcommittees. The arguments of the PAC chairman have been accepted by the other committee members in recent years, as the committee has contributed to members of Congress who might not otherwise receive the support of company employees. This conflict highlights the most important choice all PACs must make—whether to use contributions to try to change the membership of Congress or to gain access to those who are already members.

In addition to these employee meetings, one newsletter is sent to PAC contributors each election cycle. After the election the PAC sends each contributor a list of candidates who received PHH PAC contributions and their election results. Wright would like to communicate with donors more often, but limited staff resources have made this impossible.

Decisionmaking

PHH PAC's five-member governing committee operates by majority rule, although most of its contribution decisions are made unanimously. Many candidates routinely request support, but Wright argues that these solicitations have no effect on PHH PAC decisions. The PAC's highest contribution priority has always been members of the House Ways and Means and Senate Finance committees. These committees are most likely to affect the company's income. More recently, PHH has begun targeting members of the House Energy and Commerce and the Senate Energy and Natural Resources committees.

The PAC also considers the geographic location of congressional districts. Members of Congress from districts in which PHH has a large employee base are more likely to receive contributions than others, unless the committee assignments of others are important to PHH. PHH PAC contributes overwhelmingly to sitting members, with incumbent support ranging from a low of 80 percent in 1984 to a high of 95 percent in 1990.

PHH has adopted an access-based contribution posture. Its PAC rarely gives money to candidates in contested primaries, nor will it give money to both general election candidates in the same district. The PHH PAC does not provide in-kind contributions or make independent expenditures. The PAC committee meets two or three times per election cycle to select candidates for support and to be briefed on issues of importance to the company. The voluntary nature of committee work makes it unlikely that the members will question the expertise of the PAC director when making contribution decisions. Their focus on the nuts and bolts of company work rather than politics may give them a different perspective than most "political operatives," but it also means they have less information and general knowledge on which to base their decisions.

The committee has not generally taken advantage of many common sources of information about campaigns. It has little contact with political parties, does not subscribe to political newsletters, and maintains contacts with only a few industry sources.

The outside source that seems to command the most of PHH's attention is the Mortgage Bankers Associations PAC, MorPAC. PHH receives regular MorPac mailings, and Wright indicated that MorPAC research is of vital interest to PHH. The PHH mortgage business is a large, nationwide program that has shown rapid growth in recent years. Although the internal politics, and hence the priorities, of the Mortgage Bankers Association and its PAC sometimes differ from PHH's view, PHH still seriously considers the MorPAC position in its PAC contributions.[5] MorPAC does periodic mailings that provide PHH with information on candidate voting records on mortgage banking issues.

Several other sources also provide input in the PHH PAC decisionmaking process. The company belongs to about six trade associations and informal ad hoc coalitions that develop around issues of interest to the participating organizations. For example, the company currently participates in an alternative minimum tax coalition and another group concerned about motor vehicle and trucking issues. Participation in these groups helps PHH identify financially needy candidates with favorable voting records.[6]

The company no longer sends its own questionnaires to candidates. Wright concluded that the company's modest contributions led both to low response rates and to forms being returned with stock answers.[7]

Open congressional seats present unique problems for the company, since published information about candidates in these elections is usually very limited. PHH tries to make decisions on the basis of candidates' policy positions. These positions are usually determined by having an employee in the area conduct research or by having someone in the company go to candidates' campaign offices to obtain pertinent information. Sometimes the PAC committee itself will conduct in-person interviews with candidates, but this process is not extensive because of personnel limitations. The company supplements its data by using computerized information systems.

The 1992 Election

The 1992 election cycle may have caused some political action committees to reexamine their existing contribution behavior, but the PHH PAC pattern remained largely unchanged. Indeed, Wright noted that the company approached the 1992 election inactively. This was partially due to the pressure of other business issues but primarily due to the lack of significant issues in the campaign at either the presidential or the congressional level. The large number of retirements and the banking scandal in the House of Representatives had almost no impact on PHH PAC's contribution decisions (although some employees questioned PAC support of some members involved in the controversies), and the company was not involved in the presidential race.

The sole exception to this unchanged behavior was one instance in which redistricting caused two incumbents to run against each other. As noted above, the PHH PAC avoids contributions to both candidates in the same election, though this tactic is sometimes used by other political action committees.[8] As a result of this policy, the company had to choose between two friendly candidates in Maryland's first district, both of whom were incumbents. PHH chose the "friendlier" of the two candidates, Representative Tom McMillen (D), leaving the other incumbent (and eventual winner), Representative Wayne Gilchrest (R), without a contribution.

There are two additional issues that affected PHH contribution decisions in 1992: capital formation incentives and alternative minimum tax reform. Wright felt that member votes on these two issues toward the end of the 1992 congressional session came close to being a litmus test. Voting in opposition to the PHH position on these issues might have been enough to change a contribution decision. At the very least, it would have provoked contact with the member's office for an explanation.

The company's fundraising for 1992 reached its targeted goals early, and so its fundraising activities were minimal. The company made all the contributions it desired during the 1992 campaign. However, PHH did not achieve other goals. The company had planned to conduct a get-out-the-vote campaign with the League of Women Voters near its company headquarters and in other locations where it has 200 or more employees. Generally, a lack of resources and also a lack of time prevented PHH from doing this. Wright noted his disappointment about this but indicated that he wants to do voter registration drives during all future election cycles. He wants these drives to include opportunities not only for company employees but also for the public at large. Grassroots mobilization programs are becoming more important for many PACs as they look for methods of political participation beyond financial assistance to candidates.

Additionally, Wright thinks that if he could replay the campaign, he would have paid more attention to the redistricting of congressional districts in the company's home state of Maryland. He shares a feeling with other people in business that redistricting is an important matter and that his company should have been involved in the process. Although he did not say so directly, Wright may have been disappointed with the choices that were ultimately left for Representative Tom McMillen, a real friend of PHH, who wound up running unsuccessfully in an unfamiliar district. Perhaps the results would have been more favorable to PHH and McMillen with more company involvement. Once again, the failure to focus resources on political activity may have put the company at a disadvantage. Involvement in activity like redistricting requires a level of commitment and sophistication beyond that of most corporate PACs. Other than these two disappointments, the 1992 election cycle was a predictable one for the company.

What Lies Ahead

Following the election, the PAC reviewed its activities and the election results as it does at the close of each cycle.[9] PAC officials suggested that this review encouraged them to consider giving higher priority to members of Congress who serve on relevant committees, downplaying the role of the localities that members represent.

Beyond reviewing the process, a major postelection goal was to develop contacts and legislative strategies for the new Congress. The high turnover rate in Congress and the election of a Democratic president made this project more important than in previous years. Specifically, PHH prepared materials on issues of interest to the company and hand delivered these to members whose committee assignments are relevant to PHH. The company also reviewed these with staff members. PHH indicated it would be spending more time with appointees in federal agencies during 1993 because some appointees of the new administration came with preconceived notions about issues that concerned it.

PHH also planned to circulate position papers to members of Congress on specific legislation. In particular, Wright was interested in tax legislation that was vetoed by President Bush and that was ultimately signed by President Clinton. Wright noted that PHH worked in coalition with other business groups to pass tax relief for the company. This was something fairly new for PHH, although it did work with these coalitions somewhat in the 102d Congress.[10]

On campaign finance, Wright is hoping for some reform, particularly legislation that would limit the amount of money PACs can give to individual candidates as well as the amount PACs can give in an election cycle. He thinks there may be some restrictions on donations given to candidates from outside a candidate's district. If so, the PHH strategy of giving based on committee assignment would be drastically affected. In general, Wright favors anything that would reduce the cost of campaigning, including providing competing federal candidates more opportunities to debate on national television. He wants PHH to be flexible for 1994 and 1996 in order to comply with whatever campaign finance legislation might be passed.

Summary

How successful has the PHH PAC been during its first decade of operation? Wright thinks it is naive to believe that PAC contributions actually change votes in Congress. Rather, he evaluates success on the basis of being able to obtain an audience with legislators. Using this standard, he is satisfied with his operation, an opinion he thinks is shared by most PHH contributors.

The National Air Traffic Controllers' Association[11]

The National Air Traffic Controllers' Association (NATCA) PAC was formed in January 1990. The PAC and the Air Traffic Controllers' union are associated with the Marine Engineers' Beneficial Association (MEBA), which has its own PAC. NATCA itself was formed in 1987 to replace the Professional Air Traffic Controllers Organization, which was decertified in 1981 following a strike by its members and their subsequent firing by President Reagan. The NATCA PAC operates autonomously from MEBA and occasionally supports candidates whom the MEBA PAC opposes.[12] Indeed, the two operate with sufficient independence that one PAC will sometimes provide contributions to candidates with whom the other PAC does not have a good relationship.

NATCA PAC has three employees: a treasurer and senior director of legislative affairs, currently John F. Thornton; an associate treasurer; and a custodian of records. Thornton is the functional head of the PAC. He determines which candidates receive contributions, organizes membership solicitation drives, produces reports to the membership on PAC activities, attends fundraising functions on behalf of the PAC, and serves as the PAC's spokesperson. As federal employees, NATCA members are forbidden under the Hatch Act to participate in PAC affairs (beyond making contributions), so all PAC activity must be conducted by its three employees, who are not covered by the Hatch Act.[13]

The PAC's membership consists of air traffic controllers and a few employees of NATCA. Approximately 700 people contribute an average of $50 each year. All of the operating costs are paid for either by NATCA or by the NATCA PAC itself. Contributions are solicited and collected through the mail. The direct-mail solicitations also invite contributors to use the payroll deduction system. In addition, NATCA's biannual convention has contributed to its member base. For example, during its 1992 convention NATCA was able to add about 200 new contributors. Those who contribute receive mailings containing information about the PAC's financial activity and evaluations of congressional candidates. In general, Thornton is very upbeat about the growth of the NATCA PAC, which he feels is rapidly maturing. In the PAC's early days, he says, weeks went by without a payroll deduction form being submitted. Now, he notes, one arrives at his office virtually every day. The financial activity of the PAC supports this claim, as NATCA PAC reached the $100,000 level in just its second election cycle of activity.

Because of the previously noted Hatch Act restrictions on political activity by federal employees, Thornton is required to make PAC contribution decisions without the participation of NATCA members. He does, however, regularly meet with union members and officers to solicit their views on the performance of various members of Congress. Members are free to make these kinds of evaluations, although they cannot suggest that the PAC contribute to particular candidates. Thornton is considering formalizing this interaction through a series of lunch and dinner meetings.

Contribution Strategies and Information Sources

Contribution strategies for NATCA PAC center around internal congressional power. The targeted members are those on the Aviation subcommittees in the House and the Senate, along with members of the House Post Office and Civil Service Committee and the Senate Government Affairs Committee, who are responsible for federal employee issues generally. The former receive automatic contributions. Committee chairs and members of a few specialized subcommittees such as the Government Activities and Transportation Subcommittee in the House are next in line as contribution recipients. Like most other labor PACs, NATCA gives a large majority of its contributions to Democrats. However, a favorable labor voting record is also an important factor. Other criteria, such as competitiveness of an election, geography, personal friendships with NATCA members, and support on specific bills have some impact.

NATCA rarely gives in primary elections, to both candidates in a general election, or even to open-seat candidates. It does not make independent expenditures or in-kind contributions. However, NATCA made two exceptions in the 1992 election cycle. In one of the California Senate races, NATCA supported then-representative Barbara Boxer (D) in the primary. Indeed, this was the race in which the PAC was most heavily involved. Boxer has a particularly good relationship with NATCA and has supported it on some key issues. NATCA also got involved in the New York senatorial primary. In that election, it sided with former representative Geraldine Ferraro, who lost a divisive Democratic primary. NATCA then switched parties to support Republican senator Alfonse D'Amato, the ultimate winner. Thornton, noting the New York situation, said that he would have preferred to stay out of primaries altogether. But once the PAC was involved in one primary it became involved in others. Thornton did not make it clear whether 1992 was a unique situation or whether it marked a long-term policy change.

Like PHH, NATCA does not pursue outside information. The principal source of information seems to be person-to-person interviews with House and Senate candidates, which Thornton largely conducts himself. Beyond that, Thornton makes limited use of outside sources, including information from party committees. He does not attend PAC conferences or utilize political newsletters.

Notably, there is no lead PAC that NATCA follows in making its contribution decisions. The principal outside source Thornton does use is information compiled by the parent union, the Marine Engineers' Beneficial Association. MEBA provides various types of electoral information, including polling data and information about primary contests. Occasionally, this information is useful to NATCA in making its contribution decisions. However, as previously discussed, the NATCA PAC operates autonomously from MEBA, despite the fact that the two are merged legally for contribution-limit purposes. During 1992, Thornton also occasionally discussed candidate information with his sources in three other unions, including the AFL-CIO's COPE.

Additionally, NATCA began subscribing to a computerized legislative tracking service during early 1992. This program provides a wide range of current legislative information, and Thornton has found this to be helpful for data on incumbents. Ultimately, however, NATCA PAC is mostly a one-person operation run by John Thornton, who relies on his own judgment and who makes all the important contribution decisions.

The 1992 Election

Thornton had anticipated some changes in the PAC's behavior in the 1992 election cycle. Most notably, NATCA considered giving to two congressional incumbents who were challenging each other in the same primary due to redistricting. Yet in the end it decided not to do so. Instead, in a Democratic primary in Illinois that matched then-representative Martin A. Russo against Representative William O. Lipinski, NATCA chose to give only to Lipinski. Thornton met personally with both members, and his decision ultimately turned on Lipinski's record on aviation issues. Lipinski was determined to have better relations with air traffic controllers in his district as well as being likely to produce more favorable legislative results for NATCA in the long run.

Another issue that caused some rethinking of contribution patterns during 1992 was a general dissatisfaction among union members with incumbents. This problem was exacerbated by the banking scandal in the House of Representatives. More field activities were held in 1992 in order to explain the PAC's support of threatened members. For example, Thornton held meetings with union members and various regional and national branches of NATCA to discuss the upcoming races. These meetings resolved resistance from union members who were concerned about the PAC's support for a few candidates. For example, in the Great Lakes region, union members were unhappy with the way they perceived representative Rosemary Oakar (D-OH) was handling her office. According to Thornton, a portion of the membership thought Oakar had lost track of why she had been elected. After Thornton met with the membership, the resistance ended and NATCA supported Oakar's unsuccessful reelection bid. Beyond these meetings, problems with incumbency and the banking scandal did not change the PAC's contribution behavior.

Nor did the number of open seats in the 1992 election cycle change NATCA's behavior. Thornton noted that the PAC is geared to support incumbents and is concerned almost exclusively with aviation issues. Dealing with incumbents offers the PAC the advantage of knowing on what subcommittee an incumbent will sit. Open-seat candidates do not offer this opportunity. Therefore, in most instances NATCA stays neutral in open-seat elections and does not give money to either candidate.[14] The same reasoning is used in primaries, making challengers unlikely to receive NATCA contributions. The only exceptions in 1992 were one challenge to a Democratic incumbent in Georgia and the Illinois race discussed above. The limited funds available to the NATCA PAC reinforced these decisions.

In the presidential race, NATCA contributed $10,000 to the Democratic National Committee for the Clinton–Gore ticket. The PAC had originally planned to keep a low profile in this race by making only this indirect contribution and avoiding a public endorsement. Thornton was worried about angering President Bush with such a decision. However, in the end, the NATCA executive board publicly endorsed Clinton through an announcement in the NATCA newsletter. Some PAC members disagreed with these decisions and wrote to the PAC expressing their dissatisfaction. However, Thornton did not seem to view this as a serious problem.

NATCA also makes some contributions for debt retirement, including a contribution to one freshman made in late November 1992. This type of activity is an indication of the growth of the NATCA PAC. It previously did not have the money to make postelection contributions.

Only two legislative issues were of interest to NATCA during 1992—a pay raise for air traffic controllers and Hatch Act reform. However, since neither issue was active in Congress, neither formed the basis for contributions in this election.

Generally, Thornton was satisfied with NATCA's operations during the 1992 elections. The PAC had enough money to make all the contributions it wished and did not have to lower the desired amount to any individual candidates. It went all out for only one candidate, Senator Barbara Boxer (D-CA), to whom it gave $2,650 directly in 1992 and then donated another $1,500 to the Democratic Senatorial Campaign Committee, which was earmarked for the Boxer campaign. NATCA was able to approximately double the number of candidates to whom it contributed from 1990 to 1992 and substantially increase the total amount of money it contributed. However, as with PHH, NATCA reviewed its contribution process after the 1991–92 election cycle.

What Lies Ahead

Largely because the PAC is still young, the process remained informal during the 1992 cycle. Thornton was frank in admitting that "a lot of initial work was done by the heart," meaning that decisions were made without formal guidelines. He cited specifically Senate races in Pennsylvania and Illinois in which NATCA made contributions to Democratic candidates without obtaining sufficient assurances on the issues. It is possible, he said, that the other candidates in these races might have been more favorable on the issues. As a result, Thornton wants to formalize the internal process in the future. He wants candidates to tell him where they stand on certain issues or "if they do not tell us . . . we will take a pass on that race."

Another change that Thornton considered prior to 1994 was to have NATCA make its contributions later in the election cycle. He thinks the PAC has more impact with its contributions if they are made near election day. Thornton will consider implementing this change for the 1994 elections. The only "mistakes" Thornton could cite was giving money to losing candidates in two primaries, one in a House race in Georgia as noted, and one in the Senate race in Illinois to then-senator Alan Dixon (D).

In general, the 1991–92 cycle reflected a maturing process for the NATCA PAC. Thornton noted that NATCA has now been around long enough, and has a sufficient ongoing relationship with enough incumbents, so that its representatives now get both an easier and a fairer opportunity to have hearings with members.

NATCA's intentions for establishing relationships with members of Congress are remarkably similar to those outlined by Samuel Wright at PHH. Thornton's focus will clearly be on member committee assignments. After those have been determined, NATCA will set up office visits with members to make contacts. At these meetings, the NATCA representative, presumably Thornton in most cases, will discuss issues of interest to the PAC and make known the number of NATCA members in that district or state.

The legislative agenda for NATCA during the 103rd Congress will be extensive. Hatch Act reform could cause a restructuring of the PAC, as its elected president can now become eligible to replace Thornton as PAC director. Thornton sees no serious problem with such a scenario, since he thinks it proper that the president should be the PAC director. The change would be as much cosmetic as real, since Thornton would probably become deputy director and major policies would not change.

Thornton was also interested in health care reform. He believed that part of the health care changes that were likely to occur during 1993 and 1994 would include altering the method in which federal sector health plans are selected. Other areas of interest to NATCA are family leave legislation[15] and restructuring of the Federal Aviation Administration.

On campaign finance, Thornton is not optimistic about substantial reform taking place. He thinks that if anything happens it will be a watered-down version of what was discussed during the campaign and will not have much impact on NATCA's activity. He would personally like to see the individual contribution limit to federal candidates raised from the current $1,000 maximum to $5,000.

Summary

The NATCA political action committee is highly centralized in its operations. All activity and decisionmaking revolve around John Thornton. Given the growth rate of this young PAC, changes do not seem either likely or necessary. Thus, the NATCA PAC presents an interesting and useful model for studying political action committee behavior.

Conclusion

PHH PAC and NATCA PAC, two very small committees, reveal a pattern of informality in decisionmaking, structure, and information sources. Of the two, the PHH PAC has a formal decisionmaking committee, but even that operates flexibly. For both PACs, payroll deductions have proved to be the most efficient method of fundraising. Both PACs communicate with their members about PAC activities, and both emphasize internal congressional influence when making contribution decisions. PHH and NATCA have both had successful operations, measured in terms of their stated electoral and legislative objectives, and each remains an active and viable organization.

Notes

1. Federal Election Commission, "PAC Activity Rebounds in 1991–1992 Election Cycle—Unusual Nature of Contest Seen as Reason," Press release, April 23, 1993.
2. The definition of "small" when referring to a political action committee in this chapter is based on the amount of disbursements in a calendar year. For the two PACs profiled in this chapter, each had disbursements of less than $10,000 in calendar year 1990.
3. Most of the information in this section was provided by a series of personal interviews with Samuel H. Wright. Wright is vice president and general counsel for the PHH Group, Inc., and head of the PHH political action committee.
4. This situation changed after the 1992 election. As a result of a regular review of the PAC's activities, PHH decided in the summer of 1993 to hire a part-time employee with a PAC background to increase the company's internal grassroots activity. Among other things, this employee will be making trips to the larger PHH installations to generate enthusiasm for the PAC through presentations.
5. Wright explained that the Mortgage Bankers' Association currently has an internal political split between small and large member mortgage companies. The association is currently dominated by small companies, while the industry is controlled by large companies. With PHH aligned with the latter group, the MorPAC research may sometimes lack usefulness.
6. Wright also meets occasionally with other PAC directors. However, the company's membership in BIPAC (Business–Industry Political Action Committee) was recently ended for financial reasons.
7. In 1992 the company sent out requests for standard campaign information to every candidate in the House and the Senate in whose district or state the company had an office. Wright estimated the response rated at approximately 50 percent, a figure he

considers disappointing. As a result, the company had to collect its own information from relevant newspaper articles.

8. Wright says that PHH runs its committee just as an individual would make his contribution decisions. Rarely would an individual give to both candidates in the same election. PHH uses the same reasoning.

9. One change had already occurred, as noted earlier. The PHH PAC is no longer solely operated by Wright. In the summer of 1993, the company hired an additional part-time employee.

10. Passage of this legislation in 1992 was of major importance to PHH. Wright followed the process closely because of the potential impact of some of the provisions on PHH. Wright noted that support in committee was more important than actions taken by members on the floor. As he put it, the end vote was often less important than the internal process.

11. Most of the information contained in this section is taken from a series of personal interviews conducted with John F. Thornton, treasurer of the National Air Traffic Controllers' Association political action committee.

12. Despite the autonomy, the two PACs are counted as one for purposes of federal contribution limits. Thus, the two PACs combined cannot give more than $10,000 to a given candidate in any one election cycle.

13. The Hatch Act forbids covered federal employees from participating in partisan political activity. However, the three PAC employees are paid by the union and are thus exempt from this restriction.

14. Thornton cited occasional exceptions to this rule, in which someone in the union has developed a relationship with one of the candidates.

15. Federal family leave legislation was passed by Congress and signed into law by President Clinton in early 1993.

Part Four

Conclusions

21

Not So Risky Business: PAC Activity in 1992

Paul S. Herrnson and Clyde Wilcox

The case studies in this book have sought to address three sets of questions. First, how do PACs select the candidates to whom they contribute? Second, where do PACs turn for the information they need to sort out the myriad candidates and contests? Third, do PACs respond to the electoral opportunities that arise in particular elections? And did they respond to the unique opportunities that presented themselves in the 1992 election cycle? Based on the answers provided in these case studies, we are now in a position to determine whether the answers to these questions vary systematically among PACs that have different types of sponsors, varying degrees of institutionalization, or unequal levels of funding. We are also in a position to assess more fully the role of PACs in the campaign finance system.

The set of PACs discussed in this book include corporate, trade, labor, and ideological committees with different amounts of funds and varying levels of institutionalization. The PACs are generally representative of the broader PAC community on a variety of indicators. For example, the percentage of contributions these committees gave to nonincumbent candidates and to candidates involved in close elections in 1992 was very similar to the average for the entire PAC community. The PACs in our study include some that have long histories, some that were born in the 1992 election cycle, and some that died or were drastically restructured after the 1992 election. This chapter will draw some broad conclusions from these careful analyses of individual committees.

Expectations about PAC Decisionmaking

PACs faced a great deal of uncertainty during the 1992 election cycle. With a record number of open seats, incumbents weakened by scandal and redistricting, and a presidential race that frequently seemed unpredictable, it was easy to imagine a number of possible scenarios. Very early in the election cycle, when George Bush's popularity reached record high levels and it was obvious that redistricting would create many new seats in traditionally Republican states, it seemed very possible that the Republicans could make significant gains in the House. Prior to the Democratic National Convention, when Ross Perot led both Clinton and Bush in the polls, some journalists predicted a general anti-incumbent mood that would lead to the defeat of many members of Congress in both parties. After the Democratic convention, when Bill Clinton led by nearly twenty points in some national polls, it seemed perhaps that the Democrats would do better than previously predicted and possibly even gain seats. The uncertainty was magnified by a spate of late retirements and by battles over redistricting that stretched well into 1992.

The strategic politicians theory posits that PACs are political actors that seek to exploit the political environment to maximize their advantage.[1] PACs, like voters, are seen as responding primarily to the quality of the candidates, but PAC managers also consider the likelihood that a candidate will win. In 1992, a number of highly qualified challengers and open-seat candidates in both parties ran for office, and many initially appeared to have a good chance of winning.

The strategic politicians theory suggests that those PACs seeking to influence the composition of Congress would protect vulnerable, sympathetic incumbents but that they would also have seized upon the opportunities presented by the 1992 election to contribute to some of the many qualified nonincumbents. Some PACs have always responded to changing electoral circumstances by backing vulnerable incumbents when the electoral tides favored the other party and by investing in nonincumbents when the tides washed the other way.[2] Labor committees protected vulnerable Democratic incumbents in 1980, 1984, and 1988 and supported Democratic open-seat candidates and challengers in 1982 and 1986. COPE and NEA PAC both demonstrated throughout the 1980s a willingness to back promising Democratic nonincumbents, but they rallied to defend their incumbent friends when the Republicans seemed poised to make serious gains. Ideological PACs have also taken advantage of national political circumstances to back competitive nonincumbents.

Among corporate PACs, a sizable minority aggressively backed Republican nonincumbents in the 1978 and 1980 election cycles.[3] Convinced by the National Republican Congressional Committee that GOP gains in 1978 and 1980 could lead to a change in party control of the House in 1982, they backed Republican challengers and open-seat candidates in 1981 as well. As the depths of the recession of 1982 became evident, however, and as Reagan's popularity continued to drop, these conservative corporate PACs began to hedge their bets and give to Democratic incumbents. After the 1982 election, Tony Coelho, then head of the Democratic Congressional Campaign Committee, met with groups of corporate PAC directors and explained that access to Democratic lawmakers required contributions to Democrat House members, not to Republican challengers.[4] As a result, by the 1990 election cycle, more than half of the contributions of corporate PACs went to Democratic incumbents, and only 8 percent were given to Republican nonincumbent candidates.

This shift from an ideological strategy to one that emphasizes access to incumbents is evident in the contribution behavior of the Realtors' PAC, and to a lesser extent AT&T PAC, during the 1980s. These large corporate and trade PACs shifted their contributions toward Democratic incumbents during that decade. The Realtors had given one-third of their money to Republican challengers and open-seat candidates between 1978 and 1982 but gave only 8 percent to GOP nonincumbents in 1990. AT&T PAC dropped its contributions to Republican incumbents from 11 percent to 5 percent. Some PACs that had given an even higher proportion of their contributions to Republican nonincumbents also shifted the bulk of their contributions to Democratic incumbents.

Some corporate PACs, of course, maintained their support for Republican nonincumbents. Eaton Corporation's PAC remained steadfast in its support for promising Republican challengers and open-seat contestants, and BIPAC continued to channel a majority of its funds to these candidates. Such behavior became increasingly difficult in the latter half of the 1980s, as the average quality of Republican House nonincumbents declined. By 1990, most corporate PACs had become firm supporters of incumbents, including Democrats.

Most corporate PACs made peace with Democratic incumbents during the 1980s. They recognized that a tax break championed by Finance Committee chair Lloyd Bensten or House Ways and Means Committee chair Dan Rostenkowski is just as valuable as one advocated by Senator Robert Packwood or Representative Bill Archer (each of whom would have chaired one of these committees in 1993 if the Republicans had won control of the Senate or the House). For these corporate committees, legislative outcomes were more important than electoral politics. Yet if corporate PACs operate as strategic actors, then at least some of them would have returned to supporting some Republican nonincumbents in 1992. With so many open seats at stake, such a contribution strategy would not necessarily have involved giving to the opponent of an incumbent Democrat.

It is also possible, however, that PACs are institutions that are slow to change their contribution behavior and adapt only gradually to changes in their environment.[5] Having learned over the course of the 1980s that incumbents nearly always win, these PACs might not jettison that lesson in order to respond to the new opportunities that arose in the 1992 election. Because of numerous possibilities to change the composition of Congress, various theories of incremental institutional behavior and institutional learning predicted that PACs would none-theless do in 1992 what they had done in 1990—back incumbents, including those who faced little opposition.[6]

There was no reason to believe that all PACs would respond to the possibili-ties of the 1992 campaign in the same way. We thought it possible that large, institutionalized committees might behave somewhat differently from smaller committees. First, the institutionalized committees have decisionmaking boards, and these boards frequently use elaborate criteria when deciding whether to make a contribution in a particular race. These criteria have evolved to ease decisionmaking and to avoid conflict, and they may be difficult to change. In contrast, smaller "Mom and Pop" PACs with single managers who make all allocation decisions can be more flexible in responding to a changing environment.

On the other hand, the institutionalized committees are more likely than oth-ers to have the organizational resources to monitor closely a number of races. They are also more likely to have cash left over after contributing to the import-ant incumbents on the committees with jurisdiction over their key issues. This "venture capital" may enable a PAC to contribute to nonincumbents, to provide in-kind services, or to engage in independent spending on behalf of nonincumb-ent candidates.

We thought that some PACs might change their contribution strategies in 1992 for reasons other than the unique opportunities that this particular election cycle offered. PACs that are centrally concerned with the abortion issue may have changed their contribution strategy in 1992 in response to changes in the politics of abortion. The 1989 Supreme Court decision in the *Webster* v. *Repro-ductive Health Services*, and the 1991 *Casey* v. *Planned Parenthood of South-eastern Pennsylvania* decision transformed the nature of the abortion debate in America.[7] Prior to *Webster*, pro-life PACs raised more money than their pro-choice counterparts and were more aggressive in contributing to non-incumbents.[8] After Webster, however, pro-choice activists were motivated to influence the composition of Congress in an effort to pass national legislation to guarantee the basic abortion right from *Roe*. Other issues, especially health care, were central to the 1992 presidential campaign, and we expected PACs con-cerned with health care to behave differently in the 1992 election.

Expectations about Information Networks

For those PACs that chose to contribute to nonincumbent candidates, and even for those that sought to contribute to incumbents who most needed the money, the 1992 election cycle was likely to create special problems. Although many committees had developed mechanisms to separate competitive challengers and open-seat candidates from those who appeared to be obvious "lost causes," the sheer numbers of open-seat races, combined with the uncertainty created by late redistricting, the effects of scandals, and the somewhat chaotic presidential race

Table 21.1

Proportion of House Contributions by PAC Type and Type of Campaign, 1990–92

	Corporate		Labor		Trade/Member/Health		Ideological	
	1990	1992	1990	1992	1990	1992	1990	1992
Democrats								
Incumbents	49%	48%	66%	61%	52%	46%	44%	42%
Challengers	1%	2%	11%	14%	2%	4%	7%	8%
Open Seats	3%	4%	16%	20%	6%	9%	14%	15%
Republicans								
Incumbents	38%	34%	6%	4%	33%	29%	21%	19%
Challengers	3%	4%	0%	0%	2%	4%	6%	8%
Open Seats	6%	7%	0%	1%	6%	8%	8%	8%

Source: Federal Election Commission.

made all predictions uncertain. If committees wanted their money to go to the most competitive nonincumbents, they would need to gather additional information from various sources.

Some PACs provide information to others, serving as cue-givers.[9] These "lead PACs" hold meetings attended by the managers of other committees, mail newsletters and other information to PAC members and other groups, and provide information to those who call with questions about particular races. We selected four of these committees—COPE for organized labor, BIPAC for the corporate sector, NCEC for liberal ideological groups, and Free Congress PAC for conservative groups—to see what effect these committees would have on the contributions of other PACs in this cycle.

Of course, PACs have many other ways to gather information. Decentralized committees use their local branches. A number of professional newsletters, such as the *Political Report* and *Cook Political Report*, and various on-line services provide up-to-date polling information on Senate races and many House elections. The party committees hold briefings and invite PACs to breakfasts and other events to meet their most promising candidates.[10]

For those PACs that want to target their contributions carefully, information is likely at a premium. It is probable that they will increasingly consult with managers of the lead PACs, read the various political newsletters more carefully, and perhaps use other sources of political information.

Aggregate Patterns of PAC Contributions

The overall pattern of PAC contributions in the 1992 elections very closely resembled the pattern that appeared in 1990 (see Table 21.1). Corporate PACs gave 49 percent of their money to Democratic incumbents in 1992, as opposed to 51 percent in 1990. They gave 8 percent of their money to Republican non-incumbent candidates in 1990 and 11 percent in 1992. The behavior of trade association PACs follows a similar pattern: contributions to Democratic incumbents dipped from 54 percent to 48 percent, and contributions to Republican nonincumbents increased from 7 percent to 10 percent. Trade association PAC contributions to Democratic nonincumbents fell by 6 percent. Clearly, there was a very small overall shift of contributions away from Democratic incumbents and toward nonincumbent candidates by corporate and trade PACs.

It is important, however, to consider the number of candidates in each category who actually ran in the 1992 election. The number of Democratic incumbents on general election ballots fell from 249 to 213 between 1990 and 1992. The number of open-seat candidates rose from 62 in 1990 to 179 in 1992, and the number of all nonincumbents rose from 50 percent of all candidates in 1990 to 59 percent in 1992. If all contributions were randomly distributed among candidates, one would expect a 20 percent increase in contributions to nonincumbent candidates in 1992. The additional support for both Republican and Democratic nonincumbents in 1992 among corporate and trade PACs fell far short of this figure.

Labor committees were more responsive to the opportunities of the 1992 election cycle. The percentage of their donations to Democratic incumbents dropped from 71 percent in 1990 to 64 percent in 1992, and the percentage to Democratic open-seat candidates rose from 11 percent to 20 percent. But this change was no different from earlier election cycles in which many opportunities were present. In both 1982 and 1986, for example, the shift in focus of labor contributions was somewhat larger than in 1992.[11] Thus, labor PACs increased their giving to nonincumbent candidates, but not as sharply as the circumstances of the 1992 election might have predicted.

It is possible that these aggregate data mask sharp changes in the behavior of PACs that had supported nonincumbents in earlier election cycles.[12] For example, corporate PACs that had aggressively supported nonincumbent candidates in the 1978 through 1982 elections and had then given most of their money to incumbents in later election cycles might have shifted back to Republican non-incumbents in 1992. It is possible that this shift has been hidden among the contributions of more recently formed incumbent-oriented corporate PACs.

Yet our analysis suggests that even among the formerly "aggressive" corporate PACs that supported Republican nonincumbents, there was little change in aggregate contribution patterns. Fully 238 corporate PACs gave a majority of their contributions to nonincumbents in 1982 (see Table 21.2). Of the 151 that were still active in 1992, only 33 gave a majority of their money to non-incumbents—a small increase from 30 committees in 1990. These "aggressive" corporate committees gave 60 percent of their contributions to nonincumbents in 1982, but by 1990 that number had fallen to 34 percent. In 1992, these PACs

Table 21.2

Aggressive Corporate and Labor PAC Support of Nonincumbents

	1981–82		1983–84		
	No. of PACs	% given to NIs*	No. still active	% given to NIs	No. giving majority to NIs
Corporate	238	63	234	43	69
Labor	139	57	130	42	37

	1985–86			1987–88		
	No. still active	% given to NIs	No. giving majority to NIs	No. still active	% given to NIs	No. giving majority to NIs
Corporate	221	41	52	195	30	31
Labor	116	52	35	107	43	32

	1989–90			1991–92		
	No. still active	% given to NIs	No. giving majority to NIs	No. still active	% given to NIs	No. giving majority to NIs
Corporate	173	34	30	151	41	33
Labor	94	35	20	84	45	26

Source: Federal Election Commission.
Notes: Aggressive PACs are those that gave a majority of their contributions to nonincumbents in 1982.
*NIs = Nonincumbents.

channeled 41 percent of their contributions to nonincumbent candidates—a notable increase, but far short of their support for such candidates in 1982.

Similarly, 139 labor PACs gave a majority of their money to nonincumbents in 1982. Of the 84 that were still active in 1992, only 26 gave a majority of their funds to nonincumbents—an increase from 20 committees in 1990. These "aggressive" labor committees had given 57 percent of their contributions to nonincumbents in 1982, and by 1990 the figure had fallen to 35 percent. In 1992, they gave 45 percent to nonincumbents. Although this represents a somewhat sharper increase than had occurred among the corporate PACs, these committees still gave less to nonincumbents in 1992 than they had in 1986 and only slightly more than they had in 1988.

The possibility remains, however, that aggressive corporate and labor PACs increased their overall spending in 1992 and therefore channeled a greater total amount of money to nonincumbents than in past elections. A modest increase in

Millions of Dollars

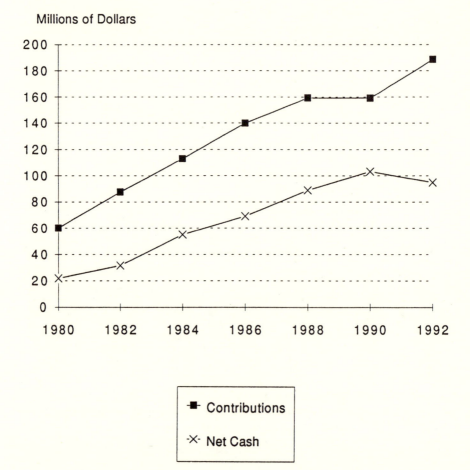

Figure 21.1. **PAC Contributions and Cash on Hand**

the percentage of money going to challengers, coupled with a sharp increase in spending, could translate into a sharp increase in the campaign budget of the average challenger. In fact, PACs did indeed contribute more money in the 1992 election than in previous election cycles, but this was part of a steady increase in contribution activity (see Figure 21.1). PACs also spent a slightly higher proportion of their available cash, for their balance at the end of the election cycle declined somewhat from the level of reserves in December 1990. In the aggregate, however, there is little evidence that PACs saw the 1992 election cycle as a long-awaited opportunity to back quality nonincumbent candidates.

If PACs did not substantially increase their contributions to nonincumbents in

1992, it is nonetheless possible that they behaved as strategic politicians in supporting those incumbents who were involved in close elections. Forced to choose between an embattled, friendly incumbent and a hopeful and potentially friendly open-seat candidate, many PACs might choose to target their contributions to help preserve the known quantity. There is some evidence that most PACs did just that.

In 1990, only 14 percent of all House members were involved in close elections (receiving between 45 percent and 55 percent of the vote), and they received approximately 17 percent of all the contributions given to House incumbents. Although PACs give more to candidates involved in close races when all other factors are equal, in practice those candidates involved in competitive races are generally less senior members with less access to agenda power. They usually receive more money than might be predicted given their rank and party, but this is balanced by the large sums that go to relatively safe committee chairs, party leaders, and policy entrepreneurs.

In 1992, 20 percent of all incumbents were involved in close elections, and they received 28 percent of all PAC contributions. Clearly, PACs did a better job of channeling their money to close elections in 1992 than they had in 1990. This is consistent with the strategic politicians thesis, although it is not definitive evidence. It seems likely that those incumbents who were threatened by the House banking scandal or redistricting knew very early in the election cycle that they could expect to face a strong opponent and were even more likely than in past elections to repeatedly solicit PACs for contributions. Thus, although many PACs may have consciously focused on incumbents in close races, others may simply have responded to persistent incumbent requests for money, most of which were made by incumbents who knew they would face stiff challenges.

There is some evidence that incumbent solicitations were largely responsible for the flow of PAC money to House members in close contests. Among corporate and trade-association committees, contributions to House members in close races had approximately the same partisan distribution as those to all incumbents, suggesting that these committees were giving to incumbents regardless of party rather than trying to protect vulnerable Republican incumbents. This suggests an attempt to preserve access, not to change the composition of Congress.

Contribution Behavior: Lessons from the Case Studies

The interviews conducted by participants in this study in the summer of 1991 revealed a startling fact: many PAC managers had yet to consider the unique characteristics of the upcoming election. The managers of the most institutionalized committees, and even the managers of some of the lead PACs, did not imagine that the 1992 election cycle would be significantly different from earlier elections. One PAC in our study, however, had clearly been planning for the 1992 elections for some time. Eaton Corporation's PAC—EPPA—had maintained its strategy of backing nonincumbent Republicans throughout the 1980s. Eaton set aside money for the 1992 election cycle, clearly hoping that the election would finally provide the breakthrough for Republicans that many had hoped for in 1981.

By December 1991, most PAC managers were beginning to receive increased solicitations from incumbents and initial requests from challengers and open-seat candidates. Because of the late decisions in drawing some district lines, many committees were reluctant to make decisions until late spring of 1992. Incumbents involved in competitive primary elections or whose districts had been radically redrawn began aggressively soliciting contributions much earlier.

What is surprising about the final contribution decisions of the PACs included in this book (and indeed of most other PACs) is how few changed their behavior in response to the large number of open seats and vulnerable incumbents. Among the lead PACs, Paul Weyrich did not resuscitate the Free Congress PAC in 1991 despite the prospects for sharp Republican gains in the House, and the NCEC continued to strengthen its ties to the Democratic party and relax its nonpartisan liberal orthodoxy. BIPAC did not change its contribution behavior, and COPE continued its historic pattern of supporting quality Democratic nonincumbents when they ran competitive races.

Among the large institutionalized PACs, both AT&T PAC and the Realtors continued to give primarily to Democratic incumbents, as well as a few Democratic nonincumbents. In both cases, the decentralized decisionmaking structure and formal rules for contributions made it difficult for the PACs to change their contribution patterns. Yet in the case of the Realtors, the potential for change existed in the area of independent expenditures, which are allocated by Washington staff. Nonetheless, the PAC did not change the way it distributed these. The NEA, like other labor PACs, supported quality nonincumbents in 1992 and therefore increased the percentage of funds it gave to challengers and open-seat candidates.

Two of the larger PACs did alter their behavior in the 1992 election, however. Both NARAL PAC and NRTL PAC distributed more funds and contributed more money to nonincumbents. NARAL PAC undertook the most radical change of any PAC in our study by dramatically increasing the proportion of its spending that took the form of independent expenditures. Most of these expenditures were made to help nonincumbent candidates, a pattern that differs sharply from the PAC's previous contribution behavior. Yet these changes were more likely a response to the *Webster* decision than to the large number of opportunities to contribute to credible nonincumbents. NARAL PAC had been content to defend pro-choice incumbents prior to *Webster* because the Supreme Court had guaranteed abortion rights. After *Webster*, NARAL recognized a need for additional pro-choice members of Congress to pass a Freedom of Choice Act or create a veto-proof Congress.

It is more difficult to assess the changes in the contribution behavior of the smaller PACs because a few contributions can result in a dramatic change in the proportion of their contributions allocated to nonincumbents. To the extent that these committees changed their contribution behavior, however, it was generally to increase the funds given to Democratic House members. This was offset by a decrease in the money given to Democratic senators. Although two Democratic Senate incumbents ultimately lost, as a group they did not face the insecurities posed by redistricting and the House banking scandal. Among smaller PACs, only NFFE PAC increased the percentage of the contributions it gave to nonincumbents, and its increase was smaller than the overall increase among labor committees.

With the significant exception of NARAL PAC, however, and to a lesser extent NRTL PAC, all of the PACs in this book behaved much the same way in 1992 as they had in 1990. Some PACs, such as the Realtors and AT&T, had dramatically changed their contribution behavior over the course of the 1980s. In the 1992 election, these committees chose to maintain their new course rather than to return to their earlier patterns of behavior.

The continuity in PAC behavior suggests that most PACs are not strategic political actors; they are not predisposed to support promising nonincumbent candidates in order to try to change the character of Congress. Most PACs, including most of those in this book, are simply not motivated by electoral goals; instead their contributions are inspired by legislative strategies. Most PACs are more interested in maintaining their relationships with sympathetic incumbents than in the far riskier strategy of trying to change the composition of Congress.

The risk of the latter strategy is perhaps most clearly seen in the fate of EPPA, which dramatically reduced its activity after the 1992 election cycle. After many years of strong support for Republican nonincumbents, the corporation saw little gain. The PAC's activity may have satisfied the ideological motives of PAC members, but ultimately Eaton Corporation executives decided that the company's material goals were not being advanced by maintaining a national PAC.

Of course, it is worth noting that many PACs in 1992 felt cross-pressured between the demands of sympathetic incumbents involved in close elections and those of strong nonincumbent candidates. Both BIPAC and COPE might have given more to nonincumbent candidates had there been fewer pro-business and pro-labor incumbents involved in close races. The fact that Democratic and Republican incumbents of all ideological stripes were involved in close elections probably dampened support for nonincumbents.

Several of the PACs in our study did channel a substantial percentage of their contributions to incumbents in competitive contests. Free Congress, BIPAC, NRTL PAC, Eaton's EPPA, and PHH all gave more than half of their incumbent contributions to candidates in close races, and the AAP, NARAL, NFFE, and COPE all gave approximately 40 percent or more of their money to incumbents in jeopardy. These committees had a history of supporting both incumbents and nonincumbents in close races, so that this activity did not represent a change in PAC behavior.

PAC Decisionmaking and Information Networks

How would PACs deal with the lack of reliable information available in the 1992 election cycle? PACs faced a more uncertain electoral climate than in previous elections because of the late redistricting decisions and rapid shifts in the competitiveness of some House and Senate contests. To effectively target their contributions, PACs needed high-quality, timely information.

Of course, this imperative was only relevant for those PACs that sought to influence the composition of Congress or for those that could afford to contribute money in a large number of House and Senate elections. Smaller PACs commonly give money to only a few candidates in any election cycle, and they did not sort out the electoral dynamics of most districts. Similarly, PACs that give primarily to powerful incumbents did not need a great deal of information about the competitiveness of most elections. They could instead focus their attention on the few members of Congress who chair committees, hold party leadership posts, or are leaders in areas of policy that the individual PAC deems important.

The timing of the different PAC contributions over the span of an election cycle lends some support to the idea that lead PACs provide other committees with informational cues. Among corporate PACs, BIPAC was generally among the first to give to nonincumbent candidates.[13] The typical corporate PAC did not give a contribution to a nonincumbent until after BIPAC had already invested some money in the race, suggesting that BIPAC's endorsement may have influenced the contributions of the corporate PAC community. Although this evidence is far from definitive, it suggests that the hundreds of corporate PACs that receive BIPAC mailings may use this information to help guide at least some of their contribution decisions.

For labor unions, however, the picture is a bit murkier. Approximately half of labor contributions to nonincumbent House candidates came before the COPE contribution, as did approximately a quarter of contributions to nonincumbent Senate candidates. It is not surprising that COPE is less of a leader than BIPAC, since COPE's decisionmaking apparatus involves representatives of individual unions. Unions that seek to place a candidate on the COPE marginal list are almost certain to have given to that candidate already, and other sympathetic COPE member unions may act before the official endorsement by the umbrella organization is made. Those PACs that are uncertain about a particular candidate may decide in part based on the COPE endorsement, but many unions are willing to act on their own in advance of a decision by COPE's marginal committees.

Of course, the fact that BIPAC or COPE gave before other PACs in the same sector does not prove that their contributions influenced the decisions of other PACs. Some scholars have argued that corporate PACs may give to the same candidates in part because of market constraints, "interlocks" on corporate boards, and other factors.[14] PACs may give to similar candidates because of these factors or because a given candidate has particular appeal to them. Yet the managers of the lead PACs in this volume believed that their information helped guide the decisions of other committees.

The interviews conducted for this book suggest, however, that these PAC managers turned to more than just the four lead PACs isolated here for direction. JustLife, for example, reported following cues from the NRTL PAC. The aggregate data suggest that NRTL PAC also provided important cues to other pro-life PACs. Although many of the candidates who received contributions from the NRTL PAC got no additional funds from other pro-life PACs, among those candidates who received at least two pro-life PAC contributions, nearly 80 percent of these contributions came after that of the NRTL PAC. NARAL PAC, on the other hand, was rarely among the first pro-choice PACs to give to a candidate—indeed, a substantial majority of pro-choice contributions came before a check from NARAL arrived. This suggests the possibility that there are a number of cue-giving committees in various ideological and other PAC communities and that not all PACs take cues from the PACs that are the most visible in advocating their particular cause.

Other interviews suggested a somewhat less hierarchical model. The PAC officials at Eaton reported that they had met on an irregular basis with other PAC managers who were supportive of Republican nonincumbent candidates to exchange information. This informal network was more a meeting of equals than a briefing by a cue-giving committee. The Eaton official reported that EPPA sometimes received phone calls about candidates and that it sometimes made such calls. This reciprocal exchange fits the pattern reported for the NRTL PAC, which sometimes led the rest of the pro-life PAC community, but frequently followed others.

The picture that emerges from these chapters suggests that in addition to lead PACs, there are other types of PAC networks that are similar to the "issue networks" that exist around the executive branch.[15] The role of Diane Rennert in the AAP-PAC fits this pattern. She attempted to maximize her influence, and those of the Publishers, by networking with other campaign finance professionals and sharing information. Although the American Association of Publishers sponsors a relatively small PAC, Rennert may have influenced some contributions of other PACs through her interactions with other PAC managers. Similarly, NFFE works with the members of the Federal Postal Coalition to share information and increase its influence. Another case in point is the role of organized labor in supporting women candidates in the 1992 election cycle. The Letter Carriers PAC, COLCEP, is a member of EMILY's List, and it shared information gathered by organized labor with other PACs who were members of EMILY's List. Finally, PACs that are affiliated with the member unions of the AFL-CIO frequently exchange information prior to meetings of the marginal committees. If a labor PAC manager wants to know about a race in Michigan, he or she may call on the manager of the Autoworkers PAC; if the race is in New York City the call may go to the Garment Workers. Thus, some PACs do serve as lead PACs—they are important sources of cues to other committees—but other information networks may be more horizontal than vertical, with committees exchanging information in a relationship of equals.

The behavior of two new PACs—WISH List and the Gay and Lesbian Victory Fund—suggests another type of leadership role for some PACs. The success of EMILY's List in bundling contributions to pro-choice Democratic women candidates helped inspire the formation of both of these PACs and helped inform their activities.[16] Bundling places a large amount of money in the hands of candidates but minimizes the PAC's control of these funds. As such, it is an especially useful technique for ideological PACs with a large number of members who are willing to write checks to support individual candidates. Another example of this diffusion of innovation is the NARAL PAC program of independent expenditures, which was probably modeled after that of the Realtors and the American Medical Association's AMPAC.

Of course, other PACs were not the primary source of information for most committees in 1992. The PACs in this study relied on a variety of information sources, including political newsletters, party briefings, and information from contributors and members. For those committees with decentralized or federated structures, local units were even more important in 1992 than in previous elections. In an election year in which local units are important for political intelligence in addition to fundraising, their contribution recommendations are more likely to be heeded.[17]

When local officials guide contribution decisions, Washington staff has less influence. At least some of the larger, federated trade association PACs may have found a way to maintain the influence of the Washington lobbyists on allocation decisions of the PAC. The Realtors' PAC, for instance, uses different decisionmaking procedures for contributions and independent expenditures. The latter procedure is more heavily influenced by the professional staff. AMPAC and, to a lesser extent, NARAL also make contributions and independent expenditures using separate procedures.[18] Some PACs that have split decisionmaking processes allocate their contributions and independent expenditures using different strategies. NARAL is an obvious case of a PAC utilizing divergent strategies, for its independent expenditures were far more likely than its contributions to go to nonincumbents and candidates in close races.[19] The Realtors' PAC also showed a sharp divergence in allocation strategies. Although only 23 percent of RPAC's contributions went to candidates involved in close elections, a full 77 percent of its independent expenditures were on behalf of these marginal candidates.

Overall, few PACs changed the way they sought out information in 1992, although many relied more heavily on some previously established sources. The NCEC, for example, continued to use its precinct-level targeting data as its main source of information. BIPAC continued to cast its net widely, relying on local business leaders and the candidates themselves for information about congressional elections. AT&T relied on its state and regional disbursement committees.

Implications for Reform

Critics have charged that PACs have become mere appendages of incumbent reelection committees, channeling millions of dollars of special interest money into the campaign coffers of members of the committees that write the tax laws that affect their businesses or authorize or fund their programs. As Robert Biersack notes in the introductory chapter, the proportion of money that PACs give to incumbents increased steadily throughout the 1980s. Reformers who advocate eliminating PACs or sharply limiting their maximum contributions have argued that these committees help make elections uncompetitive by providing incumbents with an enormous financial advantage.

Yet PAC managers such as Bernadette Budde of BIPAC have long lamented what they perceive to be the declining quality of nonincumbent candidates, especially among Republicans seeking election to the House. Some PAC managers have argued that many committees would back qualified nonincumbents if more of these candidates ran and if it seemed likely that they had a real chance of winning. Under those conditions, PACs could provide nonincumbents with needed dollars to help deliver their message to voters.

During the late 1980s, PACs began to stockpile cash. The net cash on hand of PACs increased dramatically during this period and reached an all-time record in 1992. If a sizable number of PACs had changed their contribution behavior in 1992 and had given some of their cash reserves to nonincumbent candidates, they could have potentially helped to change the composition of Congress. If, on the other hand, PACs did not alter their behavior in the face of the opportunities offered by the 1992 election cycle, then this could be taken as proof that most PACs were nothing more than a relatively permanent source of financial advantage for incumbents and one of several factors that work to the advantage of incumbents in House and Senate elections. The behavior exhibited by PACs in the 1992 election cycle suggests that they are likely to channel a substantial majority of their contributions to incumbents in future elections. In an election campaign that presented PACs with their best opportunity to support nonincumbents in many years, the pattern of PAC support for incumbents was scarcely altered.

Of course, some PACs do primarily support nonincumbents, and some of the PACs in this book provide badly needed "seed money" for challengers and open-seat candidates. Research has shown that early money from PACs does help candidates raise additional monies both from other committees and from individuals.[20] And although there may be some dispute about the marginal impact of campaign spending by incumbents, all researchers agree that nonincumbents benefit more from additional money than incumbents.[21] So it is possible that the smaller amounts of funds provided to nonincumbents have a bigger impact on elections than the larger amounts provided to incumbents.

The differential effects of campaign spending between incumbents and challengers are dwarfed by the difference in PAC receipts, however. The average House challenger received $29,500 in PAC contributions in 1992, while the average incumbent received $257,500. Among candidates who received between 45 percent and 55 percent of the vote, the incumbent advantage was $330,800 to $74,100. The magnitude of this incumbent advantage means that PACs in the aggregate are indeed supporters of incumbency reelection.

Thus, even if some PACs provide nonincumbents with critical early contributions, in general the role of PACs in the campaign finance system is to provide incumbents with additional financial advantages. PACs therefore help to make elections less competitive. If Americans value competitive elections to enhance democratic responsiveness, then the overwhelming support for incumbents by PACs is a troubling phenomenon.

During the past few years, proposals to reform the financing of congressional campaigns have frequently focused on abolishing or severely limiting PAC activity. Proposals by Senator David Boren and former president Bush have included limits or an outright ban on PAC contributions. In the 1992 presidential campaign, H. Ross Perot attacked PACs as a source of influence peddling. In June 1993, the U.S. Senate passed a bill that would ban PAC contributions and eliminate the bundling of individual donations. Because such a restriction on PAC contributions is unlikely to pass constitutional muster, the bill also includes a restriction on PAC contributions of over $1,000, should the U.S. Supreme Court overturn the ban. In November 1993 the House passed its version of campaign finance reform. It imposed a voluntary spending limit of $600,000, with matching funds available of up to $200,000 for individual contributions of $200 or less and an overall PAC limit of $200,000 per candidate per election cycle. The legislation did not change the specific PAC contribution limit of $5,000 per candidate per election. As this book went to press, attempts were being made to reconcile the very different House and Senate proposals.

Despite our concern for the tendency of PACs to channel their support to incumbents, we have strong reservations about the Senate reforms. Our reservations stem from the fact that many interest groups that sponsor PACs do so in order to advance their broader legislative goals, and these organizations will seek other ways to continue to channel funds to incumbents. So long as private money is used to finance elections, the elimination of PACs will not eliminate the role of interest groups in congressional elections. Senator Boren may not accept contributions from oil company PACs (an important industry in his state), but a substantial proportion of his campaign money comes in the form of large contributions from oil company executives. In a world without PACs but with private financing of campaigns, interest groups will find alternative ways to help their preferred candidates.

The Senate bill includes an aggregate $5,000 limit on the contributions that executive and administrative personnel from a single company can give to any one candidate. That provision, however, is almost certain to be overturned by the Court because it treats executives from small and large companies differently. Executives from a company with 500 administrative employees, for example, could give an average of $10 to a candidate under the provisions of the Senate bill, while their counterparts from a company with 50 executives could give an average of $100.

One way interest groups will continue to help candidates if PACs are banned is through independent expenditures. The *Buckley* v. *Valeo* decision establishes that groups or individuals can spend unlimited amounts in support of, or in opposition to, candidates. During the early 1980s, only a few ideological PACs engaged in substantial independent expenditure campaigns, and many of these exaggerated the amounts they spent by reporting their fundraising costs as independent expenditures. During the latter half of the 1980s, larger trade association committees such as AMPAC and RPAC engaged in substantial independent expenditure activity, and in 1992 NARAL PAC began a sizable effort. Interest groups that wish to influence legislation or elections but who find the total amount they can give to candidates severely limited will probably increase their level of independent spending.

Independent expenditures are not preferable to cash contributions, and they pose some significant problems. First, there are tremendous temptations for candidates, PACs, and the political consultants who assist them to consult with one another prior to making an independent expenditure. In an electoral system in which independent expenditures are the main vehicle for organized interests to participate in elections, the potential for collusion among these actors will undoubtedly increase, as will the probability of illegal behavior. The FEC, which is already overburdened and understaffed, simply lacks the resources to investigate a large number of complaints about collusion and otherwise enforce the law.

Second, there is the problem of accountability. In an election system characterized by substantial independent activity, candidates will not be responsible for many of the messages put out in connection with their campaigns. The potential for lies and distortions will increase tremendously, compounding the difficulties voters have in ferreting out the truth and discerning what individual candidates stand for. This lack of accountability and responsibility in campaigning would undoubtedly harm the reputation of Congress, perhaps leading to greater cynicism about this already much-maligned institution.

Moreover, even if the Court were to allow Congress to ban the bundling of individual contributions by interest-group members, a campaign of coordinated contributions by group members is clearly constitutionally protected speech. If a PAC manager believes that the PAC cannot achieve its goals within the new contribution limits, the manager may be more likely to encourage the development of campaigns of coordinated individual contributions. Such contributions will be far more difficult to trace than PAC contributions, clouding the transparency of the disclosure system.

It is also unclear whether a system in which a greater proportion of candidate funds comes from individuals will benefit nonincumbents or will make members of Congress less likely to listen to the arguments of representatives of particular groups. If PACs were abolished, interest-group members would still contribute to candidates and lobby representatives and senators. Many of these contributors would consider the same factors that PAC managers now consider and listen to the same cue-givers. It is possible that corporate money would be somewhat more ideological if it came entirely from individual corporate officials, most of whom are Republicans. Yet corporate officials recognize the benefits of access to Democratic incumbents, and many would contribute accordingly.

Thus, the limits in the Senate bill seem likely to encourage more coordinated individual contributions, which will be difficult to trace, and more independent expenditures, which may limit electoral accountability. Yet the behavior of PACs in the 1992 election cycle does suggest the need for some reform to level the playing field.

We cannot and do not wish to eliminate interest-group activity in elections. We do, however, favor greater electoral competition. Because campaign funds appear to have a larger incremental value to nonincumbents than to incumbents, and because quality candidates can use early money to attract later resources from other sources, it should be possible to increase the competitiveness of congressional elections with only a modest commitment of resources. We do not advocate additional limits on contributions but rather suggest that additional resources be provided to nonincumbents.

It is not our purpose to propose a complete set of reforms, but certain ideas seem worth mentioning. Reforms that prevent incumbents from carrying over money from one election cycle to the next might encourage better challengers, who might otherwise be deterred by large incumbent war chests.[22] Reforms that provide some additional funds for nonincumbents, especially early in the election cycle, would help quality candidates more effectively communicate their ideas to the electorate. It would probably be necessary to allow both incumbents and nonincumbents to claim these grants, but it seems likely that the electoral climate would make it more difficult for an incumbent to accept the money. Both of these types of reforms would encourage more competitive elections. Free television or radio time for candidates, reduced postage rates for campaign mail, and additional provisions to aid political parties could also help the competitive nonincumbents whom the parties generally support.

Conclusion

We began this study by posing three questions. First, how do PACs select the candidates they support? Second, where do they obtain the information needed to select among the many candidates who request their funds? These two questions are closely related, and the answers vary across types of committees. Many lead PACs and large institutionalized PACs possess the organizational capacity to thoroughly research the competitiveness of most congressional elections and to learn which candidates are committed to the PAC's policy or ideological goals. These committees are in a position to rely on their own researchers, lobbyists, and field staff for the bulk of their information. Some of them receive input from state-level affiliated PACs. Although many of these lead PACs and large institutionalized committees have enough information to reach some contribution decisions without input from others, most of them communicate with party committees and other PACs prior to making their contributions or independent expenditures. Lead PACs tend to be more on the giving than the receiving end of the information hierarchy, but the flow of information is not strictly one-way.

Almost all of the lead and institutionalized PACs have detailed decisionmaking procedures that require a PAC manager to consult with a board of directors, other PAC employees, or state-level affiliated PACs prior to distributing their committee's campaign money. Paradoxically, a PAC's decisionmaking procedures can in some cases impede its ability to use the information it collects. The need to consult with a variety of individuals can prevent a PAC manager from responding to the most current electoral information. Some PAC managers can use this information to direct their independent expenditures, however, without consultation with local affiliates or PAC members.

Smaller PACs that lack the organizational capacity to carry out their own detailed campaign research tend to rely on two strategies. PACs that focus their money on incumbents generally have few informational needs. They look at roll-call votes, and they accept input from lobbyists and other inside-the-Beltway sources. Ideological PACs that contribute to nonincumbents have greater information demands. Some of these PACs turn to national party committees and lead PACs for cues, while others engage in a more even exchange of information with committees that share their political predispositions.

The managers of small PACs tend to have a great deal of autonomy in overseeing their committees' operations. Because these PACs lack the formal structure and decisionmaking processes of the lead and institutionalized committees, their managers can exercise more freedom when devising their contribution strategies and have more discretion over how their contributions are distributed. So long as their money holds out and they stay in touch with their informational sources, these PACs can make use of the most recent information about congressional candidates and their campaigns.

Our third question focused on the changes in PAC contribution strategies. Do PACs respond to the opportunities that arise in particular election cycles, and would they respond to the opportunities that appeared during the 1992 election cycle? In the aggregate, PAC contributions to nonincumbent candidates increased only modestly in 1992. The overwhelming proportion of PAC contributions went to incumbents, as they have in all recent election cycles. Even PACs that had previously shown an inclination to support challengers and open-seat candidates did not dramatically alter their more recent pattern of contributions to incumbents. Among our case studies, only those PACs with issue agendas prominent in the 1992 elections—abortion and health care—changed their behavior to any great degree.

We conclude that despite the tremendous diversity in PAC histories, goals, organizational structures, informational resources, and decisionmaking processes, most PACs gave most of their money to incumbents during an election cycle in which there were many highly promising challenger and open-seat candidates running for Congress. The fact that most committees spent their funds in a way that was designed to maintain access to important decisionmakers, rather than replace them, suggests that most PACs are involved in electoral politics to advance lobbying goals instead of to influence the outcomes of elections.

There is tremendous diversity in the PAC community and among the committees in this study. This diversity is only partially reflected in contribution behavior, however. In an election in which the public professed to pollsters a desire to change the composition of Congress, and in which term-limit referenda passed in many states, the PAC community provided incumbents with additional financial advantages that limited the competitiveness of congressional elections. The pro-incumbent bias of most PACs reflects their access-oriented goals, the kinds of information available to most committees when they make their decisions, the nature of their decisionmaking processes, and the structure of congressional elections. These factors encourage most PACs to be supporters of the status quo, even in elections in which the majority of Americans want change.

Notes

1. Gary Jacobson and Samuel Kernell, *Strategy and Choice in Congressional Elections*, 2nd ed. (New Haven, CT: Yale University Press, 1983); Gary Jacobson, *Money in Congressional Elections* (New Haven, CT: Yale University Press, 1980); Theodore Eismeier and Phillip Pollock III, "Strategy and Choice in Congressional Elections: The Role of Political Action Committees," *American Journal of Political Science* 30 (1986): 197–213.

2. Eismeier and Pollack, "Strategy and Choice"; Clyde Wilcox, "Organizational Variables and the Contribution Behavior of Large PACs: A Longitudinal Analysis," *Political Behavior* 11 (1989): 157–73.

3. Eismeier and Pollack, "Strategy and Choice"; Diana Evans, "Oil PACs and Aggressive Contribution Strategies," *Journal of Politics* 50 (1988): 1047–56.

4. Brooks Jackson, *Honest Graft* (New York: Random House, 1988); Theodore Eismeier and Phillip Pollock III, *Business, Money, and the Rise of Corporate PACs in American Elections* (New York: Quorum Books, 1988).

5. For a discussion of innovation and stability in bureaucratic organizations, see J.M. Dutton and R.D. Freeman, "External Environment and Internal Strategies: Calculating, Experimenting and Imitating in Organizations," in R.B. Lamb, ed., *Advances in Strategic Management* (Greenwich, CT: JAI Press, 1985).

6. For an application of social learning theory to political organizations, see Marjorie Randon Hershey, *Running for Office: The Political Education of Campaigners* (Chatham, NJ: Chatham House, 1984).

7. Elizabeth Adell Cook, Ted G. Jelen, and Clyde Wilcox, *Between Two Absolutes: Public Opinion and the Politics of Abortion* (Boulder, CO: Westview Press, 1992).

8. Clyde Wilcox, "Political Action Committees and Abortion: A Longitudinal Analysis," *Women and Politics* 9 (1988): 1–20.

9. Frank Sorauf, *Money in American Elections* (Glenview, IL: Scott, Foresman, 1988); Margaret Latus, "Assessing Ideological PACs: From Outrage to Understanding," in Michael J. Malbin, ed., *Money and Politics in the United States* (Chatham, NJ: Chatham House, 1984).

10. Paul S. Herrnson, *Party Campaigning in the 1980s* (Cambridge, MA: Harvard University Press, 1988), pp. 73–74.

11. Of course, the 1982 and 1986 elections were generally good years for Democratic candidates, while the 1992 election was one in which neither party had a clear advantage. The Democratic edge created by negative perceptions of the state of the economy were balanced by the effects of redistricting.

12. Research has shown that PACs formed during different election cycles maintain a somewhat distinctive contribution strategy. See Clyde Wilcox, "PACs and Pluralism: Interest Group Formation and Partisanship," *Polity* 21 (1988): 155–66.

13. The median percentage of corporate contributions to nonincumbent candidates in 1992 that arrived before BIPAC's contribution was only 20 percent.

14. Dan Clawson and Alan Neustadtl, "Interlocks, PACs, and Corporate Conservatism," *American Journal of Sociology* 94 (1989): 749–73.

15. H. Heclo, "Issue Networks and the Executive Establishment," in A. King, ed., *The New American Political System* (Washington, D.C.: AEI, 1978).

16. Candice Nelson, "Women's PACS in the Year of the Woman," in Elizabeth Adell Cook, Sue Thomas, and Clyde Wilcox, eds., *The Year of the Woman: Myths and Realities* (Boulder, CO: Westview Press, 1993).

17. John Wright, "PACs, Contributions, and Roll Calls: An Organizational Perspective," *American Political Science Review* 79 (1985): 400–414.

18. Dong-Young Kim, *Campaign Finance Decisionmaking and Strategies of Trade Association PACs: Two Case Studies*, unpublished doctoral dissertation, Georgetown University, 1992.

19. NRTL PAC showed the opposite pattern, with its reported independent expenditures on behalf of candidates in fewer competitive races than its contributions. However, because much of the reported activity by NRTL PAC appeared to be fundraising and not advertising, this difference may be misleading.

20. Robert Biersack, Paul Herrnson, and Clyde Wilcox, "Seeds for Success: Early Money in Congressional Elections," *Legislative Studies Quarterly* 18 (1993): 535–52.

21. Gary Jacobson, "The Effects of Campaign Spending in Congressional Elections," *American Political Science Review* 72 (1978): 469–91; Donald Green and Jonathan Krasno, "Salvation for the Spendthrift Incumbent: Reestimating the Effects of Campaign Spending in House Elections," *American Journal of Political Science* 32 (1988): 884–907; Gary Jacobson, "The Effects of Campaign Spending in House Elections: New Evidence for Old Arguments," *American Journal of Political Science* 34 (1990): 334–62; Donald Green and Jonathan Krasno, "Rebuttal to Jacobson's 'New Evidence for Old Arguments,' " *American Journal of Political Science* 34 (1990): 363–72.

22. Jonathan Krasno and Donald Green, "Preempting Quality Challengers in House Elections," *Journal of Politics* 50 (1988): 920–36.

Appendices

Appendices A and B summarize the contributions and expenditures made by each PAC covered by this book over the past twelve years. For each committee, Appendix A lists the total amount contributed, the number of candidates receiving contributions, and the proportion of all contributions by the PAC that were given to each type of campaign (e.g., House Democratic incumbents). In the cases of PACs that also made independent expenditures supporting or opposing candidates, Appendix B provides the tables for those expenditures.

These tables allow for comparisons among the different committees described in the preceding chapters. They also document the changes some PACs have made over the course of these six election cycles, changing their emphasis to different types of campaigns as experience and electoral circumstances change.

Appendix A: Contributions to Congressional Candidates by Individual PACs (in dollars and number of candidates) (Tables A.1–A.20)

Appendix B: Expenditures by Individual PACs (in dollars and number of candidates) (Tables B.1–B.3)

Table A.1
AFL-CIO COPE

		1978	1980	1982	1984	1986	1988	1990	1992
Senate									
Democrat									
Incumbent	(contributions)	$62,550	$111,000	$81,275	$43,750	$49,000	$129,150	$84,950	$89,350
	(no. of candidates)	11	18	12	12	9	20	18	18
	(% of total contributions)	8	14	9	7	6	13	10	11
Challenger	(contributions)	$90,750	$42,000	$75,300	$75,150	$124,070	$85,000	$68,750	$75,000
	(no. of candidates)	14	9	10	14	16	10	8	9
	(% of total contributions)	11	5	8	11	15	8	8	9
Open Seat	(contributions)	$71,100	$21,250	$18,000	$48,500	$54,800	$56,750	$20,000	$63,150
	(no. of candidates)	9	4	3	5	8	9	2	7
	(% of total contributions)	9	3	2	7	7	6	2	8
Republican									
Incumbent	(contributions)	$17,500	$18,000	$1,000	. . .	. . .	$10,050	. . .	. . .
	(no. of candidates)	3	4	1	. . .	. . .	3	. . .	. . .
	(% of total contributions)	2	2	0	. . .	. . .	1	. . .	. . .
Challenger	(contributions)	. . .	$250	. . .	. . .	. . .	. . .	. . .	. . .
	(no. of candidates)	. . .	1	. . .	. . .	. . .	. . .	. . .	. . .
	(% of total contributions)	. . .	0	. . .	. . .	. . .	. . .	. . .	. . .
Open Seat	(contributions)	. . .	. . .	. . .	. . .	. . .	. . .	. . .	. . .
	(no. of candidates)	. . .	. . .	. . .	. . .	. . .	. . .	. . .	. . .
	(% of total contributions)	. . .	. . .	. . .	. . .	. . .	. . .	. . .	. . .

House									
Democrat									
Incumbent (contributions)	$277,891	$345,280	$217,350	$274,895	$252,476	$384,646	$348,277	$306,395
(no. of candidates)	111	111	95	123	150	191	188	152
(% of total contributions)	34	44	24	42	30	38	41	37
Challenger (contributions)	$136,350	$151,205	$300,200	$129,600	$196,000	$209,200	$102,975	$104,100
(no. of candidates)	49	51	79	48	57	49	33	47
(% of total contributions)	17	19	33	20	23	21	12	13
Open Seat (contributions)	$147,200	$87,580	$204,700	$87,250	$160,610	$134,500	$214,150	$182,250
(no. of candidates)	43	27	45	25	35	28	34	54
(% of total contributions)	18	11	23	13	19	13	25	22
Republican									
Incumbent (contributions)	$5,400	$8,200	-	$500	$1,050	$3,400	$3,275	$4,375
(no. of candidates)	5	7	-	1	3	3	7	5
(% of total contributions)	1	1	-	0	0	0	0	1
Challenger (contributions)	$1,000	$2,800	$1,500	-	-	$1,000	$300	$2,500
(no. of candidates)	3	3	1	-	-	1	1	1
(% of total contributions)	0	0	0	-	-	0	0	0
Open Seat (contributions)	-	$1,000	$5,000	-	-	-	-	$500
(no. of candidates)	-	1	1	-	-	-	-	1
(% of total contributions)	-	0	0	-	-	-	-	0
Total	$809,741	$788,565	$904,325	$659,645	$838,006	$1,013,696	$842,677	$827,620

Table A.2
Business Industry Political Action Committee (BIPAC)

		1978	1980	1982	1984	1986	1988	1990	1992
Senate									
Democrat									
Incumbent	(contributions)	$5,000	$1,092	–	–	–	–	–	–
	(no. of candidates)	2	1	–	–	–	–	–	–
	(% of total contributions)	3	1	–	–	–	–	–	–
Challenger	(contributions)	–	–	$1,027	–	–	–	–	–
	(no. of candidates)	–	–	1	–	–	–	–	–
	(% of total contributions)	–	–	1	–	–	–	–	–
Open Seat	(contributions)	$2,000	–	–	$1,109	–	–	–	–
	(no. of candidates)	1	–	–	1	–	–	–	–
	(% of total contributions)	1	–	–	1	–	–	–	–
Republican									
Incumbent	(contributions)	$14,500	$1,107	$10,958	$16,489	$19,469	$17,041	$9,754	$16,305
	(no. of candidates)	5	2	6	8	12	10	5	8
	(% of total contributions)	7	1	5	10	15	12	9	12
Challenger	(contributions)	$18,000	$24,633	$22,839	$7,643	$5,513	$12,848	$16,951	$12,222
	(no. of candidates)	8	15	12	5	2	4	6	5
	(% of total contributions)	9	17	11	4	4	9	15	9
Open Seat	(contributions)	$10,500	$7,436	$8,724	$8,994	$17,913	$9,544	$8,256	$15,257
	(no. of candidates)	5	6	2	4	7	4	3	7
	(% of total contributions)	5	5	4	5	14	7	7	11

265

		1	2	3	4	5	6	7	8
House									
Democrat									
Incumbent	(contributions)	$8,500	$2,500	$5,226	$5,287	$2,221	$5,121	$2,074	$4,129
	(no. of candidates)	6	3	4	5	2	2	2	4
	(% of total contributions)	4	2	3	3	2	4	2	3
Challenger	(contributions)	$9,000	$6,599	$2,230	-	-	-	$3,317	$4,071
	(no. of candidates)	4	5	2	-	-	-	2	2
	(% of total contributions)	5	-	1	-	-	-	3	3
Open Seat	(contributions)	$8,000	$3,107	$7,619	$2,577	$5,308	$2,764	$2,074	$1,030
	(no. of candidates)	4	2	7	2	5	3	2	1
	(% of total contributions)	4	2	4	2	4	2	2	1
Republican									
Incumbent	(contributions)	$28,000	$31,668	$54,909	$33,959	$32,937	$38,451	$12,752	$17,970
	(no. of candidates)	21	21	43	29	27	26	12	18
	(% of total contributions)	14	22	27	20	26	28	12	13
Challenger	(contributions)	$63,000	$47,612	$46,158	$64,189	$10,878	$28,163	$19,348	$29,630
	(no. of candidates)	38	44	35	34	8	23	16	30
	(% of total contributions)	32	33	23	38	9	21	17	22
Open Seat	(contributions)	$30,500	$20,353	$42,392	$29,606	$32,504	$22,555	$36,106	$32,817
	(no. of candidates)	24	22	33	18	25	17	27	34
	(% of total contributions)	15	14	21	17	26	17	33	25
Total		$197,000	$146,107	$202,082	$169,853	$126,743	$136,487	$110,632	$133,431

Table A.3
National Committee For an Effective Congress (NCEC)

		1978	1980	1982	1984	1986	1988	1990	1992
Senate									
Democrat									
Incumbent	(contributions)	$24,877	$80,869	$24,528	$55,718	$38,319	$79,901	$84,050	$68,500
	(no. of candidates)	3	11	8	7	5	11	12	16
	(% of total contributions)	13	19	6	7	6	12	14	11
Challenger	(contributions)	$25,398	$13,003	$20,714	$70,796	$97,380	$59,993	$34,050	$42,000
	(no. of candidates)	7	5	6	9	12	11	5	10
	(% of total contributions)	13	3	5	9	14	9	6	6
Open Seat	(contributions)	$9,999	$7,000	$200	$38,470	$45,498	$29,753	$12,450	$29,500
	(no. of candidates)	3	2	1	5	6	4	3	7
	(% of total contributions)	5	2	0	5	7	4	2	5
Republican									
Incumbent	(contributions)	$10,000	$3,195	-	-	-	-	-	-
	(no. of candidates)	2	1	-	-	-	-	-	-
	(% of total contributions)	5	1	-	-	-	-	-	-
Challenger	(contributions)	-	-	-	-	-	-	-	-
	(no. of candidates)	-	-	-	-	-	-	-	-
	(% of total contributions)	-	-	-	-	-	-	-	-
Open Seat	(contributions)	-	-	-	-	-	-	-	-
	(no. of candidates)	-	-	-	-	-	-	-	-
	(% of total contributions)	-	-	-	-	-	-	-	-

267

House								
Democrat								
Incumbent (contributions)	$53,240	$181,071	$193,404	$341,801	$226,028	$231,914	$239,350	$270,900
(no. of candidates)	32	57	52	73	57	47	72	103
(% of total contributions)	28	43	47	43	33	34	40	42
Challenger (contributions)	$29,801	$54,907	$115,917	$216,393	$179,614	$175,717	$126,175	$119,050
(no. of candidates)	17	27	43	48	40	34	44	44
(% of total contributions)	16	13	28	27	26	26	21	18
Open Seat (contributions)	$33,384	$77,633	$53,166	$70,944	$104,443	$107,338	$100,500	$120,800
(no. of candidates)	20	25	20	11	22	18	25	42
(% of total contributions)	18	19	13	9	15	16	17	19
Republican								
Incumbent (contributions)	$2,000	-	$1,000	$500	$1,000	-	-	-
(no. of candidates)	1	-	1	1	1	-	-	-
(% of total contributions)	1	-	0	0	0	-	-	-
Challenger (contributions)	-	-	-	-	-	-	-	-
(no. of candidates)	-	-	-	-	-	-	-	-
(% of total contributions)	-	-	-	-	-	-	-	-
Open Seat (contributions)	-	-	-	-	-	-	-	-
(no. of candidates)	-	-	-	-	-	-	-	-
(% of total contributions)	-	-	-	-	-	-	-	-
Total	$188,699	$417,678	$408,929	$794,622	$692,282	$684,616	$596,575	$650,750

Table A.4
Free Congress PAC

		1978	1980	1982	1984	1986	1988	1990	1992
Senate									
Democrat									
Incumbent	(contributions)	$181	-	$500	-	-	-	-	-
	(no. of candidates)	1	-	1	-	-	-	-	-
	(% of total contributions)	0	-	0	-	-	-	-	-
Challenger	(contributions)	$7,437	$4,625	$1,000	$1,440	-	$100	-	-
	(no. of candidates)	2	4	1	1	-	1	-	-
	(% of total contributions)	4	3	1	4	-	1	-	-
Open Seat	(contributions)	-	-	-	-	-	-	-	-
	(no. of candidates)	-	-	-	-	-	-	-	-
	(% of total contributions)	-	-	-	-	-	-	-	-
Republican									
Incumbent	(contributions)	$2,400	$450	-	$923	$5,519	$100	$2,000	-
	(no. of candidates)	4	2	-	2	1	1	1	-
	(% of total contributions)	1	0	-	3	9	1	23	-
Challenger	(contributions)	$20,493	$50,790	$16,356	$1,595	$9,665	$3,721	-	-
	(no. of candidates)	11	17	7	4	5	3	-	-
	(% of total contributions)	10	37	11	4	16	30	-	-
Open Seat	(contributions)	$9,350	$6,392	$6,000	$6,755	$1,092	$300	-	-
	(no. of candidates)	7	4	2	5	1	3	-	-
	(% of total contributions)	5	5	4	18	2	2	-	-

House

Democrat								
Incumbent								
(contributions)	$13,969	$325	$1,151	–	$300	–	–	–
(no. of candidates)	4	3	2	–	1	–	–	–
(% of total contributions)	7	0	1	–	0	–	–	–
Challenger								
(contributions)	$2,224	$3,216	$12,024	–	$2,351	–	–	–
(no. of candidates)	4	2	5	–	2	–	–	–
(% of total contributions)	1	2	8	–	4	–	–	–
Open Seat								
(contributions)	$2,016	$3,906	$13,190	–	–	–	–	–
(no. of candidates)	4	3	2	–	–	–	–	–
(% of total contributions)	1	3	9	–	–	–	–	–
Republican								
Incumbent								
(contributions)	$9,248	$8,259	$22,233	$2,603	$5,750	$1,400	$1,203	$5,400
(no. of candidates)	13	19	27	5	3	4	2	5
(% of total contributions)	4	6	14	7	10	11	14	48
Challenger								
(contributions)	$85,745	$40,735	$36,472	$10,704	$11,565	$1,698	$5,500	$5,175
(no. of candidates)	58	25	14	17	10	2	2	4
(% of total contributions)	41	30	24	29	19	14	63	46
Open Seat								
(contributions)	$54,206	$17,603	$46,197	$12,759	$23,829	$4,950	–	$700
(no. of candidates)	32	13	20	16	19	8	–	3
(% of total contributions)	26	13	30	35	40	40	–	6
Total	$207,269	$136,301	$155,123	$36,779	$60,071	$12,269	$8,703	$11,275

Table A.5
National Education Association PAC

	1978	1980	1982	1984	1986	1988	1990	1992
Senate								
Democrat								
Incumbent (contributions)	$21,400	$45,387	$84,625	$48,225	$73,250	$102,510	$127,415	$101,957
(no. of candidates)	7	21	21	16	16	24	27	23
(% of total contributions)	6	16	7	3	4	5	5	4
Challenger (contributions)	$26,000	$8,500	$59,400	$76,502	$106,000	$84,000	$60,000	$110,500
(no. of candidates)	7	8	11	20	12	11	6	14
(% of total contributions)	8	3	5	5	5	4	3	5
Open Seat (contributions)	$18,000	$5,500	$13,500	$57,210	$66,750	$73,400	$20,000	$69,000
(no. of candidates)	6	3	2	7	8	9	2	8
(% of total contributions)	5	2	1	4	3	3	1	3
Republican								
Incumbent (contributions)	$4,650	$5,300	$12,150	$11,150	$18,850	$18,500	$13,400	$1,000
(no. of candidates)	4	4	7	6	7	3	5	1
(% of total contributions)	1	2	1	1	1	1	1	0
Challenger (contributions)	-	$2,000	$7,000	$250	-	$5,300	$1,400	-
(no. of candidates)	-	1	2	1	-	2	2	-
(% of total contributions)	-	1	1	0	-	0	0	-
Open Seat (contributions)	$1,250	$5,750	-	-	-	$10,000	-	-
(no. of candidates)	2	2	-	-	-	1	-	-
(% of total contributions)	0	2	-	-	-	0	-	-

House

Democrat								
Incumbent (contributions)	$121,035	$136,721	$408,007	$889,802	$1,077,376	$1,179,716	$1,424,780	$1,092,490
(no. of candidates)	93	126	179	235	218	228	227	208
(% of total contributions)	36	49	34	56	52	56	61	47
Challenger (contributions)	$64,702	$32,300	$336,935	$292,606	$324,400	$307,287	$213,150	$343,000
(no. of candidates)	28	30	71	74	55	49	34	59
(% of total contributions)	19	12	28	19	16	15	9	15
Open Seat (contributions)	$68,950	$23,577	$216,598	$142,000	$322,500	$237,500	$322,500	$505,000
(no. of candidates)	31	17	45	30	43	28	38	65
(% of total contributions)	21	8	18	9	16	11	14	22
Republican								
Incumbent (contributions)	$4,300	$15,150	$17,000	$40,508	$51,307	$64,999	$85,135	$37,675
(no. of candidates)	7	20	27	23	31	32	31	22
(% of total contributions)	1	5	1	3	2	3	4	2
Challenger (contributions)	-	-	$2,000	$5,050	-	$3,677	-	$13,500
(no. of candidates)	-	-	1	3	-	2	-	4
(% of total contributions)	-	-	0	0	-	0	-	1
Open Seat (contributions)	$3,000	-	$26,000	$16,000	$20,000	$17,800	$50,000	$30,000
(no. of candidates)	2	-	6	3	3	4	6	5
(% of total contributions)	1	-	2	1	1	1	2	1
Total	$333,287	$280,185	$1,183,215	$1,579,303	$2,060,433	$2,104,689	$2,317,780	$2,304,122

Table A.6

American Telephone and Telegraph Company PAC (AT&T PAC)

		1982	1984	1986	1988	1990	1992
Senate							
Democrat							
Incumbent	(contributions)	$30,100	$15,405	$62,650	$134,582	$126,090	$72,425
	(no. of candidates)	25	20	21	38	33	29
	(% of total contributions)	14	10	7	10	9	6
Challenger	(contributions)	$500	$3,300	$25,500	$8,650	$9,500	$29,000
	(no. of candidates)	1	6	9	5	5	9
	(% of total contributions)	0	2	3	1	1	2
Open Seat	(contributions)	-	$8,300	$21,800	$36,550	-	$36,390
	(no. of candidates)	-	6	5	12	-	9
	(% of total contributions)	-	5	3	3	-	3
Republican							
Incumbent	(contributions)	$27,500	$27,740	$110,740	$111,662	$107,900	$60,600
	(no. of candidates)	33	29	31	29	30	22
	(% of total contributions)	13	17	13	9	7	5
Challenger	(contributions)	$3,750	$705	$6,040	$5,500	$10,000	$8,500
	(no. of candidates)	6	2	3	3	3	4
	(% of total contributions)	2	0	1	0	1	1
Open Seat	(contributions)	$5,500	$6,000	$46,500	$38,500	$21,000	$19,000
	(no. of candidates)	7	6	8	7	3	5
	(% of total contributions)	3	4	6	3	1	1

House						
Democrat						
Incumbent						
(contributions)	$55,305	$35,435	$265,445	$499,768	$655,450	$574,350
(no. of candidates)	126	114	185	227	236	225
(% of total contributions)	26	22	32	38	45	44
Challenger						
(contributions)	$2,300	$700	$6,350	$12,750	$11,700	$27,800
(no. of candidates)	6	2	8	9	7	26
(% of total contributions)	1	0	1	1	1	2
Open Seat						
(contributions)	$2,750	$2,650	$22,750	$25,000	$37,750	$69,000
(no. of candidates)	6	7	28	22	26	61
(% of total contributions)	1	2	3	2	3	5
Republican						
Incumbent						
(contributions)	$72,065	$48,607	$235,435	$394,600	$448,160	$335,370
(no. of candidates)	159	112	149	170	154	137
(% of total contributions)	34	30	28	30	31	26
Challenger						
(contributions)	$5,500	$3,050	$3,000	$6,250	$7,500	$21,700
(no. of candidates)	14	11	3	8	3	21
(% of total contributions)	3	2	0	0	1	2
Open Seat						
(contributions)	$7,225	$7,989	$34,980	$32,800	$27,275	$43,400
(no. of candidates)	20	21	29	21	20	49
(% of total contributions)	3	5	4	3	2	3
Total	$212,495	$159,881	$841,190	$1,306,612	$1,462,325	$1,297,535

Table A.7
Eaton Corporation PAC (EPPA)

		1978	1980	1982	1984	1986	1988	1990	1992
Senate									
Democrat									
Incumbent	(contributions)	-	$2,250	$100	$250	-	$250	-	$1,000
	(no. of candidates)	-	2	1	1	-	1	-	1
	(% of total contributions)	-	1	0	0	-	0	-	0
Challenger	(contributions)	$1,000	-	$1,000	-	$1,000	-	-	-
	(no. of candidates)	1	-	1	-	1	-	-	-
	(% of total contributions)	1	-	-	-	0	-	-	-
Open Seat	(contributions)	$1,500	-	-	-	-	-	-	-
	(no. of candidates)	2	-	-	-	-	-	-	-
	(% of total contributions)	2	-	-	-	-	-	-	-
Republican									
Incumbent	(contributions)	$8,800	$250	$7,250	$18,000	$24,750	$22,250	$4,000	$11,000
	(no. of candidates)	5	1	5	7	11	8	3	4
	(% of total contributions)	9	0	5	11	12	12	3	5
Challenger	(contributions)	$11,600	$46,000	$23,000	$9,000	$14,000	$27,000	$41,500	$24,500
	(no. of candidates)	8	13	7	6	2	5	7	5
	(% of total contributions)	12	29	16	5	7	15	26	11
Open Seat	(contributions)	$5,750	$8,250	$8,000	$18,000	$32,000	$28,000	$5,000	$26,000
	(no. of candidates)	5	5	3	5	7	5	3	8
	(% of total contributions)	6	5	6	11	15	15	3	12

House

Democrat								
Incumbent (contributions)	$4,550	$5,500	$4,500	$5,000	$1,500	$1,500	$5,150	$6,200
(no. of candidates)	10	10	5	8	2	2	6	4
(% of total contributions)	5	3	3	3	1	1	3	3
Challenger (contributions)	$1,000	$850	$500	-	$1,500	$500	$5,000	$5,000
(no. of candidates)	2	2	1	-	2	1	4	3
(% of total contributions)	1	1	0	-	1	0	3	2
Open Seat (contributions)	$3,000	$2,000	$3,650	$1,500	$3,500	$3,000	$2,000	$2,000
(no. of candidates)	3	3	9	3	6	4	2	1
(% of total contributions)	3	1	3	1	2	2	1	1
Republican								
Incumbent (contributions)	$13,350	$34,375	$44,650	$27,450	$54,100	$44,050	$25,050	$31,800
(no. of candidates)	14	33	61	37	33	30	23	17
(% of total contributions)	14	22	31	16	25	24	16	14
Challenger (contributions)	$36,600	$35,500	$27,050	$66,500	$30,700	$28,500	$29,000	$51,100
(no. of candidates)	26	33	26	30	17	14	14	33
(% of total contributions)	38	22	19	39	14	16	18	23
Open Seat (contributions)	$9,850	$24,600	$22,100	$23,800	$52,000	$28,000	$42,000	$61,000
(no. of candidates)	13	24	26	17	27	14	26	40
(% of total contributions)	10	15	16	14	24	15	26	28
Total	$97,000	$159,575	$141,800	$169,500	$215,050	$183,050	$158,700	$219,600

Table A.8
Realtors PAC (RPAC)

		1978	1980	1982	1984	1986	1988	1990	1992
Senate									
Democrat									
Incumbent	(contributions)	$22,950	$77,125	$83,419	$84,100	$60,600	$110,875	$92,175	$104,784
	(no. of candidates)	9	27	23	14	22	24	27	26
	(% of total contributions)	2	5	4	3	2	4	3	4
Challenger	(contributions)	$21,150	$6,500	$5,450	$8,174	$30,250	$25,950	-	$13,800
	(no. of candidates)	5	4	3	8	7	6	-	3
	(% of total contributions)	2	0	0	0	1	1	-	0
Open Seat	(contributions)	$18,700	$15,500	$1,000	$18,320	$11,000	$30,450	-	$17,800
	(no. of candidates)	7	4	3	4	3	10	-	7
	(% of total contributions)	2	1	0	1	0	1	-	1
Republican									
Incumbent	(contributions)	$63,000	$39,850	$94,650	$157,005	$152,249	$79,474	$104,300	$90,624
	(no. of candidates)	13	15	24	33	24	21	22	17
	(% of total contributions)	6	3	4	6	6	3	3	3
Challenger	(contributions)	$32,000	$80,168	$40,350	$26,250	$19,750	$14,150	$21,075	$15,000
	(no. of candidates)	7	16	13	5	2	5	5	2
	(% of total contributions)	3	5	2	1	1	0	1	1
Open Seat	(contributions)	$30,750	$23,700	$16,250	$30,450	$69,000	$52,284	$30,500	$18,300
	(no. of candidates)	8	8	4	6	7	8	3	4
	(% of total contributions)	3	2	1	1	3	2	1	1

House								
Democrat								
Incumbent (contributions)	$233,400	$323,790	$288,434	$670,578	$820,640	$1,304,202	$1,509,772	$1,227,731
(no. of candidates)	146	183	139	199	200	234	243	233
(% of total contributions)	22	21	14	28	30	43	49	42
Challenger (contributions)	$9,200	$35,025	$53,724	$31,777	$18,200	$26,350	$10,000	$39,000
(no. of candidates)	7	17	23	14	11	7	2	9
(% of total contributions)	1	2	3	1	1	1	0	1
Open Seat (contributions)	$73,500	$38,900	$75,150	$56,350	$116,900	$131,125	$110,000	$218,500
(no. of candidates)	23	14	22	19	29	19	19	38
(% of total contributions)	7	3	4	2	4	4	4	7
Republican								
Incumbent (contributions)	$293,360	$520,040	$860,799	$927,820	$1,100,419	$1,079,309	$1,039,890	$889,859
(no. of candidates)	117	135	169	150	159	166	157	150
(% of total contributions)	27	34	41	38	40	35	34	30
Challenger (contributions)	$167,000	$258,825	$337,567	$228,916	$104,650	$46,800	$17,500	$35,300
(no. of candidates)	53	67	54	45	40	35	34	9
(% of total contributions)	15	17	16	9	21	14	4	1
Open Seat (contributions)	$117,400	$121,800	$255,667	$185,700	$253,250	$144,800	$159,516	$279,440
(no. of candidates)	34	32	48	25	37	23	23	44
(% of total contributions)	11	8	12	8	9	5	5	9
Total	$1,082,410	$1,541,223	$2,112,460	$2,425,440	$2,756,908	$3,045,769	$3,094,728	$2,950,138

Table A.9
National Abortion Rights League PAC (NARAL PAC)

	1978	1980	1982	1984	1986	1988	1990	1992
Senate								
Democrat								
Incumbent								
(contributions)	$3,500	$30,700	$34,582	$10,600	$13,000	$33,000	$29,500	$31,084
(no. of candidates)	2	6	8	3	3	7	7	8
(% of total contributions)	7	16	12	5	5	12	8	6
Challenger								
(contributions)	$6,100	$7,150	$14,933	$29,763	$8,500	$12,000	$34,500	$45,500
(no. of candidates)	6	3	2	7	3	3	5	8
(% of total contributions)	12	4	5	14	3	5	9	9
Open Seat								
(contributions)	$5,000	$5,000	$10,000	$10,000	$28,000	$12,000	$6,000	$19,886
(no. of candidates)	1	1	2	1	4	3	2	3
(% of total contributions)	10	3	3	5	10	5	2	4
Republican								
Incumbent								
(contributions)	$7,432	$11,387	$8,000	$1,000	$1,000	$15,250	$2,000	$2,000
(no. of candidates)	1	2	2	1	1	3	2	1
(% of total contributions)	15	6	3	0	0	6	1	0
Challenger								
(contributions)	-	-	-	-	-	-	$5,000	-
(no. of candidates)	-	-	-	-	-	-	1	-
(% of total contributions)	-	-	-	-	-	-	0	-
Open Seat								
(contributions)	-	$5,000	$500	-	$1,000	$2,000	-	$1,113
(no. of candidates)	-	1	1	-	1	1	-	2
(% of total contributions)	-	3	0	-	0	1	-	0

House

Democrat								
Incumbent								
(contributions)	$14,100	$72,488	$86,787	$82,330	$76,022	$90,550	$132,250	$171,629
(no. of candidates)	29	34	49	64	43	59	51	53
(% of total contributions)	28	37	29	39	28	34	34	35
Challenger								
(contributions)	$5,500	$17,839	$77,384	$40,357	$84,227	$60,494	$39,447	$86,557
(no. of candidates)	4	6	32	29	19	19	18	34
(% of total contributions)	11	9	26	19	31	23	10	18
Open Seat								
(contributions)	$5,225	$23,718	$53,516	$12,450	$39,919	$21,930	$101,923	$97,683
(no. of candidates)	7	8	19	6	12	10	19	40
(% of total contributions)	10	12	18	6	15	8	26	20
Republican								
Incumbent								
(contributions)	$400	$10,726	$1,500	$9,000	$8,050	$12,950	$20,875	$13,750
(no. of candidates)	4	3	4	4	7	7	10	6
(% of total contributions)	1	5	1	4	3	5	5	3
Challenger								
(contributions)	$2,000	$9,900	$1,000	$7,500	$6,000	$5,000	$8,500	$14,000
(no. of candidates)	1	1	1	4	2	1	3	4
(% of total contributions)	4	5	0	4	2	2	2	3
Open Seat								
(contributions)	$1,000	$2,125	$9,000	$8,000	$5,750	$1,000	$5,000	$9,999
(no. of candidates)	1	2	3	2	4	2	1	2
(% of total contributions)	2	1	3	4	2	0	1	2
Total	$50,257	$196,033	$297,202	$211,000	$271,468	$266,174	$384,995	$493,201

Table A.10
National Right to Life PAC (NRL PAC)

		1980	1982	1984	1986	1988	1990	1992
Senate								
Democrat								
Incumbent	(contributions)	$2,141	$2,500	$294	$2,500	$2,000	-	$16,200
	(no. of candidates)	1	1	2	2	1	-	9
	(% of total contributions)	3	1	0	0	1	-	7
Challenger	(contributions)	$3,600	$100	$2,500	$5,000	-	-	-
	(no. of candidates)	3	1	1	1	-	-	-
	(% of total contributions)	5	0	1	1	-	-	-
Open Seat	(contributions)	$1,000	-	-	-	-	-	-
	(no. of candidates)	1	-	-	-	-	-	-
	(% of total contributions)	1	-	-	-	-	-	-
Republican								
Incumbent	(contributions)	$500	$15,833	$26,833	$77,514	$25,000	$11,000	$16,200
	(no. of candidates)	1	3	10	17	7	5	9
	(% of total contributions)	1	8	7	11	10	7	7
Challenger	(contributions)	$26,750	$53,012	$14,122	$27,162	$15,784	$14,833	$21,500
	(no. of candidates)	8	8	4	9	3	5	9
	(% of total contributions)	37	27	4	4	6	13	9
Open Seat	(contributions)	$11,498	$5,000	$9,249	$39,304	$11,478	$4,476	$10,500
	(no. of candidates)	3	1	2	5	5	1	4
	(% of total contributions)	16	3	2	6	4	4	5

281

House							
Democrat							
Incumbent (contributions)	$3,655	$21,050	$22,048	$64,319	$33,550	$6,200	$12,400
(no. of candidates)	6	12	18	30	18	7	11
(% of total contributions)	5	11	6	9	13	6	5
Challenger (contributions)	$1,411	$6,250	$23,339	$8,129	$8,527	$2,198	$8,406
(no. of candidates)	3	3	9	3	3	2	5
(% of total contributions)	2	3	6	1	3	2	4
Open Seat (contributions)	$1,200	$13,342	$15,000	$16,126	$7,937	$4,000	$5,148
(no. of candidates)	4	8	5	4	2	2	4
(% of total contributions)	2	7	4	2	3	4	2
Republican							
Incumbent (contributions)	$8,482	$31,930	$82,975	$203,446	$97,650	$42,268	$48,736
(no. of candidates)	4	16	56	54	42	22	37
(% of total contributions)	12	16	21	29	38	38	21
Challenger (contributions)	$6,214	$25,700	$143,073	$136,679	$24,596	$18,653	$62,630
(no. of candidates)	15	10	39	28	14	11	40
(% of total contributions)	9	13	37	20	10	17	27
Open Seat (contributions)	$6,386	$19,950	$51,436	$115,462	$29,582	$8,549	$44,321
(no. of candidates)	6	11	20	23	11	10	25
(% of total contributions)	9	10	13	17	12	8	19
Total	$72,837	$194,667	$390,869	$695,641	$256,104	$112,177	$229,841

282

Table A.11
National Federation of Federal Employees Public Affairs Committee (NFFE PAC)

		1978	1980	1982	1984	1986	1988	1990	1992
Senate									
Democrat									
Incumbent	(contributions)	-	$2,100	$6,000	$5,500	$1,950	$5,250	$6,400	$3,300
	(no. of candidates)	-	6	8	5	4	9	14	10
	(% of total contributions)	-	9	16	9	7	17	26	13
Challenger	(contributions)	-	-	$4,000	$9,500	$6,200	$1,500	$1,400	$2,650
	(no. of candidates)	-	-	3	5	8	4	6	8
	(% of total contributions)	-	-	10	16	22	5	6	11
Open Seat	(contributions)	-	-	$1,500	$4,000	$2,500	$500	-	$1,750
	(no. of candidates)	-	-	1	2	3	1	-	5
	(% of total contributions)	-	-	4	7	9	2	-	7
Republican									
Incumbent	(contributions)	$100	-	-	$1,000	$1,500	$250	$750	$500
	(no. of candidates)	1	-	-	1	1	1	3	2
	(% of total contributions)	3	-	-	2	5	1	3	2
Challenger	(contributions)	-	-	-	-	-	-	-	-
	(no. of candidates)	-	-	-	-	-	-	-	-
	(% of total contributions)	-	-	-	-	-	-	-	-
Open Seat	(contributions)	-	-	-	-	-	-	-	-
	(no. of candidates)	-	-	-	-	-	-	-	-
	(% of total contributions)	-	-	-	-	-	-	-	-

House								
Democrat								
Incumbent (contributions)	$2,875	$19,725	$17,650	$32,905	$10,480	$19,100	$13,250	$13,150
(no. of candidates)	12	40	36	49	18	33	35	31
(% of total contributions)	97	84	46	56	37	61	53	52
Challenger (contributions)	-	$400	$7,312	$2,250	$2,950	$1,850	$1,050	$1,000
(no. of candidates)	-	2	6	5	8	6	6	4
(% of total contributions)	-	2	19	4	10	6	4	4
Open Seat (contributions)	-	$100	$2,150	$2,250	$1,750	$650	$1,050	$1,800
(no. of candidates)	-	1	4	6	5	3	5	8
(% of total contributions)	-	0	6	4	6	2	4	7
Republican								
Incumbent (contributions)	-	$1,225	-	$1,000	$1,000	$2,000	$875	$1,050
(no. of candidates)	-	5	-	2	3	4	3	3
(% of total contributions)	-	5	-	2	4	6	4	4
Challenger (contributions)	-	-	-	-	-	-	-	-
(no. of candidates)	-	-	-	-	-	-	-	-
(% of total contributions)	-	-	-	-	-	-	-	-
Open Seat (contributions)	-	-	-	-	-	-	-	-
(no. of candidates)	-	-	-	-	-	-	-	-
(% of total contributions)	-	-	-	-	-	-	-	-
Total	$2,975	$23,550	$38,612	$58,405	$28,330	$31,100	$24,775	$25,200

Table A.12
FHP Health Services Political Action Committee

		1978	1980	1982	1984	1986	1988	1990	1992
Senate									
Democrat									
Incumbent	(contributions)	-	$3,625	-	-	$750	$3,500	$3,000	$4,000
	(no. of candidates)	-	1	-	-	2	3	1	3
	(% of total contributions)	-	33	-	-	4	12	6	4
Challenger	(contributions)	-	-	$500	$1,500	$2,200	$1,250	-	$7,025
	(no. of candidates)	-	-	1	1	2	1	-	3
	(% of total contributions)	-	-	4	14	11	4	-	7
Open Seat	(contributions)	-	-	$125	-	-	-	-	$10,000
	(no. of candidates)	-	-	1	-	-	-	-	5
	(% of total contributions)	-	-	1	-	-	-	-	10
Republican									
Incumbent	(contributions)	$50	$125	$275	-	$3,750	$8,450	$10,750	$11,138
	(no. of candidates)	1	1	1	-	4	3	5	3
	(% of total contributions)	1	1	2	-	19	30	20	12
Challenger	(contributions)	-	-	-	-	$500	-	-	-
	(no. of candidates)	-	-	-	-	1	-	-	-
	(% of total contributions)	-	-	-	-	3	-	-	-
Open Seat	(contributions)	-	-	-	-	-	-	-	$7,000
	(no. of candidates)	-	-	-	-	-	-	-	3
	(% of total contributions)	-	-	-	-	-	-	-	7

House									
Democrat									
Incumbent	(contributions)	$2,700	$4,635	$6,700	$5,465	$4,850	$8,450	$25,950	$30,800
	(no. of candidates)	6	12	12	12	10	14	20	20
	(% of total contributions)	75	43	54	52	25	30	49	32
Challenger	(contributions)	$250	$600	$450	$375	$525	$250	$500	-
	(no. of candidates)	1	3	2	1	2	1	1	-
	(% of total contributions)	7	6	4	4	3	1	1	-
Open Seat	(contributions)	$160	-	$250	$550	$500	$500	-	$7,500
	(no. of candidates)	2	-	1	2	1	1	-	7
	(% of total contributions)	4	-	2	5	3	2	-	8
Republican									
Incumbent	(contributions)	$100	$1,855	$3,765	$1,605	$4,450	$2,500	$12,000	$12,750
	(no. of candidates)	1	12	11	6	9	7	14	15
	(% of total contributions)	3	17	31	15	23	9	23	13
Challenger	(contributions)	$125	-	$235	$934	$750	-	-	-
	(no. of candidates)	2	-	3	1	2	-	-	-
	(% of total contributions)	3	-	2	9	4	-	-	-
Open Seat	(contributions)	$225	-	-	-	$1,000	$3,450	$500	$5,500
	(no. of candidates)	2	-	-	-	2	7	1	5
	(% of total contributions)	6	-	-	-	5	12	1	6
Total		$3,610	$10,840	$12,300	$10,429	$19,275	$28,350	$52,700	$95,713

Table A.13
Association of American Publishers (AAP PAC)

		1978	1980	1982	1984	1986	1988	1990	1992
Senate									
Democrat									
Incumbent	(contributions)	$900	$3,250	$2,250	$2,250	$2,600	$7,250	$6,500	$4,750
	(no. of candidates)	4	10	7	5	5	10	9	6
	(% of total contributions)	11	31	17	16	29	31	31	19
Challenger	(contributions)	$100	-	-	$1,000	-	-	-	-
	(no. of candidates)	1	-	-	2	-	-	-	-
	(% of total contributions)	1	-	-	7	-	-	-	-
Open Seat	(contributions)	$400	-	-	$750	$750	$500	-	$1,000
	(no. of candidates)	2	-	-	2	2	1	-	1
	(% of total contributions)	5	-	-	5	8	2	-	4
Republican									
Incumbent	(contributions)	$850	$900	$1,000	$1,500		$7,500	$2,500	$4,000
	(no. of candidates)	4	3	3	2		8	3	4
	(% of total contributions)	10	9	8	11		32	12	16
Challenger	(contributions)	$200	$150	-	-	-	-	-	-
	(no. of candidates)	1	1	-	-	-	-	-	-
	(% of total contributions)	2	1	-	-	-	-	-	-
Open Seat	(contributions)	$100	-	-	-	-	-	-	-
	(no. of candidates)	1	-	-	-	-	-	-	-
	(% of total contributions)	1	-	-	-	-	-	-	-

287

House								
Democrat								
Incumbent								
(contributions)	$4,650	$5,530	$6,900	$6,700	$3,750	$5,850	$8,250	$12,900
(no. of candidates)	34	27	21	19	13	15	16	17
(% of total contributions)	55	52	53	49	42	25	40	52
Challenger								
(contributions)	$100	-	-	-	-	-	-	-
(no. of candidates)	1	-	-	-	-	-	-	-
(% of total contributions)	1	-	-	-	-	-	-	-
Open Seat								
(contributions)	$200	$200	-	-	-	-	-	-
(no. of candidates)	2	1	-	-	-	-	-	-
(% of total contributions)	2	2	-	-	-	-	-	-
Republican								
Incumbent								
(contributions)	$900	$550	$2,900	$1,510	$1,800	$2,150	$3,400	$2,250
(no. of candidates)	9	4	13	6	5	5	5	4
(% of total contributions)	11	5	22	11	20	9	16	9
Challenger								
(contributions)	$100	-	-	-	-	$250	-	-
(no. of candidates)	1	-	-	-	-	1	-	-
(% of total contributions)	1	-	-	-	-	1	-	-
Open Seat								
(contributions)	-	-	-	-	-	-	-	-
(no. of candidates)	-	-	-	-	-	-	-	-
(% of total contributions)	-	-	-	-	-	-	-	-
(% of total contributions)	$8,500	$10,580	$13,050	$13,710	$8,900	$23,500	$20,650	$24,900

Table A.14
Clean Water Action Vote Environment (CWAVE)

		1988	1990	1992
Senate				
Democrat				
Incumbent	(contributions)	-	$4,653	-
	(no. of candidates)	-	3	-
	(% of total contributions)	-	20	-
Challenger	(contributions)	-	$230	$538
	(no. of candidates)	-	1	2
	(% of total contributions)	-	1	2
Open Seat	(contributions)	$2,000	-	$3,799
	(no. of candidates)	1	-	1
	(% of total contributions)	38	-	16
Republican				
Incumbent	(contributions)	-	-	-
	(no. of candidates)	-	-	-
	(% of total contributions)	-	-	-
Challenger	(contributions)	-	-	-
	(no. of candidates)	-	-	-
	(% of total contributions)	-	-	-
Open Seat	(contributions)	-	-	-
	(no. of candidates)	-	-	-
	(% of total contributions)	-	-	-
House				
Democrat				
Incumbent	(contributions)	$199	$3,505	$10,379
	(no. of candidates)	1	5	2
	(% of total contributions)	4	15	43
Challenger	(contributions)	$3,094	$2,972	$418
	(no. of candidates)	3	3	1
	(% of total contributions)	58	13	2
Open Seat	(contributions)	-	$6,546	$8,839
	(no. of candidates)	-	2	4
	(% of total contributions)	-	29	37
Republican				
Incumbent	(contributions)	-	-	-
	(no. of candidates)	-	-	-
	(% of total contributions)	-	-	-
Challenger	(contributions)	-	-	-
	(no. of candidates)	-	-	-
	(% of total contributions)	-	-	-
Open Seat	(contributions)	-	$4,808	-
	(no. of candidates)	-	1	-
	(% of total contributions)	-	21	-
Total		$5,293	$22,714	$23,973

Table A.15
Conservative Victory Committee

		1988	1990	1992
Senate				
Democrat				
Incumbent	(contributions)	-	-	-
	(no. of candidates)	-	-	-
	(% of total contributions)	-	-	-
Challenger	(contributions)	-	-	-
	(no. of candidates)	-	-	-
	(% of total contributions)	-	-	-
Open Seat	(contributions)	-	-	-
	(no. of candidates)	-	-	-
	(% of total contributions)	-	-	-
Republican				
Incumbent	(contributions)	$21,083	$13,062	$1,000
	(no. of candidates)	6	5	1
	(% of total contributions)	25	13	1
Challenger	(contributions)	$6,650	$17,300	$14,000
	(no. of candidates)	7	5	5
	(% of total contributions)	8	18	15
Open Seat	(contributions)	$16,500	$6,550	$4,000
	(no. of candidates)	4	3	3
	(% of total contributions)	20	7	4
House				
Democrat				
Incumbent	(contributions)	-	-	-
	(no. of candidates)	-	-	-
	(% of total contributions)	-	-	-
Challenger	(contributions)	$1,021	-	-
	(no. of candidates)	1	-	-
	(% of total contributions)	1	-	-
Open Seat	(contributions)	-	-	-
	(no. of candidates)	-	-	-
	(% of total contributions)	-	-	-
Republican				
Incumbent	(contributions)	$13,011	$21,550	$12,250
	(no. of candidates)	13	15	4
	(% of total contributions)	15	22	13
Challenger	(contributions)	$14,076	$18,700	$37,455
	(no. of candidates)	11	16	23
	(% of total contributions)	17	19	39
Open Seat	(contributions)	$12,011	$20,100	$26,500
	(no. of candidates)	7	9	14
	(% of total contributions)	14	21	28
Total		$84,352	$97,262	$95,205

Table A.16
JustLife Action

		1986	1988	1990	1992
Senate					
Democrat					
Incumbent	(contributions)	-	-	$2,820	$46
	(no. of candidates)	-	-	1	2
	(% of total contributions)	-	-	13	1
Challenger	(contributions)	$3,827	-	-	-
	(no. of candidates)	1	-	-	-
	(% of total contributions)	96	-	-	-
Open Seat	(contributions)	$50	$100	-	$23
	(no. of candidates)	1	1	-	1
	(% of total contributions)	1	2	-	0
Republican					
Incumbent	(contributions)	-	-	$16	-
	(no. of candidates)	-	-	1	-
	(% of total contributions)	-	-	0	-
Challenger	(contributions)	-	-	$32	-
	(no. of candidates)	-	-	1	-
	(% of total contributions)	-	-	0	-
Open Seat	(contributions)	-	-	-	-
	(no. of candidates)	-	-	-	-
	(% of total contributions)	-	-	-	-
House					
Democrat					
Incumbent	(contributions)	-	$2,977	$5,840	$1,879
	(no. of candidates)	-	3	37	23
	(% of total contributions)	-	45	27	32
Challenger	(contributions)	$75	$3,563	$9,614	$3,765
	(no. of candidates)	3	2	7	6
	(% of total contributions)	2	54	45	65
Open Seat	(contributions)	-	-	$168	$23
	(no. of candidates)	-	-	2	1
	(% of total contributions)	-	-	1	0
Republican					
Incumbent	(contributions)	$25	-	$2,807	$23
	(no. of candidates)	1	-	6	1
	(% of total contributions)	1	-	13	0
Challenger	(contributions)	-	-	-	$23
	(no. of candidates)	-	-	-	1
	(% of total contributions)	-	-	-	0
Open Seat	(contributions)	-	-	$238	$46
	(no. of candidates)	-	-	1	2
	(% of total contributions)	-	-	1	1
Total		$3,977	$6,640	$21,535	$5,828

Table A.17
Washington Political Action Committee (WASH PAC)

		1982	1984	1986	1988	1990	1992
Senate							
Democrat							
Incumbent	(contributions)	$23,700	$38,550	$61,100	$93,200	$103,000	$47,680
	(no. of candidates)	17	16	22	28	26	21
	(% of total contributions)	27	20	21	30	39	24
Challenger	(contributions)	$5,250	$33,600	$33,000	$31,250	$2,000	$1,500
	(no. of candidates)	5	9	6	5	2	2
	(% of total contributions)	6	18	11	10	1	1
Open Seat	(contributions)	$3,000	$12,250	$30,000	$18,500	-	$22,000
	(no. of candidates)	2	4	6	6	-	6
	(% of total contributions)	3	6	10	6	-	11
Republican							
Incumbent	(contributions)	$7,500	$15,750	$60,600	$41,000	$40,500	$35,500
	(no. of candidates)	6	11	18	10	12	9
	(% of total contributions)	8	8	21	13	15	18
Challenger	(contributions)	$3,000	$3,500	$500	$250	-	$1,000
	(no. of candidates)	3	1	1	1	-	1
	(% of total contributions)	3	2	0	0	-	0
Open Seat	(contributions)	-	-	$2,500	$4,000	$5,000	$1,000
	(no. of candidates)	-	-	1	3	1	1
	(% of total contributions)	-	-	1	1	2	0

Table A.17 (continued)

House							
Democrat							
Incumbent	(contributions)	$25,600	$71,350	$66,800	$76,200	$76,150	$67,900
	(no. of candidates)	59	98	88	84	80	76
	(% of total contributions)	29	38	23	25	29	34
Challenger	(contributions)	$6,275	$2,000	$4,150	$10,500	$7,700	$1,350
	(no. of candidates)	15	6	10	16	9	3
	(% of total contributions)	7	1	1	3	3	1
Open Seat	(contributions)	$5,450	$3,800	$14,500	$8,250	$8,500	$6,250
	(no. of candidates)	19	9	21	11	13	14
	(% of total contributions)	6	2	5	3	3	3
Republican							
Incumbent	(contributions)	$7,550	$8,000	$17,250	$20,500	$14,375	$15,840
	(no. of candidates)	21	20	32	29	20	22
	(% of total contributions)	8	4	6	7	5	8
Challenger	(contributions)	$1,000	$500	-	$1,000	$2,250	$1,000
	(no. of candidates)	3	2	-	1	4	3
	(% of total contributions)	1	0	-	0	1	0
Open Seat	(contributions)	$600	$750	$3,000	$4,000	$2,900	$500
	(no. of candidates)	3	2	5	7	5	1
	(% of total contributions)	1	0	1	1	1	0
Total		$88,925	$190,050	$293,400	$308,650	$262,375	$201,520

Table A.18
WISH List and Gay and Lesbian Victory Fund

		Wish List 1992	Gay and Lesbian Victory Fund 1992
Senate			
Democrat			
Incumbent	(contributions)	-	-
	(no. of candidates)	-	-
	(% of total contributions)	-	-
Challenger	(contributions)	-	-
	(no. of candidates)	-	-
	(% of total contributions)	-	-
Open Seat	(contributions)	-	-
	(no. of candidates)	-	-
	(% of total contributions)	-	-
Republican			
Incumbent	(contributions)	-	-
	(no. of candidates)	-	-
	(% of total contributions)	-	-
Challenger	(contributions)	-	-
	(no. of candidates)	-	-
	(% of total contributions)	-	-
Open Seat	(contributions)	-	-
	(no. of candidates)	-	-
	(% of total contributions)	-	-
House			
Democrat			
Incumbent	(contributions)	-	$579
	(no. of candidates)	-	3
	(% of total contributions)	-	45
Challenger	(contributions)	-	-
	(no. of candidates)	-	-
	(% of total contributions)	-	-
Open Seat	(contributions)	-	$604
	(no. of candidates)	-	1
	(% of total contributions)	-	47
Republican			
Incumbent	(contributions)	$19,172	$100
	(no. of candidates)	6	1
	(% of total contributions)	28	8
Challenger	(contributions)	$9,718	-
	(no. of candidates)	4	-
	(% of total contributions)	14	-
Open Seat	(contributions)	$39,219	-
	(no. of candidates)	9	-
	(% of total contributions)	58	-
Total		$68,109	$1,283

294

Table A.19
PHH Corporation Inc.

		1982	1984	1986	1988	1990	1992
Senate							
Democrat							
Incumbent	(contributions)	$1,250	-	$2,900	$4,750	$1,000	$1,250
	(no. of candidates)	2	-	3	5	0	2
	(% of total contributions)	83	-	21	22	19	19
Challenger	(contributions)	-	-	$100	-	-	-
	(no. of candidates)	-	-	1	-	-	-
	(% of total contributions)	-	-	1	-	-	-
Open Seat	(contributions)	-	-	$500	$500	-	-
	(no. of candidates)	-	-	1	1	-	-
	(% of total contributions)	-	-	4	2	-	-
Republican							
Incumbent	(contributions)	-	$1,500	-	$5,000	-	-
	(no. of candidates)	-	1	-	6	-	-
	(% of total contributions)	-	31	-	23	-	-
Challenger	(contributions)	-	-	-	$250	-	-
	(no. of candidates)	-	-	-	0	-	-
	(% of total contributions)	-	-	-	-	-	-
Open Seat	(contributions)	-	-	-	-	-	-
	(no. of candidates)	-	-	-	-	-	-
	(% of total contributions)	-	-	-	-	-	-

House						
Democrat						
Incumbent (contributions)	-	$2,000	$4,650	$6,750	$2,550	$4,100
(no. of candidates)	-	4	12	19	4	3
(% of total contributions)	-	41	33	31	49	62
Challenger (contributions)	-	-	-	-	$500	-
(no. of candidates)	-	-	-	-	1	-
(% of total contributions)	-	-	-	-	10	-
Open Seat (contributions)	-	-	$950	-	-	-
(no. of candidates)	-	-	3	-	-	-
(% of total contributions)	-	-	7	-	-	-
Republican						
Incumbent (contributions)	-	$400	$4,600	$4,575	$1,200	$800
(no. of candidates)	-	1	5	9	4	1
(% of total contributions)	-	8	33	21	23	12
Challenger (contributions)	$250	$1,000	-	-	-	-
(no. of candidates)	1	1	-	-	-	-
(% of total contributions)	17	20	-	-	-	-
Open Seat (contributions)	-	-	$250	$250	-	$500
(no. of candidates)	-	-	1	1	-	1
(% of total contributions)	-	-	2	1	-	8
Total	$1,500	$4,900	$13,950	$22,075	$5,250	$6,650

Table A.20
National Air Traffic Controllers Association (NATCA)

		1990	1992
Senate			
Democrat			
Incumbent	(contributions)	-	$8,000
	(no. of candidates)	-	6
	(% of total contributions)	-	9%
Challenger	(contributions)	-	$2,000
	(no. of candidates)	-	3
	(% of total contributions)	-	2%
Open Seat	(contributions)	$250	$5,150
	(no. of candidates)	1	1
	(% of total contributions)	9%	6%
Republican			
Incumbent	(contributions)	-	$3,000
	(no. of candidates)	-	2
	(% of total contributions)	-	
Challenger	(contributions)	-	-
	(no. of candidates)	-	-
	(% of total contributions)	-	-
Open Seat	(contributions)	-	-
	(no. of candidates)	-	-
	(% of total contributions)	-	-
House			
Democrat			
Incumbent	(contributions)	$1,800	$57,800
	(no. of candidates)	3	47
	(% of total contributions)	68%	66%
Challenger	(contributions)	-	$1,250
	(no. of candidates)	-	2
	(% of total contributions)	-	1%
Open Seat	(contributions)	-	$4,500
	(no. of candidates)	-	5
	(% of total contributions)	-	5%
Republican			
Incumbent	(contributions)	$600	$5,700
	(no. of candidates)	2	6
	(% of total contributions)	23%	7%
Challenger	(contributions)	-	-
	(no. of candidates)	-	-
	(% of total contributions)	-	-
Open Seat	(contributions)	-	-
	(no. of candidates)	-	-
	(% of total contributions)	-	-
Total		$2,650	$87,400

Table B.1

Realtors Political Action Committee (RPAC) (on behalf of congressional candidates)

		1980	1982	1984	1986	1988	1990	1992
Senate								
Democrat								
Incumbent	(expenditures)	-	$34,523	-	-	$228,038	$158,811	-
	(no. of candidates)	-	1	-	-	1	1	-
Challenger	(expenditures)	-	-	-	$515,836	-	-	$349,289
	(no. of candidates)	-	-	-	1	-	-	1
Open Seat	(expenditures)	-	-	$99,270	-	-	-	$98,953
	(no. of candidates)	-	-	1	-	-	-	1
Republican								
Incumbent	(expenditures)	-	-	-	$115,165	-	-	-
	(no. of candidates)	-	-	-	1	-	-	-
Challenger	(expenditures)	-	-	-	-	-	-	-
	(no. of candidates)	-	-	-	-	-	-	-
Open Seat	(expenditures)	-	-	-	$607,595	$348,498	$437,726	$169,950
	(no. of candidates)	-	-	-	2	1	3	1
House								
Democrat								
Incumbent	(expenditures)	-	$25,663	$70,200	-	$281,762	$189,295	$170,395
	(no. of candidates)	-	1	2	-	2	2	3
Challenger	(expenditures)	-	-	-	-	-	-	-
	(no. of candidates)	-	-	-	-	-	-	-
Open Seat	(expenditures)	-	$8,675	-	$288,305	-	-	-
	(no. of candidates)	-	1	-	1	-	-	-
Republican								
Incumbent	(expenditures)	$14,685	$68,947	$22,666	-	$474,123	$208,393	$230,429
	(no. of candidates)	1	4	1	-	3	2	4
Challenger	(expenditures)	$55,513	$51,252	$169,658	$10,000	-	-	-
	(no. of candidates)	3	2	5	1	-	-	-
Open Seat	(expenditures)	-	-	-	$172,895	-	$105,360	-
	(no. of candidates)	-	-	-	1	-	1	-
Total		$70,198	$189,060	$361,794	$1,709,796	$1,332,421	$1,099,585	$1,019,016

Table B.2
NARAL PAC (on behalf of or against congressional candidates)

		1987 - 88		1989 - 90		1991 - 92	
		for	against	for	against	for	against
Senate							
Democrat							
Incumbent	(expenditures)	-	-	-	-	-	$945
	(no. of candidates)	-	-	-	-	-	5
Challenger	(expenditures)	-	-	-	-	$196,356	-
	(no. of candidates)	-	-	-	-	2	-
Open Seat	(expenditures)	-	-	-	-	$137,487	-
	(no. of candidates)	-	-	-	-	1	-
Republican							
Incumbent	(expenditures)	-	-	-	-	-	$48,818
	(no. of candidates)	-	-	-	-	-	13
Challenger	(expenditures)	-	-	-	-	-	-
	(no. of candidates)	-	-	-	-	-	-
Open Seat	(expenditures)	-	-	-	-	-	$43,318
	(no. of candidates)	-	-	-	-	-	2

House					
Democrat					
Incumbent	(expenditures)	–	$2,871	–	$77,885	$1,967
	(no. of candidates)	–	1	–	1	1
Challenger	(expenditures)	$500	–	–	–	–
	(no. of candidates)	1	–	–	–	–
Open Seat	(expenditures)	–	–	–	$69	–
	(no. of candidates)	–	–	–	1	–
Republican					
Incumbent	(expenditures)	–	–	–	–	$4,137
	(no. of candidates)	–	–	–	–	1
Challenger	(expenditures)	–	–	–	$63,683	–
	(no. of candidates)	–	–	–	2	–
Open Seat	(expenditures)	–	–	–	$134,205	$144,091
	(no. of candidates)	–	–	–	35	1
Total		$500	$2,871	–	$609,685	$243,276

Table B.3

National Right to Life Political Action Committee (NRLPAC) (on behalf of or against congressional candidates)

		1980	1982	1984	1986	1988	1990	1992
Senate								
Democrat								
Incumbent	(expenditures)	$381	$5,177	$2,493	-	$94	$1,480	-
	(no. of candidates)	1	1	1	-	1	1	-
Challenger	(expenditures)	-	-	$7,420	$20,281	-	-	$2,376
	(no. of candidates)	-	-	1	1	-	-	1
Open Seat	(expenditures)	-	-	-	$189	$210,727	-	-
	(no. of candidates)	-	-	-	1	7	-	-
Republican								
Incumbent	(expenditures)	$56	$14,551	$1,748	$127,021	$60,401	$179,032	$56,383
	(no. of candidates)	1	1	2	7	3	5	12
Challenger	(expenditures)	$297	$7,696	$25,191	$18,859	$68,031	$71,036	$91,409
	(no. of candidates)	1	1	2	1	4	9	11
Open Seat	(expenditures)	$2,362	-	$38,097	$171,659	$920,315	$20,107	$47,268
	(no. of candidates)	2	-	1	3	6	2	7

House								
Democrat								
Incumbent	(expenditures)	$437	$56	$1,912	$311	$6,585	$14,914	$57,411
	(no. of candidates)	3	4	2	1	2	3	10
Challenger	(expenditures)	-	-	$824	$2,509	$1,989	-	$51,117
	(no. of candidates)	-	-	2	2	2	-	10
Open Seat	(expenditures)	$163	$5,619	-	$311	$2,778	-	$426
	(no. of candidates)	1	3	-	1	1	-	2
Republican								
Incumbent	(expenditures)	$1,360	$4,704	$1,454	$31,843	$17,096	$50,978	$127,651
	(no. of candidates)	7	8	2	15	8	18	47
Challenger	(expenditures)	$2,829	$2,411	$12,381	$13,997	$13,754	$60,749	$217,648
	(no. of candidates)	8	3	9	8	11	20	70
Open Seat	(expenditures)	$286	$261	$8,996	$14,279	$11,799	$20,140	$134,205
	(no. of candidates)	2	2	2	10	7	7	35
Total		$8,171	$40,475	$100,516	$401,259	$1,313,569	$418,436	$785,894

About the Editors
and Contributors

Robert Biersack is Supervisory Statistician at the Federal Election Commission. He has published articles on campaign finance and taught at the Catholic University of America, Georgetown University, and George Washington University.

Paul S. Herrnson is Associate Professor of Government and Politics at the University of Maryland. He is the author of *Party Campaigning in the 1980s, Congressional Elections: Campaigning at Home and in Washington,* and several articles on political parties, campaign finance, and congressional elections. Professor Herrnson has consulted for the House Democratic Caucus and served as an American Political Science Association Congressional Fellow.

Clyde Wilcox is Associate Professor of Government at Georgetown University. He worked for two years at the Federal Election Commission and has published articles on campaign finance in a variety of journals. Professor Wilcox is the author of *God's Warriors* and coauthor of *Serious Money: Individual Contributors in American Politics* and *Between Two Absolutes: Public Opinion and the Politics of Abortion.*

Denise L. Baer is Visiting Associate Professor of Government at American University. She is coauthor of *Elite Cadres and Party Coalitions* and *Politics and Linkage in a Democratic Society* and has written widely on political parties and Congress.

Martha Bailey is Assistant Professor of Political Science at Southern Illinois University at Edwardsville. She has worked for Representative Robert Wise of West Virginia and written on the labor movement and labor PACs.

Anne H. Bedlington teaches at Georgetown University and American University. She was Supervisory Statistician at the Federal Election Commission and has written several articles on campaign finance.

Mary E. Bendyna, R.S.M., is a doctoral candidate and university fellow in the Government Department at Georgetown University. As a member of a Catholic religious order, she is especially interested in religious aspects of the abortion controversy. She has published articles on religion and politics.

Joe Ferrara is a doctoral candidate in Government at Georgetown University. He has written on public attitudes toward the war with Iraq and toward defense spending. He works at the Pentagon on defense acquisition issues.

James G. Gimpel is Assistant Professor of Government and Politics at the University of Maryland. He has served as Policy Analyst for the U.S. Senate Labor Committee and for Senator Dan Coats of Indiana. He has also been a consultant for Penn and Shoen Associates, a Washington-based polling firm, and for the Department of Housing and Urban Development. Professor Gimpel has written on political parties, political behavior, and Congress.

Roland Gunn is a doctoral candidate in Government at Georgetown University. He is interested in conservative political thought in America.

Robyn Hicks is a doctoral candidate in Government and Politics at the University of Maryland. She is also Political Analyst at American Viewpoint, a polling firm in Washington, and in that capacity has worked on more than a dozen campaigns for the U.S. Senate, House of Representatives, and state and local offices.

Barbara Levick-Segnatelli is a doctoral candidate in Government and Politics at the University of Maryland. She has taught at Northeastern University and worked as Executive Aide for the Chesapeake Bay Communications Office of Maryland.

Robert E. Mutch teaches at George Washington University. He is the author of *Campaigns, Congress, and Courts: The Making of Federal Campaign Finance Law* and several articles on campaign finance. He has taught at Brooklyn College, Barnard College, and Rutgers College.

Candice J. Nelson is Assistant Professor of Government at American University and Director of its Campaign Management Institute. She is coauthor of *The Money Chase* and *The Myth of the Independent Voter* and has written several articles on campaign finance. Professor Nelson has served as an American Political Science Association Congressional Fellow.

William A. Pierce is a graduate student at the University of Maryland and Press Secretary for Representative Bill Thomas of California. He has served as Communications Director of the National Taxpayers Union; Account Executive for Hill and Knowlton, a major Washington public relations firm; and Director of Issues Research for the Broyhill for Senate campaign in 1986. Mr. Pierce has also worked for the National Republican Senatorial Committee.

John J. Pitney, Jr., is Associate Professor of Government at Claremont McKenna College. He has served as Acting Director of Research at the Republican National Committee, Senior Domestic Policy Analyst for the House Republican Research Committee, and in other political posts. He is coauthor of *Congress's Permanent Minority? Republicans in the U.S. House* and several scholarly and popular articles. He has also served as an American Political Science Association Congressional Fellow.

Craig A. Rimmerman is Associate Professor and Chair of the Department of Political Science at Hobart and William Smith Colleges. He is the author of *Presidency by Plebiscite: The Reagan-Bush Era in Institutional Perspective* and articles on American politics, public policy, and democratic theory. He has been an American Political Science Association Congressional Fellow. Currently, Professor Rimmerman is working on a book examining issues of participation, democracy, citizenship, and civic indifference.

Jack E. Rossotti is Assistant Professor of Government at American University. He has written articles on campaign finance.

Ronald G. Shaiko is Assistant Professor of Government at American University. He is the author of *Voices and Echoes for the Environment: Public Interest Representation in the 1990s* and has written extensively on interest groups and Congress. Professor Shaiko has served as an American Political Science Association Congressional Fellow.

Julia K. Stronks is Attorney at Law and Assistant Professor of Political Studies at Whitworth College. Her publications are on issues of First Amendment religious freedom.

Sue Thomas is Associate Professor of Government at Georgetown University. She is the author of *How Women Legislate* and coeditor of *The Year of the Woman: Myths and Realities.* Professor Thomas has published articles in a variety of journals and is currently at work on a book on women as state legislators.

Index